LANDSCAPE FOR LIVING

LANDSCAPE
FOR LIVING

GARRETT ECKBO

Julius Shulman

HENNESSEY + INGALLS
SANTA MONICA 2002

ART + ARCHITECTURE
B O O K S

Originally published in 1950 as an Architectural Record Book
with Duell, Sloan, and Pearce, by F.W. Dodge Corporation.

Reprinted 2002 by

Hennessey + Ingalls
1254 3rd Street Promenade
Santa Monica CA 90401

Manufactured in the United States of America

California Architecture and Architects, No.23

ISBN 0-940512-32-7

Library of Congress Cataloging-in-Publication Data

Eckbo, Garrett.
    Landscape for living/ Garrett Eckbo.
        p. cm. -- (California architecture and architects ; no.23)
    Originally published: New York : Architectural Record with Duell, Sloan & Pearce, [1950]
    ISBN 0-940512-32-7 (paper)
    1. Landscape architecture. I. Title. II. Series.

SB472 .E22 2002
712--dc21

                                                        2002017326

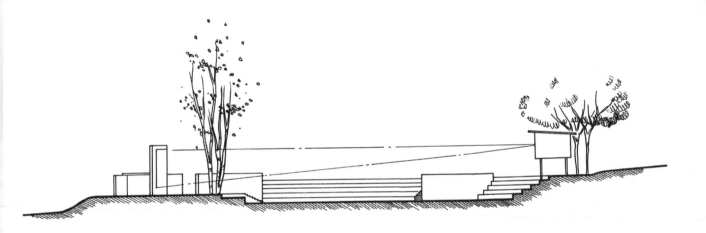

TO | ARLINE
| MARILYN
| ALISON

This book has not been written in the contemplative repose of a year's re-treat to some suburban villa. It has been produced in the middle of the city of Los Angeles, and in the midst of active professional practice and active professional teaching. That will account for many of its vices and/or virtues.

Acknowledgments for help and support, both specific and general, are so broad as to be difficult to put down. First to my family, for the fortitude and patience which has lived with the preoccupation, absent-mindedness, jangled nerves, bad temper, and clattering typewriter of the spare-time author for the past year or more. Then to my partners, Robert Royston and Edward Williams, and to my southern associate, Francis Dean, for strong and steady support; to Dean Gallion and my colleagues and students in the School of Architecture at the University of Southern California, for the opportunity to continue intellectual as well as practical development; to many clients who have borne inexplicable delays and jogs in plan and job production with great patience; and to all the professional and educational colleagues at home and abroad who made serious reply to my letters of inquiry. In the actual production of the manuscript Leo and Etta Zwell were indispensable; the special photographic assistance of Julius Shulman was invaluable; good work on drawings was done by Erwin Vogel, Robert Lesnett, William Rudolph, Tom Ballinger, Hector Rodriguez, Howard Troller, Heinz Neheimer, Frank Harris, Dike Nagano, James McEwen, Evelyn Royston, Francis Dean and Arthur Shatz. Rodriguez was also invaluable in the assemblage of the illustrations. For careful reading of portions of the manuscript and constructive comments I must thank Gregory Ain, Simon Eisner and Jack Shapiro, in addition to the Zwells. Last but not least my publishers have been patient and helpful as deadline after deadline has receded into limbo.

The work illustrated in the Practice section is the work of Eckbo, Royston and Williams, Planning Consultants and Landscape Architects, Los Angeles and San Francisco, unless otherwise credited. We consider the contributions of all three partners to be equally important to the quality of the work. We came together out of mutual respect for one another's competence and imagination, and we have remained together over 500 miles of California coastline because of the continuation of this mutual respect.

Special thanks to Katherine McNamara, Librarian of the Department of Landscape Architecture and Regional Planning at Harvard University, and to her staff, for generous cooperation in supplying bibliography and reference material.

There has been little written on landscape design in contemporary terms. One previous effort is GARDENS IN THE MODERN LANDSCAPE by Christopher Tunnard. LANDSCAPE DESIGN 1948, the catalog of a recent exhibit at the San Francisco Museum of Art, is an excellent summary of work in the San Francisco Bay Region. There have been magazine articles in similar vein; some by this writer, a series by James C. Rose in PENCIL POINTS 1938 and 1939, and a series by Thomas D. Church in HOUSE BEAUTIFUL 1948 and 1949. We understand that some of our like-minded colleagues have books in preparation. This should begin to add up to a progressive bookshelf in landscape design.

GARRETT ECKBO

Los Angeles, California
May 15, 1949

CONTENTS

Soil Conservation Service

BACKGROUND

CHAPTER I

WHY NOW

". . . men come to build stately sooner than to garden finely; as if gardening were the greater perfection."

Books must justify their existence. This book attempts a serious analysis, in terms of theory and practice, of landscape development in our culture. This analysis must be in terms of the world we live in, the allied arts, the construction industry, and society in general—as they are, and as they are becoming. None of these are the same today as they were yesterday, and none will be tomorrow as they are today. We must examine today in relation to yesterday in order to project the potentiality for tomorrow. The book is not projected as a personal expression, although personal elements in it are unavoidable. Its intent is not frivolous, sensational, or opportunist. Nor is it thought of as conclusive, definitive, or messianic. It is meant to begin discussion, not to end it.

We are concerned, in this book, with a reciprocal and changing relation between general theory expressed in prose and specific solutions presented graphically with drawings and photographs. Sometimes the solution is a specific application or implementation of an idea; some-times the theory results from the analysis of a completed solution. These are relations between analysis and synthesis, objectivity and subjectivity, research and intuition, which are present in all serious art work.

Words and graphic presentations are merely the best tools we can use to present concepts of rich, full, and useful experience out-of-doors. Landscapes can only be experienced specifically and directly. Here we are trying to establish a foundation of understanding, awareness, willingness, and broad perspective which is essential to preparation for such experience. The observer will assimilate what his cultural background prepares him for, and a little more.

A new discussion of theory and practice in the field of landscape design is necessary because the professional, commercial, and amateur designers, in their work, have failed to recognize the technical, social, and cultural changes that have occurred in the world in the past hundred years. We live in a world whose advances are based on the continuous expansion of the use of the scientific method, beyond those fields called exact, to such as esthetics and sociology. The scientific method is one which takes nothing for granted, accepts no precedents without examination, and recognizes a dynamic world in which nothing is permanent but change itself.

1

It is a process of rational analysis and creative synthesis, of continuous research, hypothesis, and experiment to prove or disprove such hypotheses.

The analogy between science and art has been recognized by many serious writers including the following:

MOHOLY-NAGY

The actual aim is socio-biological synthesis. This cannot be achieved without 'laboratory experimentation,' though this is another objection to contemporary art, voiced often by the layman. But without experimentation there can be no discoveries and without discoveries no regeneration. Although the 'research work' of the artist is rarely as 'systematic' as that of the scientist they both may deal with the whole of life, in terms of relationships, not of details.

CAUDWELL

Science and art are the frontiers of phantasy. They embody the most abstract, the most general, the most essential laws of concrete feeling and perception. They are 'pure' and for that reason they have separated out from each other. They are concerned with the new, with just those general items of social experience which negate the already existing common ego and common perceptual world, and therefore demand the extension of both ego and world (new art works, new hypotheses) to include them. This is the way practice unites with theory, because men's practical experience contradicts the already given consciousness of men and demands its modification.
Art is the science of feeling, science the art of knowing. We must know to be able to do, but we must feel to know what to do.

TEAGUE

. . . As a matter of fact, the most fruitful scientific thought . . . is borne forward by creative imagination as much as by reason, and it surprises the truth by flashes of brilliant insight long before the structure of supporting proof can be built up.

Thus there is a contrast between intuition and reason in both art and science. The popular theory that art is all intuitive and science all rational is a great over-simplification or vulgarization. It is true that today the operation of intuition in either field seems inexplicable, hence mystical or unknowable. Yet the very potential of science is that nothing is ultimately unknowable, that all our world, tangible and intangible, matter and force and energy, body and mind, can sooner or later be investigated, explained, and known. There are no boundaries to the scientific investigation of the world, to the artistic expression and projection of the potentiality of that investigation, nor to the democratic patterns of society which are implicit in their vision and insight. Sooner or later intuition will prove to be merely a phase of reason, as revolution is a phase of evolution; a more or less abrupt qualitative change or expansion, resulting from a quantitative accumulation of facts, forces, or circumstances.

ARCHITECTURAL FORUM, NOVEMBER 1948

Intuition—the faculty of knowing without reasoning—does not, however, imply the mystic ability of knowing without experiencing.

While it is true that after all the objective decisions in creative work are made subjective ones still remain, there is too much tendency to hide behind artistic intuition and subjectivity. Creativity increases with discipline, not the reverse. Romance, too, does not flee the stage when reason enters, but rather bursts forth in new richness, like Phoenix from the ashes, from the dull blanket of academic fiddle-faddle.

The potential richness of landscape design is far greater than much of the consciously developed landscape in our country. The speed and wealth of development in every field in the first half of the twentieth century is only an introduction to the potentialities ahead. While landscape design may not be affected directly or technically by the Industrial Revolution—trees still come from little seeds—it cannot evade an auxiliary or secondary reflex to its tremendous impact on architecture, engineering, and the allied arts. When architecture moves from Vignola to Frank Lloyd Wright and Le Corbusier how can landscape design stay with Repton and Le Nôtre? What of the cultural expression, in every creative field, of a world which has developed from permanent poverty for the majority to potential security for all in 200 years?

2

It is high time that these currents began to be reflected in the work of landscape architects. Run through the still if not stagnant waters of our long-impounded reservoirs of design theory, they can release unsuspected artesian sources of inspiration and imagination. We need release: on the one hand from a subservience to arbitrary authoritarian "formal" axial patterns; and on the other from an "informal" subservience to nature and its naturalistic imitation and reproduction. The first betrays a muddle-headedness about history, and a refusal to concede social progress; the second betrays a muddle-headedness about man's relationship to the material world we live in, and a kind of irrational mysticism about nature.

Historical period styles have always been a product of social discipline and stabilized social patterns in which the style became a product of all the people. Before the eighteenth century the majority participated in this social production with little or no recognition or consideration from the minority who ruled them from the top. No recognizable social styles have appeared since the eighteenth century, because democratic societies have not yet resolved the contradiction between the hangover of feudal autocratic patterns and the potential for full participation in government and culture by the majority common man. In other words we have not yet stabilized a social pattern long enough to produce a lasting cultural expression.

Landscape design is important in this general expression, as the final integrating element which gives continuity to our physical environment. Nowhere can the stability of the social structure be seen more clearly than in the quality and maturity of its pattern of landscape development. The latter is a kind of social barometer; it requires a maximum in stable social organization to keep it steady long enough to mature. Isolated advanced sections of a society can produce isolated advanced expressions which have considerable endurance—a play, a book, a painting, a building, even a fine garden. When we go beyond these individual expressions to a group of buildings with their attendant web of landscape connections, a community, a metropolis, or a region, we come to as clear and accurate a social expression as can be found. The question is clear: Is full democracy expressed in acres of rich private estates, square miles of slums and semi-slums, and occasional parks for "breathing-pores"?

Beyond the richness inherent in landscape work as it is at present practiced, there is an even greater potential in the continuously developing integration of architecture, engineering, and landscape design. These three professions deal separately with fragments of the single problem of site development. Somewhere great art has been defined as putting a number of elements together in a way which produces a result greater than the mere accumulation of these elements. This has been done in painting, in sculpture, in architecture, in landscape architecture. It is now time to do it in the broader field of site space design.

Analysis in terms of both theory and practice is very important. Theory and practice are two equal components of a single consecutive operation or series of operations. Our general tendency, under economic stress, to divide these two into separate unconnected pigeon-holes ends in sterilizing both. The esthetic poverty of our general physical environment is an expression of this divorce of practice from theory. They are not antidotes or antonyms for each other; they are complements and supplements. It is not a question of either/or; it is a question of both together. Theory is the why of doing things, practice is the how; neither functions well without the other. If practice is know-how, theory is know-why. Theory must serve practice; must answer the questions raised by practice; and must be tested by the data of practice.

The broadest objectives and responsibilities of landscape design and of each landscape architect must be these:

(1) The solution of all practical and functional problems.

(2) The provision of pleasant surroundings for active work and play, and passive relaxation.

(3) The provision of more than these, in spatial experience comparable to great

3

architecture or great natural beauty, and allied to both.

(4) The carrying on of positive research and experiment to broaden the limits of this experience.

In relation to our clients these objectives and responsibilities can be translated as follows:

(1) The resolution of all the contradictions between needs, desires and means presented by each client or group of clients.

(2) The development for them of concepts of space formation, use and experience beyond those they are able to develop for themselves.

Thus the professional planner-designer must always be both a follower and a leader in relation to his clients. If he concentrates too much on leadership he isolates himself; if he concentrates on following he becomes merely a draftsman.

This book would be calmer if it had been written in calmer times. We are living in times of major growth, of climactic developments in world history. Serenity, the avoidance of controversy, the air of intellectual aloofness, are elements of irrelevant ivory-tower dilettantism in these obstetric forties and fifties of the twentieth century of Christianity on this earth.

4

CHAPTER II

WHAT IS LANDSCAPE DESIGN?

As a conscious rearrangement of the elements of the landscape for use and pleasure, landscape design is an existing fact in our culture, and it has been an existing fact in all human cultures since people first began to stabilize in one place, build shelters, and grow crops.

It may well be asked why we use the term "landscape design." There are a good many names commonly accepted and used to refer to work in the landscape field:

landscaping
landscape gardening
landscape design
landscape planning
landscape engineering
landscape architecture

Choice among these is somewhat arbitrary, since there is as yet no legal sanction of any one term. The first two tend to refer to the more practical and limited aspects of the field. Design implies a three-dimensional relation between materials and people. Planning implies two-dimensional abstraction, and Engineering that purely practical approach which is helpless in the sea of esthetics. Landscape Architecture is used by the organized profession, which is the most established and reputable authority we have. However, this term implies an integration with architecture which does not in

truth exist now, although it has existed in the past.

In order to define and evaluate a human activity we must establish its relationship to the general cultural pattern of the society in which it occurs. That is, what is landscape design for? With what problems does it deal? Where does it fit in that pattern of production relations between people, and between people and nature, which produces the things we need?

Landscape design covers that portion of the landscape which is (1) developed or shaped by man, (2) beyond buildings, roads, or utilities and up to wild nature, (3) designed primarily as space for human living—not agriculture, forestry, etc. (Note how Colvin expands this definition to include the total landscape as the total living environment for all people.) It is the establishment of relations between buildings, surfacing and other outdoor construction, earth, rock forms, bodies of water, plants, open space, and the general form and character of the landscape; but with special primary emphasis on the human content, the relation between people and landscape, between human beings and three-dimensional outdoor space quantitatively and qualitatively.

Landscape design in our culture deals with the problems of the outdoor physical envi-

5

ronment of the American people; that is, how best to use the land once its ownership status has been determined by deeds and property lines. This means the specific kind of development, in terms of grading and paving and construction and planting, of each piece of property insofar as it is not covered by buildings or engineering structures. These are problems which have to be solved somewhere along the line in the development and use of any piece of property. If they are not solved during the planning and construction stages, they are merely left over for solution by the occupants as best they can.

The problems of landscape design are among the general problems of our physical environment. All our communities, without exception, need more properly located and organized open space (public and private), and/or proper organization of existing open space (public and private). These needs are conceded or stressed by all individuals working on our physical planning problems.

The function of landscape design is more than the direct design of outdoor space arrangements. In the larger sense it is the continuous establishment of *relations between* man and the land, tying in those hills and valleys and broad panoramas which are beyond design, through designed elements which establish a scale relation between each individual human and the large landscape, placing them so that that individual gets a maximum experience from the relationship. For this process trees and special structures are of pre-eminent importance, to the extent that they are intermediate in scale between man and the landscape and partake of the qualities of both. Thus the view garden relates man to the landscape literally; the enclosed self-sufficient garden must supply a space-and-material experience comparable to that relationship in quality. The landscape is everything seen from a given station point or series of such points, whether in the crowded city or the open desert or mountains. Therefore, landscape design must embody the effort to organize this total outlook rather than merely the design of isolated pictures, ob-

jects, groupings, or structural elements. The contradiction between this need for wholeness of view control (spatial continuity) and the actual breaking up of the formation of the view by property lines is one of the major problems in landscape design.

If the broadest definition of art covers all the best artifacts of the man-made world, as distinguished from the wilderness of nature, then landscape design is potentially the bridge between these two worlds. It has this potential because it gives human scale and organization to considerable sections of the landscape, using largely materials which retain those qualities of growth and irregularity we associate with nature. But landscape design cannot achieve this potential if it persistently segregates man as "formal" and nature as "informal"; if it persistently apologizes for man's presence in the world with the dictum that "art" must not appear in the landscape.

Today there are in general four kinds of problems which fall to the landscape field:

Private gardens—outdoor space around private homes, sufficiently enclosed or isolated for the private use of the individual families.

Public grounds—"landscaping" of all types of buildings, singly or in groups.

Parks—considerable areas of open space, organized primarily by landscape means, for the recreation, both active and passive, of the general public.

Collaboration with architects and engineers in site planning for land development—that is, the work which is primary to the detailed work of all three.

Landscape design usually deals with only a portion or fragment of the total problem of site or property development. Outdoors and indoors are inseparable; they are complementary and supplementary, two sides of the same door. The land at the beginning is programmed as one complete unit—a home, a school, a hospital, a park; thereafter it becomes separated into two or more fragments—architecture, landscape, engineering, etc. Although lip service and some actual follow-through are given to the idea of complete teamwork and co-ordinated development, the fragmentation remains. The professional division of labor, now a set of vested interests, produces and maintains a popular division of thought, and this becomes so well-established that it is difficult to work back toward the primary unity of the site. We think of "house" and "garden" but seldom of "home" as a unit greater than mere house and garden. We are caught in our own system of pigeon-holes; analysis has become an obstacle, rather than a prerequisite, to the final synthesis of problem solution.

The jagged line of this fragmentation between the indoor and outdoor portions of site development stands out very clearly in the actual work of landscape design. The core of most problems in practice is the establishment of good relations, both functional and esthetic, between a building and its site. Does the form of the building fit the form of the site, and are they so merged as to make it difficult to separate them, or does the building look as though someone dropped it there by accident, and then hurried back to pretty it up a bit?

Perhaps the first step in most landscaping—foundation planting, that great technique for moving miscellaneous nursery stock—purports to "tie the building to the ground," "soften it," "conceal the scars," etc. Landscaping is very apt to be sold as beautification which may cover up damage to nature or mistakes of architect or builder.

These colloquialisms and commercialisms express a basic fact. The integration of building and site, of the rational geometry of man with the blind irregularity of nature, is the primary problem of physical development usually left over for the landscaping process. Whether it be in terms of the crude practicality of front walk and driveway, or the refined esthetics of subtle architectural space concepts on a subtly irregular site, this is the problem which is continuous throughout man's development of the raw land.

That considerable portion of landscape design which is concerned with the development of sites and areas not directly related to buildings, in public parks and large private estates, has a good deal of freedom in its arrangement of open space and natural materials. Its primary functional problems come with the introduction of active recreation facilities. However it is only separated, not divorced, from architecture. Few estates these days are large enough to lose sight of central architectural elements. Every in-town park has a simple physical relation to the architectural elements of its community; this relation is expressed by the transportation lines which connect it to all the homes and work places which do not have adequate open space closer to them. All the slums, all the blighted old neighborhoods, all the shiny new substandard dingbat subdivisions, all the apartment houses of whatever economic level—these are the indoor space for which our systems of public parks endeavor to provide adequate complementary outdoor space.

We have nearly pure landscape design in the large out-of-town park, in rural or primeval surroundings, even as we have pure architecture wherever we have 100 per cent site coverage in congested urban centers. But, even between these extremes, there is a direct and balancing connection; each complements and palliates the other. Twentieth century transportation becomes a substitute for direct physical relationship; time takes precedence over space. The theory of park design has proceeded from the actuality of urban congestion as directly as egg from hen.

WHO DOES IT

Anyone who makes specific decisions about landscape form must be considered a designer of some sort. The people who do landscape design and planning fall roughly into three groups: amateurs, commercials, and professionals. Of these the first two are probably each responsible for at least a third of our developed landscape and the last may perhaps be responsible for as much as the final third.

Amateur landscapers are people without formal training, who usually don't get paid for the work they are doing. They include unconscious landscapers, such as farmers, horticulturists, and foresters, who in the course of working with plant propagation, production and protection may work out quite large-scale modifications of, or arrangements in, the landscape. Rural landscape patterns, as developed generation after generation by farming operations, are perhaps our most direct and continuous expression of the joint operations of man and nature.

Conscious amateurs include home owners who can't afford, or don't feel they need, professional help; dilettantes with excess time and energy; and "practical" men appointed to executive status, such as park superintendents. All of these people consciously accept the responsibility for making specific decisions about the form of sections of the landscape, and a fair portion of them carry it out quite satisfactorily. (No professional arrogance is intended here. Free participation by amateurs in all the creative processes of our society is one of the cornerstones of full democracy.)

Commercial landscape designers usually, though not always, lack formal training. They perform design services incidental to, and often as promotion for, profit from the materials and labor of their installation. They include nurserymen, who grow, sell, and install plants; landscape contractors, who do various kinds of earthwork or outdoor contruction in wood or masonry, with or without planting service; and gardeners who, in the course of maintaining installed planting, often have considerable freedom to influence, change, or expand its development.

Professional landscape architects include those who have received training at an accredited school, or have had long professional experience. They provide design and supervision services on a straight fee, time or percentage-of-cost basis, taking no direct profit on materials or labor. They are a small group, perhaps 1500 in the entire country, concentrated almost entirely in urban centers. In the San Francisco Bay region there are perhaps fifty; in Los Angeles not over one hundred. By contrast there are seven hundred qualified archi-

tects in Los Angeles; probably five hundred around San Francisco.

What are the relations between these three groups, in determining the form of our outdoor environment? We have guessed that in terms of quantity they divide it roughly into thirds. In terms of quality the professionals have a consciously developed and maintained theory of landscape design. This is taught in the schools and carried out quite consistently in most professional work. They also have a conscious concern with the quality of the design and installation of their work. The work done by conscious amateurs and commercials is nearly always derived from professional theories of form in a diluted or distorted fashion.

There is a further reciprocal relationship between professional and commercial practitioners. While the former exert pressure in the direction of quality of planning and installation, the latter exert pressure in the direction of the most production for the least cost and therefore the most profit. This pressure, subtly reinforced by the whole general climate of opinion of our society, as expressed in newspapers, radio, movies, etc., tends to reduce emphasis on design and on theory. The result is apt to be design work done in the simplest, most academic and hackneyed terms, which also reduces the time spent in supervision, because there is little if any difference between jobs. Thus, the tendency toward hack work, mechanical in form and sterile in content, tends to be a direct product of commercial pressure. The successful professional must combine (1) promotional imagination, (2) business acumen, (3) technical competence, (4) design ability. Those four together are a rare combination, and reputable practices have been built on not more than two or three of them.

Along with the tendency toward hack work done according to formulae (a theoretical justification for the capitulation of the professional to economic pressure) goes a parallel tendency toward superficiality, sensationalism, and trickery. Design, instead of being serious research and creation based on a sense of social responsibility, tends to become shallow, cynical, a tech-

8

nique for extracting from the world the living it "owes" the designers. Constant vigilance is required to avoid these two tendencies toward mechanical formulae and irresponsible tricks.

There is also a contradiction between the ideal of private practice (each professional in his own office) and the demands for more advanced and expanded technical organization implicit in the problems which society proposes for solution. In the physical planning fields, as the scale and importance of problems expand, the private office tends to become inadequate in terms of resources for research, design, and execution. Hence the growth of park departments and planning staffs as part of the government structure at every level, "competing with private enterprise."

The wasteful duplication in private office organization, in which each professional is apt to find himself secretary, bookkeeper, telephone girl, draftsman, file clerk, business manager, promotion man, contact man, publicity agent, and field superintendent, all distracting and detracting from his primary role as planner-designer-supervisor, will likewise sooner or later be recognized as more than individual problems. It is the physical separation of architects, engineers, and landscape architects, each in his own private office, which makes difficult the most complete, thorough, and productive collaboration around the general problem of site-space formation. On the other hand, the problem of preventing public design and planning agencies, with their tremendous potential for social production, from becoming sterile bureaucracies in which imagination, invention, experiment, and research are all frustrated and reduced to the lowest common denominator of dull mediocrity, will also have to be solved before either the public or the professional will consent to merging private offices in broader, more social organizations.

CHAPTER III

ON HISTORY

History can be recorded, and it can also be analyzed. In landscape history we find voluminous records, but little analysis. History is a continuous dynamic developing pattern, not a series of static pigeonholes. We are concerned with rational analysis of what has gone before, but not for purposes of adulation or imitation. We are the heirs of the ages, not their slaves.

The fundamental thesis of this book is that landscape design is a problem in the unified organization of specific units of outdoor space. This organization, when done well, is more than a collection of elements, features, pictures, or plants. Each unit—such as a garden, a park, an institution's grounds, or a planned community —can develop an overall integrated character in which the detailed elements play the part of the cast of characters in a play. The play determines the cast of characters, not vice versa.

The great bulk of landscape work done today is a collection of features and plants with little or no overall design or plan conception binding them together into a unity greater than themselves. To treat history as an accumulation of garden features—as do Richardson Wright and Mary Louise Gothein, for instance—is to leave us here in the middle of the twentieth century with a horrible potpourri of Egyptian pyramids, Babylonian hanging gardens, Roman atriums and Spanish patios, Medieval cloisters, Renaissance terraces and parterres, English landscape gardens, Colonial box gardens, Chinese pagodas, Japanese lanterns and rocks, American alpine beds. What do we do with it? What principles of organization must we establish to wade through this eclectic hash and determine a clear, clean, and beautiful way of solving our own problems on their own terms with the materials we have at hand? That is the objective of this book—to point a way out of the swamp of eclecticism and sentimentality in which the leaders of landscape architecture and horticulture have left us.

History is the body of tradition and experience from which we start. The purpose of creative design in any field is to continue the life and the vitality of tradition by developing and expanding it. This is opposed to the academic concept of defending tradition by suffocating it, embalming it, and codifying it. Compare the freedom, the richness, and the vitality of the original Renaissance gardens with the sterility of their American imitations, reproductions, and inspirations.

Even as Le Corbusier has said, the "styles" are a lie. There has never been an English garden outside of England, a Spanish garden outside of Spain, or a Japanese garden outside of

Japan. There has never been an Italian Renaissance garden since the Italian Renaissance, never an American Colonial garden since the vigorous beginning of the American States. A style is a definite form of expression of a certain people in a certain place at a certain time; "styles" are humbug and measured details. Talk of the enrichment of our garden art by eclectic borrowings is merely a cloak over esthetic laziness, esthetic immaturity, esthetic poverty.

What produces a historical style? A specific combination of time, place and social pattern, the latter also a specific combination of people, technological development, and political structure. It is true that after the earliest periods, styles have always been influenced by what went before them. We do not object to this—we too are influenced and inspired by the great works of other times and places. But we do not think that influence demands imitation, or that respect must be shown by faithful reproduction. Quite the contrary: What would Vignola, Raphael, and Bramante think of the little men who have scoured their work so persistently, measuring every detail, surveying every axis, and sending it all home in carefully rendered drawings to Long Island, Bar Harbor, and Montecito? The poverty of measured drawings! Rich America picking the pockets of historic France and Italy for their culture! We must have too much respect for history, for tradition, for the Renaissance, and for France and Italy to stoop to such meanness.

We do not think that the history of creative development in landscape design had to stop with Le Nôtre and Repton—rather, we think it is now our belated responsibility to pick up where they left off. We experience their work; we admire it; and we are stimulated to produce things as great in quality, but expressing in their specific form our own time, place, people, and technology. Never fear but that we are and shall continue to be an integral part of the great landscape tradition of the world.

CHAPTER IV

THROUGH THE EIGHTEENTH CENTURY

WEST AND EAST

The history of landscape design is simple and clear through Baroque France of the seventeenth century, or up to the Industrial Revolution. It has two basic streams—the formal axial tradition of Europe and western Asia, and the stylized nature-symbolism of eastern Asia. These two streams had little contact with or influence upon each other until the seventeenth century— that is, until near the end of pre-industrial history. Each stream has clear continuity of basic form and content throughout its development. We understand the former better than the latter, simply because the development of understanding between Eastern and Western cultures is still in its infancy.

FORMAL WESTERN TRADITION

The formal tradition is not one simple regular stream; its development was uneven and irregular. It proceeded through a series of cultural periods at different locations in time and place, although with a thread of continuity running through them. Each period tended to develop from simple informal or unself-conscious beginnings in the ordinary adaptation of people's living needs to topography and climate, through gradual accumulation and consciousness of wealth and power centralized in a fraction of the population, to a flowering in rich and controlled expression and a decadence in meaningless elaboration.

Geographically the formal tradition developed in the central latitudes of mild semi-arid climate running from central Asia through to the western end of the Mediterranean basin, with protrusions south into tropical India and north into temperate Europe. Historically its high points and clearest expressions were in Renaissance Italy, Baroque France, and the Moslem world which extended from central Asia and Mughal India through Persia, Arabia, and North Africa to Moorish Spain.

PRE-RENAISSANCE—In all the pre-Renaissance cultures there is a consistent, simple, orderly rectangularity—a direct expression of human organization within established boundaries. The site, the surrounding landscape, and nature in general, are recognized in the adaptation of the plans to topography and views, but not by any more subtle or subjective inclusion of naturalistic forms or symbols. Within this rectangular system there are two tendencies apparent: an irregular, free, or functional relation of rectangles, usually at 90 degree angles, sometimes still freer and more irregular; and the growth from this of axial bilateral symmetry, that is, the tendency to relate all rectangles on their center lines, to make these center lines more and more continuous as a basic skeleton for the plan, and to develop a continuously more elaborate and formalized or conventionalized emphasis on major and minor axes, vistas, allées, terminal features, etc.

In general, the development of symmetrical axial plan control seemed to proceed parallel with expansion in physical scale and in the material power of those who controlled such plans. It was a pregnant pattern insofar as it represented a search for the rational, beautiful and orderly organization of space for human use and enjoyment; it tended to become sterile as it became mechanical, arbitrary, and expressive of minority power and authority rather than of majority needs. Its three historical peaks are likewise peaks of centralized power: despotic Egypt, imperial Rome, and the Baroque monarchies of seventeenth-century Europe. Conversely the two limited pre-industrial expressions of democracy—that is, of man's attempts to improve the structure of his social relations—which occurred in ancient Greece before Alexander the Great and in Europe in the late Middle Ages from the thirteenth to the fifteenth centuries, produced much richer, subtler, and freer planning conceptions. While their open space developments were limited by requirements of security and topography, the intellectual activity of the Greek freedmen and the Gothic guildsmen, in their free towns, produced recognized peaks in rich and refined architectural expression. The open space relations of Greek acropolis and Gothic town square had a freedom in form and a humanity in scale that was foreign to the authoritarian expressions of Egypt, Rome, and Baroque Europe.

MOSLEM TRADITION—The Moslem tradition preceded the Renaissance in time, and was doubtless a contributing influence through trade channels. Although its great development ran from the seventh through the fifteenth centuries, the basic character of Moslem or Moorish work has remained consistent ever since.

This may be because those peoples have never experienced the cultural release and invigoration, combined with confusion and contradictions, which came to the western world with the industrial and democratic revolutions. Fine examples of Moslem gardens can be found all the way from central Asia and northern India through Persia, Arabia, and Turkey to North Africa and Spain. They were primarily enclosed gardens, insulated with walls or buildings from the aridity or the humidity of their environs and from general social contact; they were planned in axial rectangular patterns of a simplicity, clarity, restraint, discipline and delicacy not to be found in the western European tradition. Their primary elements were cool foliage, water, paving, and plants producing fruits and fragrance.

RENAISSANCE—In many ways the Renaissance marked the beginning of our modern capitalist world. Its great works resulted from the patronage of the mercantile capitalists who were beginning, by intrigue and by force, to take power and authority out of the hands of the feudal landlords. Its great artists and architects drew their strength and their inspiration from the beginnings of the modern scientific approach—the open-minded examination of the world around them, its orderly analysis, classification, and cataloging, and from this information the development of new forms, new techniques, and new combinations of old forms.

The Renaissance began in the mild semi-arid climate of Italy, and it was here that its greatest garden expressions were produced. The important work of the period was around Florence in the early Renaissance, and around Rome in the high Renaissance. We find, as earlier, a development from simple country homes to great palaces for the wealthy and powerful, expressed through a most rich, flexible, and imaginative application of the technique of axial planning to the rough topography and the exacting clientele. These were architectural gardens: the form was determined and controlled by architectural elements, walls, and steps, paving and water containers. Plants played a minor role; they were clipped and forced to conform to architectural (sculptural) form concepts. It was only with the

13

relaxed maintenance of the intervening centuries that the great cypresses and oaks were able to develop their own forms as we see them today. They were terraced gardens, in which the basic human need for horizontal ground planes on rough terrain was recognized amply and graciously. They were sculptural gardens, in which sculpture was used with freedom and strength as an integral part of the architectural structure of the garden. Many of them were water gardens, in which any available water source was tied into the central structure of the garden and exploited with a richness and imagination not since equalled, with jets and rills and waterfalls, channels and basins and water organs. All the best of these gardens of the Italian Renaissance were complete and unified form-concepts, in which the strength of the whole outweighed any of the parts, even the buildings.

BAROQUE—From the Renaissance gardens of Italy to the Baroque gardens of France and Austria was a great and final step in the development of the formal landscape tradition—in time from the sixteenth to the seventeenth centuries; in topographical space from the rugged hills of Italy to the flat lands of continental Europe; in politics from contests for power between feudal lord and mercantile capitalist to their temporary alliance in the interests of mutual security. From this alliance emerged king and nation to form a pattern within which business could proceed without interruption and turmoil.

This Baroque order, harking back to Rome and Egypt, produced the final cumulative overpowering summary of the physical expression of authoritarian control and centralized power. Nothing before or since has equalled the magnificence, the arrogance, or the impending sterility of the Baroque space concepts which reached their final expression in the limitless gardens developed over a third of a century at Versailles for Louis XIV by André Le Nôtre. The simple graphic diagram of endless center lines radiating from a central control point (Louis' bedroom), passing from garden spaces to allées dominating the countryside or avenues

dominating the city; serene, superior, aloof but watchful, bleak, inhuman, expressing the individual opposed to and in control of the community, hiding endless slums behind its sweeping skirts, was saved from its mechanical stupidity only by the panting talents of eager designers. This plumbers' planning system has since haunted the world in sterile redundance from Washington to Tokyo, from Buenos Aires to Canberra.

Nevertheless these Baroque gardens were elegant, rich and fanciful in their detail and in their application to specific sites. They developed concepts of the use of water and trees in large clear controlled quiet forms which are of continuing value as we work toward comparable scale in the control of our relations with nature.

Discussing "THE ORGANIZATION OF OUTER SPACE—The Residential Group and Nature," Giedion analyzes the other Baroque concept, a relationship of architecture to nature or to large open spaces including natural elements such as trees and water: ". . . the royal chateau . . . dominated the town behind it and the natural terrain that spread out before it. . . . An immense complex of buildings, more than two thousand feet long, has been directly confronted with nature; the grounds are a real part of the structure itself, and form with it a whole of great power and grandeur." Even though by "nature" Giedion refers to man's formalization of garden elements, he describes an important milestone in the relationship of buildings to the land. The path of development he traces, from Vaux-le-Vicomte through Versailles, the Piazza Obiqua in Rome, the "places" of Paris and of Nancy, the crescents of Bath, and the Piazza del Popolo in Rome to van Doesburg and Corbusier today, is pregnant and stimulating. It helps us to develop concepts of community open space beyond the mechanical "functional" level and to develop balanced relations in scale between site and development. Corbusier, Sitté, and Saarinen expand the analysis.

SPAIN AND PORTUGAL, during the Renaissance and Baroque periods, produced garden

14

work which was a remarkable blend of Moorish clarity and craftsmanship, Italian classic organization, and indigenous richness and flamboyance. Eight hundred years of the benevolent and productive autocracy of the Moors left marks on Spanish culture which no amount of physical destruction could erase. The typical "Spanish" garden today throughout Latin America, as well as the Iberian peninsula, is the patio—enclosed, intimate and secluded—rather than the open country villa which Charles V and four Philips tried so hard to import into Spain. Spanish gardens of the Renaissance and Baroque periods are among the best examples of that expansion in cultural richness produced by the merging of two or more strong streams. From the fine pure Moslem gardens of the Alhambra and Generalife near Granada, through the gardens of the Alcazar in Seville done for Peter the Cruel by Moorish workmen who left their distinct flavor throughout, to the Renaissance adaptations at Aranjuez, the Escorial, the Parterre of the Retiro in Madrid, and La Granja, there was established a typical garden pattern—enclosed, but with Renaissance detail —that has maintained considerable integrity and authenticity to this day. This continuity may be due to the fact that the Iberian countries and their expansions in Latin America, like the Moslem lands, have yet to go through the full and disturbing flowering of the Industrial Revolution. The fascist invasion of Spain in 1939, during which the gardens of the Alcazar were destroyed, was the last step in the chain of forcible frustration of this flowering.

AMERICAN COLONIES—The American colonial gardens of our eastern seaboard, developed throughout the seventeenth and eighteenth centuries by settlers from England and western Europe, continued the English process of breaking down the formal plan in a more functional manner. In the sparse frontier economy of the colonies, the settlers were forced to revert to the simple direct utilitarian planning which was the grass roots of the formal tradition. Although the colonial gardens in plan were geometric and at times axial, they were developed with such simple unostentatious elements—trees, grass, box-wood hedges, paths and drives—that they produced a result quite different from the elaborate frivolity of their European antecedents. Because they were functional gardens, often primarily concerned with flowers, fruit and vegetables, the plants on which their main form depended were allowed to develop their best natural characteristics. Here is one strong expression of that unity between geometry in plan and free informal growth in elevation which is of primary importance to those of us who are in search of clear and strong landscape forms for the twentieth century. Later colonial gardens, primarily Mount Vernon, combined the influences of axial planning with the irregular naturalism stemming from the eighteenth century romantic revolt to produce gardens which were formal and informal at once, which had organization that was relaxed, unobtrusive, truly functional, and truly charming. This healthy sprout from the running stolon of landscape tradition (western branch) died aborning. It produced no visible reaction in the minds of either the vigorous vulgarians of the nineteenth century, or the stale academicians of the twentieth.

SUMMARY OF WESTERN TRADITION— We can sum up the formal tradition as a tradition of unified architectural conceptions in which indoors and outdoors, structural and natural elements, were integrated to produce complete site-space organizations. It is a tradition of planned organization of open space in the most simple, direct, logical and rational manner. It is a clear and positive expression of man's separation from and/or authority over nature, of the authority of some men over many other men, and of the culture, wealth, and power of those dominant few. It was produced, in a complete and final form, before the discovery of the industrial techniques for mass production of goods and wealth, by cultures basically autocratic in social structure.

CHINA AND JAPAN

The Oriental pictorial-symbolic landscape tradition developed parallel with the western

15

formal pattern, and over a comparable period of time, in eastern Asia, primarily China and Japan. This part of the world was isolated from western Asia and Europe geographically by mountains and deserts and politically by the westward orientation of Occidental expansion, and included as great a range of climate and topography. Here a landscape tradition developed in which man and nature were considered friends and companions, at peace with one another, in which man loved nature, communed with her, and sought peace and revitalization among her forms. In this tradition formalism, regularity, geometry, the straight line, the sharp corner, reason, order and logic were rejected—or never developed—in favor of the irregular, the picturesque, the pictorial, the symbolic, and the mystic. Natural materials and elements, with their own characteristics maintained or exaggerated by sensitive representational handling, appeared in dominant proportions: at small scale surrounded by structural enclosure, at larger scale surrounding architectural elements such as pagodas and tea houses.

In China, within enclosed courtyards we find a range of character from simple paving with tubbed flowering specimens to arrangements of water, grills, zigzag bridges, fantastic doorways, water-carved limestone rockeries, and exuberant planting that are a special kind of picturesque rococo design. One bridge to the western tradition is in this Chinese domestic pattern, a system of enclosed courtyards, with living rooms facing them, basically similar to the Moslem Moorish tradition. Another we find in Hamlin: "The most marked feature of Chinese planning is its extraordinary formality and its ability to create great conceptions in large terms. In a temple, all the main halls and gates are centered on one chief axis, with roofs running across. . . . The same system of planning controls the Chinese ideals of city design. In Peking one great north-south axis carries through the entire city a full seven miles long. . . ." In this axial pattern, however, the Chinese developed a system for blocking the vista by setting openings between courts off the axes, in contrast with the western emphasis on length of controlled vista

and closer to our current concepts of baffling off portions of the space so as never to see it all at once. Apparently large formal architectural conceptions were set in the midst of, or confronting, irregular naturalistic parks in which the Lake-and-Island ("shan shui"—hills and water) concept was dominant.

This Chinese garden style which had been evolving since the second century before Christ was probably introduced into Japan along with continental Buddhism in the sixth century A.D. The Japanese took it up and proceeded from enthusiastic imitation through a translation into their own terms of talent, sensitivity and topography to the production of that complete, rich and harmonious conception—the Japanese garden. This, a thoroughly indigenous product, the object of so much shallow curiosity and blind imitation on the part of the western world since 1868, is probably the most highly refined and completely developed garden conception our world culture has known. By contrast with the architectural conceptions of the western world and the horticultural enthusiasms of the nineteenth and twentieth centuries the Japanese developed techniques and forms for the use of purely natural materials—plants, water, rocks—in landscape development which produced the most complete, careful and sensitive expression of the specific natural character of the material, and at the same time put it under the control of a larger human conception and handling which improved its form and character. The symbolism and nature representation were one of those systems of standardization which have been basic to all great cultural expressions. What is relevant to us is what we see in the physical result: the restraint, the calculation, the control; the orderly sculptural use, in infinite variety of arrangement, of rocks at every scale from sand to boulders; the precise refinement, in varying degrees, of rock in water basins and lanterns; the endless delicate training of trees and shrubs to produce an exact line or weight; the constant ingenuity in the use of stray materials, straw, sticks, stones, sand piles; the careful modeling of ground, shrub, and rock forms into continuous sculptural wholes;

and the intimate relation to an architecture of light sliding panels, which could be opened wide to the garden, and which when repeated in it established continuity with the house.

The Japanese garden, like the Chinese, was a pictorial garden rather than a space conception. They were gardens for withdrawal, repose, contemplation, and ceremony. The tradition was produced by societies which were largely feudal —that is, authoritarian—in structure. One of the techniques by which feudal authority has maintained its control for centuries has been mystic obscurantism—that is, irrational answers to rational questions. This was part and parcel of the philosophical base of Chinese and Japanese gardens. The Tea Ceremony of the Japanese is strangely like the Ivory Tower of western intellectuals: a spot of order in a disorderly world, to which we withdraw to escape its vulgarity.

EIGHTEENTH CENTURY

The eighteenth century was the century of the Industrial Revolution and of great social ferment throughout the western world. From Abraham Darby's perfection of the mass production of iron about 1750 to the industrial use of James Watts' steam engine in 1776 (the year of the Declaration of Independence and of Adam Smith's *Wealth of Nations*) the world was feeling the birth pangs of a new social structure which had been in pregnancy for three centuries before. Mercantile capitalists were finding at hand the tools to new and untold wealth, and there was a tremendous expansion in social horizons. "Life, liberty and the pursuit of happiness" and "Liberty, equality, fraternity" became the slogans with which the rising revolutionary bourgeoisie secured the support of the common people in their struggle against the restrictions of feudal society. Not since the great slave-empire of Rome fell before the new ideas of the feudal barbarians from the north had there been such social upheaval. The idea of a broader, more secure, more rational world, in which man en masse could seek freedom and individual development, grew like a lusty weed.

This expansion in social horizons brought an expansion in physical horizons. Man was secure on the land; the land was his; nature was no longer fearsome and unknown; why shut the garden off from her? The stage was ready for the great romantic idea of making all nature part of each landscape project. With this great sunrise came a dark cloud: the factories and slums of the "insensate industrial town" (Mumford) began to befoul the landscape. Formal gardening had been sterile since Le Nôtre, and now look what man was doing to the land with these filthy towns. A loss of faith in the old systems of physical order became part of the search for a new life.

The focal point for the development of new ideas and forms in the landscape moved from Italy in the sixteenth century to France in the seventeenth and to England in the eighteenth. In the first half of this century, already weary of stale formality, the stage was set for the romantic revolt by the writings of Addison, Pope, and the Earl of Shaftesbury. They extolled the beauties of landscape painting and the wilds of nature, and satirized bitterly the stupidities of geometric gardening. Then one William Kent leaped the garden wall and discovered all nature to be a garden. (Peets.) He and Batty Langley began to campaign for the elimination of geometry, order, and rational planning, the introduction of idealizations and rationalizations of nature and of every sort of picturesque, wild, ruined, romantic, irregular, pictorial element, whether of man or nature. This movement reached its climax in the mass production of clumps and hillocks by that great rugged individualist, Capability Brown. This prolific romantic outburst was accompanied by a mass destruction of formal gardens, and of all boundaries between pleasure gardens and open park lands. A typical expression was the ha-ha, a trench or depression accompanied by a retaining wall, so arranged as to keep cattle out of the pleasure garden without appearing in the view from pleasure garden into meadows and woods.

After the widespread excesses of Brown, the

17

romantic movement in landscape design settled down in the work and writings of Sir Humphrey Repton and Prince von Puckler-Muskau, men of taste, judgment and a sense of order and rational fitness, who eliminated excesses, extremes, and vulgarities and produced that organized theory of informal or naturalistic landscape development which is still followed by the academicians of the American landscape profession. It was they who swung the current away from the picturesque and pictorial, more subjective and irrational direction advocated by Uvedale Price and John Payne Knight toward the more sensible and direct ordering and representation—verging on imitation—of the scenes of nature. (See Tunnard.)

The English romantic revolt, in its time, was a vital and vigorous movement. Into the standardized bilateral symmetry of geometric architectural garden planning it introduced the whole wealth and wonder of the natural world, the continuity of the rural countryside, healthy pride in the land and its growth, and the initial refreshing richness of the irregular, the disorderly, the picturesque, the irrational and subjective. As Wright and Gothein indicate, it re-appraised the beauty of individual trees and gave the first hints of the herbaceous border and the mixed tree and shrub planting. The garden of, for, and by plants, the horticultural collection, already foreshadowed in the breakdown of overall form in the English formal garden, now began to appear.

While the romantic movement came as a part of that whole social ferment which accompanied the birth of industrial techniques and modern scientific procedures, it marked rather the conclusion of development of the pre-industrial western landscape tradition than the beginning of a new development. With it the western and eastern traditions came to full parallelism in content as a world landscape tradition. Aside from differences in detail and technique, both these parents contained the same system of opposing paired concepts: formality and informality, classicism and romanticism, geometry and biology, architecture and nature, town and country. However much their various spokes-

men may have spoken of integrating these pairs, they did not physically succeed. The world was not yet ready for such integration; the relations between man and nature were still too confused. That is the job which has been left for us to tackle in the last half of the twentieth century.

Since the eighteenth there have been no major steps, no new thoughts, in the theory of landscape design as a system of organization of outdoor space. There have been only endless academic re-hashings, some clever and convincing, some stupid and clumsy; new combinations of old patterns, new discoveries of old features and details, new measured drawings and surveys of the same old gardens, all coalescing into the incredible hash of present-day American professional, commercial, and amateur landscape design. It is high time to take another step forward, to brush away the cobwebs and the antique fishnets and examine the world around us, to leap into the broad stream of science and society, merge ourselves with the century of the common man, and play our part in expanding the frontiers of man's use and experience of the space in which he lives.

FORM AND SOCIETY

This world landscape tradition, with its eastern and western halves, is a highly selected, very fragmentary tradition. It is not at all a complete expression of man's relation to the land and to nature during the centuries of recorded history, but rather an expression of the relation of very small fractions of the population to the land and to the balance of the population of their times. Since the earliest periods of civilization we have found three distinct types of gardens:

1. The utility garden, in which special plants were raised as a crop for their produce, and in which the space for people could be the minimum necessary for cultivation.
2. The living garden, in which space for people was most important, and plants and other features formed a background for their activities.
3. The show garden, in which there had to be

18

plenty of space for people, but to which they came to see some impressive sort of picture, composition, or arrangement of plants, sculpture, or construction. The important thing in the garden space was not the activities of the people who came into the garden; it was the picture which showed the wealth, power, or taste of the owner.

All three of these have existed in all periods, whatever their system of form.

We must finally conclude that specific kinds of form on the ground—such as the formal or informal pattern—do not necessarily express different kinds of social organization, or degrees of relationship between authority and democracy. The expression has been more complicated; Chinese, Japanese, Italian, French, and English aristocrats and landowners have all been equally firmly in control of their societies, but have expressed it in varied ways, based on their own times and places, cultural and technological developments. However, we can say that authority has been expressed in an expansion in scale to the point of bleakness and inhumanity, an elaboration in detail to the point of frivolity and sterility, and/or a rapidly progressive rigidity in plan conception. Conversely democracy has been expressed in humanity of scale, simplicity and practicality in detail, and continuous flexibility in plan conception.

IN CONCLUSION

These two contrasting components of the world landscape tradition—Western geometry and Eastern irregularity, authority of man and respect for nature, the straight line and the free curve—are still in the twentieth century the cornerstones of the official theory of formal and informal landscape design as taught in American professional schools.

Further examination of the complex and varied space-patterns which make up the world landscape tradition impresses us with the fact that it contains four main streams of form and concept, rather than the two—formal and informal—which are now embalmed in our official theories. For formal geometric planning appears in two equally strong streams, the bilateral axial systems of Egypt, Rome, Renaissance Italy, Baroque France, the Hindu and Moslem world, the Aztecs and Mayas, and imperial China; and the irregular free geometry of Assyrio-Babylon, Greece and the Aegean, Gothic Europe, the Incas of Peru, and less pretentious developments in all periods. Likewise informal irregular planning has two clear strong currents—the subjective, romantic, picturesque, pictorial symbolism of China, Japan, the early English landscape gardeners, Uvedale Price and John Payne Knight; and the more "sensible and practical" naturalism of Brown, Repton, von Puckler-Muskau, Olmsted, and Jensen. To foist two of these four on our defenseless students as the only sacred static world system of landscape design is clearly arbitrary, however much it may be rationalized. Argument as to whether bilateral symmetry is the rich and mature fruit, or a sterile parasitic growth, upon irregular geometry; or as to whether the picturesque is a vulgarization of the natural, or naturalism is the picturesque made practical, is all equally academic and irrelevant. We cannot analyze history without examining it in its entirety, and we cannot continue its development and expansion in the face of dogmatic and whimsical eclecticism.

19

CHAPTER V

SINCE THE EIGHTEENTH CENTURY

INDUSTRIAL REVOLUTION

It is appropriate to pivot an analysis of the history of landscape design around that period of abrupt technological acceleration in the eighteenth century called the Industrial Revolution. It is appropriate as an analysis of landscape tradition, and it is appropriate as an analysis of the history of world culture of which landscape design is an integral part. For in the two hundred years since mass production of iron became technically possible, the human world has advanced technologically, economically, politically, and socially as much if not more than in all the thousands of years before. This sudden qualitative expansion in the long, slow, quantitative accumulation of iron handicraft made possible the development of mercantile capitalism, even then struggling out from under the control of feudal absolutism, into the industrial and financial capitalism which today operates the most tremendous system of production ever seen in our world. We need scarcely list the well-known rapid-fire technical and social advances—coal, oil, electricity, atomic power; revolutions, parliamentary democracies, secret ballot, women's suffrage, public education, abolition of slavery, trade-union organization—which have burst upon the

world in this two hundred years in which the historical timetable has maintained so constant an acceleration. Before the Industrial Revolution security, comfort, and culture for more than an elevated fraction of the population was an impractical dream far beyond the capacity of handicraft production. Now this dream for all mankind has become the practical potential of industrial organization, within the perspective of our own times.

THE NINETEENTH AND TWENTIETH CENTURIES

The nineteenth century was perhaps the most tremendous, pushing, aggressive, expansive, ruthless, and confused hundred years in world history. In this relatively brief historical period a newborn social structure took over the entire world in great strides and grew from lusty youth to full maturity while doing it. Control of production and distribution passed from the merchants and landlords to the industrialists and bankers. Free competition produced its own nemesis, monopoly. The whole territory of the physical globe was neatly and completely divided up into independent capitalist states and their colonies and dependencies. Feudal or

20

slave social relations survived only in backward sections—China, India, our own deep South—where they were useful to the new dominant entrepreneurs. Modern free wage labor appeared in masses, driven off the land and into the factories, and immediately began to organize and to argue for its rights. Science expanded with and before industry. The boundaries of the known world leaped from the shadows of the nearby woods (to which our garden had just been expanded) to the far stars of the universe and the secret cells of our bodies. The physical environment changed with an appalling rapidity. The industrial town, a collection of slums around a belching factory, grew from the small pimples which appeared with the industrial revolution to the ulcerous sores of the latter half of the century. Political morale passed from the vibrant optimism which elected Thomas Jefferson in the teeth of the Alien and Sedition Acts, to the cynicism and pessimism which followed the betrayal of the results of the Civil War in the deep South and the emergence of the great trusts as the primary power in America. Esthetic morale went through a similar cycle; with the end of the century independent design had been nearly completely stifled and isolated from an uncomprehending clientele, and artists and architects were either licking their wounds in ivory towers, or glibly selling neo-classicism, romanticism and eclecticism. (See Mumford, Huberman, Hamlin, Finkelstein.)

The twentieth century has seen constant acceleration in every facet of political, social, technological and cultural development: a century of boom and bust, of wars and imperialism, of fascism and socialism, of tremendous expansion in the monopolized control of production and distribution, of constantly sharpening contradictions between the expanding forces of democracy and the restrictive forces of reaction. There seems to be little compromise possible between Henry Luce's American Century and Henry Wallace's Century of the Common Man. It is a century of automobiles and airplanes, of electricity and atomic power, a century in which all our tremendous potential for benevolent mass production seems to hang in dreadful balance with persistent forces of destruction, decadence, and decay.

ART AND SOCIETY

The problem of the creative worker in the nineteenth and twentieth centuries has been complicated: a contrast and contradiction between the flood of wealth, good living, and new esthetic horizons implicit in machine production, and the poverty of opportunity, the scarcity of employment, with which he found himself surrounded in the real practical world. He found it necessary to fight for his opportunities, his esthetic integrity, and his livelihood in a world which had become fast, shallow, vulgar, violent, and shabby, and which seemed to have lost interest in serious values.

There were three ways to turn. One was to the taste of the new ruling business class, which had taken the place of the feudal lord and the Renaissance patron, and which was primarily responsible both for his isolation from a mass audience and for the degradation of the taste of that mass audience through the mass commercialization of their cultural media. This was the path of eclecticism, romanticism, and neo-classicism, the substitution of entertainment and decoration for serious creation, the frustration of esthetic research, the repression of esthetic integrity, and the sterilization of esthetic production.

ECLECTICISM—The eclectic school of landscape design has emphasized the pictorial or show type of garden in most periods. The professional arbiters of taste in the past century have been most impressed by the French and Italian Renaissance show places and by the romantic English landscape school. From these they built up an arbitrary and dogmatic set of design "rules," into which other periods of garden design had to fit willy-nilly. This historical study of garden design was intensely interested in what was done and how it was done, but not so much in why it was done. It made careful studies and measured drawings of existing arti-

21

facts, without paying much attention to the kind of people, the local and regional conditions, the available materials, and the particular mental atmosphere, cultural and esthetic quality, and social organization of the specific time and place which produced those artifacts.

LANDSCAPE ARCHITECTURE QUARTERLY—APRIL 1938

It is perhaps to this very eclecticism—the borrowing of styles that are native to other countries and other times—that garden design in America is most obligated for its wealth of expression as an art; for in this country there is hardly a climate or a geographical environment or an inherited American tradition to which some landscape architectural form based on European precedent cannot appropriately be adapted as a means to both utility and greater ornament.

MODERNISM—Another path for creative work in general, that of the moderns, has clung stubbornly to the principle of freedom of enterprise in esthetic endeavor; it has explored the potentialities of new techniques, new materials and new space concepts to the limits of its physical resources. In the course of this insistence on the maintenance of esthetic integrity it has tended, in varying degrees, to turn in on itself, to retreat into an ivory tower, and to reject the relevance of social responsibility and social realism. This path has been followed, through the first third of this century, by most of the minority of really serious creative workers who have rejected the academic approach. Into it has gone most of the most productive creative energies of our times; at best it has expanded very greatly the boundaries of human experience and service within reach of the graphic and spatial arts; at worst it has degenerated to empty fiddling with empty forms and colors at the same level as any hack academic art work.

The third path—the stony one of avowed social responsibility, social realism, and politics—has been followed by a few hardy souls in those fields where work was possible, such as housing, planning and recreation, or political posters and cartoons. (See Bernal in *Circle*, and Finkelstein.)

There are three primary currents which have run through twentieth century advances in the allied arts of painting, sculpture, and archi-

tecture: the space concept, the materials concept, the social concept. The first accepts three-dimensional space-form: the sphere, the cube, the room, the field, the continuity of more than one of these, as a basic element in plastic or esthetic organization. Historically this concept goes back to the discovery and elaboration of the use of perspective on a picture plane in the Renaissance and Baroque art periods. The next major step was taken by the Cubists, who elaborated and complicated the potentialities for treatment of space on canvas by experimenting with relations between planes, forms, and colors without regard to the laws of academic representation or "true" perspective. Modern sculptors took up the idea and carried it much farther in three-dimensional work, introducing all sorts of rich and imaginative space relations and openings into the interiors of what had been mass objects to walk around and look at, seldom through or into. Modern architects went on at the human scale of full enclosure and direct spatial experience, and have produced a body of work which indicates beyond the possibility of doubt the tremendous potential enrichment of our environment which is implicit in such marriages of structural and spatial imagination. The further expansion of this concept to the outdoors, with its greater scale and reduction of boundaries and controls, has barely begun.

The second current accepts the native quality and potential of the material used to organize this space as primary in determining how to use it. It roots deep into many past periods of creative production. It became lost in the distortions and superficialities of eclectic decorative work. Modern painters began its rescue in working with collages and montages, and modern sculptors, industrial designers, and architects have continued this to the point of basing large portions of their form concepts on serious study of the nature of the materials involved.

The third recognizes the existence of people in relation to the creative process in the form of the controversy "is art for art's sake—or for people?" This has been expressed in various ways—the new techniques of representation developed by the cubists, the rejection of subject matter by abstractionists and non-objective painters, the search for new subject matter by dadaists, futurists, surrealists, etc. The housing and planning activities of many architects—Le Corbusier, Gropius, Neutra—express art for people rather than for its own sake.

Independent indigenous design has persisted in America throughout the twentieth century: in the graphic and sculptural arts in a great deal of vital and vigorous work ranging from the abstract through the regional to the social: in architecture in the great and rich work of Frank Lloyd Wright and his apprentices; European emigrees such as Gropius and Breuer, Mies van der Rohe, Richard Neutra; and a host of younger men taking their inspiration from either or both these groups.

During about 35 of these years of the struggle of independent design the landscape profession either dragged its heels in unsympathetic skepticism, or sided openly with the opposition. In 1927 Elbert Peets was a lonely voice crying in the wilderness. However, about 1936–37 a few landscape architects began positive action toward bringing the theory and practice of their work up to date with the more advanced sections of architecture and the allied arts. They abandoned the old sham battle between formal axial and informal wiggly plan patterns, and began to search for new forms evolving directly from their problems and the materials used in their solution. James C. Rose, Daniel Urban Kiley, and Garrett Eckbo did thoroughgoing research in the Graduate School of Design at Harvard University. At about the same time Edward A. Williams, working in the San Francisco Bay Region, was developing similar ideas. Thomas D. Church, thoroughly established in professional practice in San Francisco, after ten years of straining against the old Beaux Art forms, abandoned them and began likewise a search, in carrying on his professional work, for new and better forms. He has been aided in this search by a number of talented younger people—Robert Royston, Marie Harbeck, Douglas Baylis, Lawrence Halprin. There is now widespread questioning among the younger generation of

the old academic formulae to which the profession still clings, and there are a good many sound practical practitioners who have abandoned them in whole or in part, without substituting any very positive new concept of landscape form for them.

Before the last war a good deal of very free work had been done in most of the countries of Europe. Dates and names are rather confused and information is difficult to obtain today. In the Scandinavian countries, Germany, and Austria there seems to have been a strong horticultural tradition and interest in plants and nature, combined with sensible, straightforward, practical planning which was not afraid of strong but irregular geometry. This appeared clearly in the work of Albert Esch and Otto Valentien. In France, Italy and Belgium garden work was much more influenced by modern artists and architects, and alternated between imagination and triviality. Canneel-Claes, Le Grand, Le Corbusier, and Guevrekian all produced interesting and relevant work. In England Christopher Tunnard made valiant efforts to reintroduce simplicity and overall form concepts to their jumbled garden tradition, before coming to America in 1939. In the Soviet Union a new park movement, immense in scale and program, synthesized the old western concepts of landscape park, playground, athletic center, public museum, and commercial amusement center into a series of projects qualitatively different from all of these components. (See Lounz.)

Since the war Cath. Polak Daniels from Holland and René Péchère from Belgium have sent us careful and sensitive statements on landscape design in the spirit, and at the scale, of the specific historically developed cultural landscapes of their long-humanized homelands. From England Brenda Colvin speaks simply and comprehensively of the total landscape of that green isle. The breadth, clarity, and consistency of her concepts have major importance, particularly to us who are still mired in the pigeonhole patterns of arbitrary land subdivision—here a garden, there a park, seldom if ever a complete unit of man and nature. She picks up again the concepts of Kent, Brown, and Repton, who solved the problem of the unavoidable boundaries of the formal conception in the total landscape. They destroyed the boundaries of the garden, the estate, and the park. These became as one with the landscape of England. The comfortable sense of security and control went unimpeded, over terrace and ha-ha and meadow, as far as the eye could reach over the tight little isle. But this concept was out of scale with the living needs of the families at the radial centers of these fine sweeps. It became conspicuous consumption and conspicuous waste. England, the struggle center and proving ground for so much of the growth of western democracy, developed a social atmosphere inhibitive to such expressions of feudal landlordism, however elegant, however refined, however tactfully merged with everything around, however elaborately rationalized with nature-loving doubletalk. This was not the integration of *man* with nature in the landscape; this was the integration, by paternalism, of the landscape with certain specific men who were separated from the majority of their fellows. Society was not yet ready for integration with the natural landscape. First things must come first. Men must be integrated with each other in democracy; then the integration of man and nature must be physically expressed at comparable scales: the individual house and garden; the community and the landscape; town and country. In the 18th century they tried a shortcut, the integration of a few men with the countryside, but it couldn't work. It remains to be seen whether the current town and country planning programs of the British Labor Government, however advanced in concept, will produce the kind of result projected by Miss Colvin, or will be dissipated and sterilized by that benevolent paternalism which is so effective a brake upon the growth of democracy.

From ravaged Poland, where cities are being rebuilt literally by hand with rubble, the following has come to us:

ALINA SCHOLTZOWNA, DECEMBER 27, 1948

I think our current tendencies in landscape design —as represented by the works of our leading personalities—are notable by their "architectureness." I mean they consider the unity of design, the proper arrangement of the elements, and the good proportions of the whole and of the details as most essential for a good work. The picturesque, the display given by the plants they consider to be of secondary value, though both—the charm and distinctiveness of the plant individual they appreciate very much. To some extent this attitude is the result of the belief that a layout should carry the mark of human work and never imitate nature, nor be only a gathering of nice-looking plants. . . .
Personally, I think in our times man should work for recovering the very nature for himself and for next generations sake with all his efforts and all his means —technical and scientific, and in the same time create new lay-outs—masterpieces (if possible) perfect in form, fully human and well situated in the landscape.

Neutral Sweden has seen a post-war renaissance of remarkable power in the sculptural modeling of landscape forms, as well as in the structural arrangement of community patterns. Recently in Brazil excellent work has been done by Roberto Burle Marx, working closely with the outstanding modern architects there, and expressing with great sensitivity the climate, people, and botany of the land. In the magazine "Arquitectura," particularly in July 1945, we find stimulating evidence of the continuing vitality of the great Mexican garden tradition. The modern movement as reflected in landscape design has two bases: one in modern art and architecture; one, like its historic predecessors, in climatic regionalism. This ties in with a persistent tendency for rich and active new cultures to develop in "backward" parts of the world.

FOLK ART

The garden of the common man is a subject on which we can find much sentimentality— "the cottage gardens of England"—but little rational information or historical record. There have been few, if any, measured drawings or photography tours of the little gardens of the peasantry, the working class, or even the middle class. Apparently the common man of history has not had the time, the resources or the space to produce a tradition durable enough to compete with the fantasy and stability of the gardens of his rulers.

Our lack of information may perhaps be a result of scholarly snobbery. Very likely an organized research program on a sincere and scientific basis would turn up a wealth of interesting material. The little garden has probably been more consistent in form through history than the big garden. Its owners have not had the means or the security basic to the esthetic experimentation and philosophic subtleties of the great garden expressions of history.

The small gardens of the lower two thirds of the population today, wherever the community is decentralized to a detached house-and-yard scale, are very likely good indicators of the general character of the small gardens of world history. Where such gardens are developed with any attention and care, we find no self-conscious esthetics, no search for "beauty," no worry over man and nature, but rather common sense, practicality, functional forms, and ingenuity in the use of available materials. We find orderly flower and vegetable gardens, healthy and well-maintained shrubs and trees, workyards, swings and sandboxes, homemade arbors for shade, occasional touches of imagination such as the use of empty bottles bottom up to edge flower beds—all the irregularities and inconsistencies of the day-to-day lives of ordinary people, with little time or energy for the "finer things in life." (See Agee and Ditchfield.)

FINKELSTEIN, DISCUSSING THE GERMINATING POWER OF FOLK ART

There is basically no conflict between folk and popular art on the one hand, and the great stream of individualistically created works of art on the other, with its schools, traditions of form, and accumulation of technique. Actually, as we shall see, there have been the most happy and fruitful relations between these two streams of culture. . . . If on the surface it would seem as if contemporary abstraction and people's movements in art are opposites, they are the opposites which can very possibly meet to produce a new flowering of art, although the resulting art will resemble neither abstraction nor what passes largely for popular art today . . . It points to the restoration of the contact between artist and audience that took place within folk cultures, but not now restricted to the narrow community and poverty-stricken life of medieval times; a contact rather taking place within the frame of social life and intercommunication made possible by contemporary civilization, so that the distinction between folk art, popular art, and the academic forms of art will disappear. Artists and audience will share a common language, and there will be only greater or smaller structures through which art will play its role of public communication.

PLANTS

Although the vulgar Victorians attempted a compromise between formality and informality, they produced only the "glorious gaudy botch" which Tunnard describes. He and Richardson Wright give us in detail the development from carpet bedding and subtropicals to the herbaceous border and the wild garden of Robinson and Jekyll: "Seven plant explorers . . . Japan opens up . . . Russian plant explorers . . . disseminating plant knowledge . . . books and magazines . . . advancement in hybridizing . . . the rage for fruit . . . changes in garden styles (conifers, willows, California and Cape plants, bedding-out, stove plants, sempervivums and sedums, orchids, water gardening, alpines . . . the rise of the experiment station." (Wright.)

All this tremendous growth in botanical and horticultural science, in plant knowledge and plant interest, although it provided us with the magnificent wealth of plant material at hand today, had a primarily destructive effect upon concepts of overall garden form. It introduced and over-emphasized the idea of the garden as a collection of plants by kinds and specimens, unrelated except botanically or geographically, without pictorial or space concepts, in which the plants are primary and people come only to look, discuss, and admire. This has established a third camp of garden arrangement, completing a triangle with the two professional schools of formality and informality, and adding further complication to the search for sound principles of outdoor space organization. Concern with space for living is the area of agreement which can unify this trio.

25

PARKS AND RECREATION

The American park movement, which began with the appointment of Frederick Law Olmsted, Senior, as Architect-in-Chief for the new Central Park in New York City in 1858, marked a very important change in the relationship of the professional landscape architect to society. For the first time in history he was not dependent solely on private patronage for a livelihood and the opportunity to produce creative work; for the first time in history he was employed directly by the people at large, through a duly elected representative governmental body, to plan the organization of a large body of public open space. While cynics may cite the limitations placed on the democratic process by the real estate and banker lobby, this fact of the emergence of direct public employment remains outstanding.

Public parks in America since Central Park set the pattern have been palliatives designed to offset the apparently unavoidable results of urbanization.

OLMSTED WROTE

Provisions for the improvement of the ground, however, pointed to something more than mere exemption from urban conditions, namely, to the formation of an opposite class of conditions; conditions remedial of the influences of urban conditions.

Two classes of improvements were to be planned for this purpose; one directed to secure pure and wholesome air, to act through the lungs; the other to secure an antithesis of objects of vision to those of the streets and houses, which should act remedially by impressions on the mind and suggestions to the imagination.

It is one great purpose of the Park to supply to the hundreds of thousands of tired workers, who have no opportunity to spend their summers in the country, a specimen of God's handiwork that shall be to them, inexpensively, what a month or two in the White Mountains or Adirondacks is, at great cost, to those in easier circumstances.

Mumford indicates the weakness of the park movement, in that it came after speculative subdivision and the inflation of land values, rather than before; it was a palliative, rather than a preventive or even a cure (the blight kept right on spreading); it was—and still is—an auxiliary appendage, rather than a central core, to the actual process of physically planning our cities and towns.

Olmsted introduced no new principles for organizing outdoor space, but rather took up the well-formulated naturalistic landscape gardening approach of Repton and von Puckler-Muskau and developed it, made it more sensible, more practical, more technically sound, perhaps more literal. As Mumford says, ". . . his plans were animated by technical intelligence and civic foresight. He was the first planner to see the necessity . . . of deliberately separating pedestrian traffic from wheeled traffic by creating underpasses and overpasses that permitted them to operate as separate systems." (See the selected papers of Olmsted and Vaux.)

The expansion of the park movement, initiated by Charles Eliot, into the setting aside of wild scenic lands as national and state parks far from the madding throng and high land prices of the urban centers, while socially valuable, has developed the idea of the landscape architect as the protector of natural beauty to the final ridiculous extreme at which he cannot introduce milled lumber or poured concrete into his design without great soul-searching and stabs from the conscience.

The recreation movement, concerned with active play, arts, crafts, music, and community activities, has developed parallel, and more or less in contact, with the park movement (concerned with settings for more passive relaxation and contemplation). It has expanded as the democratic pattern has expanded, and its limitations are imposed by forces which also limit the growth of democracy. It has developed a recreation profession composed of executives, community organizers, directors, and year-round recreation leaders, and a system of public and private organizations which parallels, largely cooperating but sometimes tending to compete with, the park organizations of the country. Recently, for instance, there has been considerable discussion as to the advisability of merging urban Park and Recreation or Playground Departments, marked by mutual fears and suspicions that each might swallow the other.

If the approach is rational, scientific, broad, and not impoverished, it is obvious that where parks and recreation are planned within one organization, each will help the other to achieve a balance of social usefulness, and of form between the functional requirements of playground elements and the plastic freedom of park spaces. While the recreation movement has not been as directly promoted and participated in by landscape architects as the park movement, it is obvious that its requirements for space, facilities, and equipment are equally relevant to the theory and practice of landscape design. Few recreation experts are landscape architects but many landscape architects have participated in the planning and design of recreation facilities. (See Neumeyer.)

CONSERVATION

Conservation needs and activities have appeared in strong and urgent form in all three divisions of our environment—urban, rural, primeval—within the last hundred years. Movements toward city and regional planning, slum clearance and better housing, parks and recreation have all been motivated, in one way or another, by the primary and obvious need to conserve our basic human resource—the people —from the destructive effects of our chaotic urban environments. In the rural or agricultural countryside the question of soil and water conservation has been brought out as the sharpest and clearest point of conflict or harmony between man and nature in the many excellent publications of the U. S. Soil Conservation Service, and most recently in that clear, timely and courageous book *Our Plundered Planet*, by Fairfield Osborn. In the primeval hinterland the struggle for conservation of forests and grasslands, of wildlife, of mineral resources, of water for power and irrigation and flood control, and of natural scenery in national and state parks has brought out the sharp contradiction between the interests of ordinary citizens and of those free enterprise elements who see no values beyond their own private profit.

In 1936 Persons wrote: "They (soil-erosion specialists) find that one hundred million once-fertile acres of farmland—equal to Illinois, Ohio, Maryland, and North Carolina combined —have been essentially destroyed for profitable farming; that another one hundred twenty-five million acres are seriously impaired; and that another one hundred million acres are threatened—all belonging to the best farmlands of the United States." In *Our American Land*, issued by the Soil Conservation Service in April 1948, the job ahead is outlined:

1,142,000,000 acres of farm land in the United States

637,000,000 acres are best suited for grazing and woodland

33,000,000 acres are best suited for wildlife and recreation

12,000,000 acres in roads and farmsteads

460,000,000 acres suited for regular cultivation

370,000,000 acres of the cultivable land require protection

773,000,000 acres in soil conservation districts

171,000,000 acres of the land in these districts have detailed conservation plans

93,000,000 acres have had conservation treatment completed according to plan

The detailed frugal technical forms developed by soil conservation activities are a fascinating catalog of practical, straightforward, often improvised landscape elements. They comprise a special branch of landscape design with its own clean esthetic based on the sound and scientific cooperation of man and nature, working toward a new balance and harmony at a higher level than we have known. In a lyric moment one might compare them, in importance to landscape design, to the improvisations of good jazz as a source for great musical forms. Check dams and whisker dams and the planting of gullies with locust and willow, kudzu vine and pampas grass; cover crops and controlled grazing practices and little farm forests; the magnificent scale and refinement in the landscape of contour terraces, strip cropping, basin listing; "auto-frame tetrahedrons," along with brush

27

and plantings of willow and elm and river-bank revetments to reduce cutting; shelterbelts and windbreaks; farm and ranch ponds and stock-water developments: all of these are relevant and inspirational.

Today the road to true and effective conservation of our natural resources, and of our human resources through city and regional planning, lies clear before us through the great and turbulent vitality of the mass movements of American political democracy. The faith that seems lacking in most professionals and intellectuals is the real American faith, the faith in the ability of the ordinary masses of the American people to find their way to life, liberty, and the pursuit of happiness through all the snares and illusions that are strewn in their way by those few whose interests do not happen to coincide with the general welfare.

Conservation is the beginning, not the end, of our overall world view. We know that we must defend what we have. But this is not a permanent contest; the principles of democracy include procedures for placing under control those minorities who persist in blocking the path of progress. Thereafter the horizons will be open and constantly expanding to the brave new world which is surely coming. We will go on from there to develop and redevelop that world at a scale which will be constantly more rich, humane, and magnificent. That must be our perspective.

CHAPTER VI

THE WORLD WE LIVE IN —MAN AND NATURE

ONE WORLD

It is time for us to expand our perspective, widen our angle of vision, and take in the world around us as a comprehensive unity. Landscape design may be perennial borders and foundation planting, parks for the many and estates for the few, and subdivisions with winding streets in practice. But its cultural hinterland is the total physical expression (wherever there is some content of outdoor space and unprocessed materials) of the relations between man and nature. These relations have a history which is basic to, parallel to, and expressed in, the historical tradition covered in the last two chapters. Final academic summation in the twin theories of man-made formality and naturalistic informality in the landscape is an admission of a confused and irrational conception of the relation of man and nature. The long view of Osborn, Brunhes, Sauer, and Mumford is the view that must become basic to the work of all members of the planning professions in the last half of the twentieth century.

The world we live in is composed of Man and Nature. Man, himself natural, has emerged from Nature to achieve separate and equal status (good and/or bad) in our philosophies. Man plus man equals the social pattern; man plus nature equals the physical pattern; the social pattern plus the physical pattern equals the world we live in. By Man we mean the human race, people, all human beings: Man is men, women, babies, children, adolescents, old folks, Negroes, Mexicans, Orientals, "white Caucasians," Jews, etc. Human nature—the character and disposition of people—is produced by a reciprocal relation between heredity and environment. Environment makes men, and men make environment—heredity and habitat play at least a fifty-fifty role in the shaping of human nature generation by generation.

The environment or habitat has two main subdivisions—the social and the physical. Between these there are likewise reciprocal relations, but the former, being composed of animate and imaginative people, is in general primary over the latter, which is composed of inanimate sticks and stones, plants and earth. Social patterns are the composite of all the relations people develop in producing and distributing the necessities and luxuries of life. These patterns vary and change quantitatively from day to day, and qualitatively from time to time through history. Thus we are able to trace the great broad developments of slavery, feudalism, and capitalism, all from the primary base in primitive communal societies. Social patterns produce physical patterns which, on raw land, are direct and clear expressions of themselves. In general, this physical housing is apt to be more durable than its producer; new social patterns emerge through the complementary workings of evolution and revolution, take over the old habitat, and gradually remodel it to suit their own needs and express their own aspirations and values. When this has happened several times, as in the older parts of the world, one gets a rather confusing complexity of pattern, whose analysis takes time and scientific precision.

In genetic terms we can speak of dominants, emergents, and recessives, which appear in the physical as well as the social pattern: new forms such as modern architecture, public housing, planned communities, emerge among the old and point the way toward a better future pattern. They are produced by emergent social forces which may forecast the future dominants. (Mumford.) The only danger lies in the assumption that forms which are merely experimental, abstract, and diagrammatic, lacking the full social content which can only come with emergence to dominance of their producing forces, are already an accomplished and established style setting precedents for posterity.

The earth is our home—a sphere of rock and raw material, with a surface layer of soil and water, and an outer layer of air, fading out into the tremendous voids of airless interplanetary space. We the people live on this surface and in the air layer above it. Our structural and landscaping activities are directed toward proper organization and control of this intangible air space for our use and enjoyment. Nature—the non-human forces which shape and form the primeval landscape—has established a primary space organization of the earth. This has considerable variation in its degree of usefulness to us. The establishment of our own constantly more refined space organizations, within, surrounded by, sometimes obliterating the primeval pattern, but then re-using its materials in our own arrangements, is our basic overall design problem, the problem of planning and designing the earth as the home of the people.

In terms of the aggregation of people and human uses of the land we may divide our world into three main zones: the urban (including suburban fringes, towns, villages); the rural, pastoral, or agricultural; and the primeval, wild, natural, or near-natural. Grazing land, in terms of area and density of use, would overlap the rural and the primeval; the latter includes such areas as mining land, lumbering land, irrigation, water-power and flood-control developments, scenic preserves and recreation areas. The urban covers the least area but includes the most people; the rural and primeval are the reverse. Hence comes that discordant contrast between the squalor and spatial poverty of the city, and the loveliness or magnificence, the spatial luxury, of the countryside, the mountains, the desert, the beaches, the forests. Hence come the Greenbelt towns and their logical extreme, Broadacre City, spreading the people out through the countryside; and hence, too, come La Ville Radieuse and the vertical garden cities, getting the structures up off the ground and separated so the countryside can creep and flow in between them, and the people so high in the air can see miles of open country.

Within this total landscape which is our total environment the urban is most completely processed by man, the primeval is least, and the rural is, for our purposes, the most golden mean we have. Note how Colvin separates the continuous materials of the landscape—land and vegetation—from those which are generally discontinuous—rock, water, structure. We might add that this is primarily true of the rural and primeval landscapes. Rock tends toward continuity in mountain and desert, and water is of course continuous over the seascapes of most of the earth's surface. In the urban landscape, structure, including the synthetic man-made surfaces of asphalt and concrete, tends toward continuity, to the exclusion of open land and vegetation.

The urban concentrates people with their needs and activities in specific small areas (relatively speaking) to the point of complete or nearly complete obliteration of the basic natural landscape by a disorderly and raucous urban blanket, with wide thin wistful suburban fringes all about. The rural supplies and surrounds the urban wherever the land is level and fertile enough, and moisture is adequate, to produce plant and animal crops, and in the process produces the embryonic prototype for an environment in which man and nature meet and mingle on equal, friendly, and productive terms. The primeval comprises all the wild land too rough, sterile, or dry to cultivate, too remote for concentrated building, the mountains, desert, seashore, forests, and jungles, useful to us for recreation and for the extraction of timber and mineral wealth and the grazing of cattle and sheep, and as an all-encompassing preserve of the forms and procedures of that wild natural world out of which human society has developed, and of which it is now almost in control. (See Rose, Kiley, and Eckbo in the *Architectural Record*.)

The airplane has given us in the twentieth century an unprecedented opportunity to examine the continuity of the face of our world. Flight is a magnificent experience. We see the totality of the landscape, of man's struggle to adjust his relationship with his physical environment, spread before us. We see the elementary richness of topography and wild growth, the magnificent spatial scale of hills and valleys, the endless dynamic variation in form produced by the inter-related workings of all the complex natural forces—climate, soil, chemistry, biology, geology, ecology. We see laid down over this, at times with the thin attenuation of water and power lines strung over wild mountains, at times with the obliterating anarchy of congested urban sprawl, the equally endless dynamic variation of human society's physical manifestation on the land: the free and balanced geometric integration of man and nature in the well-to-do rural countryside; the pitiful scratching for survival in marginal farming on poor land with no resources; the hasty disruptive greedy ulcers of extraction of oil and mineral wealth from the bowels of the earth; the magnificent arcs and tangents of major highways, bridges, and dams; the anarchic confusion of

town and city whose plan is based on speculative expediencies of profits from land and building; the crowding and congestion, the spatial poverty of great areas of residential neighborhood; the social poverty of our new better curved gridiron subdivisions (equally lacking in community facilities); and the occasional conspicuous consumption of space and materials in the country homes and estates of the well-to-do and the wealthy, sparkling with jewelled swimming pools.

But above all, we are impressed with the magnificent richness in form and color and scale of the landscape we live in; the constant variation and adaptation in form of man's efforts to improve his physical environment; the basic design inspiration of our world, more basic than history books or academic theories or ivory-tower esthetics, more basic than any form concepts based on selected portions of it.

SAUER WRITES

The natural and the cultural landscape. 'Human geography does not oppose itself to a geography from which the human element is excluded; such a one has not existed except in the minds of a few exclusive specialists.' It is a forcible abstraction, by every good geographic tradition a tour de force, to consider a landscape as though it were devoid of life. Because we are interested primarily in 'cultures which grow with original vigor out of the lap of a maternal natural landscape, to which each is bound in the whole course of its existence,' geography is based on the reality of the union of physical and cultural elements of the landscape. The content of landscape is found therefore in the physical qualities of area that are significant to man and in the forms of his use of the area, in facts of physical background and facts of human culture. . . .

NATURE

Landscape design, as the art which gives direct physical expression to the relations between man, as individual and as society, and the landscape of the world he lives on, has no boundaries save those where man leaves off changing the landscape. Specific jobs have specific boundaries, but the general field is the total humanized landscape. Thus, though we work always in backyards, we must be aware of the world of which those backyards are a part, of their relationship to it, and of those general differences in the world which create differences in backyards in various places, and hence in the forms with which we solve their problems.

The clear, rational, scientific understanding of this physical world which we are so persistently remodeling is essential. Good landscape design should understand the fundamentals of the sciences of the physical globe—geology, geomorphology, physiography; of the relations among non-human life forms—plant and animal ecology; of the weather—climatology and meteorology. Only through knowledge of the workings of the forces which produce the natural landscape which has served as inspiration for so much landscape design can we find the way to development of more advanced forms which will be greater than, but compatible with, the primeval world landscape within which we will always be housed.

Along with these natural sciences, which are so integral a part of the culture developed by 150 years of industrial capitalism, must go sound, clear, objective sciences of human nature, the relations between people, and the relations between the physical environments created by people, the land on which they are based, and the exploitation of that land: psychology, sociology and political science, city and regional planning, conservation. These are all sciences which are in their infancy, still filled with confusion, subjectivity, and obscurantism, because they are concerned with factors at the very core of our social contradictions and crises today, too controversial to be allowed a clear and objective atmosphere for work.

CLIMATE NATURE—Chief among general world differences, particularly with relation to plants and planting, are those of climate. There are typical differences between landscape design in temperate, tropical, and arid zones. It is necessary to understand the macroclimate, those general regional relations with which the weather bureaus work, and the microclimate,

the specific detailed climate of every backyard, every alley, every hillside, lakeshore, meadow, and hilltop. The first is the general, and the second the specific, pattern within which we must always work.

BLUMENSTOCK & THORNTHWAITE IN CLIMATE AND MAN

Three great patterns dominate the earth and are of tremendous importance to man—the pattern of climate, the pattern of vegetation, and the pattern of soils. When the three patterns are laid one upon another, their boundaries coincide to a remarkable degree because climate is the fundamental dynamic force shaping the other two. The relationships between these three patterns have been the object of considerable scientific study. . . . A fourth pattern laid upon the three is that of human culture, or civilization. Though modern man has some freedom to vary this pattern because of his control of other forces, he too cannot go beyond certain limits set fundamentally by climate.

(See further Blumenstock & Thornthwaite, and Salisbury.)

The precipitation types and zones of earth science are at the scale of continent or sub-continent, rather than at that regional scale at which landscape architects work most effectively. Thus within the humid eastern zone the range in specific kinds of plant material from frigid Maine and Wisconsin to semi-tropical Florida and Louisiana is very great; likewise in the subhumid midwest from Minnesota to east Texas, in the semi-arid Great Plains from Montana to west Texas, in the western arid zone from Idaho to Arizona, and in the "summer-dry" climates of the Pacific coast from Seattle to San Diego. If each of these zones were, for our purposes, split into northern and southern halves, they might begin to approximate regions in which the balance between unity and variety in readily grown ornamental planting would be such as to create the most productive atmosphere for the landscape architect. The best, richest, and most sensitive work in the field of landscape design, with its primary concern at the community scale with land and plants, will come from concentration within a region which is big enough to cover considerable variation in climate, topography, and readily grown plant material, and yet not too big for recognizable unity of major features. These are qualifications for which it is difficult to set exact boundaries, nor is that necessary. (See Mumford on Regionalism.)

Man can change the climate somewhat—locally, specifically, and temporarily. He can do this within buildings, extending to the scale of the great Willow Run bomber plant, with quite exact control; he can do it within local topographic units with much looser and more variable control. In general he endeavors to reduce extremes of heat and cold, humidity and aridity, to that narrower range of variability within which he, and the plants necessary or desirable to his living, can best develop. These equalization efforts have had wide ranges of effectiveness; from the destruction which, by accelerating erosion, has converted fertile vegetative lands into sterile deserts in many parts of the world, to the creative construction which, through irrigation and hydraulic engineering and great reclamation projects, has caused sizeable (but still relatively limited) sections of our arid west to blossom as the rose. These moderations remain surrounded by the local climax of the local climatic zone. Their continuation depends upon continuous control; only rarely, as perhaps with afforestation, land drainage, major topographic changes, or large-scale erosion, are climatic changes induced by men durable without further control. This is a statement which is truer in relation to landscape design today than geotechnics tomorrow.

Equalization vs. Expression—With the development of technology the possibilities for such equalization increase. Thus, although historically the Mediterranean garden has been grassless, today the green meadow in the desert is a technical possibility, whether or not it is desirable or appropriate. Modern plumbing and irrigation techniques have turned the trick. We are long past the self-sufficient city-state (region) of late feudalism; even the great nations of today are feeling the labor pains of the one world of tomorrow. As we have gone from steam to electricity to nuclear fission, culture has become increasingly and persistently in-ternational, in spite of curtains both iron and silken. This apparent trend of industrial civilization toward the equalization of regions, through its expansion and complication of production, distribution, and communication, is not by any means as simple as it may seem to the gadgeteers, or as dangerous as it may seem to nature-lovers. It does not necessarily move toward the ironing out of local and regional cultures under a vast bureaucratic blanket; it can move toward the accentuation, the development, and the enrichment of those cultures beyond anything possible under pre-industrial isolation and poverty.

MUMFORD

Hence the popular notion that modern technology has lessened the importance of the natural habitat is precisely the opposite of the truth: likewise the notion that 'regional differences fade out as isolation disappears.' . . . So far from disappearing with isolation, regional differences become more marked, as each new occupation, each new social interest, brings out a hitherto undiscovered color that modifies the common pattern. Primitive regional differences may diminish with intercultural contact: but emergent differences become more profound, unless the region itself is disabled by the metropolitan effort to wipe out every other mode of life except that which reflects its own image. This is a sociological fact of universal bearing.

It is within such a context that the esthetic debate on regional expression and regional equalization, as expressed physically in architecture and landscape design, must take place. In the extreme of commercially eclectic equalization—the Tudor house and English garden in Mexico, the Spanish house and patio in England—there is obviously no question about its ludicrous incongruity. But to race back to the other extreme, at which only "native" building materials, plants, rocks, forms, and arrangements may be used in the given region is equally ludicrous in the middle of the twentieth century. We cannot turn the clock back—the world of atomic power, instantaneous communication, and supersonic transportation is here to stay. Commercialism and rusticity are merely blind alleys off the broad highway of civilized progress—our culture must become increasingly inclusive, rather than exclusive. Truly inclusion means greater discipline in selection, greater clarity in articulation, greater richness and complexity in expression. Those are among the elements of our problems. The question of the use of "native" or "indigenous" plants and rocks is not a problem of *either* those *or* "exotics," but of both together, or *either*, where they are most relevant to the solution of the specific problem.

The regional climatic analysis is not yet completed. We have continuously smaller and more specific units of variation within it, culminating in the microclimate, the actual variations in climate in every community and on every site. From high to low, from slope to flat, from pocket to alley, from north side to south side, to east side to west side, near water and how much—everyone who has ever worked with planting has experienced these local variations and complexities. The cold spot, the draft, the north slope, the hollow where cold air collects— the west slope or wall, the exposed ridge—all these, in relation to local variations in depth and quality of soil, can prove baffling to the designer with the fine regular plan, and lend ammunition to the advocate of wild gardens and naturalism. (See Fitch.)

The question of climatic regionalism assumes considerable importance in landscape design when we consider the relation of light and atmosphere to our work. There is material to be gathered from various fields of art (landscape painting) and illumination on this subject. It would appear to be a matter of the strength and direction of the light coming to us from the sun (primarily) in relation to the quality of the atmosphere. Thus the light gets clearer and stronger in regions where the air is clearer and drier—deserts and mountain tops— and as we go toward the Equator around the world, because the sun's rays get more direct. With clearer and stronger light, color, shade, bright smooth surfaces, white or light surfaces tend to stand out more sharply. With an increase in humidity (atmospheric moisture, mist, fog, rain, clouds) and in air movement comes a diminution of light by screening, refraction,

reflection, dissipation, a softening of colors and contrasts, and a general complicating, subtilizing, and variability of atmospheric (visual) effects. This regional variation in what we see and how we see it is of direct and primary relevance to landscape design, both in the old terms of pictures, illusions, and vistas; and in the newer terms of sensing space, volume, distance, and circulation. Thus designers moving between humid east and arid west, or from the far north to the far south, will require a period of visual acclimatization before they are able to work with maximum effectiveness. (See Van Dyke and Tunnard.)

Important developments in the contemporary landscape field have taken place in the temperate, arid, and tropical zones. In the temperate zones of northern and central Europe and the eastern and mid-western United States, characterized by a general humidity distribution adequate to the maintenance of year-round natural green ground cover, the boundaries between developed and undeveloped landscape are very gentle and need not exist at all. Here there is possible a most real and literal continuity of form and arrangement from urban man to primeval nature, as was recognized by the eighteenth-century English romanticists. In these zones, too, are concentrated the social and cultural heritages and vested interests of western civilization. Here our social contradictions and crises reach their sharpest and most violent expression, tending so far to inhibit the potentially peaceful and easy development of man on the land. These zones have historically been the home of the informal, the romantic, and the picturesque approach to landscape design. The modern work of the Germans and Scandinavians, of Tunnard, Rose, and Kiley has been softened and harmonized by this easy relation of man and landscape. The snow, ice, and low temperatures of the winters are, of course, the principal natural inhibitors, while the humidity of the summers limits livability.

In the arid and tropical zones nature is generally more violent, more dominant or aggressive, bigger in scale, and the problems of integration and contrast between wild and humanized landscapes are therefore qualitatively different. The arid and semi-arid zones running from central Asia through Persia and the Near East to the Mediterranean basin were the birthplaces of the ancient civilizations, and it was in Italy that the great pre-industrial Renaissance cultural climax began and spread north into temperate Europe. Today the affinity of these zones with others of similar climate around the world is widely recognized in terms of plant exchange and culture. The southwestern United States and northern Mexico, Chile, Argentina and parts of Brazil, south Australia, parts of China, and South Africa are all sufficiently similar to be included. These are all zones of low humidity, light precipitation (under 25 in. annually) and high temperatures (seldom below 15 to 20 degrees in winter). In plant terms, they are broadleaved evergreen regions by contrast with the dominant deciduous and coniferous plants of the temperate zones. In all these regions there are definitely separated wet and dry seasons. The factor of artificial irrigation through the dry season for anything but hardy native shrubs and trees—and the non-existence of grasses or other traffic-taking ground covers able to remain green without summer irrigation—is the primary qualitative distinction between gardens of the temperate and arid zones. It creates a definite line of demarcation between garden and nature, by the simple fact that natural grass ground cover becomes a fire hazard in summer and must be kept away from the house by artificial control. This is true in the semi-arid zones of ten inches or more rain per year. With less than that, in true desert conditions, it is possible to let the bare ground come right up to the door, if the urge for real cooling greenery does not force irrigated development, and if the housewife can tolerate the tracking of dust and sand into the house. The comparative difficulty of producing projected results in these zones with plants, whose growth and health can seldom be guaranteed, has led to considerable emphasis on structural elements—paving, seats, screens—to carry the main form or pattern of the garden. In large scale work in the interior valleys the

absence of strong natural character at the scale of human development, plus the need for shade and greenery, has produced experiments in more or less abstract geometric patterns of trees organizing space in a refinement of the surrounding rural pattern.

The tropical zones, at the opposite extreme of too much rain and humidity and no frost at all, occurring around the world in the central latitudes, have been typed for us as regions where heat destroys energy and initiative, and where only savages and monkeys greeted the first white bearers of temperate civilization. Yet in India and in Mexico these missionaries found and destroyed civilizations that were as rich and well balanced, in gardens as well as general culture, as anything they have produced as replacement. Today in tropical Brazil a school of modern architects and garden designers, the latter led by Roberto Burle Marx, have produced vital, vigorous, and widely heralded cultural developments. Burle Marx, a horticulturist and plant explorer as well as an able designer, with his plan forms of flamboyant yet precise curves, and their development in the pinks and purples of real tropical foliage, is expressing both the great wealthy pushing of nature in regions where growth must be controlled and repressed (rather than coaxed and encouraged as in the arid, or tolerated and watched as in the temperate zones), and the subjective urge of the most precise and scientific modern architects for a new and more abstract romanticism, a new Rousseau or Robert Morris to surround their work with lush bursting naturalism.

EARTH NATURE—The parallel interrelation of climate, soil and vegetation patterns is continuous through complete landscapes. In general round ground forms appear to increase with humidity, angular with aridity.

BLUMENSTOCK AND THORNTHWAITE TELL US

Whereas the desert and polar regions are characterized by a landscape with angular breaks, steep slopes, and flat plains and plateaus, the warm humid regions of the earth where denudation is proceeding at a maximum rate are typically regions of gently rolling slopes well covered with vegetation. . . . A fine network of streams and the gradual movement of soil particles downhill soon obliterate surface breaks caused by faults or sharp folds. The vegetation protects the land against the scouring action of the winds, and the temperatures are too high for the formation of glaciers. Thus regions of warm and hot climates display a natural landscape markedly different from that of arid or polar regions.

(See Lobeck, von Engeln, Cotton, Shuler.)

Modern sculpture and painting have shown us how organically geometry emerges from nature (see Wilenski), how all relations of forms in nature are subject to basic geometric analysis. Examination of rock books reveals the basic crystalline structure of many rocks to be straight-sided geometric forms, some of considerable size. It may perhaps be accurate to say that curved lines are more characteristic of matured or aged soil forms, straight lines of young or maturing rock forms.

PLANT NATURE—The pattern of forces behind the apparently disorderly manifestations of natural vegetation have been explained and put into orderly thinking for us by the science of plant ecology. This is a field as complex in its ramifications as landscape design; nevertheless the two overlap, and members of each should have some understanding of the other. In the big landscape work of the present, and the bigger landscape work of the future, the ecologist is and will be an essential member of the designer's team of consultants. Among the books available, *Plant Ecology* by Weaver and Clements seems to be the most readable as well as the most up-to-date. It is neither too technical nor too popular; in its concept of vegetation we find a most stimulating parallelism to our own. Their chapter on plant indicators is very relevant to large-scale landscape design. In *Plant Sociology*, by Dr. J. Braun-Blanquet, a later (1932) and much more technical volume, we find a chapter on *Life Forms and Synecological Units* that is also most relevant and interesting.

Whether he is living in grassland, scrubland, or forest land, man tends to equalize the local landscape vegetatively as well as climatically. He does this because the humanized landscape requires all three levels of growth—grass (and other herbaceous cover), shrubs, and trees—for its optimum richness in development. The degrees and proportions of this equalization vary with the locality insofar as living conditions are concerned: the need for grass appears as a need for ground cover, the need for shrubs as a need for enclosure, the need for trees as a need for shade. Thus in grassland we plant trees and shrubs, in scrubland we clear for grass and trees, in forest we clear for grass and shrubs. The further developments in the use of all three in terms of greenery, color, and space organization proceed parallel with, and are symptomatic of, developments in security, culture, and civilization.

MAN

HUMAN NATURE—Since we design for man in nature, expressing relationships between them, and the use of nature by man, there is a certain danger of over-expansion in landscape design concepts which do not have some stable ratio between people and land in mind. We are not interested in tremendous landscapes of the future, to which people may come occasionally; landscape without man is irrelevant to us; we are interested in the landscapes where the people will be, most where most people will be. We are most concerned with urban landscape design, next with rural, least with primeval, even though the scale of opportunity tends to run in reverse order. We are even more interested in *relations between* urban and rural and primeval landscapes.

It is not enough for the landscape architect merely to understand nature as so many blithely assume: he must also understand man, and that is a much more complex and subjective task. There have been many stuffy, pompous, and condescending books written about "the condition of man"—these are not the route to understanding. One cannot understand nature by standing outside her (nor is that physically possible) and one cannot understand man by standing outside him. Those authorities who separate themselves in their thinking from man in general, the majority of the people, common hu-

36

manity, thereby render themselves sterile and useless as interpreters or representatives of man. Explanation can only come from understanding; understanding can only come from direct, sympathetic, analytic-synthesizing relationship. (See Graubard, Benedict, Fromm, Stegner, Dunham, Sandburg, Whitman, among others.)

FROMM

The contemporary human crisis has led to a retreat from the hopes and ideas of the Enlightenment under the auspices of which our political and economic progress had begun. The very idea of progress is called a childish illusion, and 'realism,' a new word for the utter lack of faith in man, is preached instead. The idea of the dignity and power of man, which gave man the strength and courage for the tremendous accomplishments of the last few centuries, is challenged by the suggestion that we have to revert to the acceptance of man's ultimate powerlessness and insignificance. This idea threatens to destroy the very roots from which our culture grew. . . .

SANDBURG

The people, yes, the people,
Until the people are taken care of one way or another,
Until the people are solved somehow for the day and hour,
Until then one hears 'Yes but the people what about the people?'
Sometimes as though the people is a child to be pleased or fed
Or again a hoodlum you have to be tough with
And seldom as though the people is a caldron and a reservoir
Of the human reserves that shape history,
The river of welcome wherein the broken First Families fade,
The great pool wherein wornout breeds and clans drop for restorative silence.

BUILDING NATURE—Man's primary expression on the land has been building, and little of it today gives cause for pride. The problem of urban blight upon the land has been widely considered and analyzed by many dull but respectable authorities, and by such more active and imaginative minds as Mumford and Sharp, Sert and Le Corbusier. It is a problem which has grown with industrial capitalism. It brings forth most acutely the neurotic relations be-

tween our society and the natural world. Not only do our cities, like frowsy blankets with the edges frayed into endless streamers, smother and drown the natural beauties of their sites, but in the process they also smother and degrade the majority of the people who live in them.

From our point of view—of concern with the total landscape—there are perhaps three specific pertinent problems in this major urban quandary. One is the detailed relation between advanced building technology and its precise environmental control, and the natural world of topography and climate and plants within which it must operate; another is the question of desirable relations in general, in form and space and arrangement, in quantity and quality, between town and countryside, rural or primeval; the third is the accelerating exploitive relation of town to country, taking all and returning little or nothing, in the most direct expression of that one-way siphon from land to sea which the conservationists are fighting.

On the first point Fitch gives a lucid and lengthy analysis of the extent to which buildings today can provide us with specially planned and controlled environments. *The Architectural Forum* in November 1948 gives us perhaps the most recent summary of advanced architectural thinking on the esthetics of a building technology which, while it increasingly opens up the building to the landscape with the open structure and the glass wall, at the same time seems to increase the gap between man and nature by its increasingly precise and complete control of climate and habitat indoors. Never before in history has there been such a contrast between this potentially absolute control over interior climate, and the potentially complete transparency of glass walls and doors separating indoors and outdoors.

If we are to outgrow the role of poetic defenders of the beauties of nature, which has been our fond picture in the past; if we are to take our place and fill our potential in the triumvirate of space-organizers which will develop a new and bigger art of site-space, or land-and-building, design; if we are to properly understand our job as integrators, mediators, conciliators, or harmonizers in that zone of landscaping which fluctuates in scale and intensity between structure and landscape, town and countryside; then we must take our cue as much from the conscious esthetics of man, expressed in architecture, as from the unconscious esthetics of nature, expressed in the wild or resurgent landscape. In the relation of man to nature it is man who is responsible for decisions as to the growth or decline in the quality of the landscape. His values are constantly expanding in terms of imagination and creative synthesis. Those of nature, as expressed in man's outlook on the landscape, are shifting, shrinking, becoming more rational, more sensitized, precisely because the forces of wild nature remain approximately the same, while the forces extracted by man from wild nature expand and develop at a constantly accelerating rate. Certainly the progression in the relation of man to landscape is clear: from the savage scratching his way out of the monstrous wilderness, through the Moslem lord with his precise geometric arabesque walled away from a still unfriendly landscape, the opening up and extruding of architecture into the landscape with the growing security of Renaissance and Baroque times, the eighteenth century English realization that all nature was a garden, and its literal incorporation into the domesticated landscape, to the twentieth century potential for remaking the landscape through great engineering and soil reclamation projects. The growing dominance of man over nature is graphically clear—that his sense of responsibility for the general landscape has not grown as rapidly is part of the twentieth century contradiction.

Why is the esthetics of an architecture so intimately concerned with the scientific structural enclosure of space relevant to a landscape design which is still primarily concerned with the forms and materials of the natural landscape, only touching on structure in a limited and handicraft way? Why is the esthetics of an art of the machine relevant to an art of nature? Here is exactly the primary contradiction of landscape design, which is not merely an art of nature, but an art of man in nature. Nature without man would exist, as it did before him, but landscape design in the humanized sense only exists with man. Therefore landscape design can no more ignore the machine than can architecture (or painting or sculpture) because the machine is the second major revolution in the relations between man and nature—the first being the agricultural revolution when man ceased wandering and settled down to raise crops on the land. Landscape design is not concerned with the direct design of machine-produced objects or elements, but it is directly concerned with the use of them, particularly as they become structural elements, in the landscape.

Our major objective is neither to protect the beauties of nature from the ravages of man (although that becomes at times a pressing tactic); nor to rebuild or reproduce nature to save man from himself (although that has been until recently a most convincing argument). Our major objective is the integration, the harmonization, the co-ordination of, or the establishment of good relations between, the physical forms of nature and the physical manifestations of man in the landscape. In order to accomplish this we must understand both kinds of form, and we must understand that we are not going to accomplish it alone. We work in from the natural periphery toward the refined core, the architects and engineers work out in a reverse direction, and we cannot stop where we meet without establishing a boundary that defeats our objective. We must overlap as a beginning, and become increasingly collaborative as we proceed. We must become sensitive and appreciative of the forms of architecture, and the architects must become sensitive and appreciative, not only of the forms of nature, but of the forms of landscape design which can come out of the meeting of architecture and nature. We must—and do—know as much about architecture as they know about landscape design.

Thus our typical problem is the relation of structure to site, our future problem is the relation of town to countryside, within the overall problem of relating man to nature. As the forms of architecture change the forms of landscape design must change, and even nature becomes adjusted at increasingly larger scale. Certainly England today bears little resemblance to the English landscape before Christ. When architecture reaches the extremes of abstraction and purity in form, and contrast with nature, of a Le Corbusier or a van der Rohe our bridge becomes long and tenuous—may indeed be broken or zig-zag. But always, from Greek to Gothic, from Le Corbusier to Wright, architecture has been compounded of simple geometrical forms, primarily the right angle and the straight line, secondarily other angles and arcs of circles. This has been the source of the primary reactions in landscape design, from the positive extrusion of the formal tradition to the negative withdrawal of the informal. If now it should become possible (an oversize if) for structural design to move toward more complex organic forms, as has been forecast experimentally by some architects (Scharoun, Niemeyer, and by the *Forum*), the impact upon landscape design would be tremendous. Then the informalists might finally have force to their argument that the right angle and the straight line are unnatural forms in the landscape.

It is, of course, basically unrealistic to speak continuously of architecture in nature, as though each new building were being pushed into an untouched wilderness. There are three kinds of landscapes in which architecture must develop its forms—the urban and suburban, the rural, and the primeval. If we consider building as synonymous with architecture, which it is socially if not esthetically, then its great bulk goes on in the urban landscape, already dominated by structural and engineering elements, with nature perhaps persistent in odd useless corners or resurgent in vacant lots, but with most of the little fringes of open space developed by "landscaping" of the most typical or average conception. Of the fraction of building that goes on outside urbanized areas the great bulk must go on in rural agricultural land, a thoroughly organized and humanized landscape, albeit of "natural" plants and earth, and with considerably larger fragments of wild nature

incorporated into the pattern. Thus only an occasional fragment of architecture-building goes on in truly wild or primeval surroundings—the country home, the resort or recreation center. It becomes, therefore, somewhat romantic to develop theory in terms of a relation between precise architecture and wild nature, when its realization will entail the reproduction of an authentic facsimile of that scenery. Let us rather be consistent and concentrate on the actual elements of our problems—the indoor and outdoor space needs of the people, the materials available for their development, the nature of the sites on which they must be realized, and the actual nature of the landscapes to which they must be related.

The tendency to confuse *process* and *arrangement,* as sources of the quality of "naturalness," is very widespread. The *processes* of erosion and of growth, expressing the primary life cycle of our world, are likewise the primary source of "naturalness." The *arrangement*—PLAN— of the landscape elements (plants, rocks, ground forms in spatial relations) in primeval nature is accidental. It has no direction or dominating objective; no conscious imagination projects its results. Any rich rural countryside, especially in older (longer settled) parts of the world, is a prototype for the naturalness which can come from planned orderly arrangements of plants and ground forms, allowing the forces of growth and erosion proper controlled expression. The central questions are: Can man improve on nature? And if so, just how obviously should he go about it? Whose feelings will be hurt if Art appears in the landscape?

On the question of the proper quantitative and qualitative relations between town and country (urban and rural or primeval), which is directly analogous to the time-honored landscape question of the relation between formal and informal design, we find excellent discussion, couched in esthetic as well as functional terms, coming from Thomas Sharp and Brenda Colvin in England. Here, where so many people have lived close together in limited areas and a temperate climate for so many centuries, we find a kind of small test tube of the patterns

39

produced by man on the land, their ups and downs and potentials: the conscious humanization of the landscape in the eighteenth century, the conscious de-humanization of the landscape in the nineteenth century, the conscious search for re-humanization in the twentieth. Our problems may be bigger, broader, faster, or rougher, but all their essential ingredients exist in green England and Old London. These writers point out the need for preservation of the country from smothering by suburbia, and the parallel need for re-creation of the town as a proud and handsome entity.

The antithesis between town and country is not, in the final analysis, based on shape or form or arrangement but on exploitation. If the towns did not have such a primarily parasitic relation to the countryside, devouring all its mineral, vegetable and animal produce; scarring and eroding it in the process; dumping their raw and fertile wastes into the ocean; and then, as a final indignity, sending their confused and starved citizenry out to the countryside in a destructive and anarchic search for the life-giving recreation which the towns are too irresponsible to provide—if the towns did not do all these things to the landscape they would not be as ugly as they are, and we would not have the guilt complex and the subjective conviction of the inferiority of urbanism to primeval nature that we do. In a very real sense those towns which establish plants to treat sewage and convert it to fertilizer, those communities which respect the basic organic procedure of converting every scrap of organic waste to compost for return to the soil to contribute to the growth of new organic forms, are repaying society's debt to Nature and building up our credit balance with the landscape more accurately and convincingly than any acreage of naturalistic park development or preservation of wild scenery in park preserves. In this effort to eliminate the exploitive antithesis between town and country lies a most relevant and creative expression of the conservation movement.

While the towns bear a collective responsibility for this parasitism on the land wherever and to the extent that it exists, it does not follow that each town's responsibility is then divided up evenly, on a per capita basis, among its citizens. The responsibility must be pro-rated among said citizens on the basis of their ability to meet and discharge it—that is, on the basis of their position in the community, and their relation to the processes of bringing raw materials from the land into the community, and of disposing of the wastes resulting from the use of those materials. Thus the primary responsibility must rest with those who are considered the leading citizens: the most influential, well-to-do, established, stable and secure individuals; those who benefit the most and extract the best living from the community pattern; those who profit directly from distribution of produce; the self-appointed or elected leaders; the city fathers. Certainly it is a principle of democratic society that those accepting special privilege and special benefits from it must likewise accept special responsibility.

The three constituent problems of the urban quandary—the relation of town to country in terms of machine technology to natural processes, of form and arrangement, and of exploitation—are interacting problems which require joint and parallel solution. Both the former and latter are primary to any theory of town form, and therefore to any theory of landscape design in relation to town form. Advanced concepts of the structural control of enclosed space have a direct and pregnant influence on the forms of town and landscape planning. The philosophical attitudes of individuals and social groups toward the question of urban parasitism on the land will be expressed in their concepts of town form in the countryside, and of form and arrangement of natural landscape elements in park or countryside. To speak of the "disurbanization of towns and the urbanization of the country, to achieve an abolition of the contradictions . . ." (to which Sharp objects), is to establish a theoretical objective whose complete and literal realization is not anticipated or sought. To go in the direction of such an objective from the raucous anarchy of current urban life and the sterile drudgery of current rural life is to effect constant improvements in each, bringing to the city the healthy biology of the countryside, and to the country the concentrated creative sociability of the city. We will have a long way to go, and will know when to stop, before we reach the point of drowning both in a sea of Neither-Town-Nor-Country.

The problem of the landscape architect—even as of the architect, the town planner, the engineer, and indeed all men of good will—is now, and will be more acutely every day, the development of ways and means for bridging the gap between town and country, the antithesis between urban and rural life—more specifically between the masonry, the asphalt, and the dingbat construction of the town and the quiet greenery of meadow, forest, and shore. How to open up the town to the country, how to bring the town culturally to the country—that is our primary problem, and it will be expressed and measured in terms of quantity and quality of vegetation.

MAN IN NATURE

RURAL NATURE—The rural or agricultural countryside, particularly when it is productive and well-developed, is a region in which man and nature meet, mingle, but seldom completely dominate one another. The rural pattern is the real folk art of landscape design. Here is full integration of man's orderly, geometric, functional, accurate organization of space and materials with the full, free, rich, pushing growth of nature. The form and habit of any crop plant, from wheat to apples, from lettuce to grapes, is a complete child of the marriage of the forms and processes of nature with the science of man. Here, with little or no conscious esthetic or search for "beauty," is a pattern of infinite richness in actuality and in potentiality. In the rural landscape we find innumerable definite three-dimensional space forms produced with both structural and natural materials: rectangular or polygonal fields cut from solid natural wildwoods; trees in rows or belts forming planes; the regularity of orchards; straight lines of untrimmed hedges and mixed hedgerows, and of fences and old stone walls, grown up with natural plants; free-standing clumps of trees forming natural pavilions; intersecting planes of these lines of trees and hedges and walls forming a fragmentary organization of space. It is space which is seldom completely enclosed; always there is a suggestion of its continuity, something to follow, the stimulating impossibility of seeing all of the space at once. This free fragmentary geometry of planes organizing space is clearly analogous in plan and effect to modern thought in architecture, painting, and sculpture. Here we have a pattern continuous physically around the world, and historically since man first settled down on the land; formal and informal, beautiful and functional all at once; tremendous in inspiration and impossible to copy. It is the basic democratic landscape pattern of the world, because it has been more continuous through the lives of more people than any other great landscape tradition.

The scale of site and development of the rural tradition is such as to render it more relevant to park work and community planning than to private gardens. This adds emphasis to its relevance to the future of landscape design, for the problems of the physical environment of the American people are going to have to be solved at that scale, rather than at the scale of the private garden, however inventive, ingenious, or imaginative.

MAN IN NATURE—The outstanding characteristic of nature is growth unrestrained by man. The outstanding characteristic of man is organization for a purpose. Put these two together in landscape design and you have an organization of natural materials in such a way as to serve man's purposes, yet allow the continuance of their development with a minimum of interference. This is a principle for organic form in the humanized landscape.

Art based on science rather than mysticism will endeavor to produce landscapes which are natural in the broad and true definition which accepts man and his work as part of nature. Once that definition is established we can then evaluate and choose among landscapes that are good or bad *for people*—our only objective—rather than choosing between "natural" or "humanized" landscapes on the assumption that there is a qualitative difference between them. Those who point to the ugliness of human urbanization, erosion, or mining should consider the rough destructiveness of desert, volcano, landslide, storm or fire, or the tremendous wastefulness of natural ecological processes. (Only a tiny fraction of seedlings in nature attain mature development.) To define "natural" as derived from nature without man is deliberate obscurantism, willful mysticism. Man is natural; nature includes man. Man is the only natural force which can determine its destiny, control its evolution, and thus improve on nature.

AS LAMPRECHT SAYS

Man's place in nature is an old, old problem which has been frequently and variously treated in the great literature of the world. . . . The place of man in nature is not one definite and settled affair. The place of civilized man in nature is by no means the same as that of savage man. . . . Thus the place which man may come to have in nature is still in the making. . . . In the light of the changing place of man in nature we may, however, say one thing with assurance. We may say (borrowing the eloquent phrase of Spinoza) that man's place in nature was originally one of bondage and is potentially one of freedom. In origin man is in servile status, bound by narrow limitations of time and space, bound by ignorance, crude impulse and passion. In destiny man may in part become supreme among the varying forms which nature exhibits; emancipated by disciplined imagination from superstition, brutality, and blind chance. The essential point about this passage from bondage to freedom must not be overlooked: the passage itself is natural. In man nature comes to her most significant realization. In man nature manifests some of the most splendid potentialities that have lain forever within her. Man is, if we may speak boldly while humbly recognizing the extent of our own present inadequacies, the finest product of nature's art. His arts are her arts because she made him who thereby remakes her. Nature with man left out is not the whole of nature; and even nature as it was before man appeared and developed contained already the traits which made man possible and which, brought

to focus in him and refashioned in specifically human form, are at once man's responsibility and nature's glory.

. . . The laws of nature are not, however, dictates that compel procedure—they are not statutes or prescriptive enactments. . . . Inanimate agents react to the actual stimulus of the moment; they react, it might be said, to the superficial. Intelligent agents react to more than the actual stimulus; they react to the potentialities of the actual. And these potentialities are always plural. The plural potentialities of nature are the significant basis of human choice. It is insufficient to argue that because things are as they are they will be as they will be. Rather, because things are as they are, an agent who imaginatively foresees the diverse potentialities of things may choose freely within given limits. Freedom is never total—it is not freedom from the world. But it is genuine—it is freedom within the world. . . .

FROMM GIVES US THE VIEWS OF A RECENTLY DISCREDITED (BUT STRANGELY RESURGENT) AUTHORITY ON THE RELATION OF MAN TO NATURE

The power which impresses Hitler probably more than God, Providence, and Fate, is NATURE. While it was the trend of the historical development of the last four hundred years to replace the domination over men by the domination over Nature, Hitler insists that one can and should rule over men but that one cannot rule over Nature. . . . He ridicules the idea that man could conquer Nature. . . . Nature is the great power we have to submit to, but living beings are the ones we should dominate.

The character of nature is expressed in the pyramidal forms of earth and the angular or rounded forms of rock, the gravity relation of water, and the bursting growth of plants. It results in accidental space patterns—sometimes strong, often weak or unnoticeable. The character of man is expressed in specific space organization for use and pleasure. These characters must meet and collaborate, losing neither the wayward movement of the natural elements through human arrogance or fussiness, nor the imaginative form and pattern of man through subjective mysticism about subservience to nature, apologies for intrusion into the natural landscape, rusticity, etc. Nothing in the nature of plants or rocks as a design material demands either regularity or irregularity in arranged relations between them on the ground. Nothing in the nature of earth demands any particular relations between concave, convex, and plane surfaces, save in answer to forces of weathering. But there are always specific relations of site and surrounding landscape which must be related to conscious development in forms which are specific and imaginative, not preconceived, mechanical, or subjective. In other words, we do not project a *choice among* the irregular rectangularity of the typical rural pattern, the irregular curvilinearity of the new soil conservation patterns, or the completely wayward and unlinear pattern of wild nature. We project the possibility of relations and combinations *between* all three—a maximum vocabulary with discipline, not a minimum vocabulary with prejudice.

The spread in scale is of the essence of our problem of relating man to the specific landscape in which he lives. At the scale of the small enclosed garden we can model and shape the ground surface in a manner that is directly and abstractly sculptural, without exterior referents, as the small Japanese garden, the golf trap, or the small garden sunken structurally. At this scale, with considerable enclosure, we have a maximum freedom of choice of forms, materials, arrangements, and combinations comparable to that of painter or sculptor. As our scale expands to such optimum residential units as quarter- and half-acre lots, this freedom of choice may continue on flat land which makes the garden self-sufficient of necessity, or it may be modified in any number of specific ways by the character of the surrounding landscape. Beyond that there is a split in the path of expanding scale. Private homes on an acre or more of their own land, unless they are themselves of super-private scale, are apt to leave such considerable and variable gaps between their scale and that of the landscape they overlook, as to produce a design problem that is highly plastic and free in choice of form and arrangement in a somewhat different sense than the former enclosed gardens. That is, the freedom lies in just HOW to establish relations between an isolated structure and a good deal of land. Historically the extremes have ranged from baroque chateaux to romantic parks.

The main line in the path of expanding scale is that on which there is some sort of balance maintained between the scale of structure and that of site. Thus any sort of multi-story, or widespread single-story structure should have an area of land in its site and a relation to the landscape which neither crowds it nor isolates it—that is, which is "in scale" with it. This applies to all sorts of large buildings and institutions: multi-family housing, hospitals, schools, universities, hotels, resorts, governmental buildings, factories, skyscrapers, department stores. The reader's own experience will tell him how often this balance is honored by breach rather than observance. When such large buildings have adequate open space around them it is possible to establish between them and the land adequate spatial relations, in terms of ground, water, planted and structural forms. When such open space is inadequate, the "landscaping" becomes more purely decorative—a frill around the base of a monument.

The final jump in scale is that to the cumulative collective scale of groups of buildings, expanding again from the organized group or institution—farm, ranch, university, housing development—covered by one program, through village and town to the urban metropolis. Every such unit, however vague the boundaries of its sprawl, relates to a positive site, or area of landscape beyond that which it covers. The question of the esthetic scale relations between such building aggregations or conglomerates and their sites, as well as the question of their having any coherent form, is one for the present of site planning and the future of town and city planning. Here let us merely emphasize that such relations do in fact exist, however obscured by the anarchy of individual building. The relation between structure and site at this expanded aggregate scale is the great landscape design of the future, the design which will expand the works of man to the actual scale of the ordinary landscape, and make possible the development of magnificent sculptural ground form relations at the scale of hill and valley. Already this is forecast in the projects of Le Corbusier, Wright, Sert, Breuer. Whether the garden city be horizontal or vertical, made up of scattered or continuous structures, it can still develop strength, clarity, and coherence as an esthetic unity at one with its landscape. As we learn the means toward improving our environment by changing it, the thinking on park design and on urbanism or community planning will move toward a merger. In this merger the park space will become the functional skeleton of the community, and this articulated, clarified, chlorophylled, and sunlighted community will find it finally possible to enter into communal relations with the landscape of its site. Then it will become possible to project the true unity of the city of Los Angeles with the great plain, rimmed with hills, mountains and ocean, which is its site; and the true unity of the city of San Francisco with the peninsulas to north and south of it, and the bay and Eastbay which lie before it.

Beyond this scale of urban landscape relations we do not at this time project conscious landscape design. To be sure there are the great rural patterns, the flood control and power development programs of the great river valleys, the irrigation, reclamation, and reforestation of our western lands, and many another such tremendous regional project. This is the great scientific engineering of our land, and it has developed and will continue to develop its own esthetic of man and nature in the landscape. Colvin, at the scale of the English countryside, may project the design of the total landscape as a setting for travel and recreation. But we in broad America must bring ourselves back to the scale of the individual who, in whatever number, constitutes the cellular structure of our society and our communities. We have defined landscape design as primarily the organization of the spaces outdoors in which these individuals live, work, and play. This is our great esthetic and functional problem. It is greatest where the people are the most concentrated. Our consciously designed units of town and countryside will continue to be surrounded by vastly greater areas of rural or primeval landscape, developed scientifically to serve human society, but otherwise reserved for the forces of nature.

Here the concept of the state and national park, the wilderness reserved for the occasional intensive re-creation of the urbanite, will reach its final logical expanded conclusion.

To *preserve* nature, where she exists in quality on the site, and does not obstruct projected uses or refinements, is mandatory. To literally *rebuild* nature, once destroyed by grading or construction, is a highly questionable procedure, save at the fringes where destruction stops. This contrast is analogous to that in architectural monuments: we *preserve* fine old buildings; but should we have *rebuilt* Williamsburg?

Certainly it is true that, at an overall scale, the scenes of nature are apt to be more pleasing, to seem more wholesome and appropriate, than the scenes of man. It is probably true that we have destroyed or spoiled more natural beauty than the amount of our higher and finer contributions to the landscape. It is still true today that all our cities, without exception, are sordid, ugly, and chaotic as a whole; and that the country, the mountains, and the beaches are forced to function as escapes from this ugliness. The theory of the introduction of the park as a natural breathing pore into the ugliness of the man-made city can still be argued. But this does not mean that man is by nature or by heredity destructive of beauty or productive of ugliness, or that most people are incapable of building or preserving beautiful surroundings, and that therefore only the elite deserve them. Such thinking is merely incomplete, and tends to lead to the kind of irrational mysticism which can destroy both our potential for a beautiful world, and the democratic framework within which we must build it. Paternalism breeds its own problems. People treated like children will tend to act like children, and destroy nature. On the other hand, children treated as adults will tend to act more maturely, and not destroy nature. Nature has already produced her maximum for us, while the potential creativity of human society is yet in its infancy, scarcely tapped in tiny sections of our environment; we have scarcely begun.

Man does not always spoil the landscape. In less thickly settled pastoral regions, and in those

44

countries where the processes of civilization have gone on undisturbed for centuries, one finds a most delightfully mellowed integration of the forms of man and nature. Occasionally, too, in an outburst of collective energy, man produces Pyramids and Bay Bridges and Boulder Dams, which by their breadth and scale of conception can supersede and dominate their natural environment. We must accept as an existing fact that man's activities must change and dominate the landscape. But it does not follow that they should spoil it. Although the advent of his works upsets the orderly balance-in-motion that the forces of nature maintain, it is perfectly possible for him to achieve a new balance which will have an equal sense of order and serenity.

Analysis will show that man destroys nature somewhat in the course of marginal struggles for survival (as with poverty-stricken farming) when inadequately equipped and educated; but that such destruction occurs primarily in the course of the full-bodied, unregulated—or inadequately regulated—pursuit of private profit. Consider such activities as oil drilling, coal mining, lumbering, hydraulic mining, excessive grazing and cropping—all those activities which the conservationists have been fighting for half a century; consider the atomic effect on miles of lovely open country of one strategically placed billboard; or, consider the forces which have controlled and produced the sordid chaos that is any city today—real estate speculation, building speculation, general commercial speculation. It is no more than democratic Americanism to say that such forces can be analyzed, exposed,

and placed under proper public control, and that this will have to be done before we can go on to realize our potential and our objective of fine and wholesome surroundings for all.

Pre-industrial civilization produced great wastage and destruction of the natural landscape through irresponsible or ignorant exploitation of the land. Industrial civilization has continued and accelerated this, and has added all the ugly growing ulcers of commercial urbanism and extraction of raw materials from the earth. But these truths are no justification for despair or cynicism. They do not mean that the world is static, that human nature never changes, or that things are going from bad to worse. They are only the blacker darkness which precedes the dawn of greater civilizations and more orderly and peaceful societies than we have yet experienced. We live in a dynamic changing world. Man has the methods and the means at hand to put his world and his physical and social environments in order, an order which is rational, human, democratic, flexible, creative, and dependably continuous. In spite of the prophets of doom we do not think this order is too far off. And we think it will be expressed, and can be foreshadowed, in large-scale landscape design which is a rich and balanced expression of the working of man's free creative imagination, in full harmony with the subtle and complex forces of the natural landscape from which he has come, and of which he is an integral part. We do not feel that civilization is past its prime or coasting on an even keel, but rather that it has scarcely begun.

CHAPTER VII

PRINCIPLES OF DESIGN AND PLANNING

UNIVERSAL

There have been many many outlines of the basic principles of art and design. The following is a good summary of those most generally accepted.

ADAPTED FROM JANET K. SMITH

A PURPOSE is associated with a GOAL which generates an Idea in the mind of a human being. through his Imagination operating within his Memory and Experience this IDEA is actualized into a FORM. out of Material (natural and/or man-made) by Analysis and Action by means of Tools and Processes (dependent on hand and/or machine) appropriate to its intended use, emphasizing one or another of the Art Elements (Line, Shape, Tone, Color, Texture, Mass, Space) arranged according to the Art Principles (Rhythm, Balance, Emphasis) organized by Proportion to produce an effect of Repose or Liveliness (in either case possessing vitality), so ordered as to result in HARMONY which is a consistent relationship of Unity with Variety, and in supreme instances the Art Product (embodiment of its maker's purpose) may achieve BEAUTY.

Saarinen (1948) and Teague (1940) give us perhaps the most complete recent syntheses of the overall structure of art principles. This is kindergarten material for artists working in whatever field, material which should be so thoroughly assimilated by the student in his first work in basic design as to become thereafter largely automatic as he follows the increasingly complex paths of research and creative synthesis in his own field. Nevertheless these common art principles are the fundamental base of the pyramidal hierarchy of principle which is relevant to each specific field. Thus we proceed from the broadest level of general art principles to the level of less general principles relevant to the major divisions of graphic or time-space presentation, object or plastic design, and space organization, to the most specific theoretical principles, short of actual specific work, in each field now recognized as more or less autonomous—painting, sculpture, industrial design, architecture, landscape design. No one working in any field can avoid the relevance of all three levels of principle, although as these become more general they should become more automatically and unconsciously part of serious work, because assimilated in the beginning of preparation for it.

We have seen too many dull and sterile works in all fields held up as safely successful—or successfully safe—because they conformed to all the "laws" of unity and variety, scale and rhythm. It takes more than conformance to rules, laws, principles, or any other systems to produce works of art, whether graphic, plastic, or spatial. Art once completed may be analyzed, dissected, criticized, or imitated in terms of systems of principle. It may be true that most good intuitive or conscious design can be shown to conform with them. Nevertheless design carried out in terms of unity and variety, rhythm and proportion must still grope for guidance through the dank woods of eclecticism, philistinism, and opportunism, with eyes averted from the primrose by-path of personal romanticism. The Elysian Fields of strength, clarity, and coherence, of richness and vitality, are reached only by disciplined and sensitive concentration on the concrete factors of site and space and program, materials and people and social context.

Perhaps it is true that these universal principles are the solid foundation on which we erect our structure of gay fantasy or high magnificence. If so, we are not sure whether that foundation is best built by their conscious (which so easily becomes self-conscious) inclusion in the basic design work which prepares us for more specialized design, or whether they develop, in the nature of human creativeness, during the production processes of any design soundly based on the objective factors of its problems. Thus we end with the question: which came first, design or principle? Unfair though it may be, we do not feel scholarly enough to answer it.

MODERN

FAURE

. . . What one calls 'decadence' is precisely the epoch in which the greatest number of differentiated elements ferment, decay, die, spring up or grow, and in which, consequently, new relations appear, in which unsuspected groups are organized, in which virgin forces are united for the sake of a future they will not see. . . .

The direction of modern advanced thought in the arts is toward greater concentration on space relations, on the properties of materials, on social relevance to people, and on specific local conditions. Whether these are principles or phe-

nomena we need not say. We find them projected, without reference to universal principles, by such active experimenters and developers as Moholy-Nagy, Kepes, and Schillinger.

MOHOLY-NAGY

. . . Designing is a complex and intricate task. It is the integration of technological, social and economic requirements, biological necessities, and the psychophysical effects of materials, shape, color, volume, and space: thinking in relationships. [My emphasis— G.E.] The designer must see the periphery as well as the core, the immediate and the ultimate, at least in the biological sense. He must anchor his special job in the complex whole. . . .

SCHILLINGER

The mental growth of humanity, as revealed in scientific thinking, may be stated as a tendency to fuse seemingly different categories into a complex unity, into which previous concepts enter as component parts. The evolution of thought is a process of synthesizing concepts.
Esthetic satisfaction comes mainly from the sensation of being off balance, but in an obvious relation to balance. Here a mechanical experience becomes an artistic one through the discrimination of the 'artistic differential' by our senses. . . . The element of the unknown stimulates curiosity, and the process of associating it with the known produces a feeling of satisfaction. Here lies the success of one work of art and the failure of another. . . .

KRYZHANOVSKY

'The discovery of new laws of unstable equilibrium is the end that will be attained by the innovator who reveals new paths of art.'

Modern design is not another "manner" to add to our bag of stylistic tricks; it is not a new kind of exterior decoration to be picked up by reading a couple of magazine articles of an evening, or taking a short brush-up course during the dull summer season; it is not composed of ratchets, chevrons, zigs, zags, squirms, wiggles, or other juke-box tricks; it is not a new kind of doubletalk to be lifted from the shop-window designer's jargon; it is not a matter of bending axes into spirals, or of rejuvenating nature with a new skirt-length or a new set of glands. Modern design is serious work. It begins

47

with the rejection of pre-conceived academic systems of form as being stale and irrelevant, and proceeds with a re-analysis of basic elements and problems, and an attempt to derive from that analysis principles of organization which are truly relevant and not superficial or shallow. Specific forms produced by specific designers who are endeavoring to carry on such serious re-analysis are experimental and in process of development, and are not intended as material for a new academic system and a new series of measured drawings.

LANDSCAPE

The establishment of relations between man and nature in actuality usually involves relations between buildings or structures and the landscape. That is, the relation of the more intensively used space to that less intensively used. These two factors range through all degrees of dominance and interdependence: on a city lot the garden is merely an extension of the house; in a National Park the architecture is incidental and unobtrusive. At the scale of garden this is a relation between single structures and sites. At the scale of park this is a relation between collective structures (town) and collective sites (open space—urban, rural, or primeval).

To meet this problem with the standard query of the landscaper—"shall it be formal or informal?"—is sheer incompetence. If formal design is derived from man, and informal from nature, how can we integrate the formal building and the informal site by holding them apart in permanently frozen extremes? Neither is necessary; good landscape design is both formal and informal at once, in varying degrees, proportions, and combinations. Straight lines and free curves lose force by isolation; in juxtaposition each helps the other to stronger expression. Rigidity and freedom of atmosphere are not determined by shapes drawn on a paper plan; they are determined by the character and placing of three-dimensional elements. "Formal design" forces architecture upon the landscape; "informal design" forces the landscape upon

architecture. Neither solves the real problems of the landscaping process; rather they make solution impossible by placing arbitrary, irrelevant, dogmatic preconceptions in the way.

There should not be just two kinds of landscape design; there must be unlimited variety comparable to that in painting, sculpture, or music, and dependent only upon problem conditions and the imagination of the designer. ONE arc of "means to landscape design" CAN have "the dominance and the will of man" at one pole, and "the appreciation of the power and beauty of nature" at the other. But the range of means commonly usable and relevant, and most productive of rich and vital work, is the range between these poles, the range in which the contradictions between them are resolved in various and manifold forms and combinations, not necessarily the golden mean of equal hybridization. To say that we must choose between the forms of man and those of nature is only to say that man can never possibly be at home in this world which has evolved him. It is also to say that we can never produce forms which have the ultimate strength and coherence of art forms that come out of struggle between ideas originally in opposition.

The application of the academic principle has been sensitive and judicious. In private gardens and sites dominated by buildings, hence by man, the formal has been appropriate. On larger sites —parks and institution grounds—where open space balanced or dominated buildings, the informal, nature resurgent, was the correct answer. Occasionally, as on estates, the two might mingle discreetly.

Of academic formality—bilateral symmetry —we need say little more than to wonder how it has survived the vigorous indictment of the eighteenth century English so long, a shaking invalid propped on tottering crutches. This concept, especially at a scale greater than the human figure, is only the most arbitrary, abstract, and unrealistic (the world being real) technique for achieving balance. In all the great pre-industrial cultures its emphasis marked the point at which art expression began to turn from vitality to sterility. (See Bernal, page 193.)

48

. . . Let us point out at once that 'symmetry' as defined by Greek and Roman architects as well as the Gothic Master Builders, and by the architects and painters of the Renaissance, from Leonardo to Palladio is quite different from our modern term symmetry (identical disposition on either side of an axis or plane 'of symmetry') . . . this notion of symmetry seen as correlating through the interplay of proportions the elements of the parts and of the whole . . . (as opposed to the modern static meaning usually applied to the word). . . . 'Rhythm is in time what symmetry is in space.'

"The informal naturalistic," generally recognized as having more vitality than its alter ego, nevertheless often results in no form at all, a mere hodge-podge. In fact, like charity, it has been a cloak for a multitude of esthetic sins, and has become, in practise, as mechanical and preconceived a pattern as the axial parti. Every sly or lazy practical gardener, nurseryman or park superintendent, every hack professional, makes glib use of this phrase to excuse every sort of indiscriminate sprinkling of trees, shrubs, and grass areas over the ground. Samuel Parsons, in 1915 in *The Art of Landscape Architecture,* gave us the most complete symposium of authoritative quotes and his own observations on (informal) "landscape gardening." The following two selections give us the flavor of the whole theory:

HUMPHREY REPTON

When under the guidance of Le Nôtre and his disciples, the taste for nature in landscape gardening was totally banished or concealed by the work of art. Now, in defining the shape of land or water, we take nature for our model, and the highest perfection of landscape gardening is to imitate nature so judiciously that the influence of art shall never be detected.

CHARLES ELIOT
(OF PRINCE VON PUCKLER-MUSKAU'S UNDERTAKINGS)

Nothing less than the transformation of the almost ugly valley of the Niesse into a vale of beauty and delight, and the fact that he proposed to accomplish this transformation . . . by quietly inducing nature to transform herself. He would not force upon his native landscape any foreign type of beauty; on the contrary, his aim was the transfiguration, the idealization of such beauty as was indigenous. He was intent upon evolving from out of the confused natural situation a composition in which all that was fundamentally characteristic of the scenery, the history and industry of his estate should be harmoniously and beautifully united.

IN 1936 HEGEMANN (ON CIVIC ART IN HIS OWN BOOK) SAYS

I associate this sort of feeling with the wide and deep popularity of informal landscape gardening. No art style is more widely accepted. And the basis of 'landscape' is a sentiment, a feeling that nature's art is better than man's. . . . It encourages a general softness and mere avoidance of 'artificiality,' usually taken to mean the absence of axiation and defined pattern.
Much of the popular acceptance of 'landscape' is due, I believe, to a dim feeling that this way of arranging things is opposed to art and is a new demonstration that intuition and the heart are after all superior to the arts that require genius and training. This kind of anti-art is a very deep-lying element in American thought and feeling.
. . . The severely rational and formal type of art is apparently fundamentally irritating to people who are dimly conscious of a basic irrationality and inconsistency in their own thought. Our efforts to retain religious and patriotic conviction while constantly surrounded by evidences of irrationality in nature and human conduct, necessarily destroy the easy mental balance which alone takes pleasure in a rationalized art. A kind of sadism impels people who are conscious of their own uncertainties to hate minds, and creations of mind, which have the sense of order they cannot understand. When people of this type can ascribe emotional meaning to a work of art they are avid to substitute this intelligible meaning for the formal organization which disquiets them . . . any exhibition of purely rational design unsupported by sentiment arouses the antagonism which is part of uncertain comprehension. There is something very deep in human nature which makes failure fully to understand equivalent to fear, and fear equivalent to hate. Hence the invariable success of the ridicule of poets and artists. . . .

These last are statements more profound than even their author seems to understand. He is describing the basic insecurity of people who have no real control over their environments or their destinies; who are constantly surrounded and beset by forces and interests which claim to be working for them, the people, but inevitably end up by bilking or cheating them in some

49

way; and who carry on this unarmed struggle with wolves in sheep's clothing while subjected to a constant barrage of completely and deliberately unrelated facts, opinions, distortions, and lies from the "organs of information"—adding up to complete confusion. Nor is this barrage of misinformation and calculated derogation of popular aspirations merely a shower which greets the young citizen as he emerges from the sacred halls of learning; deliberate confusion, the substitution of facts for synthesis, opinion for analysis, and authority for independent thinking, root far back into the tender school years when the adolescent and even the child are at the mercy of wise and omnipotent adults. The basic skepticism which the American who retains some mental independence develops, the sales resistance which is the major product of salesmanship and advertising, are not to be penetrated at once by the artist or designer who emerges from his isolated studio with gleaming ideas for a brave new world.

To this anti-art emotional sentimentalism we must add the sterile practicalism with which our physical environment has been cursed. This stubborn persistence in solving each problem on an emergency basis as it comes along, without thought of relationships or reference to any other problems, to the past or the future, has produced the results which are plain to see all around us. How much of it is based on common sense and how much on sharp commercial practices is an open question. Practicalism and sentimentalism aid and abet each other; each defends the other against those common enemies, "the artist" and "the planner"; neither has much connection with real practicality or real emotion.

* * * * *

It is not necessary to reject the theory of formal and informal design and start from scratch. That would be impossible; the acceptance of the necessity for some such choice is part of the garden thinking of too many Americans today. Nor is it necessary: we have only to absorb it, along with the other elements of our landscape tradition, assimilate it, and make them all parts of a body of work that is bigger

and better, richer and stronger, than anything we have produced to date. Such an expansion in concept should take place within an expansion in the actual scale of opportunity, and that too we must work for.

There are good elements in the formal tradition—order, clarity, proportion, rational planning, imagination, the uninhibited expression of human creativity—and these must be preserved. There are likewise bad elements—the tendency toward failure to recognize the specific qualities of the site and the general beauties of nature, the application of pre-conceived arbitrary formulae of plan and esthetic to specific problems, the growth of drafting-board paper planning in which most of the lines have little real meaning on the ground—and all these crutches for lazy minds must be eliminated. There are good elements in the informal tradition—basically the desire of ordinary people for informal, irregular, simple, unostentatious, unself-conscious, straightforward living; beyond this the recognition of all the richness of human experience latent in the forms and materials of the wild or pastoral landscape, and of the irrelevance of bilateral symmetry to satisfying spatial surroundings—and these too must be preserved. There are likewise bad elements in the informal tradition—the rejection of human creativity, the tendency to make man auxiliary to nature rather than vice versa, the rationalizing of every degree of sloppy and shoddy scattering of plants and structural elements about open space as being informal and therefore okay—and these we must likewise eliminate. We must learn that we cannot avoid, by no matter what persistent concentration on practicalism or romanticism, the creation of spatial form and formal relations in space whenever we do anything whatsoever to or in our physical environment. Our only choice is whether to do this well or poorly.

Thus to take advantage of the potential form and character which are latent in each site and each problem we must release ourselves from the insidious habit of the pre-conceived formula, whether formal, informal, gardenesque, or "modern." Recognition of this one essential premise (and rejection of the old ones) will do more to introduce imagination, freedom, and vitality into landscape design than any number of "modern" problems given by the same old academic minds. There aren't just two ways to solve every problem; there are innumerable ways, derived from the specific problems and designers. There are no rules of form, only principles of approach.

ART

Art cannot be nature, reproduce nature, or successfully imitate nature. Art is conscious and controlled; nature is neither. Art is positive and constructive; it cannot be negative and prohibitive. It must always vary from nature in one direction or another, no matter how carefully naturalistic. Art is either a mathematization, an intellectual explanation or representation, a geometric clarification of nature (classicism) or it must out-nature nature, bend over backwards to be irregularly picturesque or pastoral (romanticism). The path—or shall we say ramp—to new heights of creative expression lies, not through the academic choice BETWEEN these two principles of approach, but through the vitality of using both together, resolving their contradictions, over and over again, in endlessly varying proportions and combinations. The basic contradiction in any creative work is that between imagination and reality.

Systems of thought in art which insist on the necessity for choice between paired opposite extremes—as abstraction vs. representation, formal vs. informal, romanticism vs. classicism —tend in their logical extreme to sterilize that art on which they are forced. Pure abstraction or representation, formality or informality, classicism or romanticism, tends toward dullness or incoherence, over-simplification or confusion, monotony or disorder, sterility or shallowness. The reality and the life of vital art, whether graphic, plastic, or spatial, lies always between and in various combinations of these extremes. In landscape design the mechanical formality of the mall, the mechanical informality of the meadow, each so lonely and so poverty-stricken, by marriage will achieve wealth and posterity beyond their wildest dreams.

This does not mean that we lose the values of contrast and clarity in a kind of hash which is *neither* formal nor informal, *neither* classic nor romantic, *neither* town nor country, *neither* order nor disorder. It means quite the contrary: that we have *both* together, reinforcing each other, bringing each other to life, developing strength, clarity, coherence, integrated contrast, organic geometry, with a richness and flexibility beyond the capacity of the standard sterile static academic clinging to one or the other over-simplified pole. It means that man and nature, objectivity and subjectivity, the rational and irrational, meet, merge, and dance together in ever-shifting, ever-changing, ever-variable patterns that are truly the reflection and the fit environment for the dance of life itself.

Two random quotations may help to illustrate the constancy of these relations. These are both from the English *Architectural Review* of September, 1948. The first refers to the contradiction between accident and intention, the second to that between the pastoral and monumental.

COMMENT ON REFLECTIONS FROM ASTON PARK BY
CHAS. MADGE, SOCIOLOGIST

Just as the landscape gardeners of the 18th century founded their theory of landscape on the close analysis of Nature's 'accidents'—the accidents of contour and planting—and forged therefrom an art of what might be called the deliberate accidental, so the REVIEW maintains, the modern creators of townscape, whether architects or sociologists, stand to gain enormously from a study of the accidental in the urban scene.

LUCIO COSTA, IN SEARCH OF A NEW MONUMENTALITY
(SYMPOSIUM)

. . . speaks of a desirable contemporary monumentality which 'does not ignore the part played by trees, undergrowth and fields in the natural setting; for what characterizes the modern conception of urbanism . . . is that it abolishes the picturesque by incorporating the bucolic into the monumental.'

The western formal tradition developed in a vital effort to solve the contradictions between

51

man and nature in its time, by the projection of man into, over, and through nature. Conversely the informal tradition attempted the resolution by projecting nature into, through, and around the human habitat. Those were stages in the negation of the negations between the planning of man and spontaneity of nature. Now we are ready to develop a new and more advanced stage: the direct struggle, in forms of rich and manifold variability within each job and project, between the contradictions of formality and informality, regularity and irregularity, geometry and biology, line and mass, picture and space, culture and growth, ecology and livability, structure and plasticity, imagination and reality, intuition and mathematical reason. One of the ways in which the contradiction between reason and intuition is constantly resolved is that, while a process of reasoning may very often precede the more or less intuitive production of forms, the forms thus produced may very often have to be explained and clarified by further reasoning and analysis. The proof of the pudding is always in the eating; the work must finally and always justify its own existence on the ground.

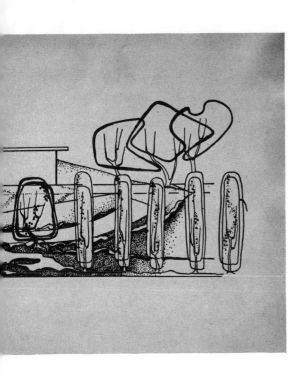

THEORY

CHAPTER VIII

THE QUESTION OF THEORY

BENEDETTO CROCE (FROM THE PHILOSOPHY OF THE PRACTICAL)

He is a true poet who feels himself at once bound to his predecessors and free, conservative and revolutionary, like Homer, Dante, and Shakespeare, who receive into themselves centuries of history, of thought and poetry and add to those centuries something that is the present and will be the future: chargés du passé, gros de l'avenir.

CHARLES E. KELLOGG, 1941

In the first place, there are two things necessary to science—facts and ideas. Simple facts and observations can only be useful to us if there are some connecting ideas; and ideas must be illustrated and supported by facts, or else they may lead us in the wrong way. Sometimes we complain that the man who is all idea doesn't get things done; that it is the practical man who really goes places. But unless the man who does things has correct ideas as well as facts, we will find that he has gone, to be sure, but to the wrong place. Thus ideas without facts or facts without ideas accomplish nothing.
Not only must we have facts and ideas, but our facts must be plentiful, else our ideas will be too narrow. . . .

Here in the middle of the twentieth century we are left with, not the sterile dichotomy of the official academic theory, but a rich and many-sided octagon of landscape tradition. Here are its parts:

The formal tradition of Renaissance and Baroque Europe and the Moslem world, with its sub-current of Greek and Gothic irregularity.
The informal romantic tradition of China, Japan, and eighteenth-century England.
The over-riding fascination with plants for their own sake, based on the horticultural and botanical advances of the nineteenth and twentieth centuries.
The conservation movement, with its emphasis on the value and wonder of the indigenous primeval landscape, expressed in our field in the American park movement.
The urban and regional planning movement, with its compulsion toward re-examination of the relations between buildings and open space, town and country.
The modern movement in the arts, in architecture, and in landscape design since the mid-30's.
The rural tradition and
The folk or little garden tradition, two notes of twentieth-century social realism.
If we examine these streams for their relevance to our work in the balance of the century, we will find that they boil back down to another dichotomy, broader, richer, and more fertile than the academic formal:informal dichotomy.

57

The great problem and the great opportunity of our times is to rebuild, on an infinitely higher plane, the unity and solidarity between man and nature which existed and still exists in primitive communal societies, and which was broken and shattered by the great sweep of history through slavery and feudalism to capitalism. This we can work toward every day on every job and every project, no matter how small or inconsequential it may seem.

On the mention of theory, two questions are apt to rise: one on the need for theory, the other on the nature of the theory needed. We must be able to answer these questions, especially here in practical America, where so much of our environment is built on the sole theory that no theory for its planning is needed—we just go out and build it.

Theory is a generalization of social experience in any particular field, or in all fields. It is at one and the same time a generalization of the past, a vitalizer of the present, and a projection of the future. If it is any one without the others it tends toward sterility, decadence, or frivolity. Only positive exploratory theory can take us beyond the precedents of yesterday. Theory is the vehicle which guarantees the continuous growth and expansion of tradition. Theory and tradition develop together and grow continuously, however unevenly or erratically, through any number of struggles with contradictions. To try to freeze them at any given time in a system of academic rules and proportions is like trying to dam a strong stream with no spillway for overflow control. Sooner or later the stream will find its way over or around the dam, wherever the joints are weakest, and come forth with a burst of vigor equal to the length of time it has been impounded.

Theory, by analyzing the past while working in the present, can project the length and character of the next step into the future. This is the process which has been responsible for all human progress of every sort. Every step forward, technically, culturally, or socially, had to be an idea—a theory—in one or many heads before it could be taken. The whole long chain of development of human tools, from the first

flint ax to the most delicate and powerful machinery of today's industry, has come about through this process of analyzing the past in the present toward the future. Theory is theory, whether it is an idea in a clever mechanic's head, or five hundred pages of windy discourse. New shelter and new clothing, steam engine and electricity, Magna Charta and Declaration of Independence and Bill of Rights: all began as theories, as ideas, some of which were called radical. The scientific process of building theory and constantly developing it by analysis, hypothesis, and experiment is basic to our twentieth-century civilization.

Theory in the arts is, of course, the stumbling block for those practical souls who have gone along with us so far. Yet art is only a process of trying to extract the maximum potential human experience out of necessary practical activities. Painting, sculpture, music, architecture, landscape design have all grown from sound, practical, functional roots in the living activities necessary to people. They have grown to cultural heights by the exact process of imaginative building on the past that we have been describing. The architect today can plan a better house than the carpenter, the brickmason, or the general contractor, because, if he is abreast of the possibilities of his profession, he is more aware of the maximum potential for an interior harmony of space, size, and form; for an exterior harmony of open and solid wall; for the most satisfying combinations of materials. Before he can produce this he must, obviously, solve all the practical functional problems in a way which also makes possible a maximum contribution from carpenter, brickmason, and general contractor. Theory—as idea—is not developed for its own sake, even though it precedes practise. It must come from practical necessity, and be based on constant observation and experience.

A good theory of landscape design, then, must be a theory of form as well as of function. It must be artistic as well as practical, in order to produce the maximum for those who will experience work influenced by it. Every work of landscape design, conscious or unconscious,

58

whether it be the utility garden of the southern sharecropper or the Central Composition of Washington, D. C., produces an arrangement of forms, colors, and textures in space which results in some sort of cumulative effect, good or bad, on those who pass through it. We cannot avoid the problem of producing form in the landscape. From the formal western school which went after it with axes and vistas, through the informal eastern school which avoided it with poetry, rationalizations, and subjective grotesqueries, to the horticulturists and the naturalists, who bury it in collections or hide it behind nature—all have produced arrangements of cumulative effect, good or bad, on us who experience them, whether or not we know their literary rationalizations. It should be noted that the good and bad is not necessarily between schools but within schools; all produce good work (pleasing to us) and bad work (unpleasant to us). The goodness or badness, for us, is not necessarily based on the theory of the particular school, but rather on certain questions of the arrangement of spaces, the development of sites, the use of materials, unity and variety, scale and proportion, rhythm and repetition, which we know or can determine are basic to our experiences in our environment.

Our theory, then, must point the way toward good form in the landscape, but it cannot define it rigidly, on an exclusive, selective basis, with dogma and formulae, rules and regulations, precedents and measured drawings. We must base ourselves upon a flexible understanding and assimilation of those basic questions of scale, proportion, unity, variety, rhythm, repetition, which have been the primary guides for good men in all fields in all times and places. We must remember that most landscape problems are so plastic, so little under the control of functional requirements, that any number of solutions is possible. For most, the final best solution is probably as unreachable as the final best solution for a square of canvas on an easel, or a block of stone in the sculptor's yard. Design, like life, has no limits to its development.

It will be said, then, on what shall we base our forms? Where shall we find them? And the answer is, in the world which is around you in space, and behind you in time. If you understand it and love it and enjoy it there is your inspiration. The more you are a part of your world the more inspired you will be, if you find those parts which are streaming steadily forward, rather than the many stagnant backwaters which exist to trap the unwary.

It must be remembered that the great pre-industrial styles of the past were produced by societies of a certain stability, a certain established structure and discipline within which artist and designer found enough security, orientation, and direction to produce their best work. The nineteenth and twentieth centuries have been a period of tremendous historical acceleration, of great flux and movement throughout the world, of huge contradictory struggles, of the rise of the common man and the democratic idea. The old relation of the artist to a clientele of the social elite has gradually receded; the new relation of artist to a democratic mass clientele is barely visible over the horizon; in between is the no man's land of commercialism, eclecticism, egocentrism, and escapism in which the artist has been wandering for lo, these many moons. Our theory must be oriented within the social, as well as the technical and esthetic, potential of the times, if it is to be relevant to the artist as producer and the people as consumers.

Our theory of landscape design for the balance of the twentieth century must be concerned with the realities of the now engrossing problems of the overall outdoor environment of the American people, rather than with abstractions about systems of axes, or poetic subjectivities about nature. We have tremendous problems, of unprecedented social and esthetic potential, ahead of us. As we prepare for them and work on them we can absorb and assimilate the old ideas, build on the strong base of our rich octagon of landscape tradition, and go on to a unified expression of integrated social and natural landscape such as has never been seen before.

This will be a theory which will be practical, functional, socially-conscious, and yet more

59

concerned with richness, beauty, magnificence, fantasy, imagination, and variety of expression than any previous theory. It must be based on and rooted in the direct elements of the problem: the physical organization of three-dimensional outdoor space, on the land, for the work, play, and relaxation of people; with a wide range of specific materials of specific qualities and properties, on specific sites of endless variety in form and character. The forms which we are to produce must come, first, from exhaustive, sensitive, scientific, sympathetic examination of these elements, and second, from the breadth of our knowledge and understanding of the world culture which is behind us, and the physical and social worlds about us. We do not project a freezing of those forms into any system whatsoever; we want only to emphasize the need for adequate foundations and root media, and for strength, clarity, and coherence —not specific kinds or classes of forms, but clear, strong, coherent forms and relations of forms.

This is a why-to-do-it book, not a how-to-do-it book. America is brimming with know-how. We can make anything, build anything, do anything. But still our cities are sordid, messy, and unhealthful; our countrysides riddled with erosion. It is the know-why that is missing, understanding why we do it before we do it. That is called planning (and design). It is the other half of the whole, America can be.

CHAPTER IX

SPACE FOR LIVING—
PEOPLE ON THE LAND

SPACE

HUDNUT

Gardens, like houses, are built of space. Gardens are fragments of space set aside by the planes of terraces and walls and disciplined foliage. Until now we have defined too nicely the differences between that space which is roofed and within the house and that which is left outside and round the house. We did not see, until the architect threw down his walls, that the space of house and that of garden are parts of a single organism: that the secret of unity lies in a unity of spatial sequences. The new vision has dissolved the ancient boundary between architecture and landscape architecture. The garden flows into and over the house: through loggias and courts and wide areas of clear glass, and over roofs and sun-rooms and canopied terraces. The house reaches out into the garden with walls and terraced enclosures that continue its rhythms and share its grace. The concordant factor is the new quality given to space.

People live ON the earth, ON the land, but IN the three-dimensional air-space, the atmospheric volume, immediately above this land surface. Plans and land-use maps may be measured diagrammatically and abstractly in square footage and acreage, but space for living is measured in cubage, in volumes of air-space enclosed or organized with tangible physical elements. The term space may be used scientifically by astronomers, demagogically by reactionary politicians, and abstrusely by artistic intellectuals, but to ordinary people it has an ordinary practical meaning—room to live in, to work in, to play in, to relax in.

Every piece of land which is set aside by legal property lines as being within the private ownership of some individual or organization is really a block of space, a volume of atmosphere, bounded by vertical planes projected from the property lines, with a third dimension adequate to include the development programmed for that land, whether it be a one-story house or a sixty-story skyscraper. The real estate, the land, is only the floor, the bottom side, of this space for living. It provides a foundation for structures, a root-medium for plants, a source of raw materials, but the volume above it is the primary element.

If the land has some irregularity or slope it has to that extent a third dimension which produces some sense of volume, determined by the vertical pull of gravity. Beyond that every element, every rock, every hole or gully, every bush or tree, every wall or pole, every object alive or dead, moving or stable, every structure, produces a physical organization and definition of space, gives it tangible comprehensible form, encloses it, puts it under control, or puts it in motion around focal elements, all with tre-

61

mendous variations in intensity, precision, strength or subtlety, and sensations resulting in the person or persons within that space. The land, the air space, and the physical elements and materials on the land are all mutually interdependent—land and super-surface elements give form to space; space displays the form of land and elements. Space sensation very simply is the aggregate of all the physical sensations one experiences in a given place at a given time.

We live continuously subjected to spatial sensation, wherever we go, indoors and out, from birth to death. The experience of space is a common and vital human experience, comparable to those of food, sleep, clothing, or sex. We all remember childhood and youthful experiences of pleasant and unpleasant spaces—backyards, sheds, attics, playgrounds, railroad yards, beaches, streets and alleys, basements—and their effect upon our growing awareness of, and attitude toward, the world around us. This sensitivity seems to get dulled, or submerged to the subconscious, as we grow older. Perhaps this happens because the spatial experiences of the majority of the population are quite poverty-stricken. The American scene—Main Street, urban housing, the standard residential suburb—has a general commercialized sterility which is far below the technical and esthetic potential of our culture. This is the richest country in the world, yet most of our buildings are put up by "practical" builders or engineers—badly proportioned, skimpily planned, and of a monotonous and deadly similarity. Even our architects tend to insufficient concern with spatial experience, and to dull, stereotyped, mechanical work. Our outdoor experiences are somewhat more varied, but there is the same tendency toward repetition of a dull and tired formula in streets, and in gardens and parks where they exist. Speculation in land and its chain of shoddy and miserly land use and space conceptions have produced the poverty of space for most American people, and the poverty of people for most American space, which is the basic contradiction of our environment. This is expressed statistically in terms of housing, slums, juvenile delinquency, fire risk, etc., and, without statis-

tics, in a general neurosis, a general worry and hostility, jangled nerves and the constant urge to get away from whatever place we happen to be in.

Space, beginning as necessity and ending as luxury, is one of the primary conditioners of human development. Measured in square or cubic feet per person, qualified by the character of its organization, it is one of the basic gauges of the quality of our living environment. A future science of the space we live in will establish standards for full American living which will be optimums rather than minimums (which quickly become maximums)—as, hypothetically, 1,000 sq. ft. for a two-bedroom house. The relation of such standards to the health of the nation has yet to be measured. Families with one or two children can be found living in any size unit from 500 to 15,000 sq. ft.; most are probably living in less than 1,000. How can we explain this spread in accommodation, save in terms of luxury and scarcity: the conspicuous consumption of space by a few, the conspicuous consumption of the many by the inadequate space left over?

Artists and architects cannot escape the impact of such contradictions. The architect is led to concern with the contradiction between our advanced building technology and our advanced housing crisis, between the potential richness and the actual poverty of our general physical habitat, in his specific struggles with the contradictions between space and structure expressed as needs vs. restrictions, biology vs. cost, and so on. Thus we find the *Architectural Forum* rationalizing the reduction, by economic pressure, of the $10,000 house from 2,000 sq. ft. in 1928 to 700 sq. ft. in 1948: "Houses . . . growing as they shrink. . . . Since the house is smaller, many areas must serve several different functions. . . ."

The concern with isolated pictorial compositions and with two-dimensional patterns, the snare of patterns of lines on paper which produce no three-dimensional result on the ground, is one of the roots of the present-day esthetic and functional inadequacy of American landscape design. This is an inadequacy of incomplete overall site conceptions, and they are incomplete because there is no concept of space, of volume, to pull all these scattered items of pictures and patterns, site and buildings, trees and views, natural and structural elements, into a unity greater and more compelling than their mere disorganized accumulation.

SPACE SENSATION

The English architect Erno Goldfinger in the *Architectural Review* for November 1941 discusses "The Sensation of Space" (see also December 1941 and January 1942). Here is an oversimplified outline of his basic analysis:

GOLDFINGER

We are always subject to a spatial sensation as we are always in an enclosed space.
Pathological manifestations are claustrophobia and agoraphobia; the normal conditions have hardly ever been investigated.
Plastic and pictorial visualization is static.
Spatial visualization is kinetic.
Sensation is determined by:
(1) The relations between two elements:
    The enclosing agent
    The enclosed space
(2) The relation of enclosed spaces to one another
(3) The relation of the enclosed person to them
(4) Automatic registration of successive images
(5) Effect of memorized analogies.

GYORGY KEPES, IN LANGUAGE OF VISION

. . . Vision is primarily a device of orientation; a means to measure and organize spatial events. The mastery of nature is intimately connected with the mastery of space; this is visual orientation. Each new visual environment demands a reorientation, a new way of measuring. Seeing spatial relationships on a flat land is a different experience from seeing them in a mountainous region, where one form intercepts the other. To orient oneself in walking requires a different spatial measurement than is required in riding in a motor-car or in an aeroplane. To grasp spatial relationships and orient oneself in a metropolis of today, among the intricate dimensions of streets, subways, elevated, and skyscrapers, requires a new way of seeing. Widening horizons, and the new dimensions of the visual environment necessitate new idioms of spatial measurement and communication of space. . . .
Looking at a landscape, at people on the street, or at any single object, as the visual field has no definite

boundaries, one can only make a spatial interpretation of the things he sees—their location, extension—based upon his own spatial position. He judges the position, direction, and interval of things seen by relating them to himself. He measures and organizes up, down, left, right, advance, and recession in a single physical system of which his body is the center and identified with the main directions in space. The ego-centered horizontal and vertical axis is the latent background, and optical differences are interpreted against this background. . . .

Gestalt psychology is also relevant to our environmental thinking:

COMPTON'S ENCYCLOPEDIA

. . . The Gestalt psychologists are opposed to the tendency of the traditional psychologists to divide the mind up into its elements, thus missing the wholeness or Gestalt quality of our experience. To illustrate: . . . When we look at a movie we do not see the thousands of separate pictures of which the film is composed but rather see persons moving about before us on the screen. In like manner most of our experiences are experiences of wholes, or 'Gestalts.' It is only by analysis that we become aware of the parts of which they are composed. The Gestalt psychology also emphasizes the relativity of our experiences. . . .

While space concepts vary among modern buildings, they agree in general in being more open in plan and in exterior walls than traditional buildings. That is, they have moved from the concept of building as a mass or block, with holes punched in the sides for light, air and access, toward the concept of buildings as free and flexible arrangements of wall planes, some solid and some open, between floor and roof planes. The early work of Mies van der Rohe is perhaps the best example of this latter concept; it eliminated more preoccupation with façade and sculptural or plastic qualities than that of other leaders.

Gardens and landscapes in general are apprehended only from within themselves; they do not have the outside walls or façades which make it possible to walk around most buildings, however modern, and view them as objects, more or less sculptural, in the landscape. Only from an airplane or a high place can one view gardens or landscapes from outside themselves, and their scale changes radically in the process of getting so far above them.

SPACE FORMATION

We are not here to advance rules or formulae for the new concept of space-form in the landscape. However, we can suggest the direction. The practical will become esthetic and the esthetic practical. The practical solution of almost any landscape problem will take the following steps: surfacing, enclosure, enrichment. Instead of concentrating on enrichment elements —pictures, "compositions," patterns, flower borders—we will tend to concentrate more on sensitive and imaginative selection and arrangement of enclosure and surfacing elements. Such concentration, while it establishes a framework or shell within which any amount of further enrichment can be woven into the overall harmony, is equally satisfying with no more than the greatest enrichment of all—human life and activity. For a really full and well-rounded scientific art of space organization, outdoors as well as in, will proceed always with two primary ideas in mind. These can be contradictory or complementary as they are interpreted by specific designers in specific situations. One is the objective of giving the richest, most plastic and satisfying form to the space which is being organized; the other is to concentrate always on that space as an arena, volume, background, and shelter for human life and activity. People are its primary content; without them it becomes an empty abstraction, exterior decoration, excess gilding, as so many great historical gardens were. People are the focal points, the terminal features, the final vitality of any spatial enclosure we may create. That is why the open center may almost be called a principle of modern design.

Let us illustrate this relation of practical and esthetic questions in more detail. On any piece of land subject to human development—most typically, a house and garden—the first practical problem to solve, once the main construction activities have been completed, is the control of all the ground areas which have been in any way disturbed. This is the problem of surfacing, and it is essential to eliminate summer dust and winter mud. The forces of nature are intolerant of bare ground and will, if left to themselves, produce volunteer ground cover on any but the most sterile surface. Such volunteer cover is typically weeds, wild grass or brush, and it is apt to be too rough for average concepts of garden use and beauty.

In ordinary garden usage, once natural cover has been rejected for more refined or intensive development, there are three primary types of surfacing: inorganic, paving of all sorts on terrace and walk and drive; organic, permanent planted cover, lawns and other sorts of mat-forming, trailing, or spreading plants; and cultivated, areas which are maintained for the growth of changing groups of flowers, vegetables, or fruits, in which the ground is regularly turned over and volunteer growth is cut down. Use of any or all these is always a specific question. The tendency of landscape design, whether academic or "modern," is to overemphasize the flat pattern of such surfacing elements, and underemphasize the three-dimensional elements which produce a sense of space or volume.

The next question to settle in the garden is the amount and kind of enclosure needed, around the sides and overhead. This arises practically with the need for control of views into the garden from outside—the question of privacy; the need for control of views within and out from it—the question of screening and framing; and the need for protection overhead from sun, wind, or rain—the question of shelter and shade. These are questions with a wide range of variation in intensity, from the minimum of the national wilderness park or the large private estate or ranch, where a superabundance of open space in itself provides a sense of privacy and enclosure, to the maximum of fifty-foot lot or small city garden, with no view out and the great pressure of the urban population converging on the garden from all sides.

These practical aspects of the question of enclosure are recognized and met, more or less effectively, by any competent designer. Beyond that there is the question of the amount of sense of being enclosed—in a room or volume of space, with a range of definition from solid masonry to the attenuation of wires or plant tracery —required by people, specifically and in general. Here the landscape field is wide open to creative general investigation, and every specific problem will benefit from the vitalizing impact of such thinking. It can be stated categorically, on the basis of our experience of great architecture and great natural scenery, that the experience of being within fine three-dimensional spatial volumes is one of the great experiences of life. This leaves us free to practice every variation in enclosure, from the flat patterned terrace in the desert to the completely glassed-in city courtyard. The contrast between various degrees of enclosure is one of the maximum sources of spatial experience.

The well-conceived scheme of surfacing and enclosure can be improved, strengthened, and refined by the integration, the weaving-in, of more elegant, colorful, or useful detailed elements, where the badly-conceived scheme cannot be saved by them. These enriching elements —flower borders, special plants, specimen trees and shrubs, rocks, pools, sculpture, murals, driftwood, ceramics, glass, furniture, movable screens, barbecues, fireplaces, game spaces and equipment—are often considered primary in garden or park, the first and sometimes the only thoughts. Practical problems of surfacing force their solution in at least a minimum fashion; the great opportunities for pleasure and beauty in the formation of enclosure and shelter are seldom even approached, save by practical accident. It is essential to good landscape design, whether professional, commercial, or amateur, to establish this classification of landscape elements in spatial terms, and thereafter to do first things first. The bottom, the sides, the top (if any), of the outdoor volume are primary; thereafter any amount of enrichment is reasonable, provided it is woven into the spatial pattern so as to reinforce it; not pushed or dropped in so as to disrupt it.

It is with the introduction of such elements that the danger of turning the garden or park into a collection, a jumble, or a "riot of color" arises. We have to remember that space in houses and gardens is for people to live in, and that a certain amount of disorder and irregularity are comfortable and relaxing. It is for us to present the alternatives and the varying relations between order and disorder that are possible; it is for the people to choose from day to day. The range from the careful pictorial fixation of the elements in the Japanese garden to the constant flux of the enthusiastic dirt gardener's flower borders is the range of human values which our arrangements of space must provide for. Every relation of internal elements to enclosing framework, from the ascetic clarity of the purist modern interior to the over-decorated clutter of the Victorian parlor, is the potential arc within which we must work. Our feeling of appropriate relations will vary from day to day according to our general experiences. We are tending to think in terms of fewer elements more carefully arranged within adequately enclosed spaces, because the general tendency in homes and gardens is to have too many elements arranged with little or no care, over-enclosed in homes and under-enclosed in gardens. All our clever details, our cute steps and paving patterns, our slick screens and plastic pools, our handsome specimen plants and broad lawns, are meaningful and effective only in relation to one another; they do not exist or function in a vacuum. It is the overall space relations which link all the garden elements up into one coherent whole, give each detail and section its role to play, and thus bring out the best in it. Without some overall concept of form our details become over-emphasized, strident and self-conscious.

A beginning at rational analysis of landscape design in terms of space organization comes with the classification of garden elements in terms of their effect on outdoor space. In such a classification the primary plane of reference is a horizontal plane at the level of the human eye, roughly 5 ft. above the ground surface. Elements standing above this plane are of maximum importance in the landscape arrangement, because they tend to obstruct or block vision, to establish baffles around which there is a movement of space and a sense of depth and continuity. These maximum elements carry the main theme, the primary melody and harmony of our spatial symphony; elements which do not stand as high as the eye-level plane are secondary, a kind of counterpoint, varying and enriching the main theme. Whereas the taller elements block both movement and vision, the lower elements may block movement but vision proceeds unimpeded over them.

This principle can be upset or disturbed by strong contrasts of form, color, or texture in the lower elements. Pattern tends to replace volume, although it too can play a role in space organization: strong contrasts on a plane surface can create considerable sense of form and movement. Thus a bed of scarlet geraniums, a small and ornate pool, or a small and shining smooth terrace placed in the foreground of a large and placid view will tend to disrupt and obscure that view by their stridence. But such a relation is again the result of an over-emphasis on detail and a failure to establish proper overall spatial relations.

We can classify our garden elements, then, as primary—all those standing at least 6 ft. high; and secondary—all those which do not reach that height. Beyond this breakdown there is an endless variation in terms of weight, density, precision of form, continuity of plane surface, color, texture, actual height, thickness, and overhead spread. Thus structural screens 6 ft. or more high can run a gamut, starting with solid masonry walls and solid wood walls and fences, through pierced masonry and open wood treillage of all weights, translucent or transparent glass, chain link metal fencing, wire or rope stretched between pipe posts, to a mere row of posts or columns, with or without a top rail. These screens can be further complicated or enriched by the growth of vines of all weights, from the tracery of clematis to the mass of the mattress vine. Boundary planting, again, can vary from the large solid hedge and windbreak through every imaginable change in pattern and solidity of structure and foliage to the thinnest continuous tracery, and again, by separating the plants so they cannot grow together, the rhythm of open rows or irregular belts of every sort of plant form—clump, bush, small

thin tree, pyramid, column, spreading shade tree. Terraces and mounds and hollows where the change in level exceeds 6 ft. become part of this spatial vocabulary, as do all sorts of special elements—sculpture, garden shelters and structures of all sorts, fireplaces, aviaries, and so on.

Within the secondary elements there is a comparable variation in the weight and form of low walls and fences and lines or belts of planting used to define areas. As the third dimension decreases and a greater area becomes visible from the eye-level the importance of pattern may be allowed to increase. Paving patterns, flower and bedding plant patterns, water forms, will play as soft or as loud a role in the garden space as the amount of continuity or change of surface on the ground plane.

LINE AND FORM

The relation of line on paper to form on the ground requires discussion. There is a remarkable amount of confusion about this simple matter. The fairy tale about geometric lines being rigid, arbitrary, and "formal," whereas the free curve is the line of beauty, nature, and "informality," is only the most common manifestation.

We must first understand the relation between lines on paper and lines in the actual building or garden. Any sharp edge gives a visual line. Any form silhouetted against a contrasting background is expressed in line. Beyond that, in a structure actual line appears as the joint between two kinds of surface material on a flat plane, or as a corner where two planes come together. This line is the result of a processing of materials which makes possible smoothness of finish and consequent continuity of edge. Such sharply refined lines, with continuity in one direction (straight) or in one changing direction (arcs) seldom occur in the natural materials of landscape work, at the scale at which we work with them. Rocks and tight shrubs may have sharp silhouettes, but even they are lines of constantly changing direction, and we are more apt to sense the rock as a mass, and the shrub as a structure, in space than to be conscious of their lines. Line can be given to natural materials by human processing: thus the tooling of rock in masonry is a process of giving it more precise form; trimmed grass and hedges can have relatively precise edges and corners, if the trimming is repeated often enough to control the natural growth. Scale is important: irregularity accumulating continuously in the same direction can have the cumulative organizing force of line.

In order to design in line we must have developed a language on paper so that we know whether a line means an actual precise edge on the job, or merely a relation of elements such as plants. Then the question of the complexity or simplicity of geometric relations in our lines and forms becomes the key to our problem. Motion in balance, stability in growth, to be expressed in an environment of strong, clear, and coherent forms and relations—this will mean that, as these forms and relations get bigger in scale they will get simpler in their geometric organization. In reverse, as they get smaller they can get more complex, more detailed, and "freer." The straight line and the arc or section of a circle, clearly articulated, are the basic line forms for the organization of larger spaces, say at the scale of public parks or large private grounds. These are the forms that are restful and stable because they are easily comprehended and assimilated. Somewhere we have seen a study proving that the straight line is the easiest and most restful for the human eye to follow. As we come down to smaller scale elements we can develop more complex relations and lines, down to the final complexity of the free curve, at the scale of patio, pool, or terrace. Straight lines, their simple or complex angular relationships, and simple or complex curves, are all vocabulary elements that help and need each other. In the proper proportionate relations—complexity controlled by overall simplicity, disorder within order, controlled fantasy—these elements can produce a maximum in richness of environment for human "vision in motion."

A garden laid out in straight lines and right angles, but without bilateral symmetry, can be interesting, stable, and restful without being dull or monotonous. A complication in angles will complicate the problem of control. Likewise a garden planned in large simple segments of circles, again without bilateral symmetry, would have a sense of plastic motion, and yet be stable and restful; the same garden laid out in all complex free curves, would be more difficult to keep within orderly control. Such projects must be thought of hypothetically as in the vacuum of an open field; standard rectangular boundary lines would give an ordering framework to all four.

There is actually no such thing as a "free" line composed of "free" curves: any such line can be reduced to a system of geometric arcs and tangents. We have merely a gradation in the complexity or simplicity of geometric relations. The free curve and the free form, with their ideological implications, become a kind of escapism—freedom from? or freedom to? There is, of course, the free curve that is not very complex but nevertheless refuses to simplify itself into recognizable arcs; this line tends to become indecisive, weak, and irresponsible. After all is said and done, there may be a razor's edge trod by the most skillful designers, a line that is neither complex nor geometric, neither weak nor strong, decisive nor indecisive, the Golden Mean, the line that is all things to all men, that is neither formal nor informal—and that is enough about lines.

Design in line is only half of our technical heritage, stemming from the formal tradition through the control and precision of modern art and architecture. It is a technique developed on paper, and suffers from the danger inherent in paper design—the possibility of becoming divorced from the reality of the site. The other half of our technical heritage, stemming from the informal tradition and the general human and natural world we live in, is design in terms of the arrangement of elements and objects in space—plants, rocks, walls, pools, the ground plane, overhead and vertical planes, and so forth. This is true spatial design. The meadow, so dear to the hearts of park designers, is an arrangement of trees on grass, consciously

67

avoiding linear relationships. This was brought to its highest peak, perhaps, in the Japanese garden—a most precisely controlled and ordered plastic composition in which there are almost no simple or geometric lines. These are sculptural gardens, arrangements of volumes and masses in space, with relations of a complexity and richness which cannot be reduced to paper.

FORM AND ARRANGEMENT

There is a quadrangular contradiction or contrast in design approaches, all relevant to our subject. These may be called the plane, the structural, the plastic, and the spatial. Each in turn is modified by its content of static (relatively changeless) or kinetic (relatively changeable) elements, in relation to time. Thus the man-made structural elements of architecture tend to be static, while the bimorphic plant structure of the landscape is generally kinetic. Plane design, the picture plane, painting and graphic art have been brought up to date for us by Kepes, Schillinger, and all the advocates of Dynamic Symmetry and the Golden Rectangle. The naïveté of the pictorial approach to landscape design has been its persistent clinging to vertical picture planes: "the terminal feature," "the focal point"—and horizontal picture planes: "the garden pattern." All of which must not obscure the fact that form and pattern on enclosing planes, whether vertical or horizontal, extend definite fields of force and impact into the adjacent three-dimensional space. It is true that spatial experience and the sensation of space are compounded of pictures. But this is an accumulation of pictures of a richness and complexity beyond the formal parti, or even the informal meadow. It is all the pictures seen in every direction from every possible station point within the space under control. It is not merely the pictures seen from one or either end of a major axis or any attendant minor axes. The meadow is much closer to our concept of spatial continuity and richness than the mall, but it is hamstrung by its rejection of geometry, its pretensions to a narrow "naturalness."

Structural design, the establishment of equilibrium between connected members enclosing space, has been described as follows:

ARCHITECTURAL FORUM, NOVEMBER 1948

. . . To the degree that we call structure beautiful, it seems to be a visible manifestation of energy. Although structure is a science of statics, sometimes the great works of architecture seem less to express than to transcend the law of gravity. . . .

Plastic design is continuous forms, masses, or sheets, which may or may not enclose spatial hollows—sculpture, earthwork, handicraft object design as ceramics, and industrial design of the streamlined shell variety. Spatial design may be considered the arrangement of disconnected structural or plastic elements in space, the establishment of spatial relations between objects not physically connected; including typically planting design, furniture arrangement, window dressing, grouping of sculpture, rock arrangements, and the grouping or site planning of several or many buildings or engineering elements.

Structural forms are limited by the necessity of physical connection and fabrication, even though their scale has expanded to Bay Bridge and Boulder Dam. In the reinforced concrete of the latter, structural and plastic design achieve by marriage an unprecedented improvement of the landscape in which we live. Spatial design, because its central factor is the three-dimensional atmosphere, is the total landscape, the total habitat control, urban, rural, and primeval, room, neighborhood, city, and region. Plastic forms are earth- and gravity-bound in nature, although they become highly mobile objects in the hands of man. Ranging in nature from pebbles through boulders to mature rolling hills, and in human design through various sculptural and industrial design forms, they are forms of mass and gravity, or of continuous enclosing shells from beetle to airplane. They are the forms of the warped plane and the complex curve, the "natural" form, the "biotechnic" form, the "free" form, which in their highest development through either human or non-human processes embody the final marriage of biology and geometry. Even as sculptural or industrial objects in the general size range of the human form they have considerable impact on the spatial sensations in their vicinity; we know them well as mobile spatial enclosures—the auto, boat, and airplane; any region of rounded rolling hills is an exemplary freeform landscape, a domain of constantly varying large-scale plastic spatial relations constantly unified by the repetition of curved planes.

Plants are natural structural elements: antigravitational, irregular in form, spatial in content, requiring no physical contact with one another save for the technical problem of ground cover or the functional problem of enclosure. It is inaccurate to speak of plants as plastic forms; they are not continuous in either mass or surface.

AS THE FORUM SAYS

In nature, we have a pure resolution of all forces whatever they may be. The tree's form is a beautiful equation in which static load, wind resistance, maximum sun and water absorption are all factors.

Spatial design is both, yet neither, plastic and structural; plastic design is spatial insofar as it establishes radial fields of force, structural design is spatial insofar as it establishes literal enclosure. Thus plastic and structural design are both components of spatial design; it is developed through the establishment of relations both functional and esthetic between elements which do not necessarily have any physical connection. There are relations in space between the plastic object in the building, and that building; and between the building in the landscape, and that landscape; between buildings and plants, and between plants and the landscape; likewise between plastic elements and landscape, with or without building. One of the highest examples of spatial design in the west is the Acropolis of ancient Athens (now overlooking such modern barbarism) as analyzed for us by Le Corbusier and Saarinen. The Japanese garden is perhaps the highest example of spatial design in the east, however unintentional its spatial effects may have been (see Kuck).

While both plastic and structural elements are components of spatial design their mere accumulation does not necessarily add up to spatial relations of any coherent quality. Both, when done in terms of isolated art for its own sake, or of rugged individualism in the landscape (urban, rural, or primeval), are merely disruptive or anarchic in their effect on the general or total space in which we live. That, in fact, is what is wrong with the esthetics of our communities: the complete anarchy of completely unrelated and irresponsible design of elements both plastic and structural. Consider merely the relation between the billboard, the neon sign, and the traffic signal. The esthetics of planning, at any scale, is simply the control of the relations between all the plastic and structural elements in our landscape, which add up to a total spatial quality, usually cacophonic, but potentially symphonic.

Thus spatial design, as a larger and more complete concept than plane, plastic, or structural design, brings all of them to full fruition by completing the circuit of spatial forces which they have begun, stabilizing them in relation to one another and the general landscape, and therefore resolving the apparent contradictions between them. Various interdependences, overlappings, contrasts, and contradictions have existed between these kinds of design through history. Structural design began with plastic masses enclosing small hollow spaces in Egypt (or perhaps with cave dwellings), and developed through the static stone of Greece and the dynamic stone of Gothic times to the light and elegant framework of modern architecture. Now the *Forum* projects for us a new plastic sheet structure which will remain light and elegant:

ARCHITECTURAL FORUM

The curved shape is an economic form found widely in organic life, but which man was unable to use extensively before the appearance of the machine and the new materials produced by modern chemistry. . . . The monococque principle of the oil tank indicates that new methods of handling stresses are now available to building. . . . Now, when we are just beginning to take full advantage of the steel cage by use of the fabricated curtain wall, there is reason to believe that future theoretical development may be in

69

the direction of emancipating structure from the right-angle frame itself. A corresponding freedom from rigid forms based on the square can be expected.

No doubt frame structure, less durable, nevertheless can be traced back through history to the first nomad tent. But the varying relations of structural and plastic form in buildings, from stone through wood and steel to reinforced concrete and plastics, trace a great curve from integration through separation back to possible integration at a more refined level. Nevertheless there remains a contradiction between the plastic and the structural designer today, perhaps best exemplified by the formlessness of many buildings designed by industrial designers. When the spatial designer has no understanding of structure, and the structural designer has no understanding of space, productive collaboration becomes difficult if not impossible.

Plastic design, in pre-industrial cultures nearly always disciplined by structural and spatial relations, tends today to be the least disciplined and the most formless kind of art production, precisely because it is divorced from structure and seldom considered spatially. In landscape design it is reasonably relevant to the treatment of ground and water forms, but becomes quite irrelevant in that cliché, "mass planting," once intended quantitatively, now used to force plants, free natural structures in space, into unnatural sculptural masses. Spatial design, separated for the moment from structural design, has its roots in all the great historical background of architectural, romantic, or symbolic arrangement of structural or natural elements in the landscape, and its current growing climate in the space concepts of modern art and architecture. Seen thus spatial design becomes greater than, and inclusive of, structural and plastic design, potentially expansive in scale to the city and the region. Yet it cannot grow toward that potential without, at one and the same time, maintaining the integrity of and resolving the contradictions between structural and plastic design forms: building frameworks by man, plant frameworks by nature, mass and sheet sculpture by man, earth, rock, and water

forms by nature. All of these can participate in spatial organization without losing their articulate character.

Structural design, because of its inherently simple geometric form relations, is thought of as obviously man-made, hence "unnatural," "harsh," "disruptive," and so on. Plastic design, with no technical compulsion to geometry, tends toward "free form," those complex and constantly changing curves in line and plane which are classified as the restful forms of beauty and nature. Sometimes, as in industrial design, these free forms become relations between tangents and radial curves that are somewhat more orderly, somewhat more intermediate between plastic and structural forms. Plastic forms are thought of as antithetical to the rigid straight-line geometry to which our buildings are forced by the persistence of post-and-lintel construction through all the expansions of industrial techniques and materials. This rectangular system of spatial enclosure, forced on us by technical necessities, is no more persistent than the theory that we must escape from it to a dominance of curved plastic forms as quickly as possible. The compulsion to build in straight-line forms produces a compulsion to romanticize or escape to curved forms.

Now, assuming that the *Forum's* theoretical projection of freeform plastic sheet structure becomes an actual mass possibility, what happens to our landscapes, urban, rural, primeval? Here is that magnificent opportunity long dreamed of by the informalist, the romanticist, the functionalist weary of geometric compulsion. Here is freedom; here is no more geometric necessity; here is the opportunity for structural design to become truly biotechnic, no longer obtrusive and self-conscious in nature, able now to consummate a final marriage with plastic design. Can you envision a plastic urban landscape, a city without straight lines or recognizable arcs? Have you seen "artist's conceptions" of the cities of Mars, or surrealist's nightmares about architecture—or fairy tales, the Emerald City of Oz? All of us, whatever our subjective prejudices pro or con geometric form, have grown up in the simple cubical

70

security of frame buildings, in the simple orientation of rectangular subdivisions of the land. Was it Le Corbusier who spoke of maintaining the integrity of the cube? And Saarinen of the importance of the room? A structural landscape suddenly gone freeform, a city or town gone plastic, projects a picture of instability and insecurity in space on the land, of endlessly complex visual restlessness in the habitat, a shapeless urban landscape in which clever designers would immediately make a killing designing clean cubical gardens as retreats from plasticity. Here, with this projection of the plastic structure, is our opportunity to clear up this contradiction between geometry and biology, between structure and wild nature.

Even so, were this new plasticity to blow through our constructed world, through our humanized landscapes, those who have been calling for biotechnic forms, for informality and irregularity, for the "line of beauty," would find themselves lost and disoriented in a world without base lines or reference corners. Luckily, this will not happen: the engineers, the real estate developers, and the building fraternity are not sufficiently interested in esthetics to make the change.

The general objective in our environment is undoubtedly a quality of equilibrium and stability, coupled with their opposites, movement and growth: controlled motion, orderly growth, balanced equilibrium, dynamic stability. Those are expressions of life and the needs of life. Within them there can be infinite variations in playfulness, fantasy, gaiety, sobriety, monumentality, disorder, carelessness, and so on. It is a question of the scale relation of parts: disorder within order is possible and natural; order within disorder is unnatural and nearly impossible. Strength, clarity, and coherence in physical forms and relations are the tools, the

means by which we can achieve this large and balanced order, this dynamic equilibrium within which all the complex pulse of life can flow and grow. This by contrast with the general environment most of us live in: anarchy, frenzied restlessness, a neurotic commercial cacophony of signs and lights and noises and salesmanship; hovering over it like an expanding storm cloud the tremendous inhuman static repressive order of monopoly—Stuyvesant Town.

Always the relation to the vertical pull of gravity, and the stability of the horizontal plane at right angles to it, are primary considerations. In architecture this is a foregone conclusion; in landscape design, working on the ground which is never exactly level, and with light structures which get easily out of plumb, stability becomes highly important to the general equilibrium, the sense of security, of the space conception. Plants tend to grow vertically, or radially around a vertical center line; structures are more stable in verticals and horizontals, although any angle or combination of angles is technically possible; water is stable when level and moving when not; the ground surface is the great variable, sloping even when it looks level, always subject to the action of surface drainage. Problems of spatial design tend to fall into two classes, those on ground which appears level, and those on ground of a noticeable slope. On the first we can develop our more classical, pure, or abstract form relationships; the latter are endlessly specific, more practical, more subjective, the slope requiring stabilizing compensation with terracing, vertical plant or structural forms, or overhead shelter.

APPROACH

We begin our landscape problem with the analysis of program and site, architecture and people; we project divisions and relations of the land and the space above it; we refine, develop, and perfect these relationships persistently, systematically, and intuitively; very early in the process we begin to think of the relation of ma-

71

als to the spatial relations we are developing; as we refine the spatial relations we refine the materials concepts, so that the final design drawings are conceptions of the use of materials as well as of the organization of space. In the plan it is a question of the general relations in the controlling overall three-dimensional pattern, which unifies the specific garden or landscape elements into a larger whole. Within that whole it is a question of the general character of each element—lawn, terrace, shelter, pool, tree, shrub, and flower groupings. Within those elements again it is a question of the relations between the parts in those elements—between the various areas or projections of lawn or pool, the bricks or stones of the terrace, the roof, supporting members, and other parts of the shelter, and the specific combinations of trees, shrubs, and flowers. Within those relations of parts again it is a question of the relations of finish in color and texture—amount and kind of processing or tooling, polishing or roughness, brightness or neutrality, and so on. These stages in refinement proceed vertically through the levels of size, form, texture, and color, and of plan, element, part, and finish. Within each level some decisions must be made; there are horizontal variations in refinement in each, from the over-simple to the exhaustive. Variations in these horizontal and vertical refinements are part of the variations among specific jobs and specific designers: one needs or tends toward concentration on form, another on texture, another on color, and so on. Ideally all are given serious weight; beyond that no rules can be established for these relations. It is finally necessary in all democratic art fields, once the reasonable limits of objective control have been passed, to allow literal artistic license to the responsible designer. In return, he or she accepts the necessity of socially-minded discipline within the range of objective decisions.

The plan is the paper projection of actual and proposed space relations on the site, at the handy scale of the drawing board. Working in plan without detailed experience of the site or allowance for adaptation and improvisation during installation is the sterile conclusion of the mechanical and arbitrary Beaux Arts approach. But working on the ground without the overall scope of the plan is the concentration on little things, the clever detail, the pictorial arrangement, the decorative, arty, romantic, subjective, irrational emphasis. Plans and sections give the overall control, the combination of bird's-eye view and precise detailed information, which are basic to the fullest, richest, clearest, warmest spatially symphonic concept within the limits of the site. Within the broad and tolerant framework of such conceptions there will be ample room for detailed improvisation during installation on the site, for elements of romanticism, fantasy, subjectivity, and apparent irrationality, disorder, or accident, and for the creative participation of those resident in or passing through the space, in terms of actual flexibility, mobility, and rearrangeability of the detailed elements.

Thus the arrangement of garden elements, of forms in space in relations which may be completely or approximately linear or irregular in the diagram of a plan, is the realistic specific half of the design process, the half that must be in the back of the planner's mind as he makes his line diagrams, even as the plan conception must, in some way, be in the back of the designer's mind as he arranges his plants and rocks, his walls and pools and steps, on the ground. These again are not either/or elements —the diagrammatic line abstraction versus the realistic spatial grouping of specific individual elements—but two complementary and supplementary halves of the complete space-organizing process. They embody the relations between planning and design, which are essential to each other. These are the opposites, the contradictions which in their unification make possible the unification of the general and the particular, of the parts in the whole.

AS LE CORBUSIER SAID IN 1922

The Plan is the generator. . . . The whole structure rises from its base and is developed in accordance with a rule which is written on the ground in the plan: noble forms, variety of forms, unity of the geometric principle. A profound projection of harmony: this is architecture.

72

A plan calls for the most active imagination. It calls for the most severe discipline also. The plan is what determines everything; it is the decisive moment. . . . To make a plan is to determine and fix ideas.
It is to have had ideas.
It is so to order these ideas that they become intelligible, capable of execution and communication. It is essential therefore to exhibit a precise intention, and to have had ideas in order to be able to furnish oneself with an intention.

AND AS FRANK LLOYD WRIGHT SAID IN 1903

. . . The plans are as a rule much more articulate than is the school product of the Beaux Arts. The individuality of the various functions of the various features is more highly developed; all the forms are complete in themselves and frequently do duty at the same time from within and without as decorative attributes of the whole. This tendency to greater individuality of the parts is emphasized by more and more complete articulation. . . .

When we try to give clarity and articulate identification to the parts of our garden and larger schemes, we are still met with the stale criticism "too busy" or "too complicated" or "why so many kinds of plants" from those to whom landscaping is still only a Beaux Arts picture, a segment of nature, or a green setting for an architectural objet d'art.

PEOPLE

CHAS. KELLOGG, 1941

Although in his researches the scientist must be calm and objective in the application of the principles he formulates from his results, the people are as important as the soil. At the same time the scientist must be no less a scientist but rather more of the artist. There can be no choice between strictly objective science without broad understanding of people on the one hand, and great human sympathy without clear understanding of the facts, on the other. The one leads to a drab mechanical existence, the other to careless sentimentalism.

People are seldom discussed, realistically and sympathetically rather than mechanically, as essential components or elements of theories of planning and design. Yet it is useless to project a science and an art of fine and handsome space organization unless we project also fine and handsome people within that space. Nor can we project the expansion of this fine and handsome space organization throughout the majority of the physical environment unless we can also project the majority of the population of that environment as being equally fine and handsome. If our concept of design is held on a higher plane than our concept of people we introduce a basic contradiction into our work which will make it impossible to continuously broaden and enrich it. Is art for art's sake, or for people? If the latter, is it for the majority or a minority? If the latter, which minority? If it is true that "landscape design can be truly appreciated only through the eye and mind which are trained to see and understand" (*Landscape Architecture Quarterly*, July 1937) how and by whom is appropriate training provided for our clientele? Is it only the individual private clients who get this training? How about the majority who experience our park designs? Do they require a course of training before they can enjoy them? Or do we reserve the finer concepts for the more understanding private clientele, and design down to the broad masses? And so on—each question begets another.

Our work is done for people, to provide settings and surroundings for their life and activities. Therefore all its forms must relate definitely to the forms of people: to their size, their shape, the way in which they move about and relax, their requirements as to air, sun, shade, the way in which they perceive their surroundings, and so on. This observation may seem simple and elementary to the point of naïveté, until one looks about with open eyes and sees how seldom our environment is really formed to fit the simple and fundamental needs of the people who must live in it. If human life on an individual and dignified scale had been considered of primary importance by the most responsible citizens our cities would never have become as congested, filthy, and sordid as they are.

Knowledge of such mechanical factors as eye-height, stride-length, and adaptability to sun or shade is not enough. People are not robots or sheep. They are all alike and yet they are all different. That is a remarkable thing when you consider that there are some two billion of them in the world. We must also understand their subjectivity, inconsistency, and contrariness, and the forces which make them greedy, intolerant, confused, mean, belligerent, irresponsible, cynical, or vulgar. We must realize that those qualities in adults are environmental rather than hereditary. We must be scientists as well as artists of the environment. From this will come a firm conviction of the basic decency, dignity, friendliness, and creativity of the vast majority. As we said in 1942, at the beginning of the great production of American war housing, ". . . every technician concerned with the development of environments for people has a responsibility toward them—not just a shelter responsibility, but one for the development of the fundamental potential dignity of every human being."

CHAPTER X

ON MATERIALS

Materials are the means to our end of fine spaces for people to live and grow in. Materials, and the techniques and processes by which they are brought from raw nature to their final refined state in our surroundings, are the practical side to our theory of three-dimensional space organization. Every space concept, however fine and beautiful, has to be brought to tangibility, has to be brought into the experience of other people beyond the designer, by development in specific physical materials, which give it specific physical form. Every combination, arrangement, or construction of such materials produces a specific quality or sensation in the space immediately around or between it. If the general forms and proportions thus given to the space are good, the general experience or sensation which that space gives to those within it will be good, irrespective of the special detail or lack of detail given to the material. Within that general practical relationship, however, there is a further dichotomy in the way the materials are used. They may be used merely practically, that is, expediently, in the simplest and most obvious manner, or they may be used with plastic or esthetic intent, that is, handled, processed, and developed so as to produce a maximum qualitative effect. Between this use of materials for their own sakes, and their use to

give form to space, there are varying relationships. With a recognizable space concept existing the materials may be so used as to express it, strengthen it, enrich it, or confuse it. Without some recognizable space concept the most refined and sensitive use of materials becomes merely a collection of objets d'art.

In landscape work we use both refined structural and unrefined natural materials. That is, we use materials with a great range of treatment, from a maximum which changes them completely, to a minimum which changes them as little as possible, from their natural, wild, or raw condition. Although the primary and typical materials of landscape design are thought of as earth and plants, in actual practice the landscape architect becomes involved with a good deal of structural work. Particularly with the growth of the theories of modern architecture, with its bursting of the box and its tendency to radiate or extrude structural elements, does the sensitive landscape architect find himself impelled to carry on with some extension of structure into the garden. Conversely the modern architect felt himself impelled to bring the garden into the house with plants and glass, rocks and water. Earth and plants are the major theme, the dominant elemental motifs, of any typical landscape unit—rocks, water, and structural elements are the minor counterpoint, adding sparkle, interest, richness. Occasionally these are reversed.

The potential list of materials for landscape design is as long as, or longer than, that for any other field. Anything which will stand outdoor exposure can be used in a garden, once we overcome the preconception that some materials are gardenesque and some are not. Refined structural elements are essential to its continuity with the house; however, as the garden area increases, the natural, unrefined, non-structural materials—earth, plants, water, rocks—assume more and more importance. Landscape design is the only field which does use both kinds of materials in considerable quantities. It thus has the opportunity to investigate in detail the relations between them.

This is a problem which has scarcely been considered, let alone attacked, by modern design thought. It has accepted unrefined materials as decorative to structure, or as objets d'art— plants, rocks, weathered wood—and left the rest to nature. Even the most progressive contemporary designers have given most of their thought to the use of refined structural materials, and little or none to the use of unrefined natural ones at the scale of space-for-use. The effect of this has been to limit the scale of design, and to isolate it from the landscape, however boldly it may have sought integration by setting itself in the middle of forest or meadow. Integration is more than contrast; it involves some mingling or merging of elements from the two or more parties being integrated.

A further result of this concentration of modern thought on structural or refined elements, set in a kind of romantic abstraction of wild or rural nature, has been to continue the concept that space is the property of architecture—that is, of structural control, even at the scale of the community. Thus in Le Corbusier's town-planning projects the buildings are expanded horizontally and vertically to scales and arrangements which completely control all the urban space, both indoor and outdoor. Within the outdoor spaces thus controlled the pattern of free verdure is

left in the hands of nature or the gardeners. F. S. Wight says, "For Le Corbusier a work of art—that is to say a successful work of man— organizes and humanizes not merely the space it contains but all the surrounding space, invading brute nature with its own field of force." How much of this is a necessity of sound planning, and how much a result of architectural (structural) preconceptions, remains to be seen.

A final result of this concentration on the product of the machine and of handicraft has been to leave considerable portions of the environment—those in which the dominant materials are earth and plants, water and rocks—in the hands of the purveyors of stale precedent, the academicians, the hacks, the bureaucrats, and the commercial operators. Yet these portions account for a good deal of our total environment, and the principal physical result of proposals for good planning is to increase this percentage of free open space. This leaves the landscape profession, whose job is to understand these less-processed materials, with the opportunity to re-analyze them in their uses, using the kind of highly sensitive and intuitively scientific approach that has been typical of advanced thought in the allied arts.

FRANK LLOYD WRIGHT, 1936

Now there can be no organic architecture where the nature of synthetic materials or the nature of nature materials either is ignored or misunderstood. How can there be? Perfect correlation, integration, is life. It is the first principle of any growth that the thing grown be no mere aggregation. Integration as entity is first essential. And integration means that no part of anything is of any great value in itself except as it be integrate part of the harmonious whole. . . .

There are three general principles which are basic to the use of any materials for any esthetic or creative purpose (that is, with the objective of improving the environment we live in):

First, materials must express their own inborn characteristics and possibilities, not have others thrust upon them, become victims of empty techniques, or be condemned for former bad associations. This is a hackneyed thought, yet one seldom realized in action. A brick is a pre-

76

fabricated modular unit, its effects are built up by repetition and combination; concrete is a plastic poured product, whose shape and volume are subject to control and direction; a plant is a living breathing creature, with a distinctive native personality for whose development we must provide.

FRANK LLOYD WRIGHT, 1908

Bring out the nature of the materials, let their nature intimately into your scheme. Strip the wood of varnish and let it alone; stain it. Develop the natural texture of the plastering and stain it. Reveal the nature of the wood, plaster, brick, or stone in your designs; they are all by nature friendly and beautiful. No architectural treatment can be really a matter of fine art when these truly natural characteristics are, or their essential nature is, outraged or neglected.

Second, materials have importance and character only in relation to other materials and specific situations; they cannot be judged singly in themselves; they cannot have importance in a vacuum. It is the combination between the specific way in which each material is handled, and the quantitative and qualitative relations which are established between that material and the other materials around it, which determines the strength and clarity of expression of each material, and the nature of its effect upon the space from which it is viewed. We can organize space abstractly, with "pure" elements, as the cubists and the early modern architects did, or we can organize space more literally and richly, in terms of specific earthy materials, as the sculptors and the later modern architects all tend to do. These are not ideas which are in opposition, but rather stages in development; the latter grows out of the former; both remain relevant. Indeed it is by controlled and balanced contrast between these smooth and plastic elements, and those of a rougher and more assertive character (such as brick and stone) which must be used on their own terms, that we bring out and emphasize the character of each.

It is in the selection and arrangement of planting that this principle of the retroactive relations between different kinds of material comes out most clearly. It is obvious that plant-

ing of all dark or light greens, all dull or glossy foliage, all fine or coarse textures, all horizontal or vertical forms, all loose or rigid structures, would most certainly be dull, static, and monotonous. This example alone is enough to bring out our point: dark and light, dull and glossy, fine and coarse, horizontal and vertical, loose and rigid, help each other to richer, fuller and more expressive participation in the general scheme.

It is by overstatement that we clarify ideas. Consider the mutually complementary relations between such plants as the purple plum and the gray acacia; the dark Austrian Pine and the light European Larch; the heather and the banana; the Irish Yew or Juniper and the Pfitzer's Juniper; and so on. It is a far cry from such mutually reinforcing relations in contrast —whether subtle or bold—to that careful concentration on mediumness—medium size, round form, medium green, medium-size foliage; neither bold and vulgar nor fine and delicate— which seems to distinquish so much landscape work.

The garden is the place where odd durable elements from many unexpected sources can be put to practical uses which can develop a considerable plastic force. This is exemplified in many ways, from the use of bottles, old boilers, and railroad ties as curbs and low retainers in America, to the endless ingenious use of fragments of straw, bamboo, wood and stone in Japanese gardens. The placing of familiar elements and objects in new relations (new uses for old forms) is one of surrealism's tried and tested techniques for impression of experience by shock. The black anthracite coal wall by Gropius and Breuer at the New York World's Fair was an outstanding example.

Third, materials are used, not for their own sake, but primarily to organize space for people to use. The more obvious functions out-of-doors, such as ground cover, erosion control, screening, shade, color, et cetera, are really all portions of this overall objective of space control. Gardens and parks are for people first and for plants second; the importance of this emphasis increases with the interest the people have in the

77

plants. In organizing the materials of the garden so as to give the best tangible three-dimensional form to its space, we make possible better movement of people in the garden, and better relations —closer contact—between the people and the materials of the garden. This concept of the indispensable interdependence between materials and the space which they organize and which in turn shows them off, is a concept which will do more to express and develop the characteristics of the material than any of the existing pictorial, romantic, naturalistic, or arbitrarily formal concepts. Coupled with the previous concepts of the relations between materials, and the special qualities of each, it will produce an esthetic of their use that will truly advance tradition to a higher plane. There will be an articulation of elements and an intensification of the use of materials that will tend to result in the organization of more space with less material. This will tend to reduce the waste of space and of plants involved in such concepts as mass planting.

Finally we must emphasize that the great range of choice in materials, the endless variety in plants and rocks and structural elements which are available to the landscape designer today, coupled with the freedom from functional or structural control which is implicit in so many landscape problems, is not a license for esthetic irresponsibility or personal expression. Nor, on the other hand, does it demand authoritarian control of the dogmatic, academic, bureaucratic type. Freedom must accept and develop discipline in order to grow and achieve its potential; freedom without disciplined control becomes merely anarchy. It is the problem of the professional planner-designer (because today he is the only citizen who has time and energy for it) to determine the nature and the forms of this discipline. In our discussion of our historical heritage we have brought out the traditional kinds—the geometric, the axial, the picturesque, the symbolic, the romantic, the naturalistic, the horticultural, the conservationist—that are contained in our background. It is the objective of this book, in suggesting forms and approaches to our landscape problems in the immediate future, to suggest the kind of discipline we must develop. This will be a discipline based on a clear sense of the brotherhood of man as a necessity of life; it will be based on a clear vision of the magnificent continuity of free spatial order which we can bring to our world; and it will be based on a sensitivity that is both scientific and intuitive, to the best and richest use of our vocabulary of materials in all the specific situations in which we work. It will be a discipline oriented toward change and growth, development and expansion, rather than toward any static system of universal values, any final paternalistic answers as to what is best for people. It will, finally, be a democratic discipline, based on rational authority (accepted from below), rather than any sort of authoritarian or paternalistic discipline, based on irrational authority (imposed from above). (See Fromm in *Man for Himself*, page 9.)

CHAPTER XI

GRAVITY MATERIALS

THE BASIC ELEMENTS OF THE LANDSCAPE— EARTH, ROCK, WATER

The rocks, the water, and the earth in all our little gardens and larger parks are part and parcel of the continuum of earth, rocks, and water which, together with the atmosphere in which we ourselves live, is the basic inorganic structure of the natural landscape. These are gravity materials, expressing mass, inertia, or downward movement. Geologic construction and the evaporation of water are their only factors of resistance to gravity. Earth is produced from rock by the action of water plus living organisms. Natural topography is the result of the interaction of upthrusting internal constructive forces and downgrading external weathering forces. The air, when in motion, becomes a force in the landscape and a factor in design; we must let the summer breezes in, keep the winter winds out, control dust and sand and leaves, and watch for those drafts and cold spots in the microclimate which can ruin our more tender plants. (See page 432—Salisbury.)

EARTH

DR. E. RAMANN, 1928

The soil is the uppermost weathered layer of the solid crust of the earth; it consists of rocks that have been reduced to small fragments and have been more or less changed chemically, together with the remains of plants and animals that live on it and in it.

Earth is important to landscape design in two ways. It is the foundation, floor, or bottom of the garden and park spaces which we develop; and it is the medium in which one half of each and every plant, large or small, lives and grows. Its form is relevant to the first, and its content to the second. We cannot just take the earth of any specific site for granted, even if it appears flat. It has to be examined very carefully, both as to form—slope or slopes, and content—the texture, organic and biochemical content of the top three or four feet. The form is a practical problem insofar as questions of drainage and of the maintenance of an adequate depth of topsoil are concerned. Beyond those it becomes functional —the question of use; and esthetic—the question of appearance. The content is entirely practical, scientific, and the province of good horticulture; the landscape architect must of necessity have a clear understanding of at least the general principles and practices involved. Reference to such authorities as Salisbury, Weir, Mickey, Osborn, and Kellogg is essential to such understanding.

This land surface, like the general physiography of the earth, is not a static thing. It undergoes constant change and development, however slowly and unobtrusively, and, as instances such as dust storms and high-pressure water erosion show, becomes at times an exceedingly dynamic and plastic element. The forces productive of this change and development, and to which the land is constantly exposed, are those of the atmosphere and the hydrosphere (air and water), and life (plants and animals, bacteria and protozoa, and man). Of these plants are the principal stabilizing elements; they contribute to and make possible the building of the topsoil on which our lives depend; their removal or weakening facilitates the loss of that topsoil. These forces operate continuously throughout the earth, in primeval nature, in the rural countryside, in the cities and towns wherever paving or construction ends, on every piece of raw land or real estate, every lot, every backyard, every park. (See Shuler: *The Plains and Grass*, and Kellogg, pages 46-47.)

USE—Since it is necessary for us to maintain our equilibrium by holding ourselves erect, or vertical to the pull of gravity, it follows that land surfaces are most useful for human living purposes when they are nearly perpendicular to that pull. That is, the floor of the space we organize for our use becomes more useful to us as it becomes more level. There is a relation between this need for horizontal ground planes and the area and intensity of use. Thus small private gardens, active sport fields and courts, areas where many people gather closely together, must in some way recognize this need for horizontal stability. On the other hand, hills and mountains, valleys and shores, whatever their slope, or however often and abruptly it may change, are part of the basic primeval landscape to which we turn and disperse ourselves for recreation and relaxation. As the topography gets rougher, the potential intensity of its use gets less, and the problems of organizing that use get greater. Practically speaking, the hillside site always costs more for comparable living space than the flat site. However, the theory is that the sense of space gained

through the view from an elevated site compensates for less actual space for living, that is, that intensified contemplation makes up for less actual movement in space. Certainly an elevated flat site, with a view but protected from the wind, and with good topsoil, is preferable to a lowland site, other relations being equal.

We may classify surfaces for use, and possible rearrangement, about as follows: level—0 per cent to 4 per cent (or feet of vertical fall per 100 ft. horizontally); easy slopes—4 per cent to 10 per cent; steep slopes—from 10 per cent up. Level or nearly level surfaces are most useful; easy slopes begin to be limited in use to free walking or running or passive relaxation; steep slopes are nearly useless, except for active physical exercise climbing them.

EXPERIENCE—In terms of space organization, as slopes increase they tend to reduce physical circulation but increase "vision in motion"; specific experiences are heightened by the increased spatial scale of their backgrounds. Insofar as slopes reduce circulation they function in the direct organization of space. There are many specific, subtle, and clever ways in which they can be exploited to develop an increased sense of privacy with fewer elements above the surface of the ground than on flat sites. Such privacy may, however, be negated by the possibility of looking down into hillside garden areas from above. All of which is to say that the organization of space on sloping sites is a great deal more complex, specific, and demanding of ingenuity and technical competence than on flat sites.

All of which is *not* to say that spatial experience of comparable richness and intensity cannot be had on flat land. These are relations in kind, rather than degree. There is an immense sense of stability, of extent and scale, of integration with the globe of the earth and the celestial sphere, and of closeness to the vital bursting fertile warmth of growth of the soil, to be had on flat land when it is developed with some sense of scale and space.

TECHNICAL—There are a number of important technical or practical problems attendant on terracing and grading operations, increasing in importance directly as the depth and scale of the grading increase. These have a direct impact upon the planning and design of the land development, and therefore must be considered at that stage. It is not our intent to treat them exhaustively, inasmuch as there are very adequate practical and theoretical authorities available for consultation on such matters:

Terracing or grading is most cheaply and easily done when nothing at all exists on the land.

Changing the natural grade creates a problem for the footings and foundations of buildings or other structures.

Changing existing grades also creates a problem through its disturbance of the natural relations between topsoil, subsoil, and bedrock. This can be avoided by a simple and reasonable process of stripping all existing topsoil from areas which are to be graded or built over or paved, stockpiling it, controlling the rough grades to allow for desirable depths of topsoil or paving on the finished site, and replacing the topsoil where it is needed for planting. On jobs which are not too limited as to budget it may be an easy out to grade without reference to existing topsoil, and bring in new soil where it may be needed. But, as the soil conservationists teach us, this is socially wasteful. There is only a certain amount of topsoil in any given region; it takes a long, long time to build it; it cannot be replaced synthetically; we are in general using it up at a horrifying rate. To bury existing topsoil and then bring in new from elsewhere is a kind of irresponsibility which should not be tolerated. Where certain large building or engineering operations occur which establish permanent structural ground cover the existing topsoil should be stripped and stockpiled for use where it is needed, rather than callously covered over, or dumped in the nearest big hole. Needless to say, the naïve Messiah who might try to sell this altruism to the practical contractors who scramble daily through the anarchy of excavating, grading, and topsoil operations in any urban center, would receive little but incredulous stares and guffaws. This is a prob-

lem for municipal responsibility at the level of local or higher government.

Changing existing slopes disturbs and alters existing surface, and sometimes sub-surface, drainage relations. The results of this disturbance, if not carefully planned beforehand, are apt to be complex, uncomfortable if not disastrous, difficult to trace, and expensive to put under control. The problem is simply to keep the water moving, but not too fast; to spread it out on the ground where it can be absorbed, provided the subsoil drainage is good; to keep it under control mechanically, if it has to be concentrated, until it can be spread again. At the big scale of flood control this becomes major engineering, but every little garden has a miniature of this engineering problem within its own boundaries. Probably the basic principle in solving drainage problems on single sites is to preserve the existing drainage relations insofar as they do not conflict with the necessities of the plan: if the water can enter and leave the property in approximately the same area and volume as before development half the battle is won. It is the concentration of water from non-absorbent surfaces (roofs and paving), and incomplete grading operations which expose raw ground to erosion, that provide the most serious problems.

There is, finally, the complication in grading when it must be done in relation to existing trees or other elements already on the site. When such elements are to be preserved they determine the level of terracing or grading in their immediate vicinity. Structures may determine it exactly, trees within a few feet. The amount of cutting or filling that can be done around a tree is always a specific problem that must be solved on the job in relation to the kind of tree, its size and form, the kind of soil and character of the subsoil drainage, the wetness or dryness of the local climate, and so forth. The old problem of when to save and when to cut the tree is also always specific, always requiring careful judgment and thorough consideration, on the job, of all the botanical, horticultural, functional and esthetic aspects of the question before action is taken.

One other practical question with regard to grading operations is the technique for moving the earth—that is, the equipment to be used. This becomes a question of what is available locally, and how appropriate it is to the particular problem. American mechanical ingenuity, and the unconscious esthetic power of its products, is nowhere more evident than in the development of earth-moving machinery. From the primitive but highly refined pick and shovel, through the delicate roto-tiller, the agile Fordson tractor or jeep equipped with hooks and blade, the snorting and clattering majesty of the big caterpillar bulldozer, to the quiet and monumental grace of the tremendous carry-all, is a roster in form and scale and power unequaled for fascination. Add to it such specialized elements as the graceful and precise motor grader, the efficient skip-loader, the octopod ditch-digger, the monstrous steam shovel, and their nimble servant the dump truck, and you have a cast of characters equal to anything the comic book artists can dream up. SOMETIMES we say—when the plant-lovers aren't around—that the most fascinating part of any job is supervising the bulldozer. Each of these kinds of equipment has its special relevance to grading problems, to be determined in conference with technically competent personnel on the job.

SURFACING—Whatever forms we create in the land, however flat, however vertical, however subtly plastic or naturalistic in their relations of concavity and convexity, will be unavoidably subjected to all those forms of natural weathering and erosion, those mechanical and chemical attacks of air and water, which are peculiar to the region. Earth left or kept uncovered is earth eroded and changed, unless under the most careful and scientific cultivation. Except in the most arid regions, with less than ten inches of rainfall, nature will cover the ground with her own volunteer grasses and weeds, if we don't. Therefore an essential part of any program of re-shaping the land is its surfacing, once re-shaped. For such surfacing we have essentially two kinds of materials, organic and inorganic, planting and paving.

82

EARTH AS SOIL FOR PLANTS—(See Kellogg and Weir). The physiological, biological, or ecological relation between the living plant and the soil in which it grows has been, and is constantly being, examined and analyzed by a great body of botanical, horticultural, and agricultural scientists. To these men and women we are indebted, and on them we rely, for our knowledge and technique for getting the best growth from every kind of plant. There is a great deal of very excellent reference material on soil science, which is, moreover, constantly changing and being brought up to date with the growth of scientific knowledge.

In general, most ornamental plants require a medium condition of soil, not too sandy, rocky, or clayey; that is, not too many large or small particles, nor much that hasn't been exposed to action by weather, other plants, animals, and man. Most plants require in their soils a good content of organic matter, derived directly or indirectly from other plants. Most require adequate drainage, that is, water must move through the soil beyond the root area within at most a few days. In fact, this drainage factor is the primary limitation for most ornamental planting.

There are, however, in terms of landscape development, plants which will grow in practically any conditions. Rock lichens and seaweed are the obvious extremes. We can find and use plants which either require or will tolerate most extremes beyond the happy medium described —clay, sand, high percentage of rock, very sharp drainage, no drainage, no organic matter (poor or sterile soils), or too much organic matter as in swamps. There are also plants which will survive in considerable extremes of acid or alkali, although again most plants like it close to neutral.

We try to provide soil conditions adequate for our plants by:

a) Adding material lacking in the soil (chemical fertilizers, earthworms, but primarily organic matter).

b) Taking care of the drainage, both surface and subsurface.

c) Where the existing soil is too bad, removing it and replacing it with good soil from elsewhere, if available.

d) Returning to the soil that which came from it, by that basic and civilized process, composting. This is the only way to heal the fatal break, initiated by industrial urbanization, in the complete life cycle which demands that all vegetation produced by the soil be returned to that soil. The thousands of tons of brush and grass clippings which are burned annually in every metropolitan region, for want of an organization responsible enough to rot them down for return to the soil, are one of the most glaring expressions of the destructive parasitism of the city.

e) Maintaining the supply of underground water, known as the water table. This necessitates slowing down and catching run-off in appropriate spots where it can be absorbed by the ground, rather than just getting rid of it as rapidly as possible. At the large scale of flood control this ground water problem develops into a contradiction between the limited practicality of quick engineering and the long-term practicality of slow, but sound, conservation.

THE ESTHETICS OF EARTHWORK—The soil is handled horticulturally, engineeringly, structurally, sentimentally, naturalistically, conservationally; but seldom as a material with a definite three-dimensional sculptural quality apart from, or in addition to, these other factors.

It consists of an aggregation of small particles, derived from the decomposition of rock and organic materials. In composition it may vary from the slight adhesive qualities of sand to the strong adhesive qualities of clay. It has always a rock base, and at times this may come to the surface in more or less dominant quantities. Although the physical properties of the earth as soil may be altered by admixtures and weathering, its basic characteristics remain essentially the same. Perhaps the strongest of these is its very obvious subservience to gravity. Because of its composition as an aggregation of particles, it can seldom be made to hold a very

steep slope; therefore the stable pyramidal quality of its forms must be most evident.

This is based on a slope known as the "angle of repose" which is the slope a given pile of dirt will assume without structural retention. Sand has the lowest angle of repose, rock the highest. Most soils fall between them. Fill slopes have lower angles of repose than cut slopes; solid rock can be cut to a vertical cliff, or nearly so. Normal angles for ordinary soil are 1:1 (100 per cent), 1½:1 (75 per cent), or 2:1 (50 per cent) (horizontal:vertical). Slopes can of course be made flatter, steeper with structural assistance, or warped in freely-curving planes of any complexity, to blend with or represent nature, or to produce plastic forms for their own quality.

Bearing in mind the pyramidal quality of earth, and the varying differential in scale between architectural elements and the local natural landscape, the sculptural potential of earthwork is endless. It is as endless as natural topography—the surface of the earth is one large sculptural project. The elements of earthwork sculpture are basically simple, as Hubbard and Kimball point out: "In ground forms large and small, the landscape architect finds the three simple fundamental form unities: the convex, the concave, and the plane." Flat planes, sloping planes, vertical planes, warped planes; levels, sharp banks, slopes, connecting walks, ramps, ramped steps, steps, retaining walls. Examples are everywhere about us, in both the wild landscape and the man-made or -modified landscape. At the reduced model scale which facilitates experiment and thought, most abstract sculpture is suggestive of garden forms. Some such work, as that of Noguchi and Arp, becomes practically a model from which graded gardens could be developed.

Make no mistake. We are not proposing a cubist landscape, with block, cone, or pyramid mountains, ground planes intersecting in precise lines, and concrete or mobile trees. We are well aware of the beauty, the variety, and the interest of nature, and we do not propose changing her forms without due cause and objective reason. We are likewise well aware that the forces of wind and weather will continue to work as persistently on whatever forms we may make as they have on Old Mother Earth to date. Past experience is not to be thrown to the winds. It must, rather, be kept alive and revitalized by new content of ideas and new combinations and relations to humanized forms. Parsons is valuable as a reference on these older theories of ground forms.

At every scale of design of and on the land, from the little garden to the community and its green- or wild-belt, there must be no arbitrary or academic separation of formal and informal, or human and natural, forms. The horizontal plane, the vertical plane, and their rotation through any other angles, are at home "in good taste" in the imaginatively humanized landscape, if handled with technical competence and esthetic integrity. Irregularity, concavity, convexity can (but need not) become as self-consciously artificial, as blindly academic, as much of a crutch for lazy minds, as any system of axes. The horizontal plane (up to three per cent slope) is the natural floor for the more concentrated activities of mankind, up to the scale, let us say, of football field or parade ground. The vertical plane, in rock or masonry, or the same simple plane at any angle of cut or fill slope, is the natural accompaniment of the need for horizontal planes on irregular topography, or of such even continuities of slope as roads, highways, and railways. These are not "bad" forms, "scarring the landscape," "destroying the beauties of nature." More often than not, when done with intelligence, reason, and sensitivity, they are beautiful forms, forms with the clear, regular, accurate creativity of man at his best. These can be, and often are, the final refinement, the ultimate expression, of the landscape, the emergence of a purer and stronger geometry from its complicated organic geometry. Terraces and ramps, cut-and-fill slopes, walls and steps, developed where they are needed for use and comfort, at a scale which is reasonable to the program, and related with adequate plastic sensitivity to the scale and form of the site, are an improvement to the landscape. They are an improvement because

they make it possible for man to experience the landscape in the comfort of normal living, rather than with the exertion of the occasional expedition. The landscape is beautiful only when people are there to experience it.

The problem of landscape design, when such grading and terracing has been found necessary and desirable, is not the shamefaced scurrying to cover up the damage, to obscure and confuse the work that man has done and try to make it look "natural" again, to eliminate art from the landscape with profuse apologies, to make it look as though no one had ever been there even though someone will have to be there again, perhaps often, perhaps in something as completely "unnatural" as a car or a house. The problem is to establish the best—the richest, the most expressive, the most beautiful, clear, strong, and coherent—relations between these forms which are necessary to the well-being of man, and the natural weathered geologic forms of the site. It is in the specific creative sensitivity of the integrating, the contrasting, the mingling and merging and emerging of the clear and simple planes formed by man with and from the more or less greater irregularity, subtlety, and complexity of the existing ground that the actual design process lies.

These questions of ground form in the landscape are, finally and always, questions of scale and specific situation. The most refined forms are produced for the most refined use. As Parsons says: "Let any one try, on the other hand, to make a level meadow. He can with difficulty make a level cricket bowling streak, or a level tennis court—much less a large meadow a mile long like the one in Prospect Park. The eye will deceive one, and the place will never look level from every point of view." A fine flight of steps may be the final clarifying and enlivening touch to a graded hillside; twenty terraces each ten feet high may smother it in monotony. While we are not unable to compete in scale of man-made plane ground forms with nature (consider agricultural terracing in Asia and the Mediterranean, the magnificent ground forms of the Incas in Peru, the scale of our own soil conservation, flood control, and irrigation proj-

84

ects) nevertheless we don't want to be big just to be big, at least outside the city limits. We develop specific refined forms in the land at the scale needed to solve technical problems, or to properly floor and enclose space for living— and no more. On the question of the scale of even such grading we will find plenty of specific controversy. It is on hillside residential development, for instance, that we are forced to find out how much outdoor leveled space people actually need to complete their home living requirements.

ROCK

Quantitatively rock is minor in its visible relations to most landscapes, and in its visible use in most landscape design. Rock emerges as a quantitative dominant in specific landscapes— mountain and desert—and may, of course, be dominant in certain concepts of landscape design. The rock garden is the obvious example.

Qualitatively rock is an important material in landscape design. It is important symbolically, structurally, and esthetically in both a sculptural and a spatial sense. Symbolically it speaks to us of the basic core of the earth on which we live, the source of our soils, which protrudes through that soil mantle wherever it has resisted erosion and weathering, in mountains and buttes and mesas. Structurally it is important for free-standing walls and special structures such as fireplaces, and for all grades of structural assistance to earthwork, from retaining walls to paving. Sculpturally it is important as a material for actual sculpture, and because of the quasi-sculptural or object-interest quality of many natural rocks, ranging in scale from mammoth boulders and outcrops to the pebbles we collect at the beach. Spatially it is important as a potentially continuous link between structure and site, as we shall see.

The earth being continuous as the material of most of our land surface forces us to discuss its forms in terms of the continuity of that surface. We are perpetually led into the scale of the general landscape. On the other hand, rock,

being discontinuous over most of our landscape, can be discussed in terms of the specific occasional enriching element which it is in landscape design. Earth, as the ground surface, is the floor of our outdoor space; rock is part of the detailed object design within the major organization of that space.

The occurrence or availability of rock varies widely with locality, and hence its specific relevance to jobs varies widely. This variance is in terms of the cost of handling and transporting the material; that is the practical basis for the question of the appropriateness of specific kinds of rock to specific sites. We are not among those who subscribe to a slavish tying-down of landscape design to only those kinds of rock which may be indigenous to the immediate locality or region, although we do agree that specific rock relations which may exist on the site or in the immediately visible landscape must be very carefully studied.

It is obvious that, in a region with noticeable quantities of indigenous rock, no great romantic rationalizing is required to maintain its regional dominance. The combined practicality and sensitivity which are requisites of any sound designer will take care of that: the rock is heavy and it is THERE; it will remain dominant in use. That does not prohibit the introduction of minor quantities of other rocks from outside the region, for use in well-designed relations to the local rock. Transportation is only one of the factors with which natural man effects changes in the natural landscape. Visit your local stone yard. It, and its attendant network of quarrying and transport, are as much a part of your local indigenous picture as the rocks on the hillsides. In fact, in a certain sense more so, because its stone is collected, sorted, and ready to use. Nor do we feel that rock is inappropriate in garden or park if it does not exist in the immediate neighboring landscape. Rock is part of our experience of the landscape and it is man's right to develop that to its maximum.

Rock has a multitude of available characteristics, based on the many possible relations between a) its native quality, and b) the handling, tooling, or processing it receives. As the latter increases the former may be brought out with greater emphasis, or it may be superseded by the character of the processing. This range of characteristics may be suggested by the following, all relevant to landscape design:

   natural sculptural boulders or outcrops;
   ground cover of rocks selected for size, shape, and color, and set evenly—merging with water-bound macadam, gravel, decomposed rock, sand;
   rough dry walls, of stone as it comes;
   rough-cut stone with or without mortar, in walls or paving;
   more and more careful hand cutting, fitting, and mortaring;
   sawn stone;
   polished granite or marble;
   sculpture.

All gradations between these levels are possible, and every sort of combination between them. The natural boulder and the polished granite wall, properly juxtaposed, can be of greater mutual esthetic assistance and reinforcement than any mystical benefits supposed to derive from their absolute separation.

Rock, at whatever level of handling or processing, is always a highly individualized handicraft material. Each job is different, each job is new. While rockwork is, in general, a matter for combined artistry and common sense, there are one or two useful principles we can suggest. One, an old standby, is simply to guarantee a feeling of stability and appropriateness by placing the rock as nearly as possible in the position it occupied in nature. This is sometimes easy to determine, and sometimes practically impossible. Thus, sedimentary rocks —sandstone, shale, limestone—which have been laid down in such thin sheets as to show the strata lines when quarried, should always be laid with those strata marks horizontal. Indeed, in the case of strata which may have been folded in some more or less upright position, we should "induce nature to improve herself" by also laying those strata horizontally. But with igneous and metamorphic rocks, which may have formed in any sort of odd-shaped

mass without special direction in the veining or crystalline structure, it is the shape of the block of stone which determines its feeling of stability. Here again, horizontality is the primary principle. Most of the blocks or pieces of stone should be longer than wide, and the long dimension should be placed horizontally. While one can find a good many very well-done exceptions to this rule, in various block, crazy-quilt, and boulder patterns, it is nevertheless the simplest and most direct way to bring out that quality of stability which is primary in rock and stone. This applies equally to the poor man's stone wall, that of broken concrete.

In relation to buildings, rockwork and stone masonry contain the maximum flexible potential for the most direct, complete, and obvious (or the most subtle) linking of structure and site. The essential nature of wood- and metal-framed structures is separation and divorce from the decaying moisture and termites of the ground. The essential nature of masonry, and particularly of stone masonry, is precisely its union with, and broad footing into, the moist solidity of the ground. Couple this with the complete flexibility in crudity or refinement of processing which we have outlined, and one begins to see various possibilities for the imaginative bridging of the gap between frame structure and site, the tying of building to ground without forcing its form or the nature of its structural elements, in any number of ways. This is not without precedent; sensitive architects, from Japanese to modern, have developed such ideas.

The above remarks apply particularly to stone construction, that is, to the merging of individual stone shapes into some larger, simpler, dominant form, within which the stone makes a three-dimensional pattern. In the alternative use of specific rocks—water- or ice-formed boulders or pebbles, concretions and igneous fragments of plastic or fantastic form— as sculptural specimens, singly or in groups, we find our best prototypes in the Orient. The refinement, sensitivity, and maturity of concept exhibited in Chinese and Japanese rock arrangements is seldom approached in our alpine beds and miniature or authentic mountain waterfalls. It is to be noted and emphasized that their use was not naturalistic, in our sense of the word. They used rocks as combinations of sculptural forms, almost as sculptural groups; their aim was the intensification and expression of nature, not her imitation. (See Kuck.) Stonehenge, too, is a very formal spatial organization of very rough rock forms. Such work goes beyond simple questions of horizontality to sculptural concepts which demand both the freedom and the discipline of all fine sculpture.

The sculptural use of rocks in groups may be defined as one in which the individual rocks are separated from one another in space. The objective of such sculptural use, whether or not the rocks themselves are actually carved or tooled in some way, and whatever the scale, is both plastic and spatial; that is, the display of specific qualities of form, size, color, and texture, and the establishment of mass and space relations between them, in terms of tension, harmony, and/or contrast. While such groupings may have content of sentimental, symbolic, or scientific nature, the expression of that content will be strengthened, and the appeal of the grouping widened, by the establishment of the strongest, clearest, and most coherent spatial relations between its parts. Those relations are developed by the application of the general design principles of unity and variety, interest and harmony, dominance and contrast, rhythm and balance. The analysis of rock arrangements as sculptural groupings is important in a considerable variety of situations; the natural outcrop, waterfall, or boulder-strewn field, small enough to rearrange; their extension or expansion; the establishment of new forms related to them; the more purely plastic or sculptural approach, comparable to the Oriental, as expressed most purely in the Ryoan-ji Stone Garden in Kyoto (see Kuck); the rock garden, for alpines or succulents; "naturalistic" rock arrangement; the geologic or tourist collection; the highly sensitized refinement in sculptural approach of Brancusi, Arp, Waring, or Flannagan. The various possible relations between such sculptural groupings, and the structural elements we have discussed, must be borne in mind. Our previous discussion of plastic (sculptural), structural and spatial design is background for this. See also Tamura, and Tung (in Henry Inn: *Chinese Houses and Gardens*).

Sculpture by carving being the ultimate refinement of rock ("Modern sculptors . . . regard direct carving as a kind of *collaboration between the sculptor and the substance*."—Wilenski), and our discussion of both earth and rock being intended largely in sculptural terms, the following remarks made in 1935 on "The Meaning of Modern Sculpture" are pertinent and relevant at this point:

R. H. WILENSKI

But it was some time before this new stage was in fact accomplished because many of the sculptors retained at the back of their minds the notion of a wild, free, ragged undisciplined 'nature' from which the Romantic artists had selected emotive fragments and which it was the function of the classical artists to 'tidy up.' At the back of their minds many presumed an antithesis between organic nature and geometric form. . . .
2. Truth to nature.
The time came, in other words, when they had abandoned the presumed antithesis between organic and geometric form and had begun to presume instead that geometric form is SYMBOLIC of organic.
. . . They began to seek and find analogies between the characteristic forms in life and the characteristic forms in art, between the formal principles in natural structures and formal order in geometry, architecture, and sculpture.
. . . the modern sculptors have arrived at the concept of the universal analogy of form, the concept of all human, animal, and vegetable forms as different manifestations of common principles of architecture, of which the geometric forms in their infinity of relations are all symbols; and at the concept of the meaning of geometric relation as the symbolisation of this universal analogy of form.
10. All great sculpture is microcosmic in formal character; and gains in meaning when increased in size.
That sculpture is a symbol of the cultural effort towards collective contact with universal life; and the sculptors are aiming not at TRUTH TO NATURE in the old sense, which they regard as useless at the moment, but at TRUTH TO LIFE in a sense that has long been forgotten.

OTHER MASONRY MATERIALS—Rock has a clear relation or affinity with man-made masonry materials (clay and concrete products) in that they are handled in a similar manner, to solve similar problems. Whether finally placed wet or dry, they are all heavy gravity materials with a direct yearning toward unity with mother earth. This by contrast with the anti-gravitational character of frame structures and plants. Even in the most refined forms of terra cotta, thin fine concrete, porcelain, or glass, these products still retain their quality of affinity with earth and rock.

The primary characteristic of mass-produced clay products (brick and tile) is their regular rectangularity, by contrast with the irregularity of rock; and their common color range through tans and reds, expressing the passage of earth through fire. Thus one is inclined to think that they should be used in regular rectangular forms, whether horizontal or vertical, and that cutting or warping them to conform to abstract curved or angular forms or lines is apt to become a distortion of the material. However this can be oversimplified: there is a relation between the scale of the unit, the scale of the form desired, and the ingenuity and skill of the mason and designer which gives considerable flexibility to the ideal of collaboration with the material. Brick cuts easily, tile does not.

Historical examples of clever detailing in brick and tile have leaned in the direction of decorative pattern and ornamental form. It is for us to explore the sculptural and structural potentialities, the mass and space or solid and void relations, which express more clearly the direct use of the material to strengthen and enrich the sense of space. Thus we are inclined to stress simple continuity of surface pattern on all planes, or a variation in sizeable simple units, rather than the fussy precious quality of eclectic Beaux Arts detailing. If we can use the material in such a manner as to develop extrusions from its collective mass into the surrounding space, and complementary intrusions of that space into its mass—as in a pierced wall, or a wall in which some units project or recede from the general plane surface—we feel that we are expanding the potentialities of the material.

The warmth of color and texture in common brick and tile has endeared it to our hearts for centuries. Of all the masonry materials brick is probably more central in the affections of more of us than any other. This may be because it combines the strength and stability of stone, the warmth and vitality of earth, and the simple restful geometry of man. In specially-colored, hard-burned, and glazed bricks we have a considerable variety in color and texture for special and more refined treatments. The old-fashioned clinkers dear to the Victorian house-builder, the waste brick so close to the fire in the kilns—or from dismantled kilns—burned so hard as to be twisted and distorted and blackened, has in itself special qualities which can be explored and expressed in a direct structural manner. These clinkers have a certain affinity with igneous volcanic rock.

Mass-produced concrete or cement-bound building units—bricks, blocks, pavers—are related to clay products by their regular rectangularity, and contrasted by their general color range from light to dark gray, the distinctive color of poured cement. The plasticity of the original liquid mix allows great freedom in the forming, and there is an endless variety in the sizes, shapes, and proportions of these pre-cast units, and likewise in the various ingenious details for interlocking and bonding. Likewise there is a considerable variety in the precision, texture, and color of the finished units, depending upon workmanship and on the kinds of cement, sand, and rock used in the mix. With special attention this variety can be enormously amplified. With all of these precast units the remarks made about maintaining the rectangularity (circularity, hexagonality) of the basic unit hold true, with the added emphasis that the concrete units cannot easily be cut or broken to conform to odd shapes. Since they are in general larger units than bricks, they are not so easily warped into curved forms. Both clay and concrete are also used in a wide variety of industrial and building units—various sorts of pipes, flues, and drainage boxes, of circular, expanded-circular, or rectangular section—which, aside from their primarily practical uses, have considerable potential for imaginative uses exploiting their plastic formal quality in the garden.

Concrete and clay products are also, of course, subject to special handling in mass or special elements, rather than as repetitive units. In this their potentiality is very great. From the terra cotta which Louis Sullivan loved so dearly, and which has not since been adequately exploited, through the endless richness of ceramics and glazed tiles, to the complete plasticity of poured concrete, is a range very tempting to our craft or sculptural senses. Particularly in concrete, a kind of synthetic stone with no quality beyond that given to it by the mix, the forming, and the finishing, and of such constant and flexible use in all sorts of construction as to be a common experience of most Americans, do we have a material whose frontiers of development and expression have not yet been reached. There is a tremendous literature on its practical, technical, architectural, and engineering aspects, constantly being brought up to date, and most rewarding to intensive study. Our handling of concrete in the landscape, usually limited in scale and quantity, can for that very reason make intensive exploration of its esthetic and plastic aspects. In fact, that intensive exploration is essential to the final slaying of the old bogey that concrete is a dead dull material which has no place in the garden. The various complicated interactions of mixing, forming, and finishing provide the concrete designer with a palette as rich as any artist's. Where budget limits the application of special techniques to the material, often some very simple emphasis will produce remarkable results. Thus coloring by acid stain is economical and effective on any concrete surface. We must remember our principle of the interdependence, for effectiveness, of materials. Plain concrete can serve as an excellent foil for other material, or for plants with strong qualities. Often the most unself-conscious handling has remarkable effect: the writer has seen old utilitarian concrete walls, haphazardly mixed and formed roughly with odd scraps of lumber, of a most remarkable broken richness in texture. With adequate atmospheric moisture concrete will weather, stain, and grow moss and lichens even as rock.

The union of metal with brick, stone, or concrete in reinforced masonry begins to take us into the technical and legal territory and the dynamic esthetics of structural engineering and architecture. The union of the compressive strength of concrete or other masonry with the tensile strength of steel greatly increases the practical and esthetic potentiality of masonry alone. This is perhaps best demonstrated in the concept of the cantilever, horizontally over space, or vertically as a retaining element.

WATER

The character of water, the most plastic and receptive of our materials, is determined by the character of its container, and by the rate and direction of movement we give it. It seeks always a level plane surface, expressing the pull of gravity, and, when at rest, complete balanced stability. It is also affected by its chemical, plant or animal content: it tends to breed life (algae and mosquitoes) as it has throughout geologic history, unless specifically prevented from doing so. It is an essential element in the landscape in some form, as part of the elemental balance in nature of water, soil, plant and animal life. It is basic to the classification of climates, from arid to humid, in their relation to temperature ranges.

We tend to use it in organized design forms (a) in more humid climates because its more or less constant presence as natural surface water tends to make it an automatic part of our design vocabulary, especially as our work approaches the scale of the natural landscape; and (b) in more arid climates because its importance to comfort and to life receives extra emphasis there. In terms of increasing the livability of our indoor and outdoor spatial arrangements and enclosures, water is most relevant in hot arid climates and least in cool humid climates. In Arizona water is the final touch which makes the garden livable; in San

Francisco it is apt to be merely boring. It is the moistness of water which makes it relevant as aridity increases, and the coolness which makes it important as heat increases. In the tropics and humid temperate zones—France, England, China, Japan, Brazil, eastern U.S.—water has been used luxuriantly and lavishly in the landscape, at a scale which takes for granted its presence and renewal. In the arid and semi-arid regions—central Asia, the Near East, North Africa, Italy, Spain, the Moslem world—water has been used delicately, sparingly, in such a manner as to wring the maximum coolness and moistness from every drop. In the humid regions its containers historically are apt to take a naturalistic form and scale—stream, pond, canal, lake—because it is thought of as natural to the landscape, and because the structural sealing of the bottom to prevent loss by absorption is not so generally necessary. Even in geometric forms, as in the great baroque parks, their scale is such as to make them integrate naturally with the landscape. In the arid regions water has been more consistently contained in obviously structural containers, which had to be sealed to conserve the precious moisture, and tended toward small-scale, precise, geometric regularity in gardens shut off from the natural landscape.

Water has a number of other qualities, derived from the form and color of its container and its rate or lack of movement, that are directly relevant to its use as a landscape element. These range from quietude, repose, depth, tension, solidity, and the reflective qualities of its use in large, or deep, still basins with dark linings, to the lightness and sparkle of its use in motion in shallow basins with light linings. The possibilities for putting water in motion give the designer control of a sort of choreography, with its own trickling or thunderous accompaniment in sound. This includes in its own way the previous range, from the graceful sparkle of the single jet, to the solid power of the heavy waterfall. Single jets or jets in rows, vertically or horizontally, rills, cascades, overflows, large fountains; the Generalife, the Villa D'Este, the Paris Fair of 1929; the great canals

and basins of the baroque gardens, the lakes and waterfalls, streams and islands, of the Chinese, the English romantics and the American landscape gardeners and park planners—the ideas of history have been vivid and various, but they have not exhausted the possibilities. New forms, and new combinations of old forms; new materials, and new combinations of old materials—the possibilities are as limitless as the imagination of mankind.

Water not only derives part of its character from the materials lining its container, but such materials, under a thin film of water, double their quality and attraction. Brick and tile, glazed or unglazed; sand, pebbles, stone, concrete; plants and animals; all receive an exaggerated emphasis in color and texture when wet. This fact is, and has been historically, an integral part of the use of water in small quantities, in thin and fragile proportions, in trickles and splashes.

Water functions as a bounding or blocking element in the organization of space, because one must walk around it, rather than through it. It is as effective as a low hedge or wall in blocking free physical, but not visual, movement. That is why the traditional placement of pools in the centers of gardens, and the current fashion for swimming pools close to houses, are both bad in terms of spatial relations. Any body of water creates a hole or trench in the garden as far as the sensation of space is concerned. Placed in the center of square or rectangular garden spaces, especially of smaller size, pools will tend to divide them in quarters, and to reduce the apparent size.

Swimming pools in the average garden, because they are such big holes in the ground, require very careful treatment. Otherwise they are apt to become completely out of scale with the garden, swallow it up, and destroy its space. This, of course, may not be too big a price to pay for the morning dip and the evening plunge. But it is usually possible to design the pool-garden relation so that both the pleasure of the water and the space sensation of the garden are improved rather than depreciated. The primary principle for achieving this is very simple: the garden must shape the pool, rather than being forced to conform to it. While serious swimming and diving demand specific rectangular proportions in plan form, and specific relations of deep to shallow in section, few private pools are used so seriously as to limit them to that purely functional form. The standardized Beaux Arts shapes of the swimming pool companies (the rectangle, the decorated rectangle, the oval, the kidney bean) all arbitrary clichés, are dropped into the middle of gardens without much regard for the use, form, or space relations that will result.

Containers for water in the garden and the landscape—channels, basins, pools—are formed in any or all of three ways. They may be dug or hollowed out of the ground, or take advantage of existing depressions; these may or may not be lined with some more or less impervious material—clay, building paper, asphalt, concrete; at any rate these tend to conform to the natural slope of the ground, the forms are large and soft, even in a rectangular reservoir, and there is no apparent change in slope at the water line, unless rocks are present. This is thought of as the natural or informal pool, in which no structure shows. The pool in which the structural container shows at the sides or bottom, thus becoming "formal," may be built of brick, tile, or other unit masonry, necessitating the sealing of the interior below the water line to prevent leakage, or of poured concrete. There is a relation between the size of the water area, the availability of water in the locality, the nature of the ground, the degree of sealing of the pool below the water line, and the degree and way in which such structural control shows itself and is expressed. All of these are or should be subordinate to the general concept in form and space pattern of the garden or park in which the water occurs.

All of these types of water bodies are plastic and sculptural elements in the landscape. In a ground-formed depression the pool has a specific form outlined by the water line, a flat shape which speaks of depth and water-space below. The sculptural content comes from the form given to the ground as it emerges from the water, and from the possible integration of rocks with those ground forms. The pool contained in a unit-masonry basin will tend most reasonably to reflect the rectangularity of those units. The cast or poured basin, which now nearly always follows Beaux Arts forms based on distortions of unit-masonry (the constant thickness of sides and coping) is in reality a completely plastic and sculptural element, which can take any form whatsoever, however severe or "free," however simple or complex, that the designer may appropriately deduce from the garden scheme, or develop through the processes of creative imagination. Such water basins are one garden element (ground and rock forms being the others) where the landscape architect and the sculptor overlap so completely as to become theoretically indistinguishable. Although the landscape man, or the architect, usually does such pools, the sculptor in complete sympathy and understanding with the overall form concepts of the garden should be able to carry the pool to a degree of refinement and subtlety impossible without his special skill.

Design of pools seems still to be dominated by the peculiar idea that irregular pools must be naturalistic, and regular pools axially symmetric. The time-honored formal:informal schism in the form and detail of pools and other water elements is as irrelevant to them as to other elements of the landscape. The ground-formed pool can nevertheless be rectangular or geometric in form, and those forms can merge or contrast with "freer" (more complex) and more irregular forms in the same body of water. The rectangularity of the unit-masonry pool can be a free and irregular rectangularity, and angular or circular relations at appropriate scale can become part of this. The poured or blown concrete pool most certainly can escape from bilateral axial symmetry in its plan forms; beyond this there is no reason, beyond the increased complexity in forming, for parallelism between the inner and outer edges of the coping, or between the inner and outer surfaces of the entire basin. Again, three sides of a pool might be Renaissance cast-stone copings, and the fourth a rough rock cliff, most effectively. Mechanical approaches must be eliminated from our thinking.

PARSONS QUOTES PRINCE PUCKLER ON LARGER BODIES OF WATER

It is necessary to study the forms of water for the details, but the principal thing is never to suffer an expanse of water to be completely overlooked or seen in its whole extent. It should break on the eye gradually, and if possible lose itself at several points at the same time in order to give full play to the fancy—the true art in all landscape gardening.

(See also Byne and Byne on Spanish pools, and Shepherd and Jellicoe on the Villas Lante and d'Este.)

92

CHAPTER XII

ANTI-GRAVITY MATERIALS
PLANTS AND PLANTING

Many many volumes of poetry and of poetic prose have been written about plants and planting. Some of this has been well-written, some badly written; some beautiful, some corny. We are in agreement with the intentions of all these writers. Plants are endlessly fascinating: endlessly gracious, endlessly lovely, endlessly strong, persistent and adaptable, magnificent and fragile, colorful and variable, rich in structure and form, color and texture, architectural and sculptural and natural all at once, filled with potentiality for the free harmony of a beautiful world.

With the consideration of plants in the landscape we leave the ground plane, the floor of our garden space, to which earth, rock, and water are unbreakably bound however they may be carved and moulded and constructed, however ruggedly and picturesquely arranged by man or nature. The larger plants live with us the people IN the air space of the landscape, resisting and eluding gravity in the upward aspiration of their growth, yet firmly anchored, with their roots entrenched in the solid earth-bound mantle rock. The plants live in space and in the earth at once, and each and every plant is in itself an organization of space, containing within its three-dimensional silhouette a most complex and variable enclosure, a structure of

marvelous articulation and delicacy, a piece of constructivist sculpture of the most tremendous richness in variety, ranging in scale from the microcosm of the moss clump to the macrocosm of the great tropical banyan tree. Earth, rock and water are bound by gravity; plants defy it; that is the essense of space sensation, one reason for our love and need for plants.

Every plant, even of the prostrate or clinging kinds, is a study in most delicate equilibrium, in a most harmonious adjustment of many parts to meet the needs of the whole. The root structure, spreading or deep below ground, balances in cubic volume the vegetative structure above ground. It anchors the plant in one place, and forms that firm yet flexible base from which the upper parts defy gravity and the vagaries and violences of the weather. From this firm clutch upon the bosom of mother earth the plant reaches toward light and air in balanced radial symmetry, often distorted by weather, site or other plants, but always in balance, always a display of the fantastically endless variety of biological constructivism, more delicate, elegant, flexible, sturdy, or massive than man has yet produced. Upon this lithe and tenacious structure, with its permanent or changing costuming in all the manifold richness of foliage—the primary food-producing element of the plant—

are borne, seasonally, intermittently, or constantly, the reproductive elements, the flowers and fruit, that collection of delicately articulated jewels of unparalleled variety in form, color, and texture, which has been one of the chief delights and pursuits of gardeners since man first settled down on the land.

As design material plants are kinetic, not static. A plant is a living, growing structure, a unit of life. From the quick annual wild flower in the desert to the mighty redwoods and big trees which antedate the Christian church, every plant changes in form and aspect from day to day or from season to season. Plants are the bridge from inert matter to organic life, the spark plug in the great life-cycle of water, soil, plants and animals. The process of photosynthesis carried on by the chlorophyll in the plants of the world is its basic production relation, basic to the growth of the landscape, basic to the animal kingdom, basic to the societies of man. Our "ornamental" planting—our shade trees and hedges and flowers, our cacti and succulents and alpines, our bog gardens and aquatics, our lawns and meadows—as it functions in forming and enriching the spaces in which we live, is at the same time symbolic to us of the wild life-cycle of primeval nature, and of the organized life-cycle of human agriculture. The productive force of green growth, and the reproductive force of flower and fruit, as given sensitive, esthetic expression in our gardens and parks, is the very essence of the basic vitality of nature, that nature which is the world we live in, and which we are ourselves.

SCIENCE

Even an esthetic discussion of plants as used in landscape design must be based on plant science: botany, ecology, horticulture, genetics. Ecology, as the science of the relations between plants and their environment, and between plants in that environment, has been little mentioned by those who bring to us the message that we must design our planting as nature does, maintain her associations, and avoid the self-

94

conscious touch of man. (Except Robinson, who has two good chapters.) Botany, the science of the structure and classification of plant life, is basic to the assimilation of plant material into a design vocabulary. Horticulture, the science of the culture of ornamental plants, is the practical science, the tool without which the landscape architect can neither produce nor maintain on the ground the great plant designs which may grow in his imagination. It is likewise the creative science, responsible for the continuous improvement, in quality and variety, of the primary plant material of landscape design.

LUTHER BURBANK, THE FAMOUS AMERICAN HORTICUL-TURIST AND CREATOR OF NEW FORMS OF PLANT LIFE, SAID

I have no quarrel with botany, and its labored classifications and set rules, but what I do maintain is that, at best, botany is the science of dead things. . . . The only living science of plants is the science of breeding and crossing and encouraging them to become more useful or more beautiful—and let the rules go hang. . . . Every living thing is what it is as the result of the action of two forces: heredity and environment. The plant breeder's work is to guide the action and interaction of these two forces to take advantage of the plant's heredity and to influence its environment.

We can speak, hypothetically, of a local ecology, a local pattern of subclimax, climax, post-climax; of dominants, associations, societies, families and colonies, in every farm, every rural region and urban center, every town, street, park, and garden. We can hypothesize, too, about positive and negative ecology—the positive ecological balance which develops because of good habitat factors, the negative ecological balance which survives in spite of bad habitat factors. We can speak of this positive:negative relation not only in the urban areas, but in the rural sections, where good, successful, conservative agriculture would be positive, and bad, unsuccessful, or erosive agriculture negative. Also in the primeval areas we might suggest that the line between the moist and dry sub-humid climates, which separates the humid or leached soils from the arid soils, also separates the same positive (or because) and negative (or in-spite-of) zones. Human agriculture or horticulture in the positive zones changes the kind of positive vegetation; in the negative zones it changes the type from negative to positive, by irrigation and cultivation. Where the science of plant ecology evaluates climaxes in terms of quantity (actual area of greenery produced by the given habitat) with the rain forest as the highest; our art of landscape design (or humanized landscape) must measure climaxes in different terms. It must measure not only in terms of quantitative relations between outdoor space and people, but in terms of the actual quality (esthetic and functional) of the forms and proportions of space relations established with trees, shrubs, herbaceous material, grass, ground forms, rocks and water, and structural elements. This will be applied and developed as an equalizing factor through the range of climatic zones in which people are or will be able to develop rich social patterns and cultural expressions: the tropical, the humid temperate, the arid temperate, the frigid.

THE ESTHETICS OF PLANTING

We mean to stress, as has all the informal or naturalistic school before us, the unbounded or unlimited character and potential of landscape design. It is the art which can and will merge and integrate man and nature, people with their regions, town and countryside. Planting design is the one kind of design which has few boundaries derived from technical or site necessities; the one kind of design in which the unit being done is linked immediately with the grass, shrub and tree vegetation which covers the surface of the earth, save for rock mountains, dry deserts, bodies of water, and cities (synthetic deserts). Structural elements, buildings, designs in refined processed materials, are always physically isolated in the world by their own nature; planting is seldom isolated, and then only by choice. It is an art of continuity, real or potential, by contrast with the art of entity which structural or refined design is. These, too, are hypothetical, rather than permanent, contradictions. Our objective is the integration of continuity and entity, by the integration of planting design and structural design in the larger art of spatial design.

Structure is thought of as THE art of spatial design, but planting is likewise an art of spatial design—the primary spatial control out-of-doors, equal qualitatively to structural design, though varying in kind; that is, subtler, looser, less positive, less continuous, or with wider variations in degree of continuity. To speak of color first, texture second, and mass third, as does Robinson, is not only to reverse the scale of importance, to stand values on their heads, but also to ignore the primary spatial essence of plants. Every plant, no matter how low, how prostrate, how massive, matted, or solidly bushy, how fastigiate or billowing, is nevertheless a construction in space and an enclosure of space. As we go up in the scale of space organization, from the grass, ground covers, herbaceous material and vines which are primarily surfacing or enriching elements, to the shrubs and trees which are the real enclosing and sheltering forms, this spatial quality becomes, of course, more obvious and more important. To stress color, texture, and mass is to concede that planting is merely decorative, to endeavor to make it into a kind of sculpture or painting which it is not, to relapse into the search for pictures and miss the great lyric opportunities of landscape design.

Plant material, as an aggregation of units of unlimited variety in form, size, color, and texture, has esthetic possibilities which have scarcely been scratched. The variety and richness of plants as a material for creative organization are limited only by questions of culture and maintenance, and by the scope and freedom of the plan conception. We are offered a richness of vocabulary, a wealth of palette, not surpassed by the material range of any other sort of creative work. This variety proposes a problem of discipline in selection which is difficult to achieve. But the ingredients of this discipline are to be found in the problems of culture and maintenance, and in the need for development of a new and more dynamic esthetic of plant arrangement in relation to site-space form.

95

Planting design is primarily the grouping of a number of forms, varying in size and proportions, in a three-dimensional arrangement. Within this grouping there can be formal and space relations comparable, in degree but not in kind, to those in sculpture and painting.

Most planting is done practically, pictorially, sentimentally and/or commercially. Practically to solve such problems as ground cover, erosion control, windbreaks, screens, shade, et cetera; pictorially to provide "pictures to look at" (the terminal feature, the garden vista, the naturalistic glade, all heavily propagandized in professional and amateur garden publications); sentimentally to recall an emotion (the rock garden, the old-fashioned garden, the bog garden, the English garden); and commercially to move nursery stock (foundation planting is a standard technique). These objectives are all valid when properly interpreted in relation to the planning problems which exist; without such relation they become fragmentary or irrelevant. The usual concentration on them tends to minimize or overlook the tremendous potential for symphonic spatial experience latent in landscape design. This potential has scarcely been scratched in our times, save in a few great parks and estates. It has been foreshadowed in some of the great historic gardens, in some of the unconsciously dynamic planting carried out in the rural countryside, and in such natural features as meadows and groves of trees. But it has yet to be exploited consciously, boldly, and with the full sweep of man's creative imagination, allied with the rich variety of free natural growth.

SELECTION

Planting must be worked out in terms of *selection, arrangement,* and *maintenance.* These are all three mutually interdependent and retroactive. There are certain factors basic to the *selection* of plants for use:

The plan (desired *arrangement*).
Cultural requirements (*maintenance*)—soil, drainage, moisture, sun and shade, heat, frost, air movement, pruning, pest control.

Ultimate size and rate of growth.
Natural form, or silhouette and structure.
Texture—size, form, and arrangement of foliage and structural members.
Color—foliage, bark, flowers, fruit.
Fragrance or odor.

(Discussion of the first two follows this section on selection.)

SIZE—Plants are, in general, a series of units circular in plan, varying in diameter or spread from a few inches to 100 ft. or more, and in height from one or two inches to 300 ft. or more. With due regard to the selection factors listed (which are the only ones relevant) these units are independent of each other for arrangement purposes. The primary reason for placing ultimate size—modified by the rate of growth (slower plants can be crowded more than faster ones)—third in our list of selection factors after plan and culture, is that plants should always be placed so that they can continue to grow and develop with a minimum of restriction.

The relation between ultimate size and rate of growth points up the distinctive character of plants as living and obviously changing design material, by contrast with most others which are inorganic, however refined and processed. The rate of change and development of most plants, and their flexibility in adjusting to their habitat, make it necessary to project and visualize three-dimensional arrangements, not only from the drawing board and designer's imagination to the site, but on the site ahead in time six months, five years, or fifty years. With annuals we can project ahead a season's effects, but with major shrubs and trees we are, or should be, making a spatial arrangement which will develop and accumulate character and maturity year after year. There is therefore a relation between the length of time it will take a given species of shrub or tree to develop reasonably mature character, and the length of time that occupancy of that given portion of the site can be guaranteed to that plant.

This is where the stability of land use becomes an important factor. There is no use planting fifty-year trees on land whose use may

96

change in ten years. We have seen too many magnificent specimens chopped down on abandoned estates by the eager-eyed subdivider with the one-track mind. No land is safe from, or sacred to, these happy speculators, "developers," and "home builders." Every in-town park in America would be cut up into lots if these gentry had their way. Each reader will be aware of, or can easily track down, examples in his own community of this ruthless and persistent attack on every piece of well-located raw or lightly-used land. Thus in San Francisco the McLaren Park site was at one time potentially 1,000 acres of developed park space, serving the southern half of the city as Golden Gate Park serves the northern half. Through neglect and active attack it has been whittled down until, in 1944, the maximum possibility requested by the Park Department was 375 acres, while the Board of Supervisors was considering 250, and the Associated Home Builders was requesting that all but 175 acres be turned over to them for "beautiful residential development."

The net result of this instability of land use, this vulnerability of land to subdivision and re-subdivision, development and re-development ever more intensely, is a kind of instability of plant use, a tendency to concentrate on the quicker-growing kinds, however short-lived, and to avoid the slower, more stately and permanent material. The latter is reserved for those areas whose stability seems fairly well guaranteed in this most unstable world: cemeteries, parks, estates, public building sites. The general landscape pattern of our communities is so installed and arranged that it looks well for perhaps five to ten years, then begins to deteriorate, either in old age or overgrowth for its position.

There is an absolute relation to human scale and the plane of eye level, roughly five feet off the ground plane when standing (the greatest vertical extension into space with the feet still on the ground). Those plants which reach above that eye level plane are most important in the garden space—other things being equal—simply because they block the vision most effectively, and also obstruct physical movement. Plants growing below the eye level must assume

progressively less importance in the general picture, UNLESS some particular strength of color or texture—which often appears—helps them to assert themselves beyond their size. Thus the primary space organizers among plants are the trees and tall shrubs.

There is probably a zone in scale most close to that of the human figure, in which plants seem more intimate and hence more important than those larger or smaller. This is a relation similar to that which makes the furniture and interior design within the house seem more intimate and primary in interest than the house itself. The range in plant size from herbaceous material one to two feet tall, to small trees of twelve to fifteen feet, balances fairly equally above and below human size. These might be called the domestic, private, or garden scale elements. Those smaller are scarcely noticeable without special effort except as surface under foot; those larger become somewhat removed, less intimate, more at the scale of house or shelter enclosing both the person, the smaller plants, and the furniture. This is part of the constant problem of establishing scale relations between the individual and the world around.

There is no particular point in super-human size at which plants suddenly stop being relevant to ordinary environments, and must be reserved for special environments. This is merely an association derived from the artificial separation of our urban environment into areas of high and low population density (people per acre). In the high density areas, because of the unnecessarily high building coverage, there is room only for smaller plants, if any; the big trees must be used in those low density areas where they can have room to grow and spread their roots. But the range in plant sizes is part of the range in spatial experiences which is every citizen's birthright, though most of them rarely see it. Small rooms, small houses, crowded neighborhoods, small trees if any, crowded work and recreation spaces: this is the habitat of the common man. Contrast this with the big rooms, big houses, spacious neighborhoods, big trees in quantity, comfortable work and recreation spaces which are the reward of that 30

97

per cent which can afford the "American standard of living." No easy rationalization about big
trees for big people and little trees for little
people can destroy this contradiction; the daily
experience of the spatial richness of the spreading oak, the spatial aspiration of the giant pine,
should be available to everyone.

The complexity of visualizing the maturity of
the planting scheme five to fifty years ahead can,
of course, be offset by the use of over-size or
full-grown material, moved in with all the ingenuity and skill of the up-to-date nurseryman
or big tree specialist. This is a highly touted
procedure, somewhat sensational, and thoroughly intriguing to the great American preoccupation with know-how. But it is an expensive proposition, and too often employed
merely to fill up the gap where the designer's
imagination failed him. The mature tree or the
specimen plant are useful in special positions,
or to fill a special need, as shade on that hot
terrace right now. On most jobs a few specimens
are a reasonable inclusion, and great stabilizers
of the new landscaping.

The longer a plant grows in one location the
more carefully and delicately does it become adjusted and adapted to the special soil, moisture,
atmosphere, and light conditions of that location, and the greater becomes its retroactive
effect on those conditions. To then come in with
mechanical equipment, however ingenious and
powerful, and lift that plant bodily from its
closely integrated habitat, no matter how large
the root ball, and replant it in a new location
whose conditions cannot duplicate those from
which the plant came, and may be very different,
is a severe shock to most plants. The subsequent
nursing of the plant back to health and vigor
may last one to five years. As we concentrate
more and more on larger initial sizes in our
plant material, we reduce more and more the
list of kinds from which we can choose. This
reduction stems not only from the technical diffi-
culties of the moving, but from the economic
problems of the nurseryman, who cannot afford
to maintain large stocks of oversize material.
(These remarks are probably most true in the
negative—dry, semiarid and arid—regions.)

FORM—As we go further into the detail of
plant forms their richness in variety expands
rapidly. The variations in ultimate dimensions,
in height and spread and rate of growth, become
simplicity itself when we consider the fantastic
variability in general form and structure within
the ornamental plant world. With the circular
(unless distorted by external factors) plan form
of the single unit as a common denominator, we
have a range of form in elevation from those
which are horizontal in the proportion of as
much as one unit high to ten or twelve spread,
through every imaginable intermediate variation to those which are vertical in the proportion of one unit of spread to as many as ten
high. Structural forms go through all variations
of symmetry and irregularity. From horizontality to verticality, from regularity to irregularity, from symmetry to contortion, from
rigidity to pliability, from erection to prostra-
tion, from climbing to crawling, from the open
tracery to the dense mass, the variation is endless. (We can speak of plants which are tracer-
ies, and of plants which are massive, but we
must remember that no plant, save such occasional specializations as the barrel cactus, is in
its overall relations a mass.) In relation of
three-dimensional silhouette to supporting structure, and in relation of these to size and rate of
growth, the variability becomes so complex as
to get beyond rationalization or classification.
We can list among trees the round-headed, the
spreading, the irregular, the vertical oval, the
slender upright, the fastigiate, the vertical with
horizontal branches, and so on. But to further
break these down into all the angular and curving, regular and irregular, opposite and alternate relations of twig to branch to trunk becomes a task for a future academy of plant
design with research resources beyond any existing. This is perhaps the point at which the
rational becomes irrational, the objective subjective, and the scientific artistic.

Most trees take one form when they are
young, another as they mature, and a third as
they grow old. Shrubs, too, change character
with maturity. Especially the larger and more
erect species tend to open up and lose their

lower branches, becoming quasi-tree forms. This tendency is subject to considerable control by pruning. Most permanent shrub and vine forms tend to develop woody lower structures of considerable character and interest, comparable to trees, as they mature and age. Design can take advantage of this tendency rather than foster the frantic gardening efforts to conceal legs and stems.

To speak of natural form is incomplete—we must ask, natural form where? under what conditions? The single pine in the open meadow, the pine crowded with many others in a dense grove, the pine on exposed mountain top or sea shore, will scarcely be recognizable as the same species. We must establish a relation between the visualization of a certain kind of form, the selection of a kind which tends to develop in that direction, and the creation of conditions which will encourage it. This is what we mean by collaboration between material and artist.

TEXTURE—From variations in structure and silhouette to variations in texture is a step from complexity to infinity. It is from this relation between foliage and structure that most of us recognize and identify plants as they are generally used in landscape design, rather than from the more scientific procedures of botanical taxonomy. This is particularly true of the larger material, the woody and semi-woody shrubs and trees, the sizeable herbaceous material, the climbers, trailers, and sprawlers.

In size foliage ranges from the tiny scales of heather and juniper, through all the intermediate variations of "ordinary" garden plants, to the startling extremes of Magnolia triflora, palms, elephant ears, gunnera, and philodendron. In form foliage can be classified in a range typified by linear (pine needles), lanceolate (lance-shaped), ovate (oval), obovate (fat oval), cordate (heart-shaped), and so on. Complicating these are intermediates (linear-lanceolate, cordate-obovate); variations from symmetry in the individual leaf; variations in the edge (simple, toothed, holly-like, lobed) and in the point; special forms; variations in thickness and stiffness, and varying combinations of these (thick-soft, thin-stiff); variations in veining;

variations in pinnation, that is, dissection of the leaf into a few or many smaller leaflets; variations in the texture of each leaf (smooth-glossy, smooth-dull, fuzzy, crinkled, etc.); variations in the length and angle of the petiole connecting leaf to twig or stem; and so on. The variation in foliage, like the variation in rocks, is endless and endlessly fascinating. Unlike rocks, it has been difficult to preserve, save in the dusty pages of the herbarium. Plant specimens can now be preserved intact in cold poured transparent plastic blocks, and we can look forward to the day when such a library will be part of every school of landscape design.

Each step in variation in plant form is a multiple variation by virtue of its cross-reference with all the previous variations. Thus the progression in complexity is geometric rather than arithmetic. In foliage arrangement, as related to plant structure, we have further wide variation: from thin-scattered to dense-crowded, from even-all-over-the-plant to grouped-in-bunches-or-tufts, from erect through horizontal to pendant, from stiff to pliable to tremulous, from sprinkles through fronds to clumps, the range can scarcely be cataloged. Consider these in relation to variations in leaf form, leaf size, plant structure (producing silhouette), size and rate of growth, as well as color, and the limitless richness of the plant palette becomes increasingly obvious.

A further most important variation in the textural quality of plants appears in those which are deciduous, that is, which develop a permanent woody structure but lose their leaves in winter. The great virtue, richness and interest of deciduous plants lies precisely in those continuous seasonal changes which are associated in so many minds with the cold and storms of eastern winters. "They look so dead." From the fresh light greens and bronzes of bursting spring, through the rich mature greens of summer and the gorgeous reds, browns and yellows of fall, to the complete exposure of trunk, branch, and stem structure in all their elegance, strength, refinement or fantasy during the winter, deciduous trees, shrubs, and vines put on a continuous show which is not to be matched for variety and interest by any of the evergreen plants save perhaps those with showy flowers. There is a kind of cultural lag expressed in our typical concentration on greenery and flowers, to the exclusion of interest in structure and texture. We don't have to reject any of these; rather it is necessary to include them all to rescue our landscapes from dull and mechanical design.

Plants can be classified as foliage plants if the leafage covers the structural parts, as structural plants if they are exposed and dominant in character, as both if the two tend to balance, as in many trees. Some trees may be foliage plants from the outside, and structural when one goes under and within them—as olives and avocados. Some may be foliage in summer and structural in winter.

Another aspect of the relation between foliage and structure in trees, with considerable bearing on their location, is the following:

VAN DYKE

The only power of motion possessed by a tree lies in its growth upward, downward, and outward. It is capable of being moved, however, and the great mover is the wind. . . .

COLOR—We come then at last to color. It can be said that American gardens (English gardens? French gardens?) are color-happy. This is not to depreciate the value of color, which makes the world understandable, vibrant, and magnificent for us. But color, in its purer and stronger forms, comes in our world in fractional quantities, save for special or seasonal bursts, within a general framework of greens, browns, and blues, each grayed with some admixture of the other and with the changes in light and atmosphere relations. The purer and stronger the color we introduce, the more carefully considered must be its quantity, and its relations with other colors and elements around it. The "riot of color," that romantic vision of the garden beautiful, is too often, like "informal design", merely an excuse for sloppy, haphazard, irresponsible planting. We advocate the use of color, but we advocate its use in a disciplined and controlled fashion which will strengthen,

rather than disrupt, the spatial concept of garden or park.

Color in plants is normally thought of as flower or fruit color, because those are the most striking. But foliage and structure likewise have color, of considerable range: in foliage from gray, blue-gray, and brown-gray through gray-green, light, medium, and dark green, to various purple and red shades, not to mention variegations of silver, yellow, and red; from the lightness of Russian olive and silver poplar to the darkness of evergreen, magnolia, avocado, purple plum, or copper beech; in bark from the white birch through many dull grays and browns, to the reds of madrone and manzanita and some near blacks, such as the Australian ironbark. These colors are generally grayed and toned down by contrast with the clarity of flower and fruit colors. They are also subject to considerable variation under varying conditions of soil, atmosphere, cultivation, climate, and season. Even some of the evergreens have considerable seasonal variations: the myrtle family has noticeably bronze or gray young growth; Chinese photinia and sweet viburnum sport occasional bright red leaves in fall and winter; the plume cypress (Japanese) and one variety of prostrate common juniper turn respectively rich bronze and rich purple with winter. Color and texture are brought out by order and clarity in the development of contrasts of varying degrees of strength and proportion. We can have a limited symphony in light and dark greens, or we can have a strong symphony in near-blacks and -whites. The limited symphony can, of course, have its seasonal crescendos of red and yellow foliage, or pink and white blossoms.

There is a climatic or zonal relation of these colors, particularly in foliage. The strong clear greens and variegations seem to be produced by the positive ecological zones, the humid tropical and temperate forests. As we move into the negative zones of heat and aridity or frigidity the foliage colors in trees and shrubs tend toward grays, gray-greens, brown-greens, and the general landscape quality becomes thinner, paler, browner or grayer. Likewise textures seem to vary zonally: the fine glossy surfaces

100

develop in the positive zones, the dull and fuzzy ones in the negative zones where they are protective coverings.

This is where the function of man as equalizer of his environment comes in. In the positive zones, particularly where the humidity rises to a point of discomfort (as in the tropics), or where coolness and fog prevail (as our northwest coast), the darker, heavier, and glossier greens, which are most at home in such climates, tend to accentuate the oppressive or discomforting qualities of the atmosphere. Here we are apt to encourage the lighter, clearer greens, the thinner forms in cool zones, and even silver and gold variegations in zones where the atmosphere is dull and dark. In the negative zones, on the other hand, where light, heat, and dryness press upon us, we tend to promote the growth of the darker, brighter, glossier, or clearer greens, the larger and richer foliage which feels cool and moist. This we do by artificially increasing the humidity, i.e. by irrigation. Thus we seek two values in every landscape: one, the expression of the native quality of the landscape, the other, the development of maximum human livability. The latter is the equalizing value, but it is not incompatible with the former, except in the old-fashioned mystical formulation which makes man subservient to nature.

The relation of atmosphere and light to landscape design has a more specific relation to planting design. The above climatic zones are distinguished by variations in these qualities: the bright humidity of the tropics, the dull humidity of the cool coastal zones, the harsh brightness of the desert, the myriad atmospheric variations of the humid temperate east. See Van Dyke's discussion of the effects of these variations on foliage color.

We must design with plant form, texture and color, partly in relation to general and local natural ecology—"most plants are green"—and partly in relation to a scientific evaluation of maximum human livability. Even as there is a developing science of indoor color, concerned with psychological reactions, so there can be a science of outdoor color and texture, concerned with such things as the oppressive quality of the dark heavy tree, the cheering quality of the light sparkling tree. If our landscape conception calls for a grove of copper beeches, perhaps contrasted with a block of silver box elders, the former related to a larger background of light clear greens, the latter to dark heavy greens, we will not seek justifying precedent in wild nature, but only in our own imaginative appraisal of the given situation. We must evaluate form, texture, and color in terms of their effect on the general outdoor space which is being developed, rather than in terms of how "natural" they are, or what illusions or pictures they may create.

Flowers and fruit must be considered in two relations—one, on the plant which bears them, and two, cut and arranged in containers in the house. Flower arrangement is a rich and fascinating art in its own right; it is a kind of microcosm of decorative planting design, without either the cultural problems or the potential permanence of the latter. We will not attempt to consider it here. Flowers grown in the garden should first be separated as to whether they are primarily to be seen there, or to be cut for house use. The latter are difficult, though not impossible to use in the garden scheme: maintenance procedures are apt to be simplified if they are grown in functional rows in the workspace or service yard. This applies to all those, such as hybrid tea roses, whose principal asset is their flowers, and to those, such as many annuals, which require steady care and frequent changing to keep them looking well.

We are concerned primarily, then, with flowers and fruit on plants in the garden or park, and hence with the size and form of those plants which produce showy color in these reproductive parts. We can separate first the woody plants from those which are herbaceous. The latter include the general run of garden annuals and perennials, bulbs, alpines, bog plants, aquatics, succulents, annual and perennial vines, and so on. This herbaceous material is in general smaller—below eye level—more seasonal, and less permanent than the woody material. There are exceptions to each—large size, continuity of effect, long life and persistence—but

101

seldom all three in the same plant. Thus there are large annuals and biennials—sun flowers, hollyhocks—which are persistent by seeding themselves, but in unexpected places. There are perennials, bulbs, succulents which are quite persistent with proper care, but which come and go with the seasons. Morning-glories will cover considerable areas, but disappear each winter, and so on.

This herbaceous material we must consider, in general, as being enriching—rather than surfacing, enclosing, or sheltering—material in the landscape scheme. This means that it must play its part within a spatial framework of greater continuity and reliability. With that framework once well established, the herbaceous material can be woven in either incidentally, to satisfy horticultural interests and ambitions, or in carefully interlocked spatial relations, whereby a sizeable block of low but strong color can play a dominant role in the spatial harmony. The danger is, of course, that we may plan for the incidental first, and get something with the strength of the second, with disruptive and disharmonious results. The place of this herbaceous material in the general theory of landscape design, when we cannot establish sure control of its use, comes within an inevitable and quite desirable category of unplanned, accidental, possibly disruptive, but highly vital design elements. The really disruptive or overpowering herbaceous forms are few in number; most of them are subject to easy inclusion within a relatively permanent and dominant background framework. Seasonal bursts of color—as the daffodils in spring or the chrysanthemums in fall—can play the role of seasonal dominance of herbaceous societies in grassland climaxes.

Climatic regionalism is relevant to the selection and use of herbaceous material. In temperate Europe Baroque parterres and Victorian carpet-bedding climaxed in the English wild garden and herbaceous border, those crowning achievements of Robinson and Jekyll since become English institutions. The greater extremes of the temperate eastern U. S. makes the herbaceous border more difficult, but still possible. In the semi-arid and arid climates it becomes a

struggle and a test of caretakers' skill and faithfulness. In these climates for color we tend to fall back on such reliable and hardy elements as geraniums, lantana, the larger bulbs, and succulents. Certain persistent annuals and perennials tend to acclimatize themselves, too—hollyhock, alyssum, nasturtium, coreopsis, morning-glory. In tropical Brazil, in the rich and flamboyant work of Roberto Burle Marx, painter turned landscape gardener, working with the pinks and purples, the fantastic forms and textures, of tropical plant material, we find coming to great fruition in a new cultural climate the separate but analogous traditions of Chinese-Japanese painter-landscaper and English herbaceous romanticism.

The woody plants, being the more durable forms which are able to survive extremes of cold, heat, drought, or neglect, are the primary structural plant forms in the garden, those which can be relied on, together with earth, rock, and construction, to establish a reliable spatial framework within which the active and varied counterpoint of seasonal herbaceous material, as part of general human living activities, can play. Woody plants, too, produce showy color: from the spring blossoms and fall foliage of the east, through the camellias, rhododendrons, and berried pyracantha and cotoneaster of the west coast, the magnolia and crepe myrtle of the deep south, to the hibiscus, oleander, and trumpet vines of the semi-arid or subtropical southwest. Most such color is strictly seasonal; it is only in the far southwest and southeast that woody plants blooming continuously, intermittently, or for long seasons are common.

As plants get larger and more permanent they must be selected more carefully for specific situations. We can plant anything we want to experiment with in our seasonal borders without great loss in time or money. There we can play with pure color to our heart's content. But with five-year shrubs and twenty-year trees we must be more judicious; we must consider not only the color they can produce for us, but the full size, the rate of growth, the form and structure, the texture, whether deciduous or evergreen, and so on. The tree which is good for summer shade and winter sun, the shrub which will give us enclosure and privacy, may not also be the kind to produce flowers and/or fruit for us. Other things being equal, we can certainly tend to choose those trees and shrubs which give us also some strong seasonal color, in flowers, fruit or foliage. But the other things are seldom equal. The flowering trees are apt to be too small for shade (in which case they can of course be fitted in more incidentally), too evergreen for the winter, too subject to pests and diseases, too messy for the neat garden-housekeeper, and so on. Flowering and fruiting shrubs seem, in general, to tend toward an open, loose, irregular or arching habit which makes them useless for screening or solid enclosure. Consider the forms of lilac, mock orange, bridal wreath, hibiscus, cotoneaster, pyracantha. Those ingenious characters who turn to the hedge shears at this point are merely going to ruin good shrubs to make a bad screen. While these remarks are not by any means one hundred percent true (since there are flowering shrubs such as the oleander, which make good durable screens; flowering trees such as the jacaranda and yellow wood, which are good for garden shade; fruiting trees such as the apricot, the fig, and the chestnut, which are likewise good shade), nevertheless they are sufficiently true to reinforce our emphasis on the selection of plants for specific situations ON PLAN, in terms of size, form, texture and color in that order. We do not have to follow the Japanese and concentrate our interest on the form and foliage of plants, nor do we have to follow the garden clubs and concentrate our interest on flowers: we can have both, with adequate imaginative flexibility in our planning.

On the limitless fascination in form and color of flowers and fruit, both ornamental and edible, we need hardly elaborate. Better poets than we have given us lyric and delicately subtle word-evaluations, and the great horticulturists and gardeners of our times have concentrated their energies on the production of constantly improved varieties, larger, more double, brighter and clearer. If we were to raise a still small voice

it might only be to wonder if sometimes the flower doesn't run away with the plant, as in the proliferation of hybrid tea roses. But that is a matter of a general climate of opinion. As long as most of us think that lovely flowers and fruits are the peak product of the garden, its *pièce de résistance*—as indeed they are—those who sell us our plants will continue to breed for flowers and fruits primarily. As we become convinced that this *pièce de résistance* demands an appropriate environment, a suitable setting, a strong spatial framework which will carry on for it when its burst of creation is done; so will the horticulturists and nurserymen concentrate on form, structure and texture as well as flowers. This, of course, they do to a considerable extent today.

The colors of flowers and fruits, especially the herbaceous material, run the gamut. The complex delights of planning the perennial border for all seasons and all color relations have been explored for us in endless garden books and manuals. True blues, especially in deeper and stronger shades, are the choicest and most scarce colors in flower and fruit. Otherwise the general range, through red, pink, yellow, orange, lavender, purple, and white, with all imaginable intermediate variations, is well known and often described. The subtle variations—as pure pink which is merely pale red, carmine pink which has blue in it, salmon pink which has yellow in it—are subject to subtle and delicate handling even as the oils and water colors of the painter's palette. While we occasionally see color combinations which make us somewhat seasick, we are inclined to be skeptical of academic systems. We think stronger and more contrasting color combinations than those normally considered "good taste" are perfectly good and reasonable, and that such combinations are somewhat like food: it's a question of what you have been educated to and are used to. A new food can be examined, sampled, and finally assimilated if we are flexible enough to get over our fixed preconceptions. Those who condemn certain color schemes as "Mexican," "primitive," or "vulgar" are merely guilty of self-sterilization. Those who go to the Mediterranean in search of local color are really in search of humanity.

Design in the pure color relations of paint or flowers is a kind of highly specialized and sensitized department of the general categories of space and object design. In general landscape or architectural practice it becomes a special detail which can be minimized or exaggerated according to individual taste. As we move toward the clear and rich spatial order out-of-doors which we have been discussing, we are sure to need such special detail to complete, intensify and subtilize our big conceptions. At this sitting it seems generally safe to say that those colors having some content of the general landscape colors—brown, green, blue—are best in exposed quantities, while those of more primary or synthetic quality should be held to smaller quantities and more specially planned locations and relations to other colors. In the language of Munsell, hues become safer, or less disruptive, in quantity as they become lighter or darker in value and weaker in chroma. Clearer values and stronger chromas can be used, with greater care in their quantitative and qualitative relations and in their known psychological reactions on the observer.

FRAGRANCE—One further factor relevant to the selection of plants is that of fragrance or odor. This exists in great variety and variations of strength, produced mainly by flowers, but also by damaged fruit or vegetative parts in many plants. It may be pleasant or unpleasant; naturally we endeavor to avoid the latter. Careful fragrance relations are another delicate refinement of the planting scheme, tending to be quite subjective and vulnerable to personal reactions. Thus some may prefer strong fragrance, some mild fragrance, some none. Such touches as the use of rosemary and myrtle along paths and steps, where brushing them releases the fragrance of the foliage, are highly pleasant and seldom controversial. The scents of flower and garden and blossoming tree are part of the fine poetry of flowers, on which we need not elaborate.

UNITY AND VARIETY—All this richness of plant material can be used so as to obscure, con-

fuse, and smother it, or bring it out with clarity, strength, and coherence, in endless varied kaleidoscopic patterns. The techniques by which it is lost are simple; we are surrounded by them. They vary from the irresponsible-commercial or -informal, which mixes any and all forms and textures in a haphazard pepper-and-salt patchwork which adds up to complete confused indigestion; through the formal-design, which considers interest in the material merely sentimental; to the careful-professional, which avoids all extremes to stay with safe medium sizes, medium forms, and medium textures which won't prove objectionable to anyone. The techniques for expressing and expanding this richness are largely waiting to be developed; they involve combinations of imagination, self-discipline, boldness, and understanding that are seldom stressed by our schools today.

The argument over the appropriate length of the plant list is an old one in landscape circles. We are taught in our schools that design is a relation between variety and unity: variety within or leading to unity, unified variety, and so on. But the teaching and the practice in professional circles tends to end up with the elimination of variety in the achievement of a simple, easy, and sterile unity. The extreme example of this is the academic dictum, "the shorter the plant list the better the planting plan". This is a widespread conviction in academic, professional, and practical circles. The brevity of the list is supposed to be an indicator of professional restraint, control, and dignity; the long list is amateurish, naïve, uncontrolled, disorganized, commercial, or horticultural. Once again an irrelevant rule-of-thumb becomes a cultural control: the hack who boils down to thirty kinds of plants in order to get the work out faster in order to get more work becomes the professional standard; the serious and imaginative designer who endeavors to explore and exploit the magnificent wealth of plant material becomes an impractical dreamer. The naïveté does not lie in the length of the list; the naïveté lies in the simple mind which can assume that good or bad design can be gauged by such omnipotent rules-of-thumb. In 1908 Frank Lloyd Wright said "Simplicity

104

and repose are qualities that measure the true value of any work of art. . . . But simplicity is not in itself an end nor is it a matter of the side of a barn but rather an entity with a graceful beauty in itself from which discord, and all that is meaningless, has been eliminated. A wild flower is truly simple. . . ." Simplicity can be organized from any number of elements; it is merely more difficult as the number increases.

The relation between the wealth of variety in the plant palette and its analysis in terms of size, form, texture and color points the way to endless systems, of varying complexity and subtlety, for the achievement of unity. The length of the plant list is quite irrelevant to the determination of whether or not this has been achieved. Three badly-selected plants can produce cacophony, fifty well-selected plants a symphony, in the same volume of space. The plant list must first be analyzed in relation to the size (cubage) of the area to be planted. Thereafter it must be analyzed in terms of size, form, color, and texture, and of quantities of each kind of each. Thus we can have a unity by size: one or a few kinds of larger trees or shrubs can dominate and unify many more kinds of smaller woody or herbaceous plants. Variety decreases as we go up the size-scale, increases as we go down. We can have unity by form: stronger forms, as the fastigiate or the weeping, may establish a dominant framework for a variety of looser forms. We can have unity by texture: the large-dark-glossy or the thin-light-fine may predominate throughout one size of plants, or through several sizes. Likewise we can have unity by color. The relations by combination among these patterns for unity become endlessly varied; the only comparable arts are those of sound—music —or of color—painting.

The patterns of unity must be related to spatial eye-level patterns. There is a ground-cover pattern, of grass, herbaceous materials, and low woody planting, as related to inorganic surfacing. There is an eye-level pattern of tall herbs and grasses, medium and tall shrubs, and small trees, as related to structural enclosures. Finally there is an overhead pattern of tree structure and foliage, as related to constructed shelters, and the sky. These patterns can be unified within and/or among themselves.

The standard theory that cost increases with length of plant list is quite unfounded in fact. Prices on the great bulk of nursery stock run quite closely together for similar sizes and conditions of plants; only a few kinds fall at the extremes of cheapness or expensiveness. The contractor who is primarily interested in getting his money and getting off the job may whittle the price a little if he has fewer kinds to locate, but this seldom affects the overall cost greatly, on jobs of any size. It is one thing to meet the necessity of a programmed budget; that is part of the designer's responsibility. It is another thing to design in assumed cost differentials of a few cents or dollars, when that means whittling the quality of the job. In America, the richest country in the world, our design approaches are in the majority poverty-stricken (they call it "economy of means") by pressure of budget, or general "business-like" atmosphere. Who benefits from it? We all have to live in this environment we are sterilizing so persistently by design. NATIVES—One aspect of selection, which has considerable connection with maintenance, is the relation between native or indigenous and foreign or exotic plants. This has been a source of controversy in landscape circles ever since the elder Olmsted began the rescue of native species from the obscurity of local wild nature in the eastern U. S. The two extremes in this controversy have been approximately as follows: "A" rejects all local or regional wild plants as "weeds," common, vulgar, coarse, and so on; clears the land (perhaps a hangover from colonial days); and brings in refined garden species without reference to their original homeland. "B," on the other hand, rises in righteous indignation to the defense of the beauties of the local landscape and vegetation; condemns foreign introductions as disruptive of the local loveliness, inappropriate, blatant, gaudy, gauche, and so on, and as sickly exotics which will never be really healthy no matter how carefully pampered; whereas the lusty natives will grow and thrive with little or no care. This is another either/or controversy in which both sides have elements of both reason and prejudice. Here again the solution to the controversy lies in the selection and merging of the elements of reason, and the elimination of the elements of prejudice, from each side.

The range of plants useful to general landscape design extends from those surviving with reasonable health the normal local conditions—humanized-natural—through those surviving the local wild conditions. This entire range may include plants of both local and foreign origin. The variation in the proportioning of the two from the humanized to the wild habitat will depend on the degree of modification man finds necessary in the local climate and soil. Thus in a semi-arid climate like California the limiting factor on the use of native shrubs and trees in ordinary garden or park space is the amount of summer watering they will survive, in spite of their adaptation to summer-dryness. Certain technical problems of propagation and nursery handling also affect their availability and use. In the negative ecological zones the proportions of indigenous and introduced plants will vary considerably as we go from areas of intensive human cultural modification to wild areas; in the positive zones these proportions need not change greatly.

We come down, then, to specific problems of selecting the plant which will grow best while doing what we want it to do in a specific planned location. This selection will be based on our best analysis of soil and microclimate in that location, and our best prediction as to the future continuity of those conditions. Such selections should be made from the broadest possible list of available material. Restriction of the choice list is apt to eliminate the most relevant plant for a particular spot. The original nativity of the plants on the list is only relevant insofar as it may give us a clue to their adaptability to local conditions.

The esthetic aspects of the relation between native and foreign plants are more complex because more subjective. We must not fall into the trap of considering the local landscape we want to express as limited to that which existed before the white man came. The regional culture which exists at any given place and time is, as the geographers and planners point out, a complex of wild and humanized factors, and it is the humanizing which makes it a culture. At any specific given time—as 1950—when some of us decide to sit down to reconsider the situation in landscape design, we must consider the landscape we are living in, with its plant ecology—urban, rural, primeval—as a completed unit, a *fait accompli*, the site and the framework within which we must work. The past is history. We can learn from it, but no amount of nostalgia will bring it back.

In California today the landscape between urban and primeval is dominated more or less equally by the ragged verticality of the eucalyptus, a rankly persistent foreigner, and the sturdy horizontality of the live oak, an equally persistent native. These two forms help each other greatly by contrast in the landscape. Either dominant without the other would tend toward monotony of a thin or heavy cast. As a further example, we have four trees similar in use in the landscape: the live oak, a native; the olive, carob, and camphor, all exotics. The oak and the carob are similar in color, texture, and form; the carob is more limited by coolness. Olive and camphor are similar to the others in general form, but vary in color and texture: the one a billowy gray, the other a dappled light green. Their tolerance of heat and frost, hence their range, is somewhat greater than the others combined. The four together are rich and integral parts of the southwest tree culture; their origins are of only academic interest, except that they constitute a symbolic bridge from the old world of central and west Asia and the Mediterranean to the new world southwest.

ARRANGEMENT

Selection and arrangement have, of course, a mutually retroactive relation in the determination of the final planting. Selection of plants may be made to carry out the general space-form concepts of a freely-conceived plan, or a plan arrangement may be made to accommodate

106

specific plants or plant interests demanded in the program. Parallel emphasis on space and materials as being of equal importance to the highest development of landscape design insures the possibility of fine work from either beginning. However the problem is approached, programmed, and developed, at some point someone has to make a specific decision as to the exact placement of each and every plant, and as to the selection of the kind of plant for each and every location. No amount of naturalizing, informality, good fellowship, or soft-pencil scribbling can evade this necessity. Each plant has a specific relation to every other plant in its vicinity. If this relation is not carefully considered and directed at some time before the plants are actually put in the ground, it becomes merely haphazard.

The concept of plant form as inseparable from space form, of the two as mutually dependent factors which, in combination, produce something richer than their mere addition, will eliminate much of the clumsiness, redundance, and heaviness of traditional kinds of planting, and still allow proper expression to the romantic search for pictorial and decorative quality. It will reduce the total quantity of plants used, give each plant proportionately more importance and character, increase the amount and feeling of space, and give it a clarity of form and richness of expression seldom achieved out-of-doors. It will tend to increase the direct relation between people and plants, i.e., make it possible for people to establish more or less direct contact with each of the larger plants, rather than to bury many of them in "mass planting."

Even though plants do have a structural use in the sense of giving form to space, their use is governed by few such laws or problems as those which force the fabrication of a building as one continuous shell or framework. Plants don't have to hold each other up. The relations established between these plant units, the ground, and structural elements depend entirely upon the plan-and-space concept of the designer. The plants can be spaced so far apart as never to touch, always to remain detached circles. Or

they can be so crowded as to form continuous mats on the ground (lawns), masses above ground (screens) or canopies overhead (woods). They can be spaced regularly and geometrically, or completely irregularly, or any variation or combination between. Combinations of definite geometric plan skeletons with irregular clumps and groupings are both possible and desirable. Anything goes in plant grouping and arrangement if the people who are to see it like it, if it will grow well, and if the maintenance required is consistent with the nature of the plants and job program.

Arrangement of planting on most sites will proceed through the basic stages of surfacing, enclosure, shelter, and enrichment. These are the most practical stages, in terms of erosion control, screening, shade, and color. They are also the most esthetic stages in terms of the development of rich site-space form through the structural yet spatial use of plant material. In other words, we don't solve the practical problems first and then beautify them; we develop beautiful solutions for the practical problems in their broadest definition, which includes the human values needed in the landscape.

SURFACING—Organic surfacing is planting, commonly known as ground cover. This is essentially plants set so close together that the ground can't be seen from above, and, more important, the rain cannot hit it directly. There are four general types of planted surfacing: grass, or grass substitutes, which will take traffic and mowing; spreading trees, so spaced as to form complete coverage above the surface of the ground, and thus control volunteer growth and erosion without blocking traffic; ground cover, which will not take traffic, or will obstruct traffic (mat-formers, trailers, horizontal shrubs of any height); and cultivation, the continuous maintenance of specific areas of bare ground around selected and more or less changing flowers, vegetables, crops, or special shrubs or trees. These are all cheaper to install than hard paving or most inorganic surfacing, but most require maintenance which eventually adds up to offset the saving in installation.

Grass in small areas makes special surfaces

to sit or lie on, specially shaped carpets or patterns of green, which also reduce heat, glare, dust, noise. In large areas, such as parks and general public grounds, grass is the most pleasant and easily maintained ground surface control, establishing spacious continuity of surface (the meadow) and symbolic or ideological continuity with the grasses which are the primary control of the land surface of the earth. Use of grass beyond these primary kinds of areas, as on steep banks or extended tortuous strips and bays useless for sitting or pattern, tends to be an irrational and wasteful use of the material.

There is a considerable range in the finesse or refinement in treatment of grass areas, from the roughness of the natural wild meadow to the cultural precision of the bent-grass putting or bowling green. The ornamental counterpart of the latter, the *tapis vert*, the smooth lawn of one kind of grass, maintained by meticulous weeding, watering, fertilizing, mowing, and edging, is held up to us as the ideal, the peak objective for all grass-covered areas to aspire to. While this exact green carpet has its place, we are inclined to think it is a little mechanical in general application. Various mixes, of bluegrass and bent-grass and fine fescues, plus nurse crops and clover and daisies, seem to us to offer a richer palette for the grass area than the pure and unadulterated stand. They are, moreover, closer to a microcosm of the natural meadow, a more informal and easygoing surface. We have seen, in garden magazines, advocates of much more careful and complex miniatures of meadows, alpine and otherwise.

It has been said that a weed is merely a plant in the wrong place. Certainly in grass areas those invaders which grow in rosettes which destroy the continuity of the surface—as dandelions and plantains—or which freeze out and leave large bare patches in the lawns are definitely in the wrong place. But many mat-forming weeds in lawns—oxalis, chickweed, achillea—develop surfaces as pleasant as the grass itself. Dichondra, now popular as a grass substitute in the southwest, was once merely a "weed." The general idea of exploring the kinds of plants

which will adapt themselves to the special conditions of traffic, mowing (however high), and constant sprinkling in most lawn areas, seems to us most pregnant. The surface must be smooth enough and resistant enough for comfortable walking, it must maintain a fairly constant color and texture; within those limits there should be considerable room for experiment.

Mat, trailing, and shrub covers are useful on areas which will not be used for living purposes because of slope, bad location, or in some cases a surplus of land. Thus, fill and soft cut banks, or probably any slope greater than fifteen per cent, are most practically planted with such covers. They are apt to be more interesting in color and texture, and more tenacious and persistently green with less maintenance, than grasses for slope control. Particularly as the slopes become dry, sterile, or rocky, these mat, trailing, and shrub covers become more reliable. Around buildings they also reduce heat, dust, noise, and glare.

Beyond such practical considerations ground-cover plants constitute a design element of considerable importance. The larger kinds of shrubs which grow up to or above eye level, become also enclosure elements, obstructing or baffling vision as well as movement. Below eye level there is still a considerable variation in heights, say from three inches up to four feet, within which very rich and interesting junior spatial relations in form, color, and texture are possible. Here we begin to overlap the herbaceous border. The distinction between the two is simply that ground-cover planting is relatively permanent, herbaceous border planting relatively impermanent. The two can, of course, work together. Ground-cover plants, in the mat, trailer, and spreading shrub forms, run the gamut of textures from fine to coarse, and have also a considerable range in color of foliage, flower, and fruit, particularly in the milder regions. In addition to the more obvious examples these forms include such hardy elements as bulbs and tubers—day-lily and iris—and many succulents and cacti in the southwest. Thus, building on the French parterre, Victorian carpet bedding, modern German and Swiss alpine gardens, and the English color border, even as Burle Marx, we have broad opportunities for design in free modern three-dimensional patterns, below eye level where they can be understood. The ground-cover area is somewhat comparable to water in spatial terms, in that it tends to block physical but not visual movement. Bearing in mind the primary relation of people by quantity to space for living by square footage and cubage, such patterns can become rich contexts, surrounds, borders, and inserts in the general usable surfacing of grass and paving. Where, to conserve water or labor, grass is eliminated, paving, ground cover, and trees can be expanded and related in new proportions and patterns of shade, greenery, color, and spacious surface.

ENCLOSURE—As we move to the consideration of plant forms relevant to the enclosure of garden space at the sides, we move toward plants of more erect growth, whose vertical dimension tends to exceed their horizontal; whereas in ground-cover plants the horizontal tends to exceed the vertical. There are, of course, certain radial clump forms which fall between and can be used for either. Enclosure plants will have, in general, an equal or superior relation to the eye-level plane, that is, from five feet up. Their height, density, and evergreenness will be gauged by the need for screening, privacy, and protection from intrusion by life or wind. At a certain point in intensity of land use—as, probably, the fifty-foot or smaller backyard—planted screens become ineffective or unreliable as guarantors of privacy or controllers of movement. At this point structural control becomes functionally relevant, because reliable.

Within such conditions it will be seen that the range of choice in form, texture, and color is as broad as the available range of larger herbs, grasses, and shrubs, of trees, and of vines supported structurally. All the shrubbery border material—facer, filler, background—the hedge material, the smaller trees, the vines, the larger odds and ends that have been consigned to the wild garden, the cactus garden, the tropical or desert garden, or some other pigeon-hole, take

on new vitality, new interest, new richness, when we consider them thoroughly and creatively in relation to this concept of enclosure, of qualitative space formation.

When we combine this variety at expanded outdoor scale with the space-form concepts of modern art and architecture, based as they are at their best on careful distillation of the primary space-form relations of our world, new vistas and potentialities for beauty in the landscape open up before us. The free and creative organization of planes, masses, and structural patterns in space above the ground plane, as an abstract or diagrammatic basis for the development of actual practical plant and structure relations on the site, will exceed in the beauty and variety of its production any mechanically haphazard (informal) or haphazardly mechanical (formal) academic system now in use. The gamut of three-dimensional relations—rectangular, angular, circular, or more complex—is richer than any sterile axes, any "informal" sprinkling or squiggling, that has been offered to date.

As the demands of screening, privacy, and protection decrease, our range in choice of enclosure material will expand. The solid plant screen gives us primarily variations in color and texture of foliage. As its necessity for solidity recedes—as it becomes, perhaps, more playful or fantastic space elaboration within a general enclosure—variations in structural pattern, in relation of foliage to ground, and in fruit and flower color become part of the spatial palette.

SHELTER—The line between trees and shrubs is arbitrary, and there are many kinds which overlap it under varying conditions of growth. If we say that a tree is a plant which gets up high enough and spreads its branches widely enough for us to walk under them, we will find that there are single-trunked forms (as small flowering fruits or dwarf maples) which are not tall enough, or (as Lombardy poplars or Italian cypresses) broad enough to qualify. On the other hand there are many-stemmed forms—carobs, olives, privets, crepe myrtle—which do. Many of these can be either shrub or tree form, depending on soil, moisture, pruning, and so on. There are many good small tree or semi-tree forms which are commonly forced into the role of shrubs, with inevitable distortions from crowding and trimming. Likewise there are good large shrub forms which are often distorted by training into unhappy imitations of trees. Such distinctions come down to specific decisions with specific plants and cultural practices. Woody plants develop through juvenile, mature, and aged forms, and many of them may pass from shrub to tree form after the first or second of these. Thus the relation between shrub and tree forms is not really as simple as the nursery catalogs. It is a question of spacing, based on understanding of the relation between ultimate size and rate of growth of the specific plant, and of the distinction between trimming and pruning, which we will discuss under maintenance.

Definition of tree forms as those spreading foliage over our heads is a result of the classification of plants in terms of space relations. Shrubs give enclosure at the *sides* of our garden or park spaces, to any height, and with any degree of thickness or thinness. Trees give additional enclosure, or *shelter,* overhead. This again varies through all the degrees of darkness, heaviness, lightness, and thinness, plus the seasonal alternations of deciduous forms, plus the variations in structure from simple radial symmetry to complex several-trunked irregularity, plus the richness of flower or fruit in many kinds.

There is a specific functional value in deciduous trees, which we tend to ignore in our milder south and west zones in concentrating on evergreen material. This is the fact that they provide shade in the summer when it is needed, and let in the sun in winter when it is needed. This simple fact makes deciduous trees (sycamores, elms, maples) the most relevant large trees for use anywhere close to buildings (except perhaps on the north side) or over garden or park spaces which are to receive fairly intensive use. The space beneath the big evergreen tree, cool and breezy in the hot summer, becomes dank and forbidding during cold and wet winter months.

110

Certain aspects of the landscape are susceptible to wide and flexible manipulation, the health and comfort potentials of which have been scarcely tapped by contemporary designers. Two illustrations will suffice: the use of trees and use of lawns in urban areas. Above and beyond their beauty, the scientific use of deciduous trees will accomplish any or all of the following:

Deflect, absorb, and reduce the heat radiation. . . .

Reduce the free air temperatures. . . .

Filter the atmosphere. . . .

Reduce intensities and glare. . . .

Increase visual privacy. . . .

Reduce the transmission of airborne sound. . . .

In general, trees have a stabilizing effect upon their immediate surroundings, reducing all environmental extremes. Rudolph Geiger, in his excellent study on the micro-climate, found that a mixed forest growth of spruce, oak, and poplar cuts off sixty-nine percent of the sun's heat from the ground. He found that forests are cooler in summer, warmer in winter than clear land; and that a belt of trees would reduce wind velocities by as much as sixty-three percent. . . .

Certainly trees have been the friends of man ever since he first settled down on the land, providing him with shade and greenery, color and shelter, fruit and timber, and improving the local soil and climate in the process. We can scarcely improve on the many rich words which have been spoken and written in appreciation of trees. Our definition of them as elements both in space and enclosing space may seem somewhat arty or intellectual, but it will add a new dimension and a new coherence to their use in the landscape. At the scale of park, neighborhood, and community, trees become potentially the primary integrating and co-ordinating pattern, linking together buildings, roads and open space —architecture, engineering, and landscape— into a continuity of space pattern and ground organization impossible without them. This potential is seldom seen in actuality in our urban landscapes, but it is present in any well-developed rural landscape.

Many planners and architects feel that it is necessary or desirable to bring about and preserve a contrasting separation between town and country "to prevent the drowning of both in suburbia." In England Sharp, Colvin, and others have sought to achieve this separation by architectural integration of dwellings into multi-family or row houses, whose larger masses contrast sharply with the countryside and tend to emphasize the relative concentration of towns. This idea, however, is in conflict with the great American dream of a detached house for each family on an ample plot of ground. It is noteworthy that trees in organized patterns (not necessarily regular or geometric) furnish a way to resolve the contradiction. Used thus, they can pull together and give unity to the heterogeneous collection of single-family detached houses that make up our American neighborhoods, welding them into coherently integrated communities that stand out distinctly against the adjacent open lands.

The tall trees—poplars and elms and pines, eucalyptus and palms, cedar and cypress—make the major spatial backbone, the uplifting skeleton of our general tree patterns. The spreading, irregular or round-headed forms—oak and mulberry, camphor and olive, rubber and fig—make the secondary horizontal shelter or overhead enclosure pattern. The small trees—flowering fruits and citrus, birches and small palms and tall shrubs—make a third intimate detailed partial-enclosure pattern, the fanciful counterpoint, the final color and interest and richness. Trees, along with structures and vehicles, are the basic tools for establishing secure and stable scale relations between people and landscapes large or small, serene or picturesque. They provide measures with which the individual can determine sizes and distances, and thereby establish his relationship to the world around him.

Finally, we must reject that most childish of naïvetés: that the symmetrical tree with the prominent leader should be used "formally" (regularly), and the more irregular tree "informally" (irregularly). This is the kind of oversimplification which stops all design processes before they have fairly begun. We must contrast with this dictum the proposition that the most regular trees should be placed most irregularly on the ground, the most irregular in quite regular arrangements, and then go on

from there to the real rich complexities of spatial planting design.

The anarchy of tree pattern in our towns and cities is an expression of an anarchy of land use which is becoming socially wasteful and therefore obsolete. Control of street tree patterns within public rights-of-way is a beginning but merely accentuates the anarchy within the blocks. Truly democratic organization of our general community tree patterns, block by block and neighborhood by neighborhood, can be projected for an expanding future. Current spots of mechanical irregularity in parks, and of the sterile formality of authority, will be swallowed up in this tremendous tree symphony of the future. Designers of planting for housing projects and planned communities who have taken the easy way of the haphazard sprinkling of trees throughout the site have undoubtedly missed a golden opportunity to project such great patterns as these.

In ecological terms, the climax vegetation most suited to man's habitat is a varying combination of forest and savannah (tree-sprinkled grassland). As human sociology (ecology) moves toward the delicate and harmonious balance-in-motion of plant and animal ecology, the vegetative pattern of the urban environment will tend to lose its disorder, its distortion of material, its haphazard anarchy, and move likewise toward the coherence, the clarity, and the strength of the primeval and rural patterns. As this happens the rural pattern, too, will grow richer and stronger. In due time, as democratic processes achieve constantly greater portions of their potential for human welfare, and develop expanding stability and cultural expression in the landscape, the present scale of landscape values will tend to reverse itself. Instead of moving from the ugly city toward the peak of wilderness beauty, it will be possible to move from the wilderness, through constantly more magnificent and orderly rural refinements of the face of the earth, to urban communities composed of structures, paving, grass, shrubs and trees, which are rich, sparkling, crystalline nuclei in the web of spatial relations that surrounds the earth—peak expressions of the re-

111

integration of man and nature; the final conservation of the earth's resources.

PLATT

The Forest is a corporation of many kinds of plants.
The most conspicuous are trees, . . . The Forest is an
organism always in motion with all its parts inter-
related and acting on each other. These parts are
dense thickets; warm, dry, open hillsides; lakes and
streams; bogs and bottomlands; open glades with
carpets of wild flowers; moist, cool ravines deep in
ferns—all are within the Forest.

Even so, the humanized savannah-forest climax will be rich, varied, complex, yet orderly;
including the dwellings, the workspaces, and the
recreation spaces, indoors and out, of a healthy
democratic population. Even so, the magnificent
concepts of community pattern will not forget,
but rather will be based on, the relation of man,
woman, and child to tree, bush, flower bed, and
grass plot. The scale relation between open space
and the enclosing or organizing elements—the
horizontal and the vertical—will be primary.
The latter must not encroach on the former to
the point of claustrophobia, nor the former on
the latter to the point of agoraphobia. In the
negative ecological sections we push and promote post-climax tree growth out from organized centers in orderly patterns; in the positive
zones we push the subclimax grassland and
more refined open spaces out against and into
the resurgent forest blanket.

Surfacing, enclosure, and shelter are the primary elements of the garden, the park, or the
humanized landscape, even as they are of our
more refined structural habitations and workplaces. These establish the primary form, character, and space relations of the outdoor space.
If they are conceived with imagination and
sensitivity the space will be beautiful and satisfying with no more material added. If they are
conceived in haste and "practicality," or in the
sterile blindness of the academic approach, they
will be lucky to become pleasing by the grace of
the growth of the plants in them. Otherwise all
the "beautification," the flower borders and
foundation plants in the world will not save
them from dullness.

112

MAINTENANCE

The most sensitive selection, the most imaginative arrangement, are irrelevant without
adequate careful maintenance follow-through.
The key to the success of any planting program
is the closeness of its integration with the maintenance program which must carry it on to full
development. This program must expand as the
local soil and climate become less favorable to
the kind of development desired. This has been
the chief failing of public housing programs.
Certainly if maintenance is not a guaranteed part
of a landscape program we must go to some sort
of permanent structural control of surface and
enclosure, or to the limited range of plants
which can be depended upon to perform without
maintenance. Cultural considerations are the beginning, not the end, of planting design; but
first things must come first. Selection and
arrangement must be synchronized with maintenance through a determination of the amount
of maintenance that will be available, followed
by a careful check to see that the plans do not
demand more than this amount. Determination
of the areas to be left in the hands of nature,
those to be controlled by structural surfacing
and enclosure, and those to be developed with
planting which will require maintenance, must
be done in relation to this factor.

There is, of course, wide latitude in the
amounts of maintenance inherent in planting
design. A great deal of the ordinary kinds of
planting development forces the performance of
thoroughly unnecessary amounts. Little attention
has been paid to the design of planting for
minimum maintenance, especially in relation to
maximum effect. The squandering of cheap
labor for purposes of ostentation and conspicuous consumption for so many centuries has
gotten us into bad habits.

Plants should be selected which will grow well
in the given location without more care than can
be provided, and which will have room to grow
to their full ultimate size without persistent
laborious trimming. In general, a careful analysis of the nature and amount of maintenance
operations required for various kinds of plant-

ing should be made, and this analysis should become a part of the design process.

Elements requiring most maintenance work are:

a. Lawn—particularly in its more refined tapis vert forms, in small areas and complex shapes with edges difficult to trim.
b. Annual and perennial flowers
c. Trimmed hedges
d. Trimmed shrubs and trees
e. Plants requiring special soil, continuous watering, continuous spraying for pests

The low-maintenance answers to these are:

a. In small spaces, substitute ground covers, such as ivy and periwinkle, or paving for grass, except where you want it to walk and sit on. In areas large enough for power mowing grass is still the most practical and pleasant surface. At that scale, detail of mix is less important, intruders can naturalize, edges can be rough, mowing keeps both weeds and grass down, water and fertilizer keep the grass healthy.
b. For color and enrichment concentrate on relatively permanent perennials—such as geraniums and day-lilies—or colorful shrubs and trees, structural elements, sculpture, murals, et cetera.
c-d. Study plant growth to avoid laborious and deforming trimming, by selecting materials whose ultimate natural size and shape will be correct. Most plants, however, require occasional careful and intelligent pruning.
e. Skip these unless you can care for them.

Good practice in watering and weeding, cultivating and fertilizing, pruning and spraying, seeding, planting and transplanting, and all the other rational technical aspects of gardening, horticulture, and landscape maintenance vary from region to region and locale to locale. Much excellent reference material, many lectures, study groups, schools, and organizations are at hand to advise, help, and guide the neophyte in the garden. We need not try to parallel them here, in a design book, but we must stress and emphasize the dependence of most landscape design upon good maintenance. This does not necessarily mean a continuous horticultural program, but rather a programming of maintenance as part of the design, however simple or elaborate, and then the organization of the continuity of that maintenance. This is a simple principle which becomes most complex in practice.

The maintenance man who follows the landscape design originator is far more important and influential in the final success of the work than in any other creative field. Insofar as the landscape concept is based on planting design, the gardener or groundskeeper can promote it vigorously toward final maturity, or he can whittle and hack at it and finally destroy it, in whole or part. The fact that he does participate in the actual growth of the design, and very often has opportunities to make additions or adjustments which can either improve it or disrupt it, lends considerable justification to the more or less concealed conviction of many maintenance men (as well as nurserymen and horticulturists) that they are really artists themselves. This is not a problem to be solved by professional arrogance or smugness, nor by bluster or spite from the groundsman or plantsman. While personal solutions are worked out every day sooner or later this, like many other problems, will have to go through the mill of organized negotiations by duly selected representatives of the fields concerned.

Design and maintenance are more closely interrelated and interdependent in the landscape field than in any other of the arts. It is necessary to emphasize this relationship, and the unavoidable implication that garden and grounds maintenance is subject to the same sort of intensive, rational, scientific-artistic analysis and reorganization as has combed so persistently through such fields as furniture and industrial design. The landscape architect armed with such analytic perceptions should be able to go through any park, institution grounds, or large garden done with the traditional wasteful reliance on cheap labor, eliminate many man-hours of irrelevant, wasteful, and frustrating maintenance operations, and improve the esthetics of the planting in the process.

The question of neatness in the garden is another aspect of the maintenance problem. We have wide ranges in attitude: from the horticultural busybody who never lets a weed get past seed leaves, a dead leaf or twig lie on grass or terrace, or a dead flower remain in the border, to the sloven whose garden is overrun with weeds, brambles, animals and children. Desirable practice for most of us will obviously lie between these extremes. There is a relation between design for sound horticultural practice, and design to express a relation between man and nature. This is a relation between the neatness of the well-kept flower or vegetable garden and the neatness of "unspoiled shires of the forest . . . varied and balanced organisms" (Platt). Maintenance is neither good nor bad as a design control; it is simply a factor for analysis in the program. We can design landscape schemes for maximum maintenance or horticultural activity, and we can design landscape schemes for minimum maintenance; each extreme can be of equal esthetic quality and human livability.

The one maintenance activity which contains elements of artistic intuition and sensitivity, as well as of rational scientific analysis and experiment, is pruning. It requires intelligence and understanding of the material, while trimming requires little of either, merely the tools. The ultimate formal development of a plant, other things being equal, is entirely dependent upon the character of pruning it needs and receives. There are plants which will develop a mature specimen character with no pruning whatsoever, and there are those which will take no form at all without constant vigorous pruning. Most plants lie between these extremes. The frequency with which their needs are considered may be judged by the frequency with which one encounters shrubs which have matured all their innate qualities of form and character. The pruner should approach his material with all the care and circumspection exercised by a sculptor in approaching a block of stone.

The process is quite analogous: both consist in the removal of portions of the material to produce a more perfectly expressive form. It is only a short step from the experiments of the constructivist school of sculptors, to the intelligent pruning of plants. Pruning is an art requiring a great deal of thought and good judgment. Each plant has to be studied as an individual, have its esthetic possibilities analyzed, and then be given that treatment which will best further those possibilities.

CLASSIFICATION

Selection is based upon concepts of arrangement and maintenance worked out together. The tool for selection is the choice list or set of lists, classified in terms most relevant to the problems dealt with. The plant designer can, no more than the lawyer or the doctor, carry all the knowledge of all his tools and materials around in his head.

We must establish the importance of classification of our plant material in the terms of landscape design. Botanical classification, for absolute identification and understanding of plants in themselves, is in terms of the detailed technical structure of the plant, particularly the reproductive parts. In actual practice, "in the trade," plants are known and obtained by their generic and species names—two, in that order—followed sometimes by a third or varietal name. This is the procedure which is technically correct; but, all too often, we find plants identified by only one of these three names, or by common names which vary from region to region.

Ecological classification, for the understanding of the patterns of vegetation and their control in agriculture, horticulture, forestry, grazing and soil conservation; first in terms of survival adjustments, as developed by Raunkiaer and Braun-Blanquet; and then in terms of all the many practical local details of soil and water, temperature and wind, chemical and organic relations, pests and diseases, sun and shade, frost and pruning, transplanting and dividing; is basic to the practical esthetics (or esthetic practicality) of landscape design. "The

114

right plant in the right place," that final yard-stick for the success of any planting, is achieved only by a real integration of rational understanding and creative intuition.

Landscape classification, the final refined tool of the planting designer, must be in terms of the physical reality of the plant in the landscape for the average observer. That is, it must be in terms of ultimate size and rate of growth, form and structure, texture and color and fragrance, in all the manifold complexities of their endlessly varying interrelations. We must bring order out of the kaleidoscope in order to make it usable, but we must not lose the color and vitality of the material in doing so. Landscape classification must be based on local ecological classification, by regions and sub-regions, because the form of the plant is produced by the varying relations between heredity and environment. Trees and shrubs which are adaptable to more than one climatic region may develop different sizes and forms with variations in climate. Within one region variations in size and form also occur with changes in soil, water, and exposure which may stunt or encourage the plant. Thus we must classify plants for the landscape in terms of optimum cultural conditions, and must back that up with knowledge of the maximum and minimum variations from that optimum that can be expected of specific kinds. Some are widely flexible and adaptable (with more or less change in size and form); some very limited in range. Urban and primeval ecologies are similar today in that only the most adaptable plants survive in any quantity; rural ecology, based on more scientific and rational control of habitat factors, selects vegetation much more for production than for adaptability. Obviously even the rural pattern is tied to the basic conditions of the climate. In the future urban ecology may be as scientific as rural.

For examples of classifications see Hamblin, Hoyt, Taylor, Bailey, Rose, nursery catalogs. Landscape classifications, because of their esthetic or artistic content, which implies some subjective judgment, cannot be finally standardized, nor is that necessary. We have a hierarchy of specialization: all those concerned in any way with any plants (including landscape designers) must base themselves on botanical classification; all those concerned with plants growing in the ground, for whatever purpose (including landscape designers), must base themselves on ecological (horticultural) classification; all those concerned with the relation between growing plants and space for people to live in (landscape design) must base themselves on landscape classification. All of the examples above (except Rose) confuse these three levels.

ANIMALS IN THE LANDSCAPE

We cannot close this chapter without reference to that other half of biological science, zoology. If plants are the primary framework of landscape design, animals are one of its major enrichments. Think for a moment of the black Scottie, the red Irish setter, the spotted Dalmatian; Siamese and Persian cats; the flash and sparkle of aviaries; fine saddle horses, muscled work horses, golden Palominos; the pheasant, the rooster, the guinea hen, the swan; goldfish and frogs and dragonflies. Consideration of animals as design material implies both their use as elements of form, color, and movement for the enrichment of a space, and the development of areas and shelters necessary to them in a manner which will express the character of the animal, and provide it with an appropriate background.

115

CHAPTER XIII

ANTI-GRAVITY MATERIALS
STRUCTURAL ELEMENTS
OUT-OF-DOORS

Construction has been the physical manifestation of man's conquest of nature ever since the first crude sleeping platform was laced into the boughs of the jungle tree, the first skin tent pitched on the limitless steppe. This symbol of conquest expanded through history, as technology became more complex and population more concentrated, to the quantitative extreme of our urban agglomerations today.

The construction with which the landscape designer is usually concerned spans from minor architecture to minor engineering. That is, it may include small buildings, seldom completely enclosed; small bridges, retaining walls under six feet in height, earth-fill dams, and all the miscellaneous outdoor construction—steps and walls and paving, arbors and fences. There are landscape architects who do more architecture and more engineering, but they do it by becoming licensed in those professions, or by hiring licensed personnel. Within the bounding extremes of completely enclosed, wired, plumbed, and equipped buildings on the one hand, and more open structures of a high degree of technical complexity in design and function (transformer stations, large masonry dams and retaining walls, suspension or cantilever bridges) on the other, this variety of structures can expand to include all the types

of garden, park and recreation structures. It may include as well many more specialized: from private bath-houses, game rooms, and potting sheds, through all sorts of public park, bus stop, and commercial shelters, even to the fascinating forms of farm construction—barn, silo, chicken house, root cellar. These become a considerable accumulation of heterogeneous items, partly left over by the architect and engineer, partly projected as functional or esthetic needs by the client or landscape architect. This practical existing division of labor tends to negate or obscure that larger conception of spatial landscape design which must include all buildings and engineering elements in its integrated pattern. The logical projection of the thinking of all three space-planning professions tends to completely overlap by including the total landscape.

This division of labor with regard to structures in the landscape is a craft, as well as a technical, division. The elements and members of engineering construction are most completely industrialized, in both production and installation. Architects work in a complex and varying blend of handicraft installation of more or less industrial products. Landscape construction is almost entirely handicraft, that is, site-fabrication of raw materials. The extent

116

to which a really integrated industrial pre-fabrication of building parts, panels and assemblages might affect the highly specific problems of landscape work is one of our more fascinating, though utopian, fields for speculation.

We must avoid preconceptions as to structure being "unnatural" or merely practical in the landscape. Although, particularly as the scale expands, our dominant materials are earth and plants, the potential of structure in garden or park is lyric, plastic, and spatial in the highest degree. It is the final refinement and clarification of our environment. The quantity and character to be introduced will depend upon the conditions of the problem, including the architecture involved, and the judgment of the designer. Bearing in mind the essential dominance of his primary materials, he has at his disposal perhaps a wider range of materials than any other designer; everything from the roughest stone to the most polished metal and glass; in short, anything that will stand exposure. Walls of brick and stone and wood are familiar and charming; a progressive esthetic will grant equal favor to glass, concrete, and metal. A pergola of light metal members could achieve a grace impossible with stone or wood. Mirror walls in restricted garden areas would double the feeling of space; a justifiable illusion if honestly done. As Tunnard has said, concrete ramps, glass walls, and metal shelters will be thoroughly at home in the gardens of tomorrow.

There are wide gradations inherent in the degree of architectural refinement in landscape structures. These are typified by the range from painted surfaced wood to rough split stakes and shakes, from cut polished stone to dry walls of rough fieldstone. The extension of structural elements from buildings into the garden or landscape is one of the basic procedures for establishing the integration of structure and site. It is probably more relevant and successful than the reverse procedure, bringing plants into the house (although they are not mutually exclusive), because it involves an actual expansion of refined space,

rather than its submission to the forces of the surroundings. Such extrusion of structure from building into site can only be fully successful when designed and built with it in one operation, with the same materials, detailing, and craftsmanship carried through all construction. Specific examples in these pages will illustrate the difficulty of establishing structural extension from buildings completed without thought of such a possibility. Ordinarily the change from building to landscape construction means a change in degree and kind of skill, to more handicraft and less complex operations, and that change must be recognized in the designed relations between such primary and secondary construction.

In relation to the earth, structure is either founded on it, or assists in shaping it. The fact that the soil is a region of moisture and organic decay suggests a separation of structural materials into two kinds—frame and masonry. The frame type, of wood or metal, decays or corrodes from contact with soil, hence must be lifted or insulated from it. Masonry needs no insulation, is at home in the earth, links structure and site. The frame type is a more refined, abstract, "unnatural," off-the-earth construction, and should express that in its forms. Masonry is its bridge back to nature and should appear in some way integrated with both the frame structure and the site, tying them together. Redwood and other decay-resistant woods (by nature or by pressure-treatment), fall somewhere between these two extremes, standing contact with the earth but not as reliably as masonry. Their durability seems to be founded in the constancy of moisture and temperature relations in the local climate, also in specific soil conditions.

Frame structure, wood or metal—essentially a light, off-the-earth, spatial element—contrasts with the heavy, cold, massive back-to-earth stability of masonry elements. This is obvious at the level of handicraft construction. However, wood is not necessarily a light frame element; it may be used in very heavy, massive, sculptural forms, recalling the tremendous live weight of the bole or crown of the tree rather

117

than the tracery of branches and twigs which it supports. In ancient architecture the transition from heavy wood to stone construction was very gradual, and did not upset the continuity of form. Even as wood forms can quite appropriately approach the mass, if not the weight, of stone forms, so can concrete, that plastic synthetic stone, approach the thinness of light wood by virtue of metal reinforcing. The thin and elegant forms, structural and sculptural, which can be produced by refined reinforced concrete workmanship, are in truth a negation of the concept of heavy masonry. Indeed it is in modern reinforced concrete techniques that metal frame and concrete masonry are merged, resolve their contradictions, and unite their opposites in a material greater than the mere addition of its parents.

The analogy between plants and frame structures, both being free elements defying gravity and defining or clarifying space, is quite strong. Thus plants work with masonry, rock, or earth forms by contrast, lifting over them, even as frame structures do. It follows that plants should work with frame structures in the delineation of space in a parallel and supplementary way, whereas the contrasting relations with the earth materials are complementary. Therefore plants are naturally or organically decorative to masonry, rocks, and earth, but should have a spatial relation—space between them—with frame structures. Plants are now used almost entirely to decorate or conceal structure, whether frame or masonry. These are legitimate uses within a larger concept, but should become minor rather than dominant. Regular spacing and geometrical arrangements will establish relations with the forms of frame structures, and are not incompatible with free natural growth, informality, and other qualities associated with nature.

The functions of landscape construction are, in general, parallel to those of planting, but more intensified and at a smaller scale: privacy, windbreak, retaining cut-and-fill banks, connections between levels. Specific functions may include any number of semi-enclosed shelters, utility elements, and recreation facilities

118

of the scale of tennis courts and swimming pools.

The principal factor limiting construction in the landscape, especially at private garden scale, is cost. Structural surfacing and enclosure, paralleling planting in a more thorough and durable way, will always cost several times as much per unit measurement installed. However, this cost differential bulks largest at the point of installation. The continuity of maintenance labor and expense through the months and years will sooner or later bring the cost of the planting up to equal that of the construction. One does not have to mow a brick terrace. Even the Sunday morning labor of the home owner, however wholesome and healthful for him, has an hourly value which is cumulative.

The amount and kind of structure in garden or park is determined, then, partly by subjective esthetic factors, and more by the intensity of the specific practical problem—screening, drainage, surfacing—and the still more objective factor of the amount which can be budgeted for installation, immediate or in stages. Failing this last the client may, of course, buy the materials and do the installation himself.

A functional classification of structural elements as they relate to the solution of site space problems is essential as a frame of reference within which to examine specific details, however clever or sturdy. This classification, even as for planting, must base itself on the separation of flat from sloping sites or areas, and within each on the relations between surfacing, enclosure, shelter, change-of-level elements, and others more specialized.

On flat sites, or flat areas on sloping sites, inorganic *surfacing* can be classified as hard or soft, the latter being considerably cheaper but less stable. Soft surfacings include stabilizing the soil with various lime or cement techniques (depending on soil texture and local atmospheric humidity); fine decomposed rock or water-bound macadam of crushed rock, wet and rolled for stability; sand or gravel spread thin (but nevertheless movable and trackable); and various grades of asphaltic concrete, bitumuls, or macadam, that is, oil- or asphalt-bound surfaces. These are all relatively cheap surfaces which can be used to stabilize considerable areas where the maintenance of grass is impossible or undesirable. Their practical uses, for vehicular surfacing, playfields, farmyards, large walk-systems in parks and institution grounds, and so on, are obvious. They are probably more relevant in drier climates, where grass is more difficult and expensive to maintain, and volunteer weeds on bare surfaces are more easily controlled. For intimate use, private or public, these soft surfaces have to be handled with some care. All but asphalt are subject to surface loosening, and consequent tracking of dust and grit into buildings. Therefore they must be separated by considerable areas of hard paving, sufficient to clean off shoes before doors are entered. Asphaltic surfaces are clean and flexible to use; but one does encounter certain prejudices against them, because they are common to the streets which monopolize such an unnecessarily large percentage of our community areas. All of these soft surfaces are flexible as sheet materials which can be spread in any size or shape area. These are surfaces which are useful under trees, whose shade will keep them free of weeds and glare. Here the dry surfaces, which do not seal up the ground to air and moisture, are better for the trees. We can project with these soft surfaces an adaptation of the Mediterranean dry-country garden of paving, foliage, and water, in regions where the maintenance of grass becomes undesirable for one reason or another. The design problem in such a garden or park would be to break up the dry surface with enough areas or groups of ground cover, shrubs, and trees to compensate for the absence of green grass.

The hard surfacings are unit materials, or poured concrete. Units include brick, stone, tile, concrete blocks, stabilized adobe, and wood blocks. Wood decking can also be used outdoors in various size units, fixed or movable. Variations in pattern are matters of design ingenuity and workmanship. Fussy decorative Beaux Arts patterns should be rejected in favor of simpler relations of area and line that work with the general design concept of the outdoor space.

Contrasts or directional forms in the paving should reinforce, rather than disrupt, the general space relations. Sheets of overall pattern indicate specific units or blocks of garden space; lines or bands, of concrete or brick, give direction and connect units. Wood headers or grids can function either way.

Wood paving blocks and log sections are pleasant and useful for surfacing, provided adequate attention is given to the problems of decay. Milled blocks of heartwood, impregnated with creosote or other preservative, are most reliable. Log sections, however beautiful their pattern, are considerably less reliable because of their sapwood content. Both are most reliable in regions without extremes of heat, cold, or drought. They are best laid on a thick sand base, which will tend to equalize moisture relations. Experiments are now being developed with blocks of thick redwood bark, a waste material which should be quite durable. All such wood block pavers are laid with the grain vertical, and make a pleasant walking surface, of greater resilience than masonry. The cost is about comparable to flagstone; both run higher than brick or concrete.

Another useful surfacing technique is the introduction of resilient fibrous material—cork, wood chips, shredded redwood bark—into the soft sheet surfacings, macadam or fine rock, either by mixing or in layers. This adds resilience to the surface, and is most useful for children's play yards and athletic elements such as cinder tracks.

Poured concrete, as a sheet material, is more flexible for irregular areas than the unit pavers. There are many possibilities for giving it character by stain, tooling, and special aggregate. The final refinement, many-colored terrazzo, may seem too slick for landscape design, but that is merely a hangover from its commercial associations. Such brightness and richness can make an elegant foil for certain dark, bold, solid and rugged rock, plant or wood forms. The final refinement of terrazzo is mosaic paving, the contribution of a specialized artist.

Enclosure elements are subject to endless variation in detail through varying relations

119

of materials, design, ingenuity, common sense, and craftsmanship. They can be classified by spatial relation as follows:

Low, blocking movement but not vision
   Railings or open grids, of wood, metal, bamboo, tile, etc.
   Low solid walls and seats, of wood or masonry
   Pools and canals
Tall, blocking movement and some vision
   Rows of poles, with or without top rail
   Trellis or lattice frames, with or without glass or other fillers
   Louvered, split-wood, or other open-joint fences
   Masonry with openings
Tall, blocking movement and all vision
   Solid wood
   Solid masonry
   Other sheet material, as cemesto board and transite

It is well to separate vertical and horizontal planes by a change of material (but not always); and it is well to maintain continuity of a given unit or length of enclosure element by not breaking it up with panels and piers. Beyond that the forms and relations of such structures are not to be tied down in further words.

Shelter elements in the garden or landscape can be classified, parallel to our tree classification, as structures which establish horizontal planes overhead in addition to vertical elements off the ground. Within this definition we can distinguish between open structures (pergolas, arbors, lath-houses) and semi-closed structures (garden houses, bath-houses, casinos, pavilions, overlooks, and all the other miscellany of minor sheltering structures). Further cataloging of kinds is irrelevant, but some words as to the approach to their design are needed. That approach seems most productive today when based firmly on the general theory of modern architecture, stemming most typically from Frank Lloyd Wright in North America and the Bauhaus and International school in Europe, as modified by newer generations. That is, the approach to the design of landscape structures must be in terms of function, structure, and

space, rather than in terms of picture, precedent, and authentic details. The trail has been blazed, the perspective opened, by many, many modern architects. Such structures as the Barcelona pavilion (van der Rohe), Taliesin West (Frank Lloyd Wright), the Polish, Finnish, and Japanese pavilions at the Paris Fair of 1937, the Pavilion d'Esprit Nouveau (Corbusier), are typical prototypes insofar as landscape design is concerned. Suggestions are also plentiful in much exhibit and commercial interior work.

A further complication in landscape structures may come with the deliberate introduction of *changes in level* on flat sites, to increase the interest and richness of garden or park space. This can be done through earthwork: the development of excavations and mounds, of which golf traps are most typical. Structure may participate in the retention of some or all of the sides of such earth elements, thus passing into sunken gardens and raised terraces of increasingly structural or sculptural form. Beyond these, frame construction may be introduced to develop wooden and/or metal decks and towers, constructed off-grade but working with the general garden or park space. Such off-grade structures may of course also be developed in various sorts of masonry, including reinforced concrete.

On sloping sites, bearing in mind our earlier remarks about the need for some degree of leveling to make them useful, we find relevant all the above level area elements, plus certain special structural forms. These are primarily retaining elements at changes in level, and connecting elements between such levels. As they are irrevocably in contact with the soil, they must be of rock, masonry, or decay-resistant wood.

The need for retaining elements, which are apt to be quite costly, appears in general where areas are so limited that space cannot be allowed for planted banks at the normal angle of repose between levels, or where soil and moisture conditions make that angle quite unpredictable. At times, retaining elements may also be introduced for more esthetic objectives, as to expand a building into its site by the extension of

120

the foundations beyond the walls. Such structural assistance may take various forms which merge one into another. Beginning by incorporating rock with the face of a bank in a more or less natural (irregular) manner, the rock can be distributed with increasing regularity and evenness, up to a surfacing of pebbles sorted to size, or cobblestones, flagstones or masonry units. This can be combined with planting to develop any sort of pattern on the raised plane of the bank surface.

As slopes requiring retention approach the perpendicular without greatly exceeding six feet in height, such surfacing merges into dry walls and bulkheads. These are defined as retainers of open joint construction, which allows hydrostatic pressure (the principal nemesis of retaining walls) to dissipate itself by continuous water drainage. Typically they are constructed of rough stone or boulders, broken concrete, or other miscellaneous masonry elements. The planted dry wall is the happy and practical home for the collection of alpines, succulents, and similar small plants requiring sharp drainage. Bulkheads of redwood or other decay-resistant woods are satisfactory in cool, mild, moist regions; they become less reliable as extremes of temperature or moisture develop. For loose fills, open cribbing of precast concrete, railroad ties, or heavy durable timbers, constructed before or with the fill, is both practical and handsome, and is flexibly integrated with the natural ground surface. This, too, can be planted.

As the problem of bank retention grows more demanding, because of height, soft material, moisture, or intimacy, we go to solid masonry retaining walls. These have also their progression, from stone, brick, or concrete block, laid up in mortar, with or without reinforcing, to that last word in engineered reliability, the poured concrete wall. All of these must provide drainage release for water pressure. Below six feet and without complicating conditions, walls can be of the gravity type; solid masonry which stays in place by its own weight. With a higher bank, or with special conditions of soil or moisture, the reinforced vertical cantilever, on a broad footing which is held by fill behind the wall and resists overturning in front, is most reliable because most completely bonded, but must be carefully engineered.

This technical progression is likewise a progression in responsibility: dry construction is relatively simple and direct, can be worked out practically on the job with good workmen, and offers little resistance to water pressure, but it is limited in the heights and loads (varying stability of soils) it can carry. Wet masonry walls can be developed to meet practically any height and load requirements (a dam is a retaining wall for water) but, as they increase in size, their demands for technical excellence in design and installation (hence cost) increase with at least equal steps. Problems of retention are an apt field for structural ingenuity. Where there is space horizontally, the simple gravity or reinforced wall which is serpentine or sawtooth in plan will carry much greater loads than a straight wall.

Connections between levels, a special field for ingenuity and common sense in design, may be by steps, ramps, or their combination, ramped steps. These are functions of the relation between specific vertical and horizontal dimensions on the job. It is best, in terms of design scale and physical comfort, to spread such connections horizontally as much as possible. There is, however, a relation between such spreading for comfort and compressing for convenience. Often it is well to have both, to be able to go down fast but come up slowly. In steps the relation of six-inch riser to twelve-inch tread (in general the minimum slope indoors) should be the maximum slope outdoors. Outdoor steps are better looking and more comfortable if lower and broader. The maintenance of proper relations between tread and riser is of crucial importance. We have all experienced flights of monumental steps up which one could not walk in comfort, because this relation had gone awry. The direction or line of circulation, especially on broad steps, must also be analyzed. Is it perpendicular or diagonal? The general correct proportion in broadening from the six:twelve

121

ratio is about this: five-inch riser, fifteen-inch tread; four-inch riser, eighteen-inch tread; three-inch riser, twenty-four-inch tread. Beyond this we go to the ramped step, most typically risers three to six feet apart with some slope between. Maximums are six-inch risers and one-foot rise in six between. The maximum slope for a simple ramp is fifteen feet per hundred. Within these general relations many obvious interpolations and variations are possible, but the general proportional progression in broadening must be followed to produce functional connections. Steeper steps, even prefabricated iron spirals and wooden ship's ladders, may be used in special spots for quick connection or special space sensations, but only occasionally.

The materials for these inter-level connections are compounded of those for surfacing and those for retention. Thus we can have wood risers with grass, sand, or gravel treads, wood risers and treads on the ground, massive steps of log-sections or large blocks, and free-standing framed wooden steps. Likewise we can have masonry steps of solid blocks laid dry, smaller blocks, as brick, in mortar, and poured reinforced concrete.

Steps and paths must be generally considered as more than mere circulation elements. Design in those terms alone invariably makes them too small and cramped, more obvious in the general landscape because they are obviously out of scale with it. Most extreme example is the stepping stone, that coy speckling of little pieces of stone or concrete across lawns, too small and improperly spaced for walking, calling attention to themselves by their very self-conscious spottiness. This must not be confused with the legitimate and well-designed use of large pieces of stone or sections of concrete, distributed regularly or irregularly throughout grass or other softer areas. Scale is the primary problem. Steps, paths, and scattered units of paving must all be carefully related to both the scale of human use and the general scale of the specific landscape. This sense of form develops with experience. It cannot be codified, but the scale will generally be better if the elements are made larger rather than smaller. Steps, particularly,

are abstractions of natural contours, and can play a major role in both the sculptural expression of ground forms and the integration of buildings and outdoor construction with the site. Subjective resistance to "monumentality" tends to negate this potential.

A general problem in landscape construction, particularly of the most decentralized surfacing, enclosure, and change-of-level elements, is in the relation between the truly plumbed levels and verticals of the building and the more or less subtle gradations in slope of the site. The typical building operation establishes its own plane of reference, the floor level, and tends thereafter to proceed more or less abstractly, without reference to natural grade, until the problems of finished grading and drainage demand solution. This general problem must be solved by very thorough analysis of the exact manner in which the space about the building will be used and experienced by people. If the fence or wall will be seen primarily against or in close relation to the building, then it should be truly leveled, even if that demands certain structural complications. If seen primarily in relation to ground forms, or partially leveled terraces, then it can quite safely follow those slopes if they are under 4 or 5 per cent. Beyond that, with steeper slopes, the fence or wall should probably either be stepped or planted out; there is something very disquieting about a vertically serpentine structure, until it approaches the monumental scale of the Great Wall of China. When the structure is seen in relation to both building level and slight ground slopes the problem becomes quite complex; sometimes the difference may be split; sometimes stepped levels must be developed.

There is a point, varying from job to job, beyond which the true verticality and horizontality of the building or comparable architectural element must not be softened or muddled. Sometimes almost indefinite extensions of the building structure into the site are desirable, particularly on flat land. As slopes develop, such extensions become increasingly difficult, and must not be allowed to destroy the stable clarity of the main structure. This is a problem which

122

each designer must work out for himself, on each job.

The preservation of true, or nearly true, horizontal and vertical relations is no matter of abstract esthetics. It is of primary importance to the sense of equilibrium, hence of stability or repose, of each person involved. Our negative relation to the vertical pull of gravity is one of the primary conditioners of our lives and space experiences.

Special elements in landscape construction are quite various in specific character. Mention of a few will indicate the general spread. Here again detailed design is a relation between technical understanding, common sense, ingenuity, and sense of plastic or structural form. These special problems include:

Drainage—Surface and sub-surface, as discussed under earthwork. These are important functional structures of a minor engineering character, and information on their design is available in any good technical handbook.

Furnishing and Equipment—The garden which is to be lived in has these problems, even as the house, although in much simpler form. Here too we must choose between built-in furniture (seats, tables, and so on) designed to fit the general garden scheme and our standards of form, and the many miscellaneous varieties of wood and metal garden furniture, mostly clumsy if comfortable, some atrocious by any standards. It is as difficult to find good outdoor furniture, combining comfort with fine plastic form, as indoor. Most of the offerings are clumsy, cold, or corny. The special problems of design for exposure to all weather, and to the roughness of outdoor usage, have been attacked by only a few designers, notably Hardoy, Royston, and Van Keppel-Green.

The barbecue-fireplace, in all its various simplifications and complications, is undoubtedly the single most complete and consistent source of form monstrosities in landscape construction. As commonly built, of stone, brick, concrete, or all three, in all their massive obtrusiveness, it dominates every small garden into which it sails or is dropped with the effortless gaucherie of the overdressed and overjeweled dowager at the Junior League party. These structures are the epitome of the esthetic incompetence of practicalism, and of the bungling mischief it wreaks in the landscape. Those who feel themselves coming under the spell of the slick barbecue department at the big downtown store, of those fetching stories in the garden magazines, of the general back-to-the-wilderness-campfire-in-your-own-backyard romanticism should think twice, and then twice again, before phoning the local brickyard or mason. Too many elaborate barbecue fireplaces have turned out to be merely oversize incinerators.

All of which is not to say that cooking and eating outdoors in your own garden may not be one of your most re-creative activities. Careful analysis of certain problems of function and form should first be made, however. Such an element presents a problem of design in specific detailed functional relations, in good masonry and flue forms, and in fine plastic or sculptural forms, in relation to the general form of the garden or park. If generally visible it can become the final vitalizing enrichment, or the complete disrupter, of the landscape conception.

Service Area—The clotheslines, the garbage can or cans, and the incinerator are the orphans of most residential developments. No one thinks of them before the house is built, and often not until the family moves in, and then they become haphazard and obtrusive, the touch we think of as slummy. Even these service elements have both a practical and an esthetic aspect. Secluded in the service yard which is planned for them they can be straightforward and functional. How many feet of line does your family need? In a tree, a reel, or stationary tees? If the latter, do you want them to crank up and down? While the service yard of adequate size is the most satisfactory home for these elements, they can be fitted into more restricted spaces. Clotheslines, as sets of taut horizontal wires at head-height, can become parts of more fanciful and elegant arbor-screen constructions. Patented sunken garbage-can units are unobtrusive, and incinerators can be designed and built as well as, or with, barbecue-fireplace units. With all such service facilities, adequate

123

size and space is the primary requisite to maintaining them useful and clean. This has proved particularly true in group housing developments, public or private. At the expanded scale of park or institution this service orphan becomes the maintenance or corporation yard.

Recreation—In terms of active play provision for recreation includes a great variety of specific field and court spaces, equipment and apparatus, and such special elements as swimming pools. For most of these, quite specific standards have been established by recreation authorities, and these are available in reference works, as well as the catalogs of reputable equipment distributors. While the functional requirements of these elements are rather rigid and binding on the forms of their arrangement in plan, there is still ample room for the exercise of badly-needed imagination in recreation planning and design. The recreation field has the same tendency toward bureaucracy and dogmatism that is exhibited by the park field. The planning of game courts and fields in proper relation to one another and to sun and winds, and the expression of this planning in the third dimension with such elements as bleachers and field houses, backstops and screens, trees and hedges, can produce spatial arrangements of a high order of richness and interest. The development of play apparatus for children of all ages has become quite mechanical, especially in its blindness to the needs of children for creative participation in the forms and arrangements of their play. The complaint of the manager of a planned community, overheard by the writer some years back, to the effect that the children of his community seemed to prefer the town dump to their carefully planned recreation facilities is indicative of a failure to provide creative outlets. There is plenty of room in the apparatus and equipment field for such intensive design research and creation as has produced fine modern furniture. The sculptor Noguchi has done pioneering work in this direction, as well as in developing imaginative plastic contoured play areas and settings for such apparatus. Even public swimming and diving pools, rigid though their functional require-

ments may be, have numerous plastic possibilities beyond the standard rectangular layouts which only serve to confuse swimming and diving activities. The self-righteousness of the unimaginative recreation "expert" who makes his plans from the catalogs of the supply houses is as obsolete as the self-righteousness of the park planner whose tree arrangements appear to have been scattered from an airplane.

Work Spaces—These include a great variety of outbuildings and functional exedras of many sorts, up to the ultimate functionalism of farm structures: potting sheds and propagating yards; glass houses and lath houses; storage space for tools, material, play equipment, outdoor furniture, and all the other miscellaneous impedimenta which accumulates about most homes. The outdoor storage wall developed by John Funk, architect, an extension of brilliant work indoors by George Nelson, becomes relevant here. This must solve the perennial question of where to keep the lawn mower and the garden hose or hoses, so that they will be most accessible to spaces where they are needed.

UNITY—With all outdoor structural elements the dominant unity of the specific space or spaces, garden or park, for which they are projected must be borne in mind. The landscape, as an overall comprehensive concept, must determine the form and character of the elements in it, even as the play determines the cast of characters. Otherwise, if they are done for their own sakes alone, we get what we have generally today in homes and streets: a nerve-racking jumble of completely unrelated and incompatible elements.

There are two general sources of form or points of view from which we approach the question of structure in the landscape: constructivism and practical technique; fantasy and know-how. Constructivism is that particular form of modern art which works between architecture, sculpture and industrial design, by using various combinations of refined structural members and parts in more or less abstract, functionless, structuro-sculptural arrangements. These are generally of an open character, enclosing considerable space within their patterns.

They merge by degrees with light metal sculptures, Calder mobiles and Archipenko's concave-convex relations, and through them with stone and wood sculpture of considerable spatial content, as that of Henry Moore and Noguchi. On the other hand, they merge by easy degrees with both the light fantastique of the International and Redwood schools, and the more solid and plastic forms of the followers of Wright. Likewise they merge equally easily into the many precisely refined functional (or streamlined) forms and polished synthetic materials of industrial design. (See Biederman.) In landscape construction, falling as it does quite normally between function and form for their own sakes, the ideas of constructivism establish a practically permanent usefulness, in the continuous struggle to merge the contradictory ideas of pure form and pure function, and get from them something greater than both. This is a continuation of the historical struggle at the more static sculpturo-structural level, which was responsible for all the originally fine garden elements—Italian caryatids; Moorish tiled pools; Spanish carved grilles; French treillage; Japanese rockwork, water basins, and lanterns; Chinese gateways—which have accumulated into the constipation of eclecticism.

Practical technical know-how teaches us that structural design is not plastic; that is, cannot be freely formed; and is not merely an expression of the nature of the materials, important though that is. It is that and much more: a science and an art of exploiting the properties of those materials to their limits, by incorporating them in a system of variously connected members, which spans and encloses space and achieves equilibrium which is static but may seem dynamic. Structural design has its own laws, its own principles, the meat of architecture and engineering. These are best exemplified by sound handbooks, like Gay and Parker's *Mechanics of Materials:*

GAY AND PARKER

Architecture employs in its structures only forces which are at rest. All the forces which act upon the structural framework of a building or upon any of its parts are consequently in equilibrium. It is well, then, first to consider briefly the laws of statics or the science which treats of forces in equilibrium.
A stress may be defined as an internal resistance that balances an external force. A unit stress is a stress per unit of area. When a force acts upon a member, a change in shape or volume of the member results. This alteration is called DEFORMATION. . . .
The stresses which occur most frequently in structural members are TENSION, COMPRESSION and SHEAR.

LIGHTING—A special impact of the industrial revolution on garden and landscape has been the development of artificial outdoor lighting. Lighting in the garden is a refined and intimate problem, whose possibilities have been explored both practically and romantically. The practical problems are those of giving light where it is needed, at the right strength, without at any time shining it directly into the eyes of people in the garden, and in places to which conduits can be run inconspicuously. The romantic or plastic possibilities are pictorial and dramatic in the highest degree: the spotlighting of special plants, the silhouetting of trees and shrubs, the bringing out of special colors, the use of various colored lights, the control of light horizontally or vertically in quite precise forms, light through glass and water—all that kind of elaborate chiaroscuro, that electric stage-setting, which has been the property of indoor lighting experts, in theater and movie, bar and night club, for so long. Outdoor lighting is expensive and technically complicated, but full of great possibilities for spatial drama in the night. It shades off into those more transitory spectacles of fireworks and lights which accompany festivals and fairs and holidays. Little has yet been done with the design of fixtures comparable to good modern indoor fixtures. Rather the outdoor lighting men tend persistently and aggressively toward bronze lily pads, frogs with lights in their mouths, and strange lantern forms of uncertain origin. Straight commercial fixtures are in general better than any of these.
COLOR—One further aspect of processed structural materials in garden or landscape is the use of synthetic color in the form of paints or stains. This is a special and complex field of design. It has been explored with considerable thoroughness, if we are to judge by the volume of printed

125

theoretical material, by painters, interior designers, industrial designers, advertising men, sales managers, industrial engineers, psychologists, architects, and so on. And yet the general physical habitat of the American people, even at its more comfortable levels, is strangely bare of color; strangely dull, flat, neutral, barren, grayed, or pastelled. The fear of color which seems so evident in outdoor "design in good taste" is perhaps a reaction and shrinking from those color orgies perpetrated by advertising and commercial design in general. Parallel to this is that kind of dull snobbery which calls clear, bright, or strong colors vulgar, and classes those who take pleasure in them as common and coarse. History tells us that the fine old temples of Greece and China and many other ancient civilizations (more primitive and child-like than ours?) were gaily and brightly painted in clear primary colors. The delicate sensitivity of the eclectic mind is here made evident: it has given us the form without the rude, gaudy color. Such are the advances of civilization.

There is a great body of theoretical material on color, scientific, practical, and esthetic, to which reference can be made. Munsell's color qualities (hue is the name of a color; value is the light of a color; chroma is the strength of a color) provide a common language for rational discussion. Beyond that we suggest reference to Guptill, Moholy-Nagy, and Kepes, among others.

As thinking on the spatial quality of colors becomes involved with all the textural-color complexities of structural materials, plants, earth, rocks, and water, the problems of research and analysis become infinitely diverse and complex. The specific relations between pigment colors and flower, fruit, and foliage colors are most delicate, and can only be worked out on the spot. Regional variations in the quality and intensity of atmospheric light will tend to render specific solutions primarily local in their relevance. All of this may tend to suggest that we forget the problem of pigment or synthetic color in the landscape. But we must make ourselves aware of the fields of spatial experience into which exploration is possible and relevant

to our general field of landscape design, because we can never tell when such exploration may suddenly become an implicit need of some specific field of work in which we find ourselves.

The practical aspect of the question of pigment color in the landscape is, of course, to what do we apply it? We have agreed with the modern architects in stressing the importance of maintaining the character of frame and masonry structural materials. Thus, ideally, brick, stone, and wood should not be painted. Paint seems foreign to concrete, and often shows it by peeling. This leaves only stucco, that completely characterless material, to serve as a vehicle for painted color. However, the theory which is respected with 100 per cent literalism becomes a dogma, and we cannot design by dogma or fixed rules. One bridge between the need for color and the need for maintenance of the surface quality of wood or concrete is the use of colored stains, which soak in rather than seal the surface, and give color without changing the texture of concrete, or destroying the grain pattern of the wood. Again, much paint color is apt to seem harsh in garden or park: a little trim color, on fence cap or bench, will go a long way toward giving that sparkle we are in search of. Other industrial sheet materials, such as cemesto board and corrugated transite, may suddenly become relevant vehicles for color where we feel its need.

Of course the ultimate refinement of the use of pigment in the landscape is the painting applied directly to a structural wall. The art of mural painting, fresco or otherwise, seems somewhat foreign and strange to us, lost since the Renaissance, and now a startling intrusion into our quiet garden spaces. But the art has remained alive; has indeed passed through a rebirth in our neighbor south of the border, and here in North America such artists as Falkenstein and Refregier are giving it a specifically sound, modern, northern social expression. It is not impossible to project the expansion of great mural painting from post offices into our open spaces, our parks and gardens. The relation between subject matter and abstraction, that great semantic struggle, is well exemplified by the

126

work of the two artists mentioned. One is led naturally also from murals (or shall we say spatial color relations on wall planes, with or without specific content) to the rich potential inherent in mosaic, expressed so boldly for us in Brazilian azulejo work.

Thus the range in use of structural elements, and their auxiliaries such as paint, runs in park and garden from the indispensably practical to the experimentally esthetic. In the general landscape they will be minor in quantity outside of specific buildings and engineering structures, although by their precision in form they tend toward dominance of considerably greater quantities of softer or looser natural forms around them. In small gardens, or in central intensively used public spaces, they may control the forms of considerable volumes of outdoor space with complete architectural clarity. Consider the great series of public squares and plazas mentioned earlier. Always the undercurrent of structure in the landscape will be the resolution of the apparent contradiction between refined processed and unrefined natural forms.

Japanese pavilion San Francisco World's Fair: designer unknown

PRACTICE

CHAPTER XIV

SPECIFIC SITE CONDITIONS

The richness and wonder of the world we live in come from the endlessness of its physical variety, within the overall unity of the generalized morphology of the landscape—cities and towns, factories and farms, hills and valleys, mountains and plains, forests and grassland. Wherever there is vitality in the forms and arrangements of our environment, it is there because of the solution of problems on their own terms and conditions. Conversely, wherever we find sterility we find the preconceived parti, the mechanical plan (whether formal or informal), laid down with little or no attention to local color, topography, needs, desires, and so on. Every site is different, every region is different, every climate is different: hence every problem in the organization of space on the land must be solved individually, independently, on its own terms, though drawing from the reservoir of experience and theory built up on all jobs.

The individuality of each job, assuming it to be identified in some way with its regional culture, depends upon the sensitivity and clarity of its expression of specific site conditions (topography, climate, existing plants, structures, water, rocks, character of surrounding land use) and the needs and desires of its clients. Sites tend to vary almost as much as people. The architect gets these two together

and adds his own special variant solution. Thus every problem presented to the landscape architect, particularly at single domestic scale, is bound to be different. And yet all are united by certain general contexts: generalized units of average humidity, temperature range, topography, and social structure; the three typical "natural" landscapes within which we may find ourselves working (urban, rural, primeval); and the three typical client relations we may find—private domestic client direct; private commercial client, self-appointed to represent all the people who will use his facilities; and the public client, the administrator appointed by the elected representative of the public. In the last case the administrator, whatever his personal attitudes, actually represents the particular combination of political pressures which has put the official who appointed him in office.

In these specific situations there is infinite variation, within the main divisions of flat or sloping land. Thus we have small city lots, or city parks or institution grounds with completely urban surroundings; the same elements in the suburbs, where the urban blanket thins out and more natural elements are able to poke through; country estates, in wild or agricultural land, where the acreage owned exceeds the area needed for development; the agricultural countryside, usually flat or gently rolling, where man develops new forms with natural elements; and finally the great and dominant forms of wild nature—mountains, forests and jungles, deserts and great plains, strong hills and valleys, streams, rivers, lakes and oceans and their shores—which we can respect and admire without being apologetic through rusticity, and where indeed our own forms can only become appropriate through comparable strength, clarity and richness. Always our primary rule must be the development and extraction of the maximum specific quality latent in site and surroundings, before or parallel with the application of broader inspirations from our general background.

The landscape architect must consider first the nature of the building and the site as given to him to develop. These relations alone have endless variants: the symmetrical Beaux Arts palace on the flat or gently sloping site, beloved of the Harvard school; the rustic stone and log cabin in woods or rocks, beloved of the romantics; the sparse, rich, or sparkling elegance of the Le Corbusier or van der Rohe type modern house, on meadow or hillside; the Williamsburg Colonial on the city lot; the contractor's dingbat, of any size from 500 to 5,000 square feet, on any lot; the civilized barniness, or the rusticated elegance, of the California Redwood school, among the dry wild oats or chaparral; the carefully and organically related sculptural richness of Frank Lloyd Wright, at every scale of landscape from the spread of Arizona desert or Wisconsin prairie to the miniature rocky hillsides of New England.

The danger of words is that they can distort and distract. They can make the haphazard informal park sound like the beauty of all nature, the stuffy formal garden sound like magnificent clarity. Drawings and photographs are somewhat more accurate, but only in relation to the reader's ability to interpret them and synthesize them. They can never convey the real character of the job, although they may convey certain conceptions of form and arrangement on an intellectual level. One can no more experience a completed job by proxy than one can solve the

raw land problem without visiting the site. On the other hand, we all see the world around us through glasses that have been ground by our education, our experiences, our mental growth or lack of it. Therefore it is our hope that the words in this volume may have added a new dimension to the reader's vision. Perhaps from now on he will look at gardens and landscapes—formal or informal, traditional or modern, old or new, good or bad—with a deeper perception.

Generalizations must develop specific forms by application at specific times and places. We have presented a general theory in words on the general aspects of all the important elements in our field: Space, People, Materials. Now we must deal with specific conditions. In words even this is a generalization of sites; small, medium, large; flat, sloping, steep; private or group housing; public buildings; parks. The Specific Theory for each site is embodied in the plan for that site. It should embody complete concepts of specific existing site conditions and site-space, specific people, specific material as selected or available. It involves the resolution of specific contradictions between space and materials, space and people (too much or too little of either), any or all of these three and the site.

On the question of Inspiration (where do you get those forms? how do you arrive at them?) which is sure to arise, we can only say this: Designers must draw from, and express, the world they live in, the world which feeds, shelters, and clothes them. This is true in its maximum interpretation. There is no other source of inspiration; those who express only themselves have little to say. Talents being equal, the richness and strength of designers' work will increase with their understanding of, and sympathy for, the world. Even great talents cannot avoid this responsibility; in fact, their greatness is usually a measure of their understanding of at least some selected aspects of the world. It is true that selection among the multitudinous manifestations and phenomena of our world is imperative. Some are emergent, some are dominant, some are recessive. But such

132

selection, too, must be based on understanding and sympathy.

What, then, more specifically, are the main sources of inspiration for good landscape design? First, the general elements outlined hereinbefore: People (all the people, not selected sections); Space (analysis of the experience of partially or wholly enclosed space wherever it is encountered); and Materials (the whole tremendous palette of weatherproof structural elements, earth, rocks, water, and plants). Second, the history of landscape design; that is, what has been done in the world before now. Third, the general cultural heritage of mankind. There are other sources of inspiration which cannot be ignored: all the wonder and beauty of wild nature; all the rich and varied production of modern painting, modern sculpture, and modern architecture; all the complex pattern of an industrial civilization, where it has not been tainted or sterilized by the commercial touch—dams, bridges, oil refineries, electric transmission stations, earth-moving machinery—as well as assorted miscellaneous elements—women's hats, New Orleans jazz, folk singing—which are clear expressions of different sections of the social structure for those who can read.

It may be noted that the practice illustrated is not entirely consistent with, or does not entirely live up to, the theory outlined in this book. This is as it should be. If our practice were as good as our theory something would be wrong with the latter. That marks the beginning of decadence. Practice can seldom equal theory, even as the present can seldom equal the future. Theory is the projection of the future from the present and its past; practice is the expansion of the past in the present.

133

Halberstadt-Martin
figure by Falkenstein

GARDENS

"Outdoor space around private homes, sufficiently enclosed or isolated for the private use of the individual families." As an arbitrary classification we are calling these Small which are under ⅛ acre (total lot size); Medium from ⅛ to ½ acre; Large from ½ to one acre; and Estates or Farms over one acre. Further subdivision must be in terms of topography: Flat under 4 per cent slope; Steep over 10 per cent; and Intermediate all slopes or combinations between.

Most discussion of home planning ends with the design and construction of the house. However, this is really only half the problem, and it must be tied in with the other half, the land-, site-, or garden-use problem, which completes the private home problem. This must consider the relation of the house to the site topography and space, and to the natural materials or other structural elements which may be relevant to its

development. The structural problem and the land-use problem tend to be solved in a spirit of mutual exclusiveness (this has resulted in the former being much closer to technical solution than the latter) whereas they really have to be solved together, as one problem, because each reacts on the other.

The building of a house is essentially the enclosure of a certain cubic volume of air space in order to make it more usable to people by keeping rain, insects, and vermin out, controlling the temperature, light, privacy, et cetera. That is, home is thought of as a house, and a house is thought of as a shelter for convenient living (by most of us at least). This requires, in most parts of the world, complete structural enclosure of space, with certain definite objectives —the control of:

precipitation (rain and snow)
humidity

134

temperature (heat and cold)

light

cleanliness

vermin

sanitation

air circulation.

Families are variable, and so are their needs and desires. However, most home-planning seems to be based on the following main elements:

Public access, by foot and by car—garage, porch or stoop, entrance or vestibule.

General living space—living room, dining room, rumpus room, hobby room, library, music room, play room.

Private living space—bedroom, bath, study.

Workspace—kitchen, laundry, workshop, study, studio.

AS FITCH SAYS

The contemporary designer runs the risk of accepting electrical air filters as a satisfactory substitute for clean fresh air; of feeling that electrically operated louvers are preferable to natural foliage; of preferring sound insulation to plain ordinary silence . . . this is no adequate basis for the mechanistic conclusion that we don't need nature any more. . . . It is rather the necessity for integrating the two at the highest possible level. . . .

When one buys a lot one buys a cube of air space to live in, the bottom side or floor of which is the earth of the lot. It is a mistake to follow the standard practice of designing the house as a box of living space, placing it more or less appropriately ON the lot, and then landscaping it (adding beautification, or exterior decoration). It is more sensible, and productive of better results for the residents, to plan the use of the entire lot at once, as a co-ordinated series of rationally connected and related indoor and outdoor rooms. This is the only way to avoid the waste and inconvenience of the majority of our homes—useless side-yard and driveway space, front yards larger than necessary, rear garden accessible only through kitchen and laundry porch, clothes-lines and garbage cans cluttering up the back-yard and too far from kitchen and laundry, no place for kids to play without damaging the garden, etc. An optimum solution of the home-planning problem must accept the basic premise that the four general units enumerated above are really indoor-outdoor units, because they all require complementing or supplementing by outdoor elements, about as follows:

Public approach or access—front yard or lawn, walk, driveway.

General living—outdoor porch, terrace, patio, court, or garden; space for games.

Private living—sleeping-porch, private sun-traps.

Workspace—service yard: drying, garbage, wood and general clutter, kids' play yard (including garage in wet weather), growing cut flowers and vegetables.

The modern house provides for the mechanics of civilized living—sleeping, eating, entertaining, cleansing, studying, relaxing. But this does not mean that it provides a complete environment for life. An extension into outdoor space, an integration with its environment, a union with the processes of nature, are necessary to complete it. The garden must be something more than an "outdoor living room" if it is to be worthy of its name. It must do things to its possessor—amuse him, stimulate him, delight him, relax him—before its existence can be justified. It must provide him with that revitalizing contact with the growth of plants and the fecundity of the earth, without which man loses his strength and his inspiration. It must, like a bride, be perennially attractive, perennially gay, perennially delightful. Every visit to it must be an adventure and an experience. Gardens must be the homes of delight, of gayety, of fantasy, of imagination, of adventure, as well as of relaxation and repose. Every resource of imagination and ingenuity must be called upon to make them not only livable, functional, and spatial; but delightful, entertaining, and amusing. Maximum delight, minimum maintenance; every detail right, every plant a specimen, every feature a thing of beauty and a joy forever.

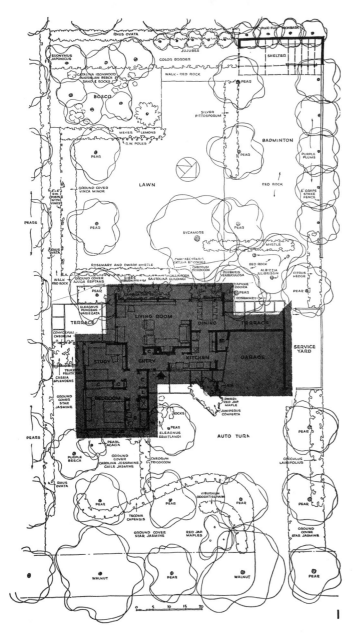

1

2

Childress-Halberstadt

GARDEN IN MENLO PARK, CALIFORNIA   1940

Architect—Frederick L. Langhorst
Photography—Stone, Fein, Halberstadt
(Courtesy Sunset Magazine)

3

4

5

1–10—Site a medium-sized, flat lot in a recently subdivided pear orchard. Surroundings rural, becoming suburban. House new, redwood with shingle roof, well planned and well placed in relation to lot space and existing pear trees. Paved entrance court combines approach by car and afoot, and guest parking. Balance of front yard in rough ground cover planting and rough hedges. . . . Living and dining spaces relate easily and naturally to large rear garden, organized with straight rough hedges and structural extensions from the house into a kind of free rectangularity, reminiscent of de Stijl-van der Rohe planning. Shady area and badminton court surfaced with fine rolled crushed rock. Pergola and split redwood fence extend house into garden on dining room side. From the open center lawn one passes behind one rough hedge to a sanded rectangle, where strong-growing Australian beeches (Eucalyptus polyanthemos) will make a small bosco. Posts and trellis were planned to extend the house into the garden on this side. Maximum use was made of the existing pear trees, eliminating them only when necessary to open up the garden, and adding some other larger trees for shade and interest.

Special notes:

5—Pear, pergola, fence, hedge of Pittosporum tobira variegata.

2—Dining terrace, pear, Daphne odora marginata, rolled crushed rock surface.

3—Design sketch to suggest baffling of garden space with rough hedges, to increase sense of volume.

10—Ribes viburnifolium at the window ledge, hedge of Myrtus communis compacta beyond.

6

7

9

10

8

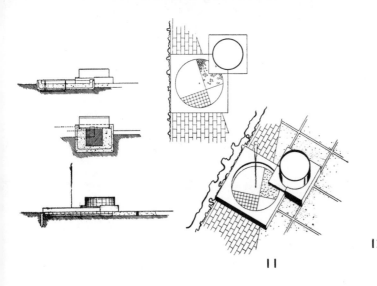

11

12

13

GARDEN IN LOS ANGELES, CALIFORNIA   1947

Design collaboration—R. Coelho-Cordoza
Photography—Maynard Parker
(Courtesy House Beautiful)

11–14—Small, flat, in-town garden. Front yard in patterns of paving, ground cover, succulents, shrubs, and trees. Narrow entrance court visually widened with free paving and step pattern. Intimate patio with living and bedroom glass walls on three sides, lucite pool, paving and foliage, louvered screen; cool and secluded. Special note
11—Detail of lucite pool

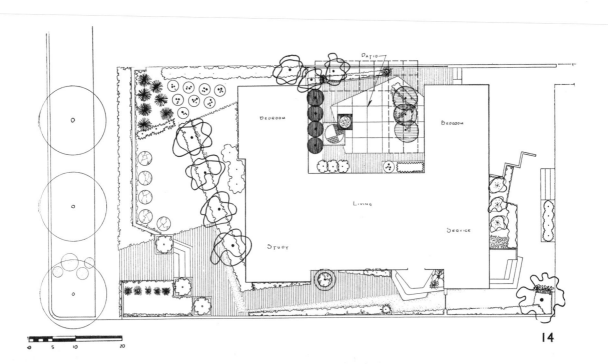

14

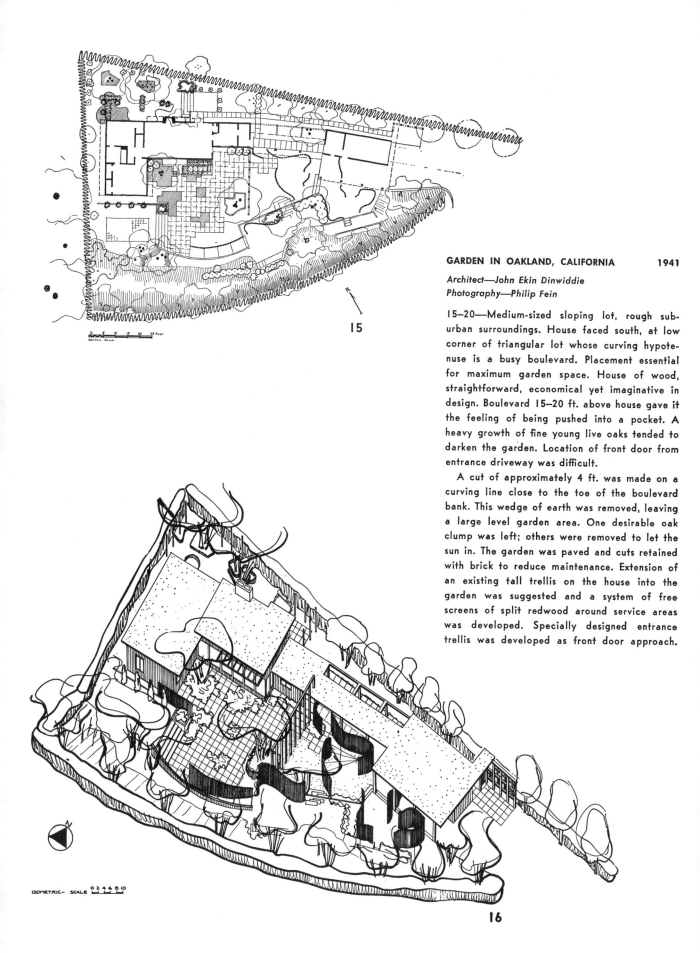

15

GARDEN IN OAKLAND, CALIFORNIA   1941

Architect—John Ekin Dinwiddie
Photography—Philip Fein

15–20—Medium-sized sloping lot, rough suburban surroundings. House faced south, at low
corner of triangular lot whose curving hypote-
nuse is a busy boulevard. Placement essential
for maximum garden space. House of wood,
straightforward, economical yet imaginative in
design. Boulevard 15–20 ft. above house gave it
the feeling of being pushed into a pocket. A
heavy growth of fine young live oaks tended to
darken the garden. Location of front door from
entrance driveway was difficult.

A cut of approximately 4 ft. was made on a
curving line close to the toe of the boulevard
bank. This wedge of earth was removed, leaving
a large level garden area. One desirable oak
clump was left; others were removed to let the
sun in. The garden was paved and cuts retained
with brick to reduce maintenance. Extension of
an existing tall trellis on the house into the
garden was suggested and a system of free
screens of split redwood around service areas
was developed. Specially designed entrance
trellis was developed as front door approach.

ISOMETRIC - SCALE

16

17

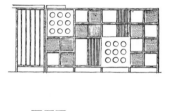

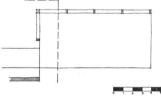

18

19

20

21

22

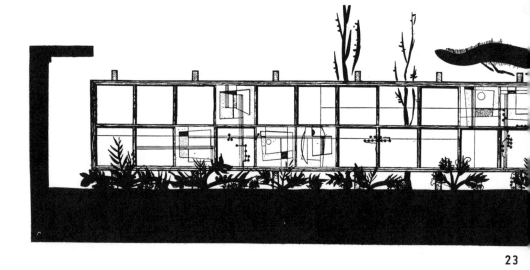

23

24

25

TWIN GARDENS IN MARIN COUNTY, CALIFORNIA
1948

Architect—Joseph Allen Stein
Photography—Childress-Halberstadt
Sculpture collaboration—Florence Swift

21–25—Rough suburban surroundings. Two optimum-size modern houses built side by side on a broad terrace cut into a wooded hillside. Floor plans which make the garden part of the house; garden plans which make the house part of the garden. Structural ingenuity and sensitive planting combined. Sculptural screen reintegrates art with the garden. On the uphill sides, secluded, enclosed, warm, intimate gardens; on the downhill sides, open exposed breezy view terraces.

26

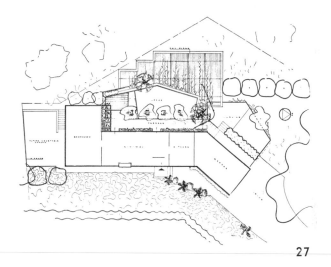

27

HILLSIDE GARDEN IN MARIN COUNTY, CALIFORNIA
1948

Architect—Gryffyd Partridge
Photography—Childress-Halberstadt

26–28—Small garden on a steep hillside in rough suburban surroundings. A small living terrace, retained with log cribbing, develops an enlarged sense of space and security through the extension of a ground-plane pergola, careful placement of screens, and the over-lapping of these garden elements from terrace to pergola.

28

29

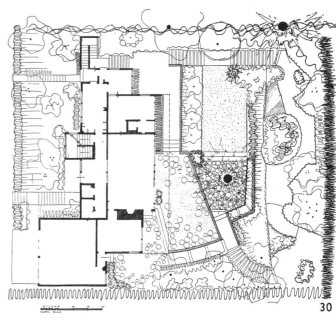

30

HILLSIDE GARDEN IN SAN FRANCISCO, CALIFORNIA
1939

Architect—John Ekin Dinwiddie
Photography—Stone & Steccati

31

32

33

—Paving of redwood log sections. Steps of
o-inch lumber.
—Chard in terrace bed, large tree fern below,
dge of Pittosporum crassifolium on rear line.
—Fuchsia in box, Clianthus puniceus on wall.
—Japanese anemone and Hydrangea hortensis
the top of the south steps.

—34—Large steep hillside lot in St. Francis
oods. Garden terraced below the house in
ree levels to develop maximum living and
rdening space for clients who were collectors
rhododendrons, azaleas, fuchsias, and allied
ants. Terrace forms reflect original contours.
ouse was new, straightforward modern. Steps
d ramped steps so arranged as to provide free
d pleasant circulation. Central level developed
ound large existing Monterey cypress. All con-
ruction of redwood.

34

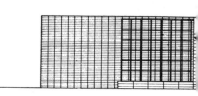

ENTRANCE GARDEN IN PASADENA, CALIFORNIA
194•

Architect for carport—Georgius Cannon

35–39—Small entrance garden for the one-story front of a large stucco hillside house. Developed in conjunction with a new carport and driveway to convey a feeling of scale and spacious hospitality beyond the ordinary narrow entrance walk. Existing trees and shrubs, and wall along side walk, were incorporated in the design. Steps and paving of concrete stained rust color. Screens, plant boxes, header boards are redwood.

37—Crassula aborescens in box, Thunbergia grandiflora on trellis.

35

36

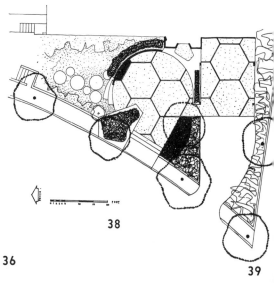

38

39

37

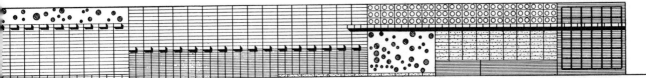

40

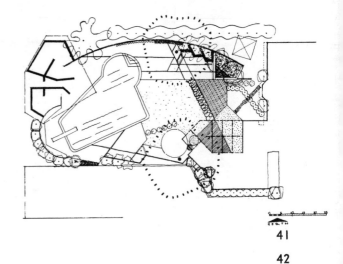

POOL GARDEN IN BEVERLY HILLS, CALIFORNIA
1948

Structural consultation—Edgardo Contini
Photography—Julius Shulman

40–48—Large flat lot in town. Large period
house had its living room extended into the
garden by the addition of a conservatory-play
room. Program called for swimming pool, bathhouse, lawn and living terrace in somewhat restricted area of rear garden. Long masonry wall

(continued on following page)

41

42

43

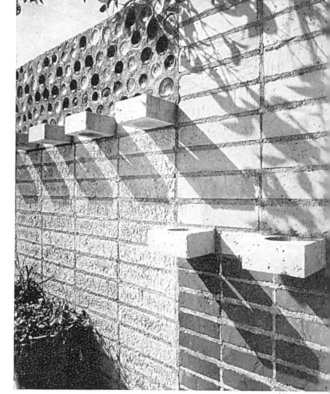

45

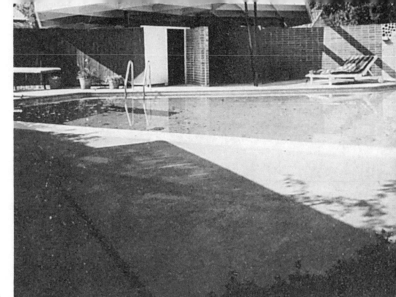

46

(continued from preceding page)

on north side was developed to link together these elements, expand the bathhouse, and provide a warm suntrap background. The wall, of brick, pumice blocks, and bottles, endeavors to extract a maximum expression from the materials by an expanded structuro-sculptural-mural treatment. Pattern of paving and pool intended to expand the sense of space within the structural enclosure. Considerable foliage will become incorporated with this enclosure as shrubs and trees grow. Entire north wall backed with Callistemon viminalis, and Cercis canadensis under existing Jacaranda ovalifolia. Form of pool allows for serious swimming in lengths with turns. Paving combines brick, concrete with crushed brick aggregate ground smooth, and plain concrete. Redwood screens on south side and around diving board meet and mingle with masonry in the bathhouse. Roof lattice carried on three steel columns and a length of pumice block wall.

Photography—Julius Shulman

47

48

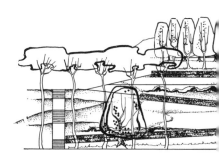

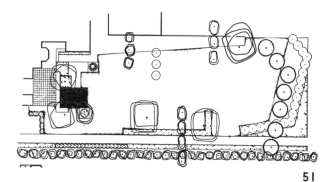

49

51

GARDEN IN BEVERLY HILLS, CALIFORNIA 1947

Design collaboration—John Bostic
Photography—Julius Shulman

49–51—Terrace extension for a large period house in a large flat garden with fine old trees— oriental planes, peaches, Eugenia myrtifolia. Pattern reflects and combines existing materials, and integrates covered terrace and open garden. Tree and shrub pattern suggested to provide continuity, closure, at open end of garden.

GARDEN IN HOLMBY HILLS, LOS ANGELES, CALIFORNIA 1947

Architects—Spaulding and Rex
Design collaboration—R. Coelho-Cordoza, John Bostic
Sculptor—Abe Liss
Pool mosaic—Torrey Spannagel
Photography—Julius Shulman

50

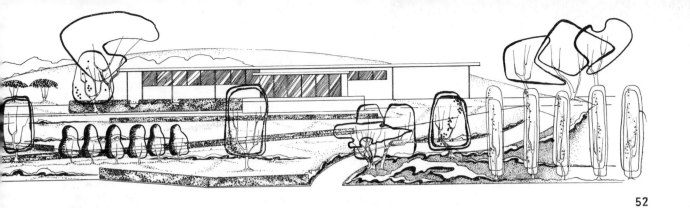

52

53

52–55—New terrace and remodeling of existing
large hillside garden, in connection with remodeling of recent modern house. Terrace incorporates pale dull terrazzo, shallow pool with
jet, concrete sculpture built on a steel armature
on the job, marble chip pattern in pool. Pool and
terrace pattern extended into garden with low
split redwood curbs. Flagstone terrace was
existing. Front planting scheme dealt with the
problem of the large street-front bank.

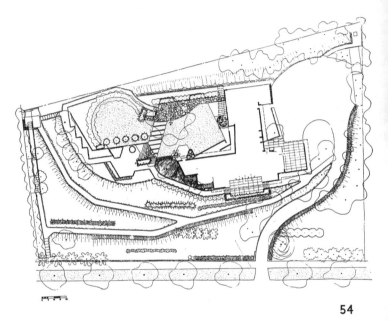

54

55

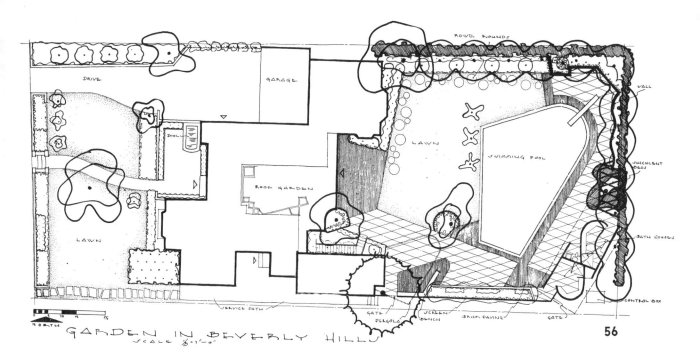

DRIVE

GARAGE

RDWD. ROUNDS

POOL

LAWN

WALL

ROOF GARDEN

LAWN

SWIMMING POOL

SUCCULENT BEDS

BATH HOUSES

SERVICE PATH

GATE
PERGOLA

SCREEN
BENCH

BRICK PAVING

GATE

CONTROL BOX

NORTH

GARDEN IN BEVERLY HILLS
SCALE ⅛"=1'-0"

56

58   59

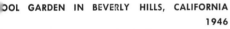

POOL GARDEN IN BEVERLY HILLS, CALIFORNIA
1946

Structural consultation—Jack Zehnder
Photography—Julius Shulman

58–61—Large flat lot in town. Tile-roof stucco
house of rambling plan. Swimming pool—bathhouse development programmed. Angles reflect
outlook direction derived from house form.
Screen of redwood and cello-glass on south side
complements large existing cypress hedge on
east and north. Paving of concrete stained rust
color, and of brick laid dry. Bathhouse of six-foot
brick walls: solid for privacy, open at top for
ventilation. Roof a grid of 2 x 8 timbers, supported on short pipe columns and center wall,
alternate squares topped with t & g boarding
and cello-glass. Magnolia grandiflora spaced
around north and east sides will develop background unifying bathhouse and brick suntrap
behind diving board.

Plant notes:
7—Psidium cattleianum in lawn.
8—Metrosideros tomentosa in box.
9—Ficus nitida along screen.

60

61

62

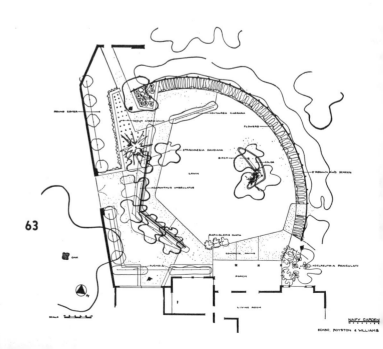

63

NAIFY GARDEN
ECKBO, ROYSTON & WILLIAMS

65

ARDEN IN WOODSIDE HILLS, CALIFORNIA 1947
hotography—Childress-Halberstadt

2–67—Garden in the country. A shingled home
the wooded hills of San Mateo County. Fine
urved wood-structure abstraction in the midst
f heavy foliage. Concrete paving, pole-and-wire
rellis in flower bed area, beds raised with wood
urbs. Shingled wall in 67 was existing.

66

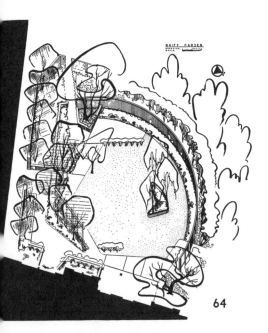

64

67

68

69

7

70

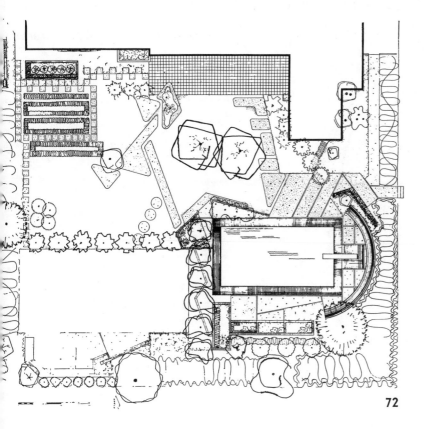

72

GARDEN IN HOLLYWOOD, CALIFORNIA   1949
Photography—Herbert Christie

68–72—Long one-story house on large flat lot, surrounded by magnificent cedars, pines, and palms. Existing rose garden (site for future studio), barbecue and badminton court; swimming pool had just been put in. Construction just completed at this writing; planting not yet rehabilitated and expanded. Client, Marguerite Brunswig, a very good sculptress in her own right. Redwood celloglass screen at new pool entrance. Brick boxes, bench and plant wall develop structuro-sculptural continuity within heavy foliage enclosure, provide containers for collections of succulents and other small plants, pebbles, and rocks, driftwood, sculptural natural sandstone concretions from the Salton Sea, and actual sculpture. Paving pattern establishes continuity and reproportioning of garden elements on ground plane. Plant wall is honeycombed with pockets for small plants.

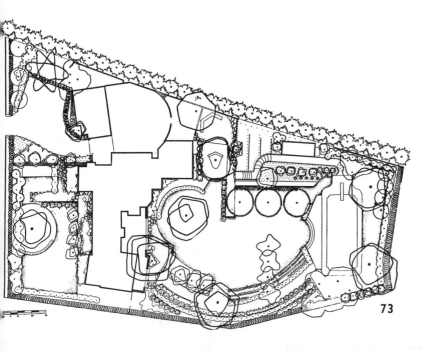

73

LARGE GARDEN IN BEL AIR, LOS ANGELES, CALIFORNIA   1949

73—Remodeled large garden, sloping gently down to an existing swimming pool from a large slate-roofed house of fine yellow-ochre cut stone. Path and foliage pattern to develop maximum spatial character from a fine park-like beginning. Areas of rolled decomposed granite under good existing olive and oaks, to preserve the roots from excessive moisture. Long curving border of bold foliage on south side to reflect mass of house and establish strong connection to pool.

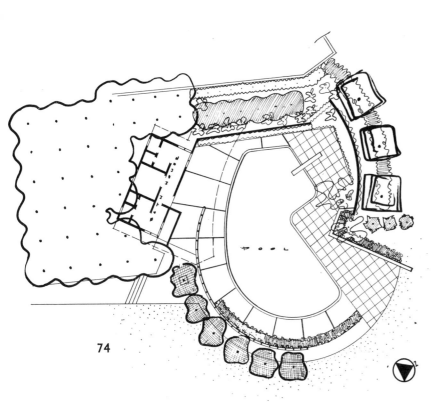

74

COUNTRY HOME IN MARIN COUNTY, CALIFORNIA
1946

Architect—Angus McSweeney
Photography—Childress-Halberstadt

74–76—Large private home grounds on Paradise Cove, facing north from a natural bowl in the hills. Swimming pool and its structural-planted radiations a fine abstract entity developing continuity with the large enclosure of site and Bay.

RANCH HOME IN CENTRAL VALLEY OF CALIFORNIA
1945

Architect—Mario Corbett

77—Ranch home on 10,000 acres in the great openness of California's Central Valley. Comparable in scale of landscape to the Midwest, or perhaps baroque France. Pattern in three dimensions developed to combine a sense of enclosure and security with that of radiating integration with the great space around, and the view across thirty miles of flat land to the Coast Range hills.

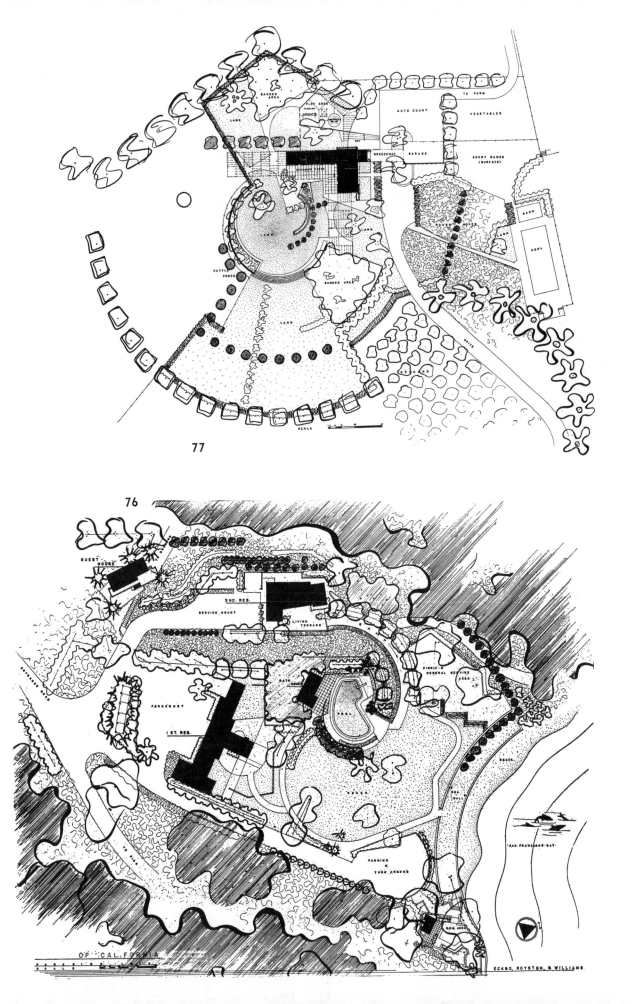

77

76

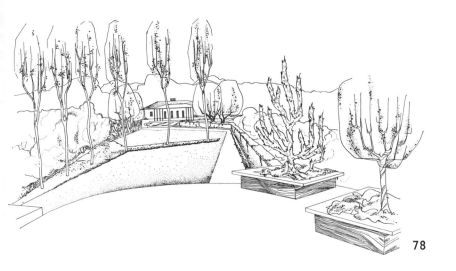

78

LARGE HOME IN HOLMBY HILLS, LOS ANGELES, CALIF. 1947

Architect—Gordon Kaufman (1932)
Remodeling—William Haines
Sculptor—Bernard Rosenthal
Design collaboration—John Bostic

78–87—Site a long broad sloping ridge in rolling hilly land. Remodeling of house, forecourt, and parts of the grounds of a 15-year-old suburban estate, totaling about six acres. Forecourt reorganized to provide maximum parking space, plus maximum three-dimensional hospitality—an entry for autos, an extension of the house. Sculpture-pool garden off library to complete the floor-to-ceiling glazing of that room. (Sunshade by office of Austin, Field, Fry, and Criz, architects.) Remodeling of main living garden (78) projected to eliminate flat static character of existing garden, increase sense of space, movement, and interest. Play terrace and structures developed as overlook for valley view.

79

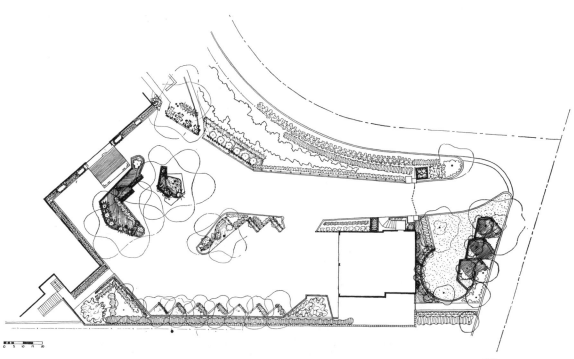

80

81

82

83

84

85

86

87

88

Myron Ehrenberg

89

P. A. Dearborn

90

Myron Ehrenberg

91

COUNTRY HOME IN WESTCHESTER COUNTY, NEW YORK 1945

Architects—Harrison, Fouilhoux & Abramovitz
Sculptor—Isamu Noguchi
Photography—Dearborn, Ehrenberg

88–94—Large estate projected, but never built. Strong cross-slope (15-foot retaining walls top and bottom) and fine outlook over rolling hills, woods and meadows. The old problem of relating the large house to the open landscape, with the new content of the widespread low informality and openness of modern architecture. In general a progression from refined living terrace through rougher play terraces and lower terraces (abstractions of meadow elements) to the wild site.

92

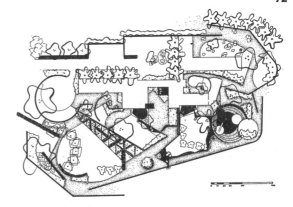

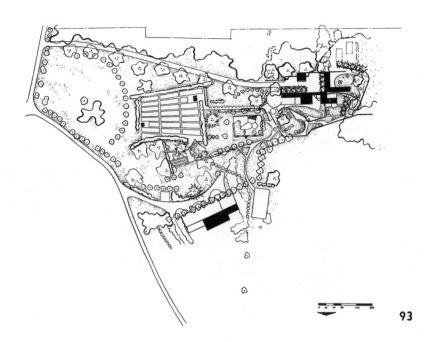

93

Special notes:

88—View from house site

89–91—Site development studies by Noguchi, before the landscape architect was called in. In 90 the lower terrace was enlarged, at our suggestion.

93—Softer and freer terrace forms shown in this general plan result from a feeling that those in 92 and 93 were sharp and abrupt.

94

PARKS

"Considerable areas of open space, organized primarily by landscape means, for the recreation, both active and passive, of the general public." Arbitrarily, as for gardens, we call **parks** Small from one to five acres; Medium from five to 50 acres; Large from 50 to 200;

Reserves over that. Similar topographic distinctions apply.

We are ridden by a mechanically literal interpretation of Olmsted and Vaux's very simple adherence to "the highest practicable ideal of pastoral scenery," not only in parks but in

164

housing, institutional work, and every landscape problem large enough to be construed or badgered into being a meadow. This mechanical sprinkling of trees about the margins of large grass areas shaped in ovals or collections of ovals is a sterilization of the intent of those great and sensitive men who initiated our park movement. The park, and there are many, that looks as though its trees and shrubs had been tossed casually from an airplane circling over the site can scarcely be called great or even good design. The fusion of the romantic heritage of Repton and Olmsted with the dominant conservationism of the big national parks has produced a kind of careful and limited naturalism which will not allow any fantasy of even the romantic or picturesque species, let alone fine flights of human imagination involving forms or arrangements which appear "unnatural." A man with the sensitivity and talent of Jens Jensen can produce distillations of the prairie landscape which approach the level of high art; more generally this theory of the naturalistic serves as a screen for tired mediocrity and hack work. While we project the contrast of the naturalistic in-town park with the urban landscape, we fail to project the reverse contrast of architectural precision in the wild landscape (except isolated examples of modern architecture).

We can agree that "there are certain kinds of scenery which experience shows to be most satisfactory in a town park, which require an extensive aggregation of their elements . . . that class of scenery already referred to as the original and typical scenery of parks and which is termed pastoral. It consists of combinations of trees, standing singly or in groups, and casting their shadows over broad stretches of turf, or repeating their beauty by reflection in the calm surface of pools. . . ." (Olmsted and Vaux.) This is to say no more than that the primary elements of landscape design, beyond the scale of the small garden, are grass and trees, with which water in sizeable areas associates most happily. While at that time there was only one possible interpretation of such a program, in terms of an imitation or representation of the forms and arrangements of nature, today it would be possible to interpret it in a number of different and more imaginative and creative ways, based on our rejection of the segregation of forms produced by man and by nature, in favor of their reunion, blending, mingling and hybridization to produce forms stronger and richer than either of the parents. Geometry in plan is not necessarily incompatible with a pastoral or woodsy quality in elevation.

The question of scale is of great importance. A rectangular garden space thirty by sixty feet will have precise rectilinear boundaries, whether planted or structural. A park space three hundred by six hundred may still have specific form from regular or irregular arrangements of trees or other large elements, but a space three thousand by six thousand does not have a precise shape to the mind of the observer— only a general proportion of length to width. There can be considerable variation in regularity or irregularity in the arrangement of its bounding trees without appreciable effect on its general character. Much more important will be the number of kinds of trees, the number of each kind, the amount of contrast in form, color and texture between the kinds, and the amount of segregation or mixing of the kinds in their actual placement on the ground. Argument between geometry and "free" irregularity may be relevant in the garden or small park and irrelevant in the larger park.

Instead of applying the same formula—"informality" dominant, with touches of "formality" here and there—to all parks, no matter what their context or program, we must become more specific, more imaginative, and much more respectful of *both* nature and human tradition. The park surrounded by city, town, or suburbs on all sides; the park *between* urban and rural or primeval patterns (like garden between house and meadow); the park surrounded by rural patterns; the park *between* rural and primeval patterns; the park surrounded by primeval scenery; all of these are *different* design problems. They are not subject to common solution by mechanical pre-conceived formula.

CITY PARK IN SACRAMENTO, CALIFORNIA   1947

Architect—Harry Devine (garage only)

95–96—One flat city block in downtown civic center area. Projected site for underground car storage structure. Summer climate of Sacramento makes relief and coolness of shade and water particularly welcome. In addition to the provision of shade trees the design incorporates a structural shelter in the shade of which are benches for the observation of the water and other features of the park. Fountain in large pool provides sparkling interest and coolness. Lawns for relaxation and lunching. Park provides passive recreation with active area for youngsters; privacy from streets; dignity and restfulness. Changing levels permit privacy, interest, and soil depth, and create visual composition of various planes and masses.

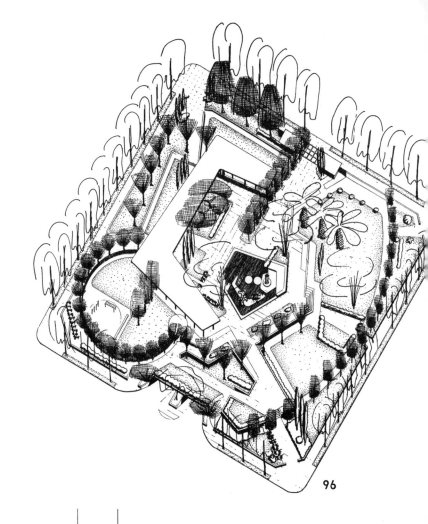

96

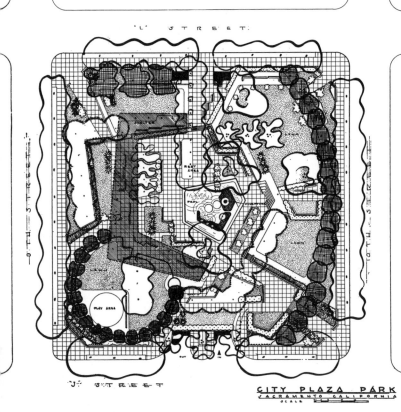

CITY PLAZA PARK
SACRAMENTO CALIFORNIA
SCALE

RECREATION AREAS FOR PUBLIC HOUSING   193█

Supervisor—Frederick A. Gutheim

97–103—Hypothetical project for United State█ Housing Authority, incorporating three smal█ park areas in which the general concept of free█ yet stronger space design was developed.

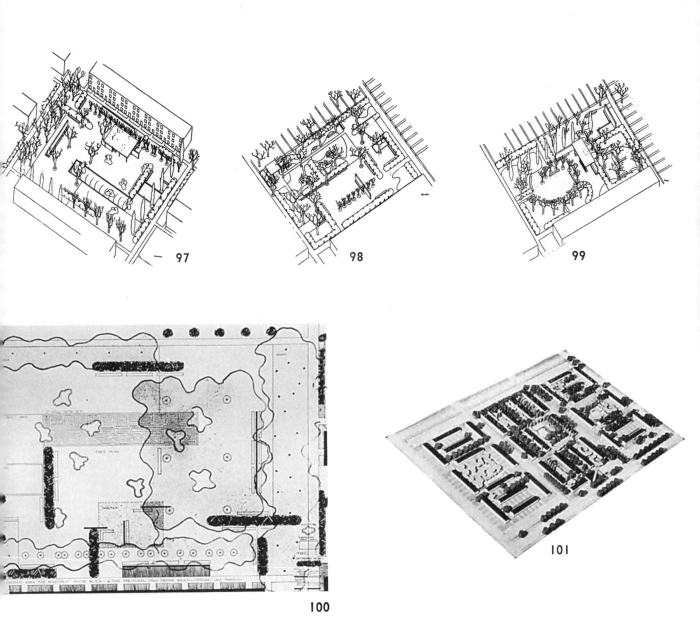

97

98

99

100

101

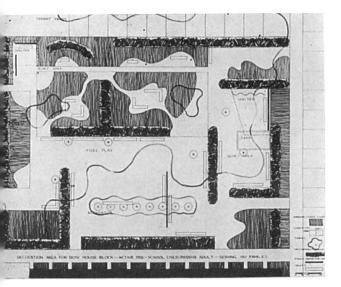

102

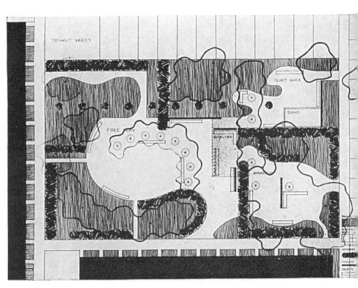

103

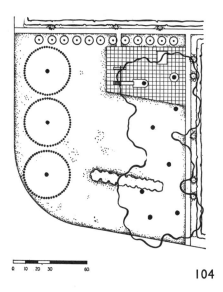

104–105—SMALL PARK NEAR WINTERS, SACRA-
MENTO VALLEY, CALIF.   1939

0   10 20 30   60

104

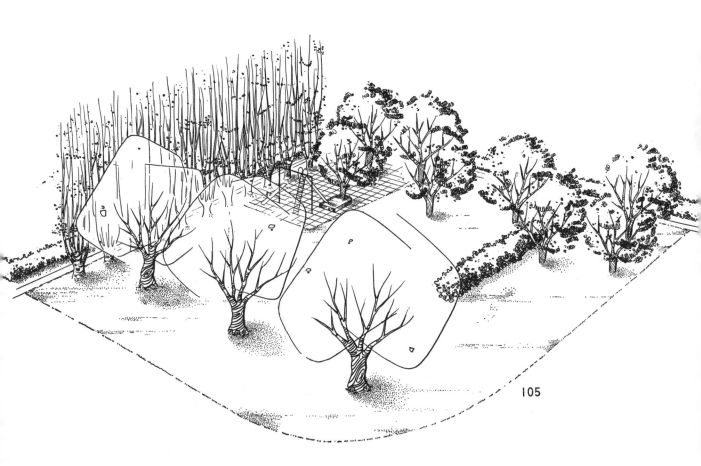

105

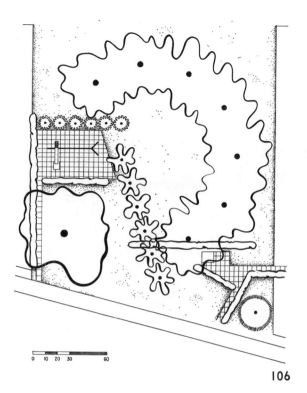

106–107—SMALL PARK NEAR ROBSTOWN, TEXAS
1939

0 10 20 30   60

106

107

108

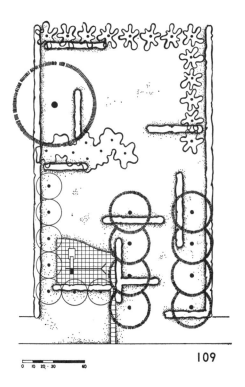

0 10 20 30   60

109

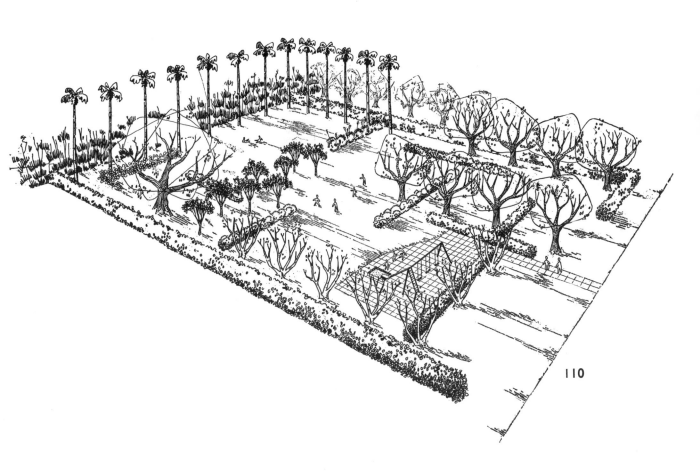

110

108–110—SMALL PARK NEAR GRIDLEY, SACRA-
MENTO VALLEY, CALIF.   1939

111–112—SMALL PARK ON MINERAL KING CO-
OP RANCH, SAN JOAQUIN VALLEY, CALIF.   1940

Small parks developed as centers for blocks of
about 25 houses—a part of the rural housing
program of the Farm Security Administration. In
flat, open, rural country. Minimal combinations
of active play facilities, open grass and trees,
shrub screens.

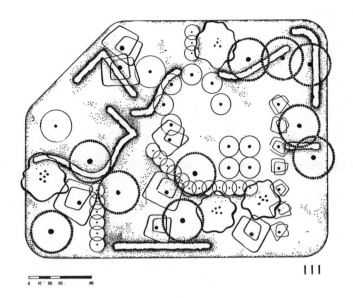

0 10 20 30.   60

111

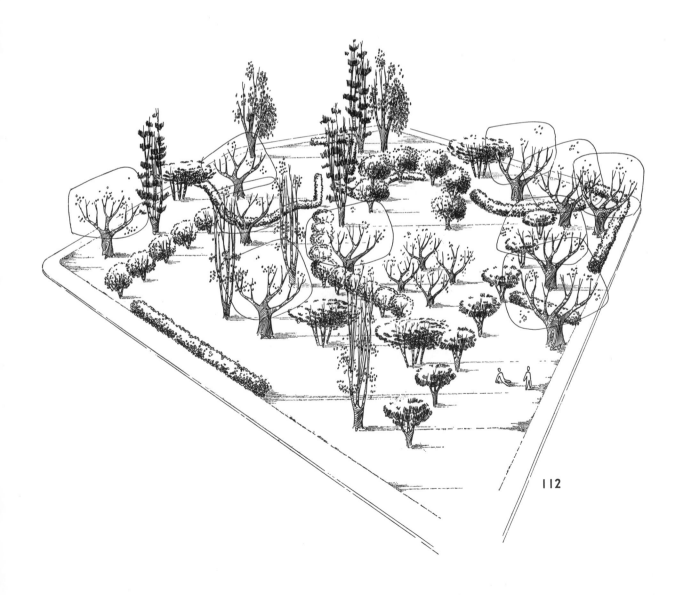

112

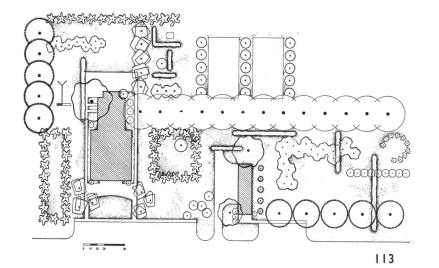

113

**COMMUNITY CENTER NEAR WESLACO, TEXAS
1939**

113–126—Community center, open space development for 50 permanent row-house units, adjacent to 200-family migrant workers' camp. Also by FSA. Nos. 115–125, inc., are study patterns indicating the potential variety of grass: shrub: tree relations which can be developed beyond the standard interpretation of "meadow."

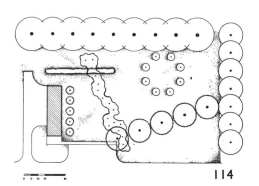

114

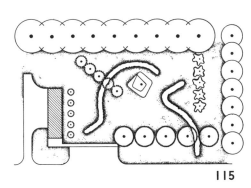

115

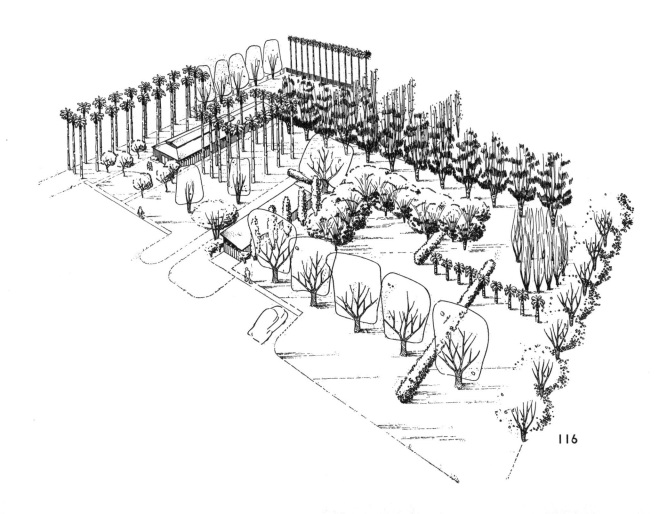

116

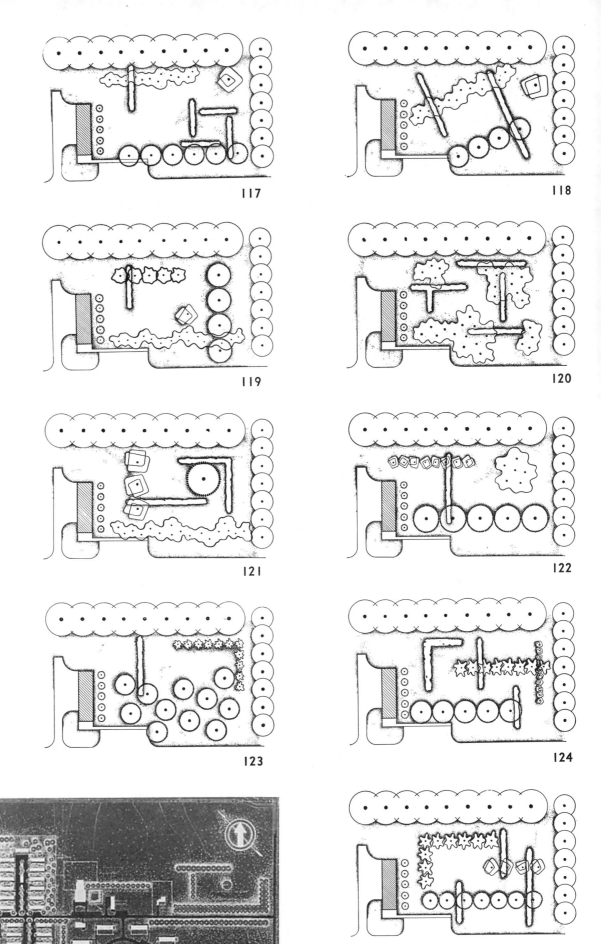

117

118

119

120

121

122

123

124

125

126

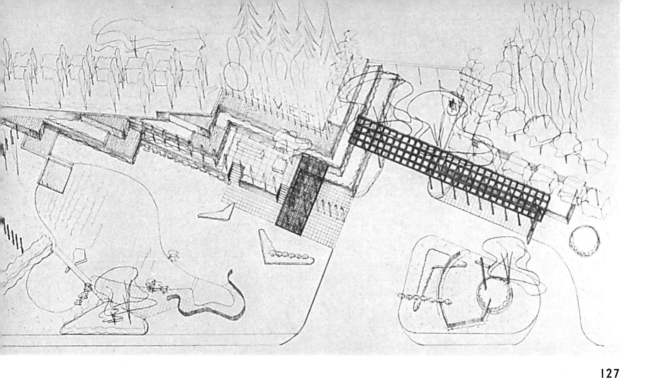

127

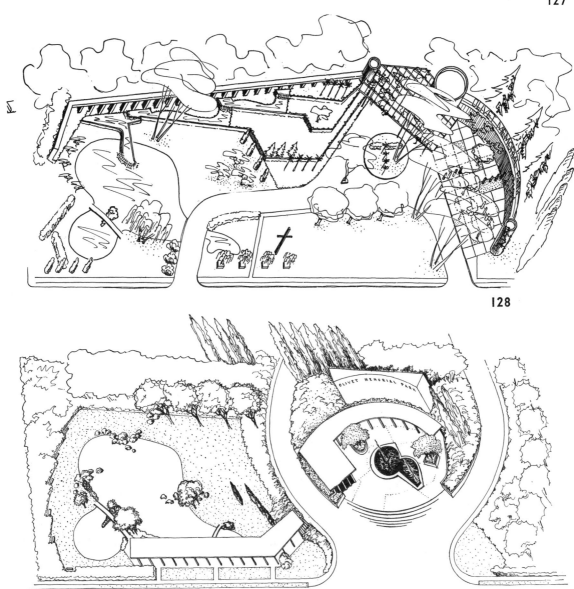

128

129

CEMETERY ENTRANCE NEAR SAN FRANCISCO, CALIFORNIA 1946

127–129—Entrance Development for a large cemetery which was isolated from the main thoroughfare by a built-up railroad line. The small lake existed.

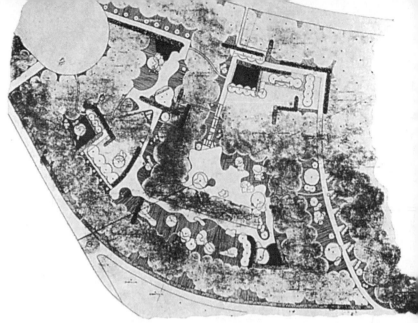

130

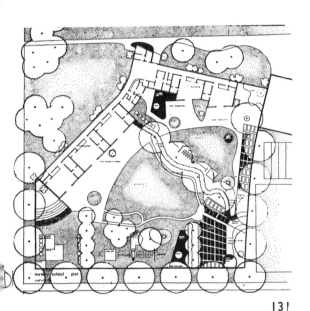

131

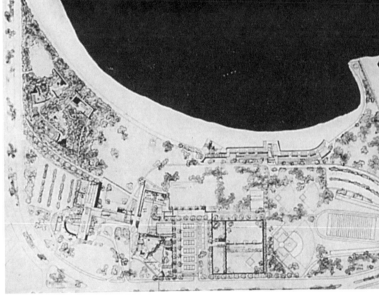

132

SOUTH BOSTON RECREATION CENTER 1938

Architectural collaboration—Saunders, Robinson, Currie, Crain

130–133—Graduate research, with four architectural planners, on a complete cultural recreation center. Facilities include main community center, nursery-kindergarten, playground, sports fields, beach club, meadow, and public gardens. 133 is an air view of the site.

133

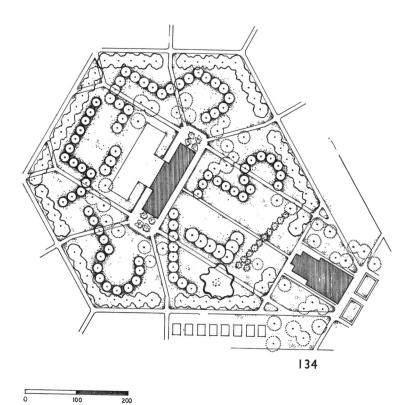

134

134–135—CAMP PARK SPACE NEAR FARMERSVILL
SAN JOAQUIN VALLEY, CALIFORNIA   194

CAMP PARK SPACE NEAR HARLINGEN, TEXAS 194

136–137—Tree-space patterns in large fre
central open spaces, in camps for 200–30
migratory agricultural worker families.

0   100   200

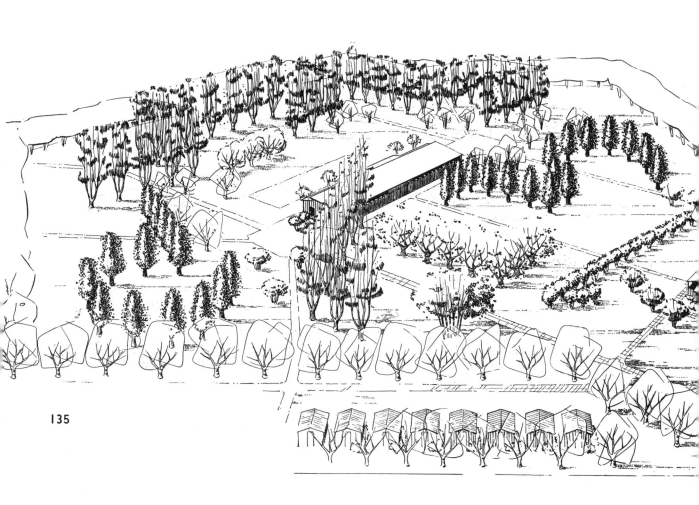

135

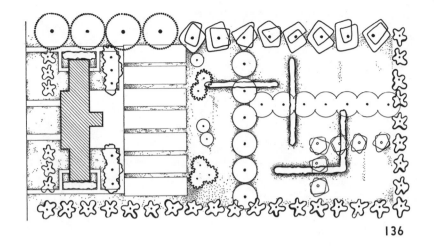

136

0 10 20 30   60

137

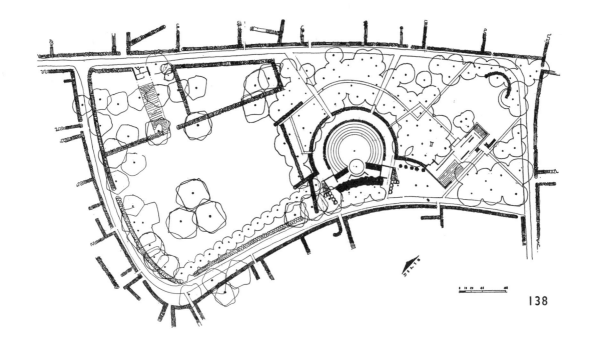

138

139

140

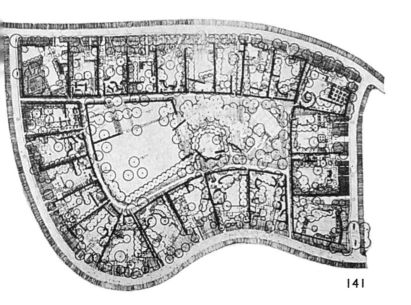

141

HYPOTHETICAL SUPERBLOCK PARK   1938

138–141—Pavilion adapted from Mies van der Rohe MLA Thesis. Central park space of 10–12 acres for a superblock of 23 half-acre lots. Playground, outdoor theatre, grove, pool and pavilion, tennis court. The Barcelona pavilion achieves (or descends to) functional community use. (No. 138 represents a preliminary stage of the final plan shown on 141.)

COMMUNITY RECREATION SPACE IN CERES, CENTRAL VALLEY, CALIFORNIA   1940

District Architect—Vernon De Mars

142–143—Expanded community center open space development for permanent FSA rural housing for 51 families, with a projected expansion of 29 or more families. Large tree patterns at the baroque scale of cheap rural land.

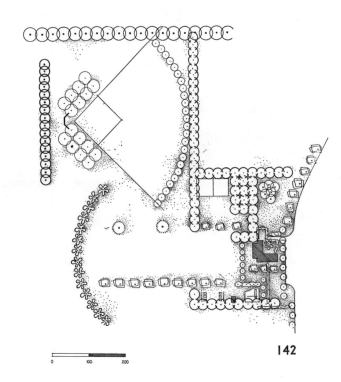

142

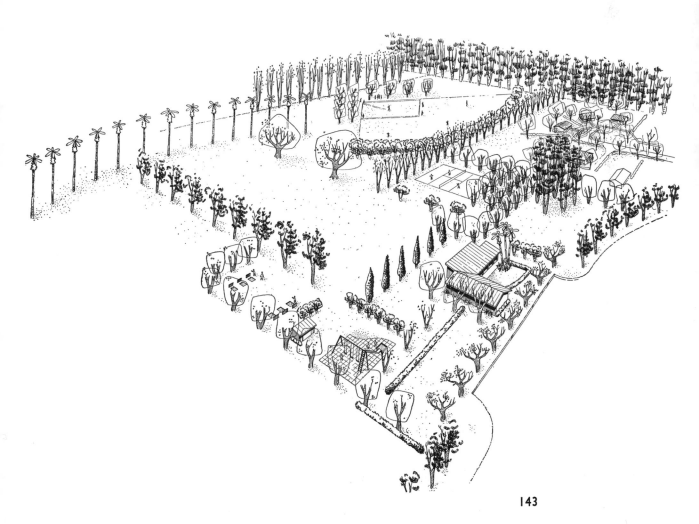

143

144

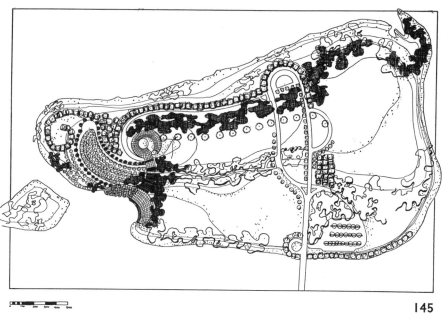

145

146

147

148

MONUMENTAL ISLAND PARK AT WASHINGTON, D.C.   1937

144–150—Graduate research project. Typical Beaux Arts program: a monument on an island in the Potomac. Tower of reinforced concrete, glass, and steel, balanced in an asymmetrical mall with three loose tree belts—locust, oak and maple, hawthorne—which reflect the form of the land, and one regular row of beech trees. Broad monumental steps, an apple tree walk, and a spiral collonaded ramp connect with a boat landing. Cars pass through far end of mall.

149

150

ROOF GARDEN IN BRAZIL

Landscaping—Roberto Burle Marx
Mural—Paulo Werneck

PUBLIC BUILDINGS

In this group we include all buildings, single or grouped, to which the public, or considerable sections of it, has free access. In other words, buildings which serve large and fluctuating groups of people, regardless of the nature of their ownership. This will include hospitals, schools, colleges, churches, clubs and community centers, exhibition and fair buildings, restaurants, markets and stores of all sorts, and recreation buildings of all kinds, public or commercial (movies, gymnasia, bowling alleys, etc.).

The problems of function and circulation vary greatly among these buildings, and must be solved on specific objective grounds. There is a general problem of planting arrangement which is common to all of them that have sites large enough to leave adequate free space around the buildings. This problem is ordinarily solved in the monumental, park-like, or picturesque way; the building is treated as an object in a setting of verdure. The latter is carefully plastered up around the base, a few specimen trees and shrubs are artfully spotted in the grounds around the building, perhaps a mall or allée is tied to the main entrance, and the whole entity is then turned loose to float quietly in a sea of green lawn. There are variations from this treatment, but it is quite generally consistent. The external observer is favored over the insider looking out, and no attempt is made to develop the integrity of the entire site space as one coherent unit indoors and out. Building and site remain two distinct elements—the jewel and its setting, the mass and its base. This is a concept which has hung over from academic to modern architecture, and which has helped neither. Great historic buildings with open space around them were carefully integrated with it.

In the various public building jobs shown as illustration we have endeavored to develop a really thorough and clear integration of building and site in terms of space, form, material and function. Again the introduction of the concept of site-space-form as of primary importance tends to make all the heterogeneous and unrelated elements fall together into a whole that is greater than their mere addition. Trees and shrubs placed so as to form clear strong spatial relations with the building, and based on its form, achieve a quality and importance impossible when they are merely plastered against it, or dotted about. Careful analysis of the way the building is used, which people it is most important to, places the outsider looking in and the insider looking out in proper relation to each other. None of this statement is intended to eliminate broad lawns, specimen plants, fountains, et cetera, from use around public buildings, but only to suggest how these same elements can be used in a stronger and freer way to achieve a new level of experience and expression.

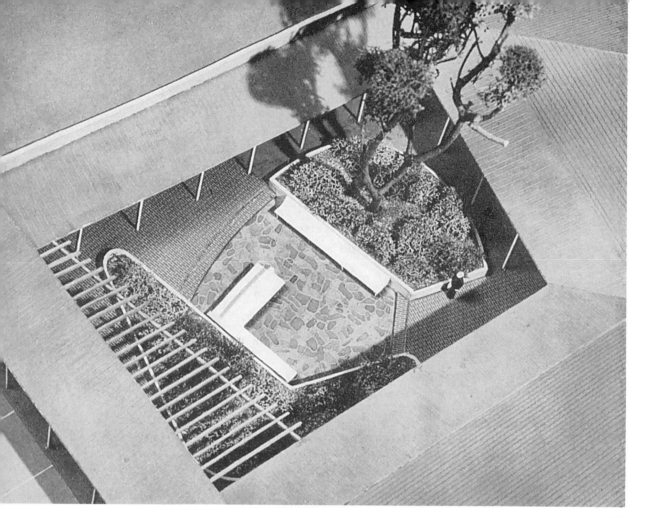

151

SHOPPING COURT IN PASADENA, CALIFORNIA
1945

Architect—Walter Reichardt
Photography—Lloyd, Pasadena

151–153—Shopping court extension to a neighborhood market. Suburban neighborhood, rough hilly land. Quiet sunken central area for resting or waiting. Planting in raised boxes for protection and three-dimensional interest.

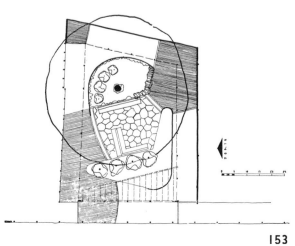

152

153

154

155

WORLD'S FAIR PAVILION IN NEW YORK   1938

Architect—Stanley C. Reese
Photography—U.S. Housing Authority

154—156—Small pavilion for housing exhibits.
Quiet corners for sitting out, playful small screen
and ground patterns, sculptural plant groupings.

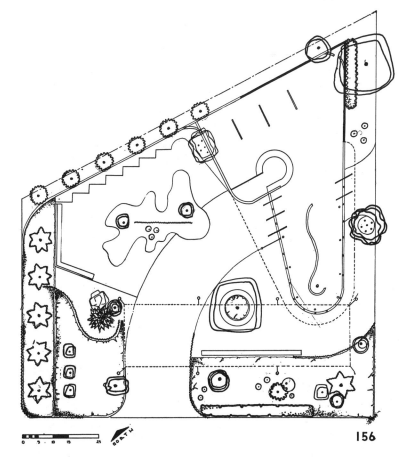

156

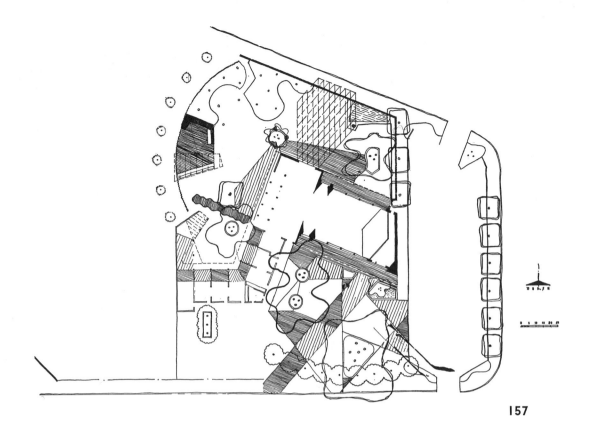

157

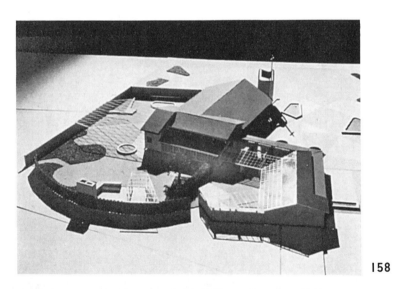

158

CHURCH IN LOS ANGELES, CALIFORNIA   1946

Architect—Robert E. Alexander
Photographer—Duke Shoop

157–165—Preliminary studies for a church now being built to different plans. Model constructed in the office of the architect. 160, 161, and 162 are sketches from the new church studies, also from Mr. Alexander's office. Site flat, at the north toe of a large block of hills, exposed to cool winds from the ocean, heavy soil. Articulation of spacious entry, quiet enclosed intimate corner for chapel, arbor for open air meetings using social hall stage, outdoor social area centering around a barbecue terrace, and special yard for Sunday School classes. Future church not a part of this study.

159

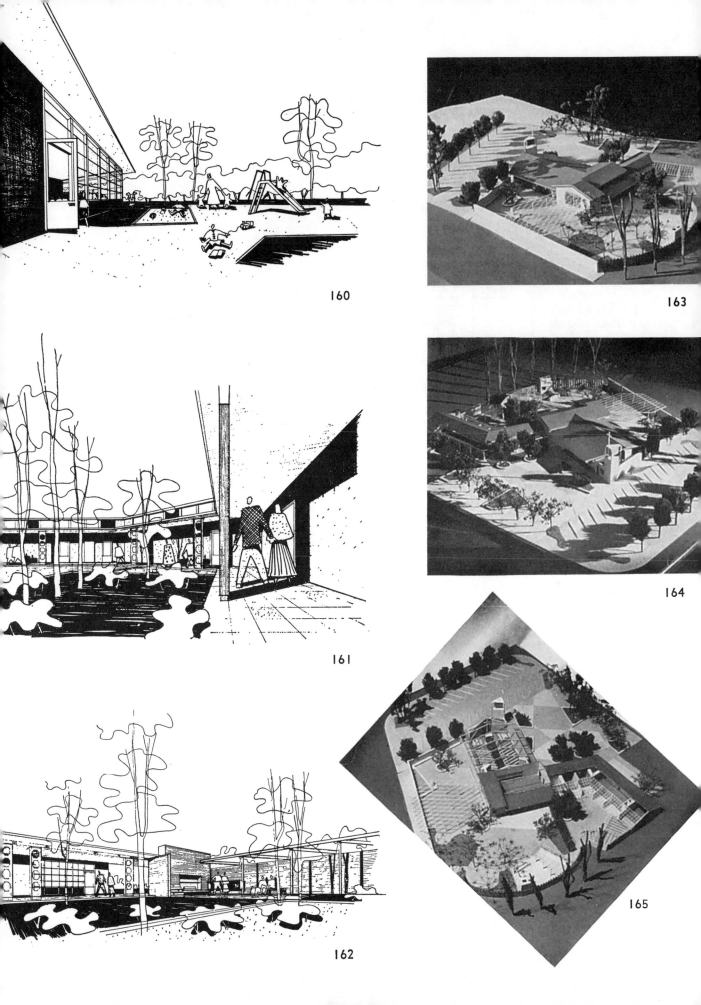

160

163

161

164

162

165

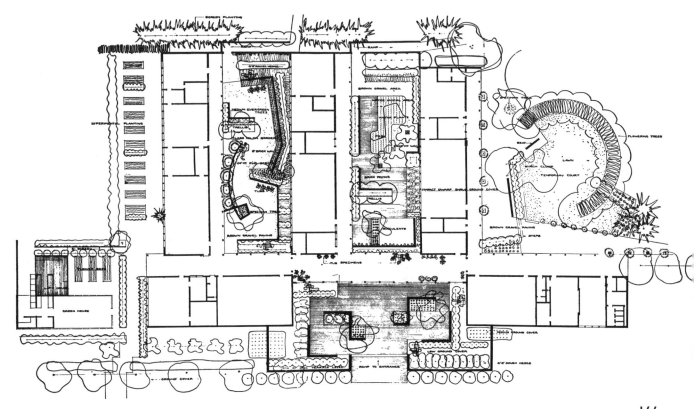

COLLEGE SCIENCE BUILDING IN OAKLAND, CALI-
FORNIA   1947

Architect—Clarence Mayhew

166–169—Court and entrance treatment for a
simple functional pavilion-and-gallery type building. Outdoor laboratory material integrated with
careful spatial organization of courts which are
too long for their width.

167

168

169

170

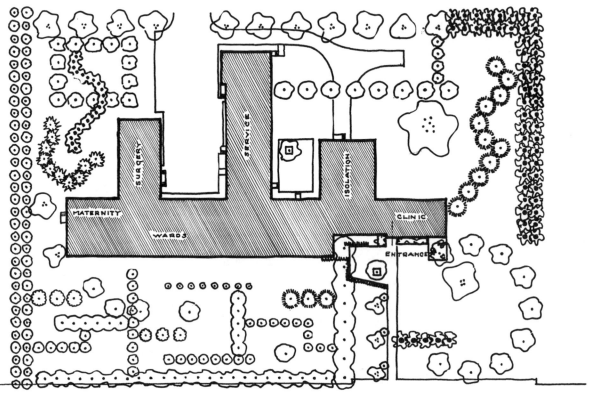

171

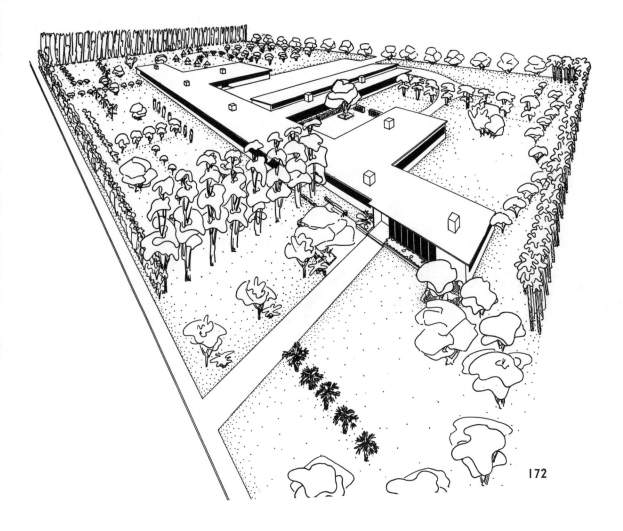

172

RURAL HEALTH CENTER IN FRESNO, CALIFORNIA
1942

District Architect for FSA—Vernon De Mars

170–172—In the hot, flat, productive San Joaquin Valley. Hospital for farm workers planned by the San Francisco District Engineer's office of the Farm Security Administration just before the war, and stopped by that event before construction. The main elements of the building —reception and clinic, general ward wing, service and surgery—are carefully and clearly articulated. The landscape plan endeavors to reflect this clarity. The main entrance, with its semicircle of olives, wide walk and entrance court, shade trees, colorful smaller clumps and rock and sand arrangement, presents a wide and welcoming opening from the street.

Break at general ward wing emphasized by strong plane of white-trunked manna gums.

Beyond this, the main lawn space is considered primarily as outlook from the ward windows, rather than as a foreground for the building viewed from the street. The strongest and tallest planting is concentrated at the property lines, and feeds in toward the building in free, irregularly geometric arrangements of lines and planes, employing such contrasting elements as Irish junipers, weeping mulberries, and persimmons.

It is felt that this strong, orderly, yet irregular arrangement will create a greater sense of tangible space, and greater interest in and expression of the qualities of the materials, than will any weaker, more hodge-podge arrangement.

(published in "The Modern Hospital" July, 1947)

**SMALL OFFICE BUILDING IN HOLLYWOOD, CALI-
FORNIA   1948**

Architect—Gregory Ain

173–174—Collaborating architects—Joseph
Johnson, Alfred Day. Site an 8 per cent slope in
a cove of the Santa Monica Mountains, fronting
on the secondary access lanes paralleling one of
the major freeways connecting Hollywood with
the San Fernando Valley. (173 indicates the
nature of the surroundings.) A light, clear, spa-

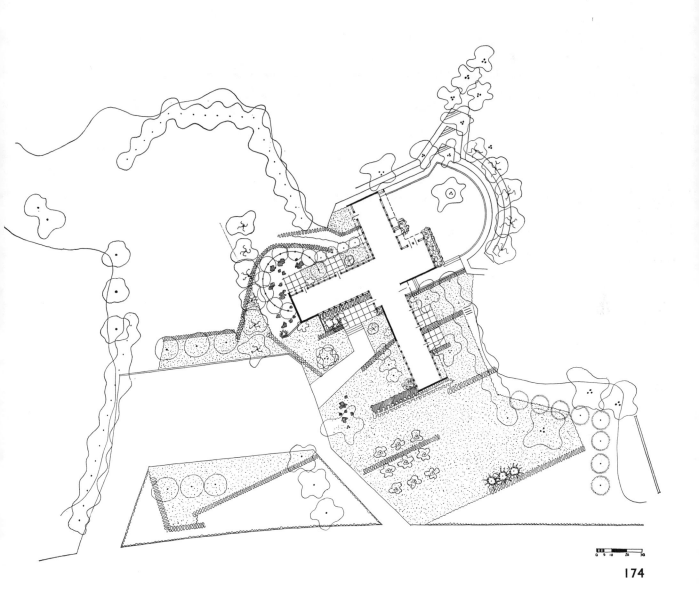

174

cious building, following gracefully the slope of the land. Planting pattern endeavors to reflect its articulated character and link structure to site. Offices have small outdoor terraces. As-sembly terraces to rear reflect and express the natural contours. Profusion of large rocks on the site suggested a garden of rocks, sand, and suc-culents at the northeast corner.

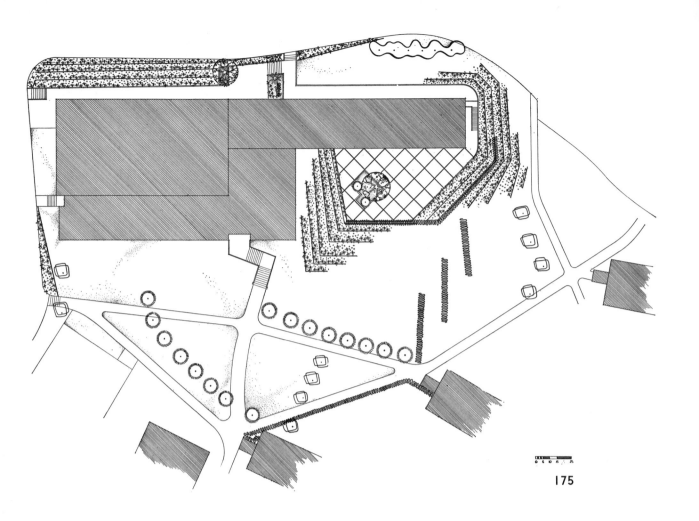

175

DURATION DORMITORIES

176

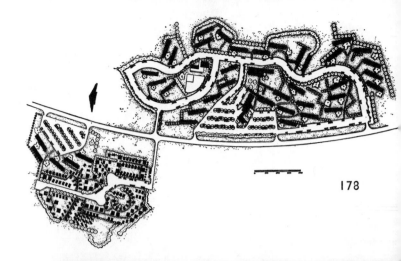

178

TENANT ACTIVITIES BUILDING FOR WAR DORMITORIES AT VALLEJO, CALIFORNIA 1943

Architect—Theodore Bernardi
Associates—Wickenden, Langhorst, Funk
Photography—Roger Sturtevant
Architect for dormitories—Vernon De Mars

175–181—Community facilities structure for a war dormitory project which, beginning with 3000 men in the FSA development, expanded to 4500 with later additions by FPHA. This activity building, on a rather rough portion of the site, took full advantage of the slope. The landscape plan endeavored to continue this and integrates structure and site within the economic and material limits of wartime work. Treatments of cuts and fills, and the choice-groupings in the plant list, were direct expressions of this situation. The general plan 178 suggests the character of the total project (without FPHA additions) and the sketch 176 by Vernon De Mars does this still better.

179

180

177

181

NURSERY SCHOOL IN WEST LOS ANGELES, CALIFORNIA 1946

Architect—Robert E. Alexander

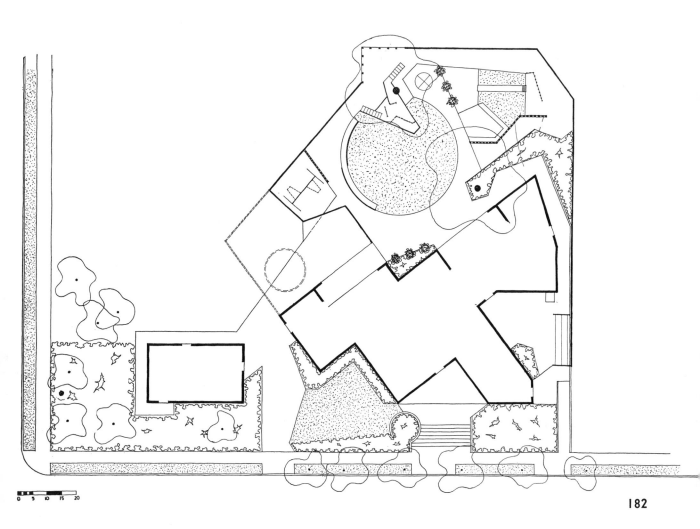

182

182—Private nursery school projected by a church organization. Site mostly flat, sloping sharply upward at the north side. Two fine large California sycamores established a natural play yard location. Ramps, slide, sandbox take advantage of the slope. Two-level playhouse under one sycamore. General pattern of benches, screens, cylinders developed to provide a quality of spacious creative playfulness. Play yard enclosed by solid screen except at one corner.

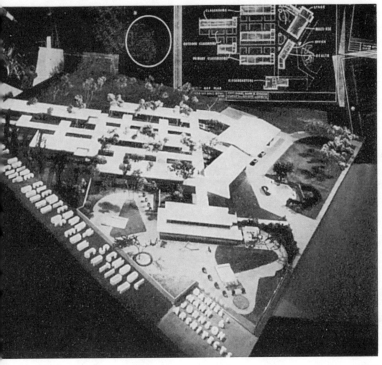

183

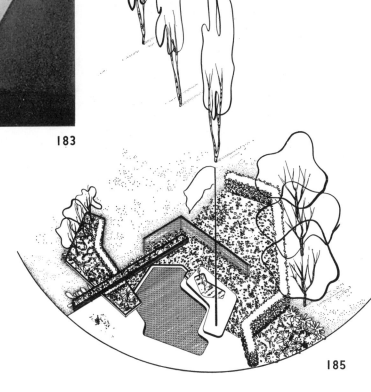

185

ELEMENTARY SCHOOL IN CULVER CITY, CALIFORNIA
1948

Architect—Daniel, Mann and Johnson
Photography—Stein of Camart

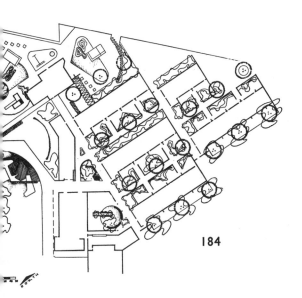

184

183–185—New school embodying many advanced planning and design concepts. Details of flagpole area, administration and lunch courts intended to develop a play of imaginative and interesting plant and structural forms within the simple clarity of the building. Kindergarten an extension of the idea of promoting creative and imaginative play: play-house, mounds and hollows, sandbox with shelves and shelter, and pipe tunnels. Outdoor classrooms have since become almost all paving, which seems more practical. Grid of tall thin trees (lemon gums, locusts, or palms) projected to rise out of the classroom grid, give it a three-dimensional expression and a sense of space and elevation.

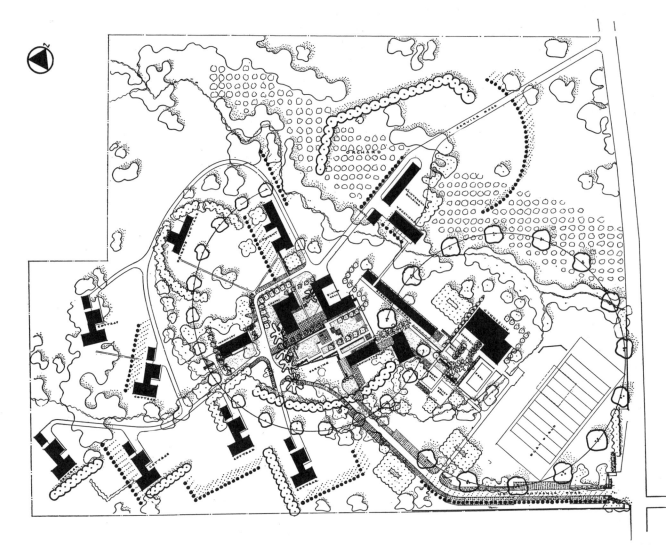

186

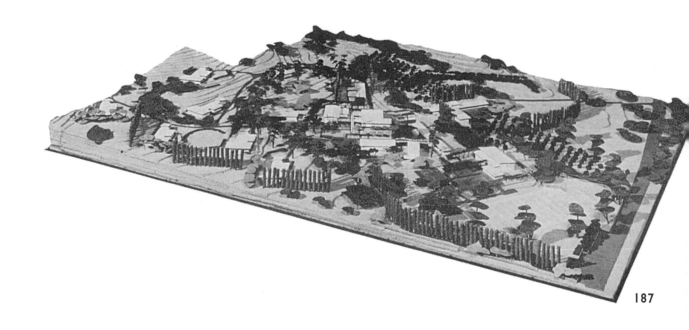

187

**PRIVATE SCHOOL IN SONOMA COUNTY, CALI-
FORNIA   1948**

Architects—Bolles and Ward
Photography—Childress-Halberstadt

186—189—Setting in rolling pastoral land makes
possible large free bold tree patterns expanding
the school grouping into the surrounding landscape and linking the two together, through the
blending of large simple geometry with loose,
irregular groves, clumps, and drifts. Formal and
informal, man and nature, meet and mingle on
equal balanced terms.

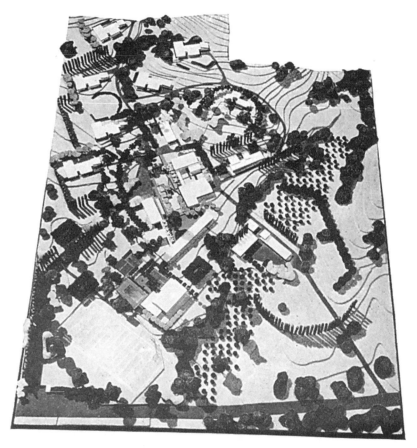

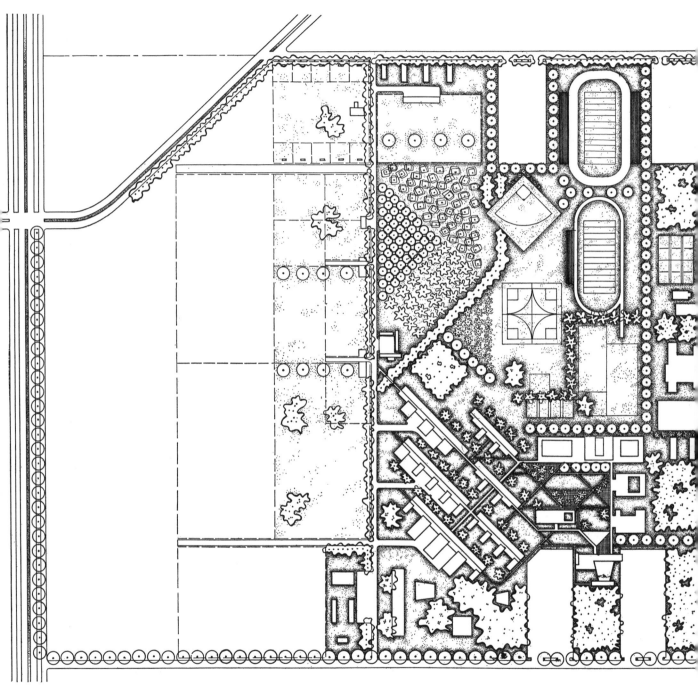

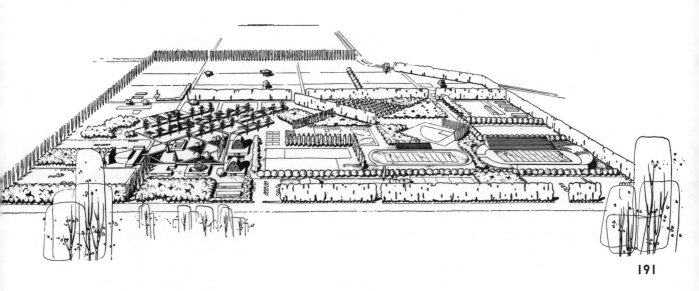

191

STATE COLLEGE IN ORANGE COUNTY, CALIFORNIA
1949

Architect—Robert E. Alexander
Associate—Richard H. Pleger

190–191a—Establishment of a basic site plan for a new college developing on a section of a wartime airfield. The architect played the primary planning role, the landscape architect functioned as consultant to him—a very productive collaboration. A complete and integrated college plant, satisfying both functionally and esthetically. Site flat and fanned by persistent southwest breezes which are cooling to the point of establishing a need for windbreaks. General pattern of buildings and trees will do this. Central quad pattern of paving, grass, water and trees is small enough for intimacy and warmth, large enough for spatial imagination. Tree pattern quite tentative: large strong windbreak backbone of eucalyptus and pine will enclose smaller and freer patterns of more colorful kinds. Grid of tall trees to rise out of academic units as for Culver City.

191a

GROUP HOUSING LANDSCAPE DEVELOPMENTS

This term can cover anything from the tar-paper shacks of the Hoovervilles that still fringe our cities, to the sumptuous homes and broad lawns of Hillsborough and Beverly Hills. Any collection of houses becomes group housing, especially if developed all at once by one operator or agency. Small groups up to 25 units; Medium up to 100; and Large up to 500 become parts of existing neighborhoods. Over that they tend to become neighborhoods themselves, and to bridge over into community planning problems. Topographical classifications apply here too, as well as the primary density groupings: single-family detached homes; row-houses, in which each family has direct access to the ground; and apartment houses of two or many stories. All of these are housekeeping units, by contrast with hotels and dormitories.

We have had a good deal of experience with group housing of all types, including that provided by public agencies for low-income groups and for war workers in general; private speculative or rental housing; and co-operative developments. For the Farm Security Administration the writer has done some 50 rural projects all over the western United States. These consisted, typically, of camps for 200–300 families of migrant agricultural workers, homes for 25–50 of these who were in process of settling down, community facilities, and farm groups. These were all done in the more extreme interior climatic conditions of the western regions, and under much more severe budget limitations than other types of public housing. For the Federal Public Housing Authority, plans and supervision were provided for another 50 war housing projects, mostly along the coast of central and southern California. While these were somewhat freer as to budget, and were in sections milder climatically, they suffered from shortages of materials and labor that became progressively worse as the war went on.

Speculative developments are notoriously minimal in their approach to landscaping; the potential of co-operative activity, in terms of physical quality and neighborhood character, is unlimited.

The writer was responsible for the site planning of 30 of the housing projects mentioned, and collaborated on the planning of another 30.

In all these types of housing, consideration of any kind of planting beyond basic ground cover, screen and windbreak elements runs immediately full-tilt into questions of theory and esthetics. To be sure there are other conventional kinds of planting which are generally acceptable and "done"—street, shade, color, foundation, and border or boundary planting. But all of these commonly follow mechanical and academic formulae, with insufficient analysis of the nature of the problem and the possibilities latent in the materials to be used. This superficial approach stems from a failure to properly evaluate and accept professional responsibility, from the acceptance of a minor role as exterior decorator placing frills around buildings, rather than the assumption of a major role as space organizer on a par with the architect.

What is the esthetic problem in the landscaping of a group housing development? Essentially it is the same as that in a private garden, extended in scale and complicated with more elements of building and site. The problem is the giving of clear, coherent, functional, rich form to all the three-dimensional space within the site boundaries, accepting the beginnings of this form already developed in the site, building and circulation layout. It is this landscape-space development which completes the overall form concept begun with the architectural and engineering plans, co-ordinates and integrates all the site elements, and ties the whole development up in one neat finished package. In doing this, it can produce the final complete integration of buildings and site, structural and natural materials, man and nature.

To the extent that this problem of complete

202

space organization and co-ordination is not dominated as much by questions of specific functions, structural necessities and economics as is the architectural and engineering design, the landscape development is a more purely plastic and esthetic problem, requiring greater concentration on questions of pure form and material, and approaching somewhat closer to painting and sculpture in the freedom of its form concepts. This plastic freedom implies the responsibility of disciplined handling of relations between space and materials, and the effort to reach philosophical clarity on such questions as the relation of man to nature, and man to man in nature.

The relation of indoor to outdoor space in housing depends on neighborhood form and control. In our homes we need to feel privacy, security, and stability. To extend these to the outdoors we must feel some reliability in the neighborhood. People feel a need for bigger lots because they have no secure control of anything beyond their lot. With guaranteed neighborhood open space, community facilities, and stability, we probably wouldn't feel the need for so much private space. Most of us can't develop or maintain a half-acre lot as our private public park. Many an urbanite moves to a suburban half-acre or a rural acre for more space for living, only to find that he doesn't really need it all, or know exactly what to do with it. But it is insulation—a greenbelt—between home and an unplanned, unpredictable, chaotic world, and until we have some guarantee of controlled neighborhood planning in which we have democratic participation, we will doubtless continue moving to suburban half-acres and rural acres—that is, the relative few of us who can afford it. The rest will just sit home and wait for city planning and urban redevelopment to happen.

There is a complementary, or duplicating relationship between private home facilities and those of the neighborhood, whether publicly or privately owned. Street and driveway, sidewalk and front walk, are extensions of each other, the connection between private home, community,

and the world. Kitchen and dining room parallel the local restaurant; laundry porch and drying yard the local launderette or commercial laundry; rear lawn the local park, kids' play yard the local playground; vegetable garden the local truck farm. This parallelism of facilities is the basic relation between home and neighborhood even at the poverty-stricken level of slum or blighted area. The expansion of community facilities to the point at which they supplement as well as complement the home, and become enriching elements raising the standard of living of the people, while it is implicit in all efforts toward good planning, is only an expansion of the existing inverse parallelism between home and neighborhood. The concept of neighborhood as a minimum home-planning unit is not a figment of imagination; it is an existing fact of life, like kitchen, bedroom and bath in the average house.

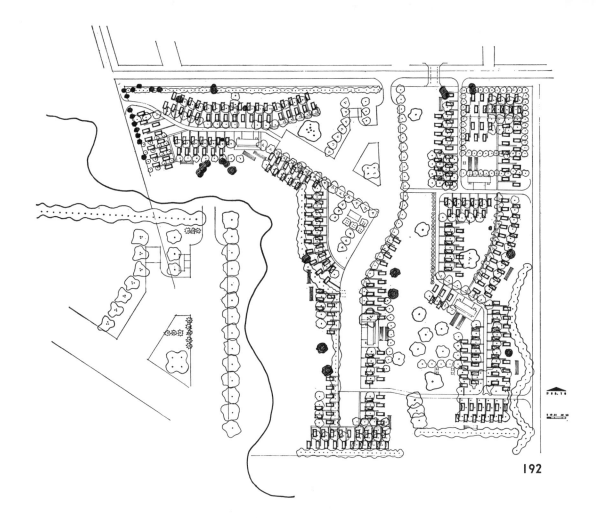

192

193

194

195

TRAILER HOUSING PATTERNS IN SAN DIEGO AND VALLEJO, CALIFORNIA   1942

District Architect—Vernon De Mars

192–198—Wartime emergency housing from the FSA District Engineer's office. These are relevant today because they suggest one approach to the problem of site planning for a large number of identical small housing units. Two sites are rolling, one is flat. The general theory is the grouping of the units in articulated cellular patterns in which the cells achieve special identity by virtue of the strong formal relations established within them. The total grouping achieves a spatial organization of the site with considerable movement and quality. Tree patterns and building colors can of course expedite this identifying articulation a great deal, as these plans indicate. Comparison of these site patterns with any of the "operative builders' planned communities" will bring out our point. Some degree of freedom from the mechanics of subdivision in which every square foot of site must go into an equally salable lot, and from mechanical concepts of the relation of house to car and street, are implicit in this kind of site thinking.

Special notes:

193—Same Acacia and Casuarina as 194. Ailanthus glandulosa was existing.

194—Casuarina stricta and Acacia baileyana—same age, same place.

195—Four-year-old Lombardy poplars at San Miguel trailer park.

197—Photo of model of Vallejo project.

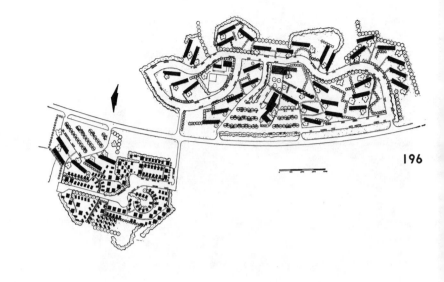

196

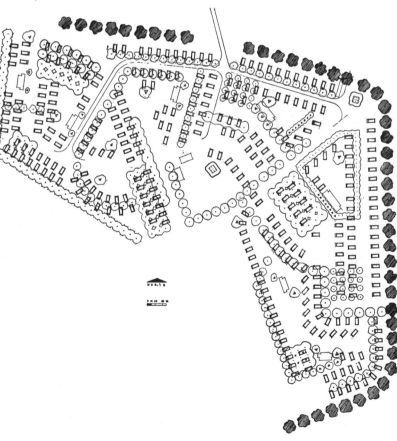

197

198

199

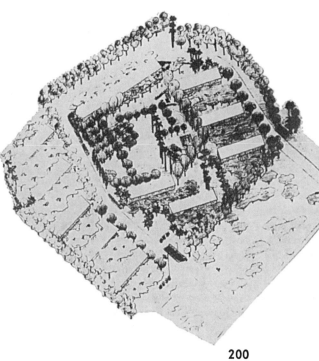

200

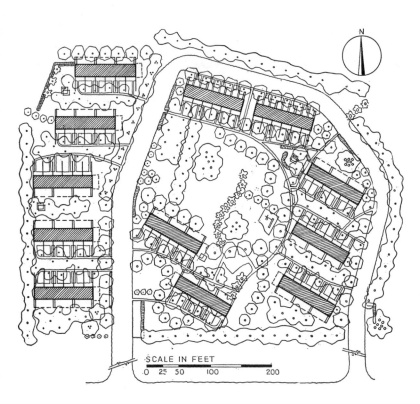

SCALE IN FEET

0 25 50   100   200

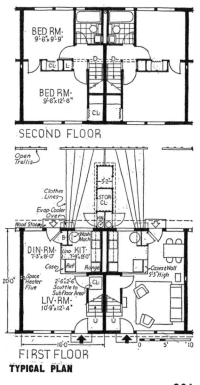

BED·RM·
9'-6"x9'-9"

BED·RM·
9'-6"x12'-6"

SECOND FLOOR

Open
Trellis

Clothes
Lines

Evap·Cooler
Over

Wood Stoop

STOR·
CL·

Wash·
Mach·

DIN·RM·
7'-3"x8'-0"

Lino·KIT·
7'-9"x8'-0"

Ref·   Range

Cases

Cases & Wall
5'-5" High

Space
Heater
Flue

2'-6"x2'-6"
Scuttle to
Subfloor Area

CL·

LIV·RM·
10'-9"x12'-4"

16'-0"

FIRST FLOOR

TYPICAL PLAN

201

PERMANENT ROW HOUSING IN TAFT, CALIFORNIA
1941

District Architect—Vernon De Mars
Snapshots by Imogen Cunningham
Plan courtesy Architectural Forum May 1942

199–204—Seventy-two family units in an oil town in the hottest and driest southwest corner of the San Joaquin Valley—average precipitation 3 to 5 in. annually, annual temperature range 15 to 120 degrees. Ironically this is one of the few rural or war housing projects done by the author in which trees and shrubs not only survived but grew remarkably well. The answer, of course, is conscientious maintenance; and the rebuttal to the voluble alibis of all the housing managers in more favorable parts of the state is clear.

The project is surrounded by a lunar landscape of sand, oil wells, and raw mountains. The site planning endeavored to group the buildings in a pattern which would not only meet the exacting orientation problems of the climate but effect a visual closure of the site space, and make possible the production of a sheltered oasis. Heavy tree planting continues the oasis idea. Reverse curve of Washingtonia palms is the backbone of the block. Extension of semi-private outdoor living space was suggested with trellises, screens, and low fences.

All planting four years old from ordinary nursery stock at photographing.

Trees in photographs:
199—Robinia pseudoacacia.
202—Ulmus pumila.
204—Olea europea, Casuarina stricta, Melia zedarach umbraculiformis.

202

203

204

205
206

207
208

209
210

205—Eucalyptus rudis, Robinia pseudoacacia, and Tamarix parviflora in clumps.
206—Robinia pseudoacacia.
207—Sterculia diversifolia in foreground.
208—Prunis pissardi, Ailanthus glandulosa.
209—Ulmus pumila.
210—Washingtonia gracilis, Ligustrum japonicum.

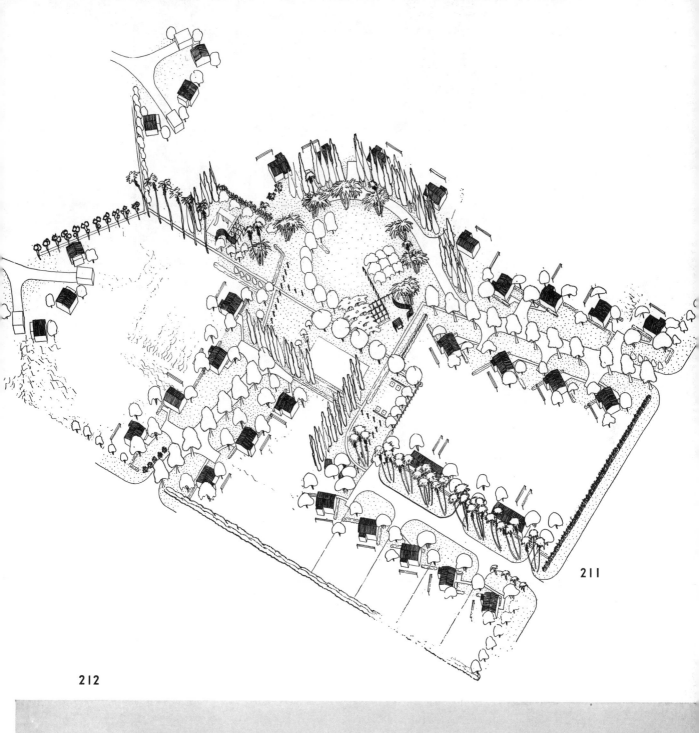

211

212

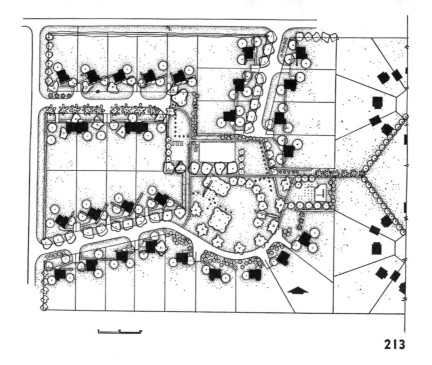

213

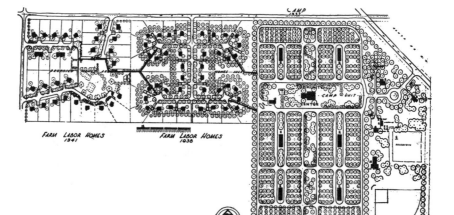

FARM LABOR HOMES
1941   FARM LABOR HOMES
                              1938

214

215

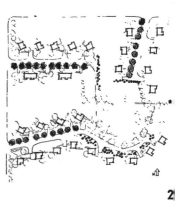

FARM WORKERS' HOUSING AT SHAFTER, CALIFORNIA 1941

District Architect—Vernon De Mars

211–221—FSA permanent single-family housing in the hot flat San Joaquin Valley. No. 214 indicates the progression: from the 1937 camp for migrant families through 40 permanent houses without park space in 1938 to 29 additional houses in 1941, focusing on about two acres of park space designed to serve all 69 permanent families. The other drawings indicate the detailed development of the park space, with open lawn center, basketball court, horseshoe pits, apparatus and shelters for children. They also indicate the careful attention that was given to planting design of maximum interest, richness and spatial quality. No. 212 is a street in the 1938 homes section. The other photos indicate the type of light frame trellis-and-screen structures—abstractions of typical practical agricultural crop structures—developed to enliven the play areas. The small arbors were developed by the architects as part of the general construction (as were the paving and recreation elements). Post-and-rail and screen structures, and all planting, were installed for a lump sum contract of $3500 in 1941.

216—Tall trees.

217—Small trees and shrubs.

218—Medium trees.

219

220

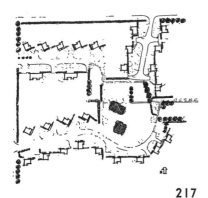

217

218

221

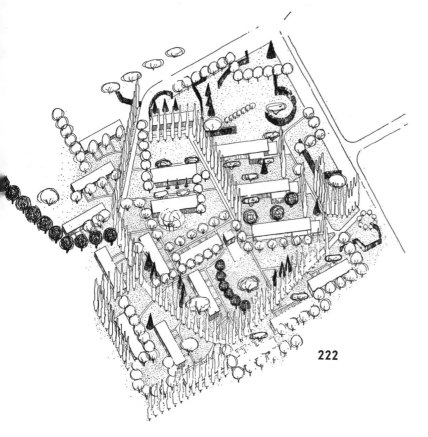

ROW HOUSING AT MANZANAR, CALIFORNIA 1942

District Architect—Vernon De Mars
District Engineer—Nicholas Cirino

222–223—Staff housing designed by FSA for the WRA relocation program in the high, clear mountain air of the Owens Valley. Surrounded by tremendous open spaces. Winter temperatures of 10° or lower required hardy plants.

222

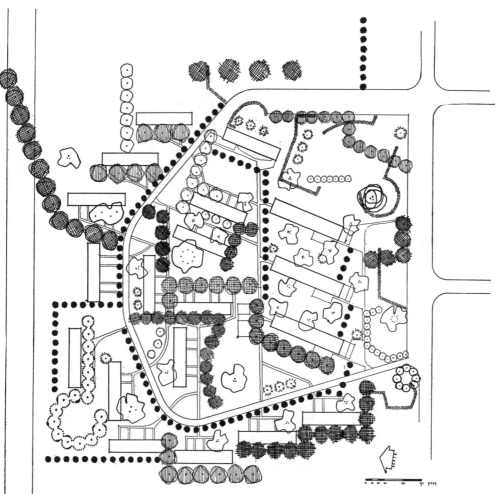

223

FPHA WAR HOUSING AT RIVERBANK, CALIFORNIA
1943

Architect—Russell de Lappe

224—One-story row housing at the north end of the San Joaquin, near the center of California's Central Valley. Site planning by the architect, planting and recreation layout by the landscape architect, on most FPHA work. Variation on tree grass plan for hot open country.

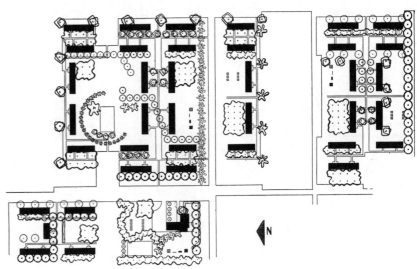

N

224

FSA ROW HOUSING AT SINTON, TEXAS   1939

District Architect—Burton Cairnes

225—Two-story row housing for farm workers in the Texas citrus belt. A plan in which regularity and irregularity are more carefully mingled in the tree pattern than in many others.

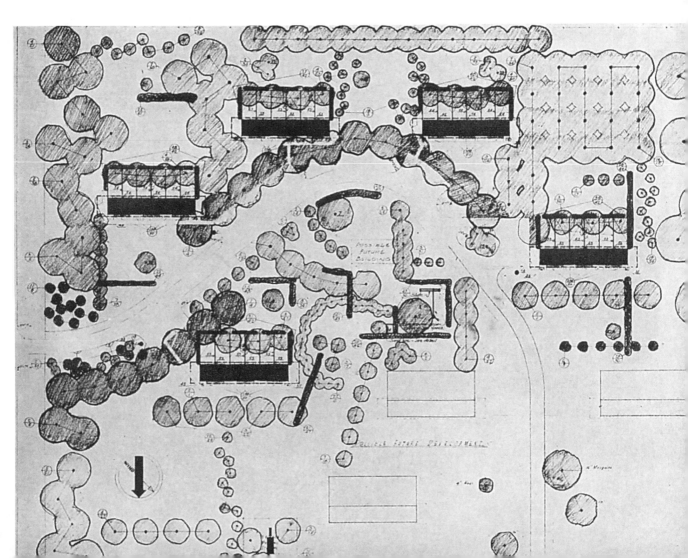

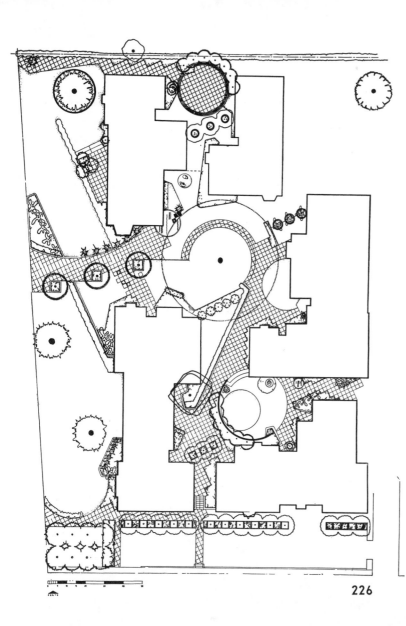

226

LUXURY APARTMENTS IN PASADENA, CALIFORNIA
1947

Architects—Cecil Rhodes Curtis and Associates
Photography—Roger Sumner
Design collaboration—R. Coelho-Cordoza

226–228—Project for a group of high-class apartment buildings, designed as prototypes for the salvation of a famous residential neighborhood from oncoming rooming house-hotel blight. Conservative architecture, suggested by the neighborhood, is complemented by a rich and fanciful outdoor pattern which develops a series of semi-private outdoor rooms.

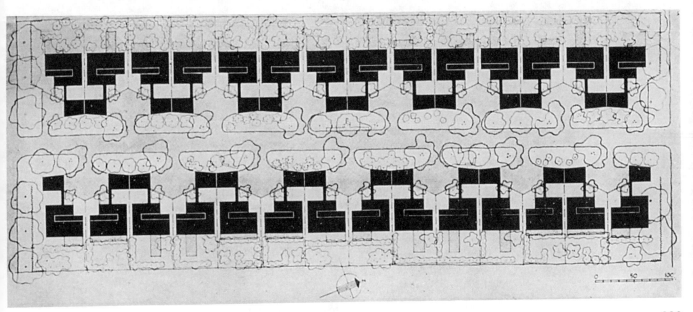

229

**HOUSING TO SELL IN ALTADENA, CALIFORNIA
1946**

Architect—Gregory Ain

229—Plan courtesy Progressive Architecture
July 1947. Twenty-eight speculative houses, all
from one identical plan, reversed in pairs along
both sides of one block of a north-south street
on the 10 per cent slope of the alluvial base of
the west end of the San Bernardino Mountains.
Lots were terraced level. Planting design for
the street frontage, punctuated by paired blank
garage side-walls of varying colors, developed
a variety of tree and shrub grouping within the
unity of regular clumps of Melaleuca styphe-
lioides, M. leucadencron, and Eucalyptus si-
deroxylon rosea. Plans for the rear gardens—
half facing east and half west—developed three
standard patterns of paving, grass, fine rolled
rock, color borders, shrub and vine screens, small
trees forming planes, and shade trees, for each
half. These plans were so combined with a planting chart as to produce a different combination
of plant material for each garden.

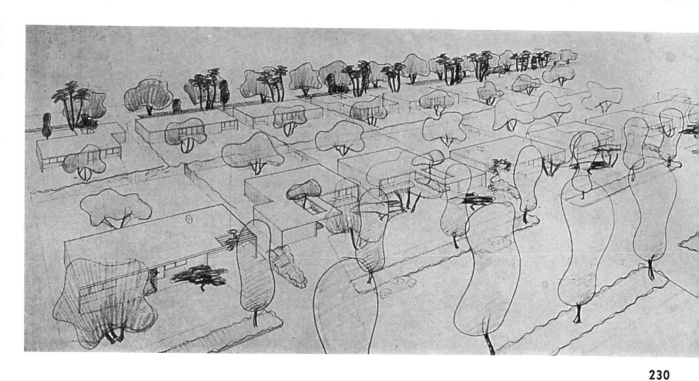

HOUSING TO SELL IN WEST LOS ANGELES, CALIFORNIA 1948

Architect—Gregory Ain
Collaborating—Joseph Johnson and Alfred Day
Courtesy Arts and Architecture

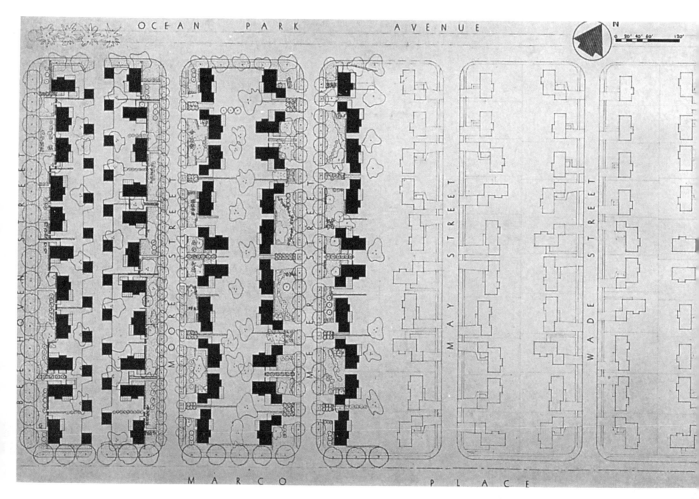

230–236—All drawings but 230 courtesy of the architect. One hundred houses projected to be built to sell by a progressive developer. East half of tract slopes, west half nearly flat. On the cool and breezy side of Los Angeles. Fifty-two houses actually built and planted; balance of property sold. All houses same basic plan, with varying placement in relation to each other, the street, and garages, and with varying use of entrance canopies. Planting, confined to the front yards with some trees in the rears, endeavors to develop a spatial park-like quality, rather than the standard two-dimensional "foundation planting." It also endeavors, by exploiting the wealth of plant material, to expand and integrate the spatial relations established architecturally, and at the same time to further individualize the houses.

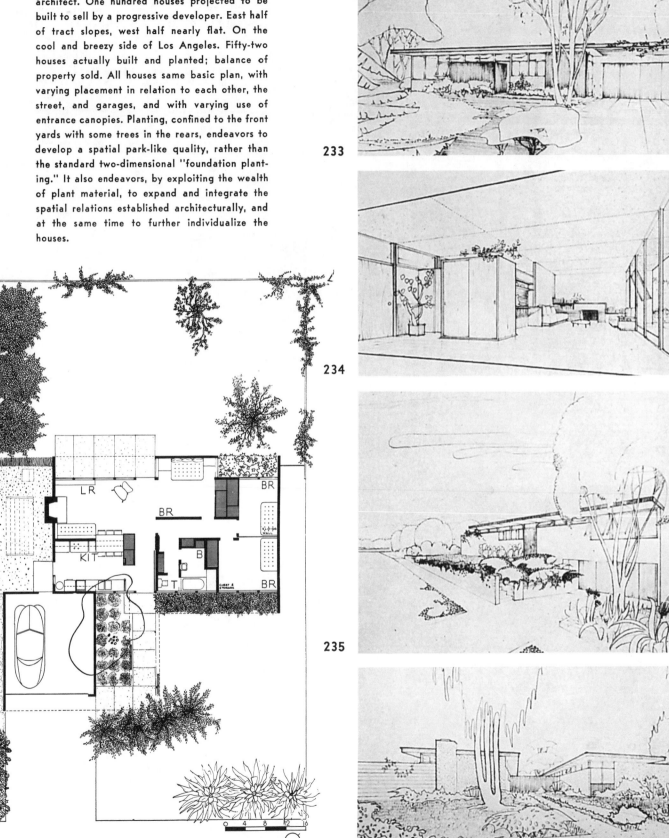

233

234

235

232

236

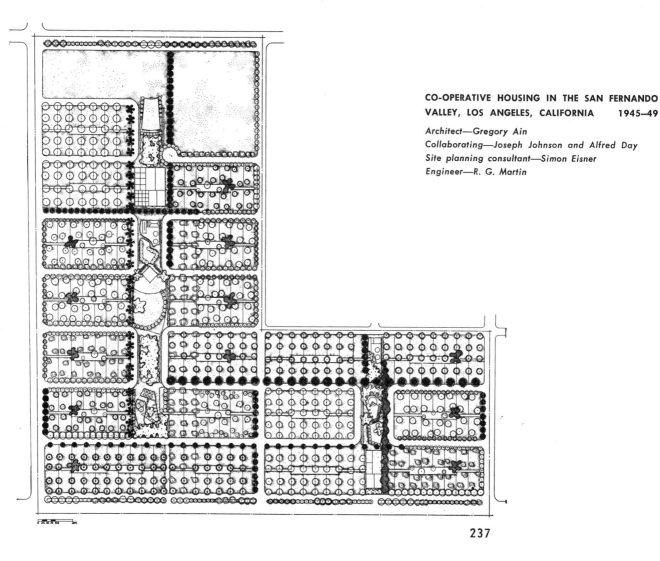

CO-OPERATIVE HOUSING IN THE SAN FERNANDO VALLEY, LOS ANGELES, CALIFORNIA 1945—49

Architect—Gregory Ain
Collaborating—Joseph Johnson and Alfred Day
Site planning consultant—Simon Eisner
Engineer—R. G. Martin

237

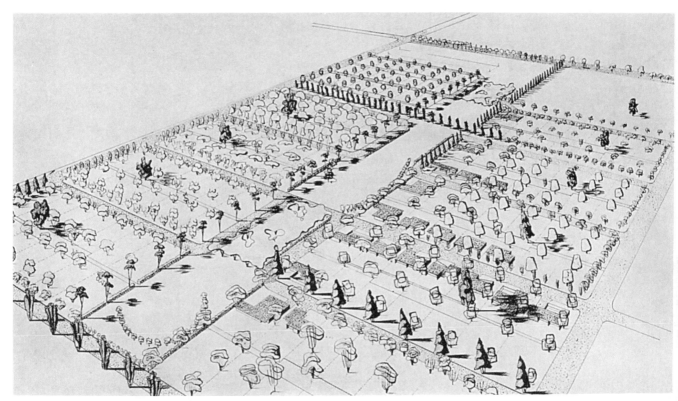

238

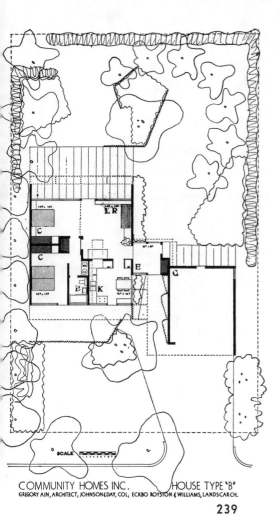

COMMUNITY HOMES INC.　　HOUSE TYPE "B"
GREGORY AIN, ARCHITECT, JOHNSON & DAY, COL; ECKBO ROYSTON & WILLIAMS, LANDSCARCH.

239

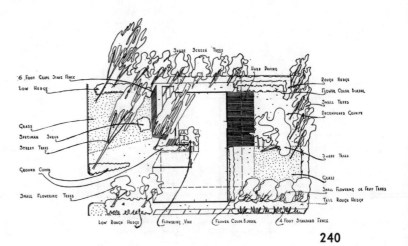

6 FOOT GRAPE STAKE FENCE
LOW HEDGE
GRASS
SPECIMEN SHRUB
STREET TREES
GROUND COVER
SMALL FLOWERING TREES
SHADE SCREEN TREES
HARD PAVING
ROUGH HEDGE
FLOWER COLOR BORDER
SMALL TREES
DECOMPOSED GRANITE
SHADE TREES
GRASS
SMALL FLOWERING OR FRUIT TREES
TALL ROUGH HEDGE
LOW ROUGH HEDGE
FLOWERING VINE
FLOWER COLOR BORDER
4 FOOT STANDARD FENCE

240

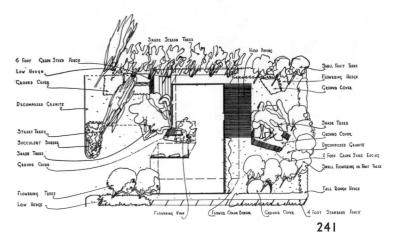

6 FOOT GRAPE STAKE FENCE
LOW HEDGE
GROUND COVER
DECOMPOSED GRANITE
STREET TREES
SUCCULENT BORDER
SHADE TREES
GROUND COVER
FLOWERING TREES
LOW HEDGE
SHADE SCREEN TREES
HARD PAVING
SMALL FRUIT TREES
FLOWERING HEDGE
GROUND COVER
SHADE TREES
GROUND COVER
DECOMPOSED GRANITE
2 FOOT GRAPE STAKE EDGING
SMALL FLOWERING OR FRUIT TREES
TALL ROUGH HEDGE
FLOWERING VINE
FLOWER COLOR BORDER
GROUND COVER
4 FOOT STANDARD FENCE

241

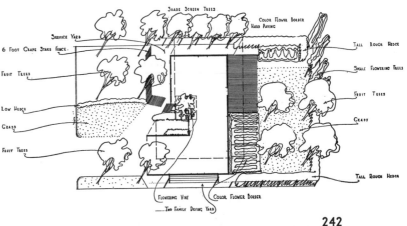

SERVICE YARD
6 FOOT GRAPE STAKE FENCE
FRUIT TREES
LOW HEDGE
GRASS
FRUIT TREES
SHADE SCREEN TREES
COLOR FLOWER BORDER
HARD PAVING
TALL ROUGH HEDGE
SMALL FLOWERING TREES
FRUIT TREES
GRASS
TALL ROUGH HEDGE
FLOWERING VINE
COLOR FLOWER BORDER
TWO FAMILY DRYING YARD

242

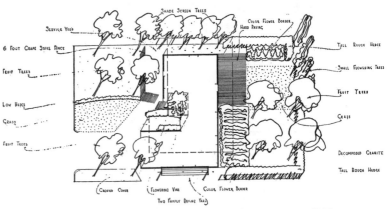

SERVICE YARD
6 FOOT GRAPE STAKE FENCE
FRUIT TREES
LOW HEDGE
GRASS
FRUIT TREES
SHADE SCREEN TREES
COLOR FLOWER BORDER
HARD PAVING
TALL ROUGH HEDGE
SMALL FLOWERING TREES
FRUIT TREES
GRASS
DECOMPOSED GRANITE
TALL ROUGH HEDGE
GROUND COVER
FLOWERING VINE
COLOR FLOWER BORDER
TWO FAMILY DRYING YARD

243

237–249—Two hundred and eighty single-family homes on 100 acres of flat land in Los Angeles' "interior valley"; 10 degrees hotter and colder than the balance of the city. Sixteen acres of park space in central strips and inner-block "finger-parks" makes possible a balanced and integrated pattern of recreation for all ages. The general master tree plan, implementing a policy of controlling all major tree planting for the benefit of all residents (approved by thoroughly democratic processes), develops an expression in foliage, structure and space of the comprehensive integration of the neighborhood unit. It accepts the good gridiron of loop streets embodied in the site plan, and draws from the still rural character of much of the valley around it.

A "backbone" pattern of strong planes of tall forms in which verticality dominates—slender fan palms, Canary Island pines, Lombardy poplars, incense cedars, Italian cypress, eucalyptus—will dominate as years add growth. At the median level of ordinary shade tree height about

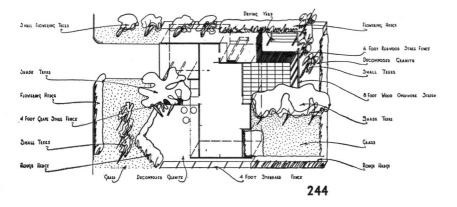

SMALL FLOWERING TREES
DRYING YARD
FLOWERING HEDGE
6 FOOT REDWOOD STAKE FENCE
DECOMPOSED GRANITE
SMALL TREES
SHADE TREES
FLOWERING HEDGE
8 FOOT WOOD OPENWORK SCREEN
4 FOOT GRAPE STAKE FENCE
SHADE TREES
SMALL TREES
GRASS
ROUGH HEDGE
ROUGH HEDGE
GRASS
DECOMPOSED GRANITE
4 FOOT STANDARD FENCE

244

half the blocks are planted as "groves," of London planes, Chinese elms, fruitless mulberries, cut-leaf silver maples, weeping willows, and Siberian elms, planted in a large-scale grid on the lot lines (approximately 70 ft. on centers). In the balance of the blocks a variety of shade trees are planted very irregularly, and in the central park two large blocks of trees will make picnic groves. Throughout all blocks and park areas a considerable and irregular variety of small colorful flowering and fruiting trees will lend interest and richness. The tree list totals 79 kinds, but these will be unified by the dominance of the larger kinds and stronger forms, the "backbone" and "grove" trees.

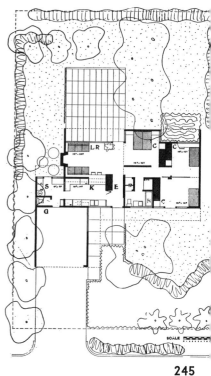

245

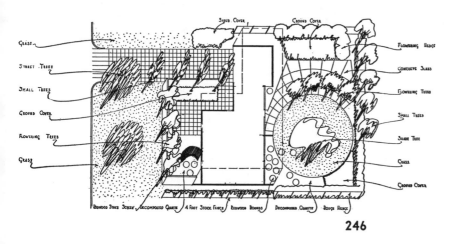

SHRUB COVER
GROUND COVER
GRASS
FLOWERING HEDGE
STREET TREES
CONCRETE SLABS
SMALL TREES
FLOWERING TREES
GROUND COVER
SMALL TREES
FLOWERING TREES
SHADE TREE
GRASS
GRASS
GROUND COVER
REDWOOD STAKE SCREEN
DECOMPOSED GRANITE
4 FOOT STOCK FENCE
REDWOOD ROUNDS
DECOMPOSED GRANITE
ROUGH HEDGE

246

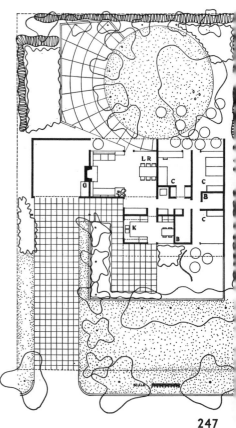

247

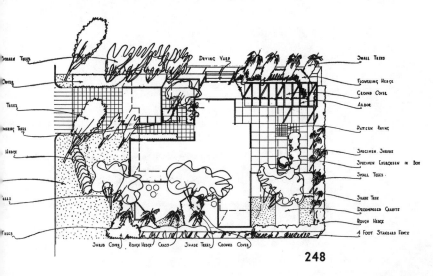

Labels (clockwise from top right): Small Trees, Flowering Hedge, Ground Cover, Aloes, Pattern Paving, Specimen Shrubs, Specimen Evergreen in Box, Small Trees, Shade Tree, Decomposed Granite, Rough Hedge, 4 Foot Standard Fence

Left labels: Screen Trees, Cover, Trees, Flowering Trees, Hedge, Trees, Trees

Top label: Drying Yard

Bottom labels: Shrub Cover, Rough Hedge, Grass, Shade Trees, Ground Cover

248

Six typical house plans have been projected by the architects to meet the varying needs of the residents. Following these a variety of typical garden plans, developing the ideas begun in 229, have been projected. 240–243, inclusive, project a variation in required maintenance to suit all needs, from the active home farmer-dirt gardener to the lazy one who just wants fun in the yard. These garden studies have barely begun, and will find themselves limited initially by budget problems. However, adequate fencing, reflecting a balance between neighborliness and privacy, and adequate planted surfacing, enclosure and shade will be provided at the beginning.

(As of September 1949 this project will remain permanently on paper. A coalition of real estate-finance-FHA interests forced its cancellation.)

249

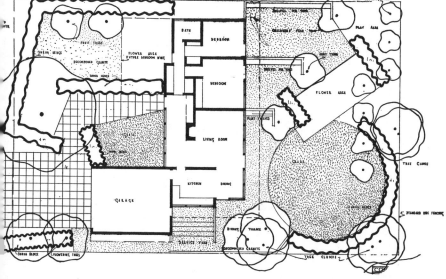

250

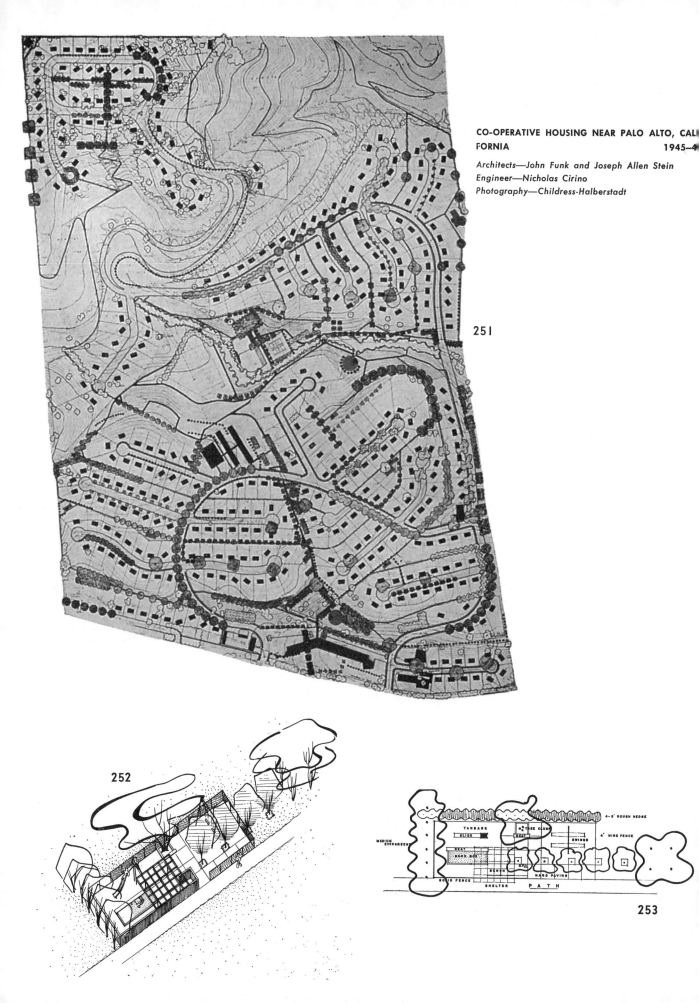

**CO-OPERATIVE HOUSING NEAR PALO ALTO, CALI-
FORNIA** 1945—4

Architects—John Funk and Joseph Allen Stein
Engineer—Nicholas Cirino
Photography—Childress-Halberstadt

251

252

253

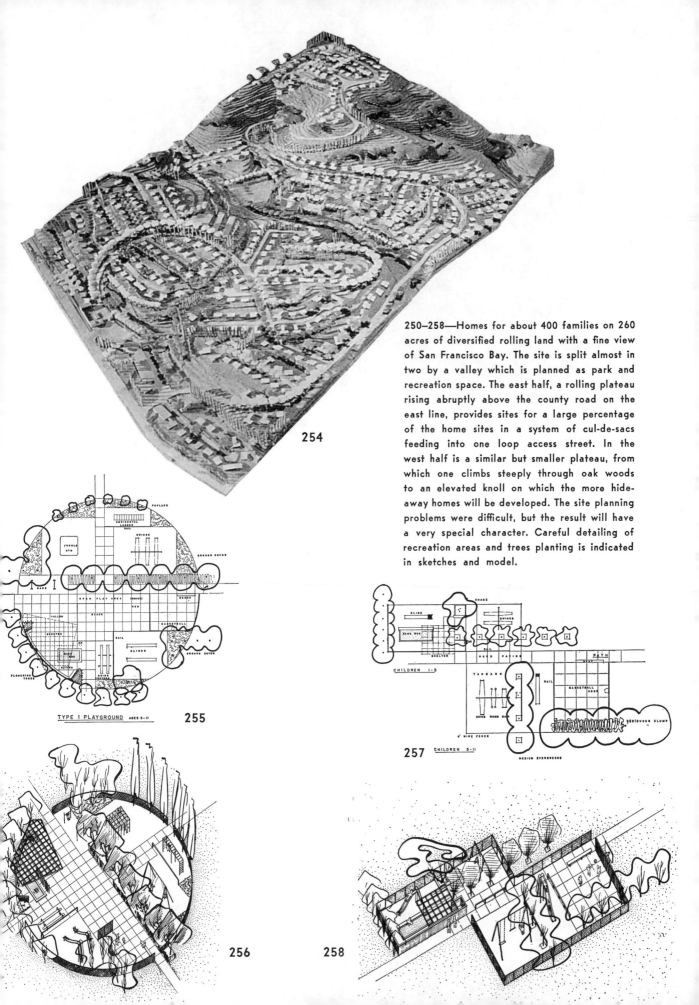

254

250–258—Homes for about 400 families on 260 acres of diversified rolling land with a fine view of San Francisco Bay. The site is split almost in two by a valley which is planned as park and recreation space. The east half, a rolling plateau rising abruptly above the county road on the east line, provides sites for a large percentage of the home sites in a system of cul-de-sacs feeding into one loop access street. In the west half is a similar but smaller plateau, from which one climbs steeply through oak woods to an elevated knoll on which the more hide-away homes will be developed. The site planning problems were difficult, but the result will have a very special character. Careful detailing of recreation areas and trees planting is indicated in sketches and model.

TYPE I PLAYGROUND AGES 5-11   **255**

CHILDREN 1-5

257 CHILDREN 5-11

256   **258**

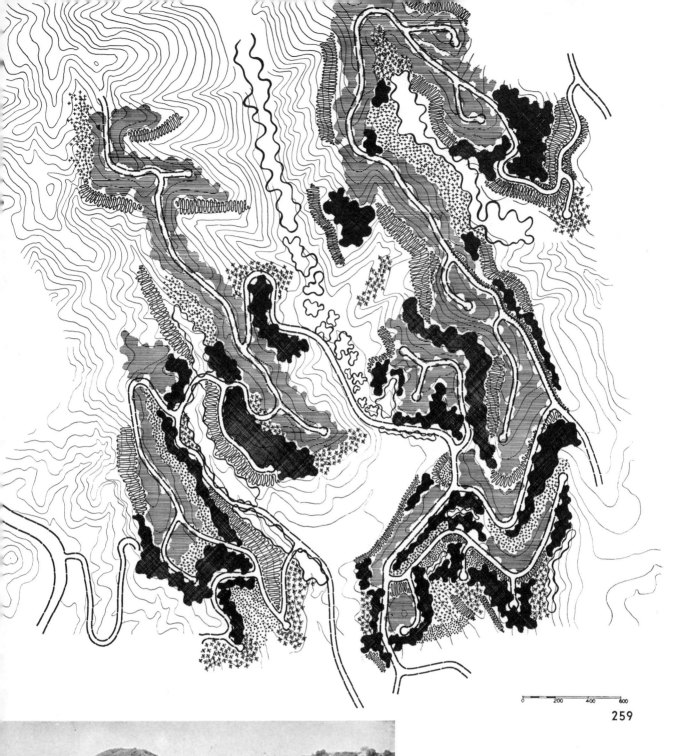

259

260

 EUCALYPTUS

 AVOCADO

 OLIVE

 CYPRESS-CEDAR-PINE

 PALM

 POPLAR-SYCAMORE

 MIXED

CO-OPERATIVE HOUSING IN WEST LOS ANGELES
1946–49

Architects—Whitney Smith, A. Q. Jones
Engineers—Edgardo Contini, Seaboard Engineering Co.
Photography—Emiel Becsky

259–270—Homes for 500 families on 800 acres in the rough lower ridges of the Santa Monica Mountains. Site comprises roughly one main valley and two smaller, bounded by ridges averaging 300 ft. above valley floors, with 30 per cent side slopes. Some easier rolling land at the lower end. Valleys and ridges run north and south. Homes were planned generally on the ridge-tops and easier slopes, valleys left to community use. Considerable earthwork was found necessary to make the site usable: well over 500,000 cubic yards of earth have been moved.

The tree pattern, suggested diagrammatically only, endeavors to articulate the various topographic units which emerge from the site engineering, and also to equalize somewhat the extremes of slope and convey a sense of security and balance by using taller thinner forms on lower levels, lower more spreading forms higher, and intermediate forms on the slopes between. Eucalyptus, avocado and olive (typical of these three groups) dominate quantitatively in the plan, and would dominate visually were it carried out. Generally the trees are thought of as being scattered irregularly among the houses, wherever they fall appropriately in garden spaces. In a few sections, where they could be continued approximately on the contour, thinner planes or belts of trees have been projected as elements of spatial organization.

The site is of a rough primeval character on the up side, merging into well-to-do residential neighborhood below. The tree plan has been rejected as being "unnatural." It has been said that "nature has no pattern" therefore we should have none. Also "too many kinds" and "too many exotics" were projected. Once again, apparently, nature is to take precedence over man. The natural interest of people in the rich variety of plant material, man's potential for imaginative projection and development of unprecedented spatial relations and humanized landscapes, is to be rejected in favor of a mechanical pepper-and-salt naturalism, a romantic Victorian suburb hidden away in chaparral and live oaks. (Actually there is a clear natural pattern on the site: chaparral—native broadleaf evergreen shrubs—on the south and west slopes, live oaks and native black walnuts among them

261

262

263

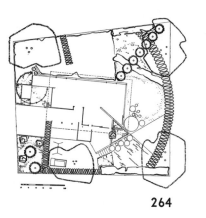

264

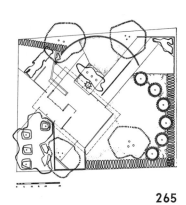

265

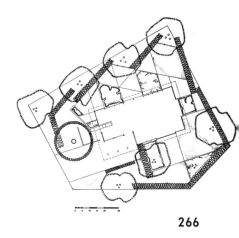

266

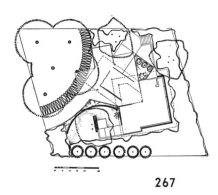

267

on the north and east, California sycamores in the moist valley floors. To south and west the site abuts on all sorts of horticultural introductions by unnatural man.)

Garden plans are preliminary studies to accompany houses of uncommon interest and imagination in plan. These gardens, too, are "unnatural"—they have "form." Photographs give the character of the site at conclusion of rough grading.

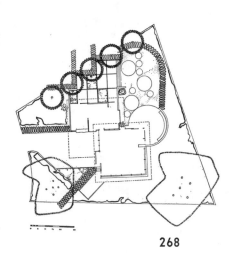

268

269

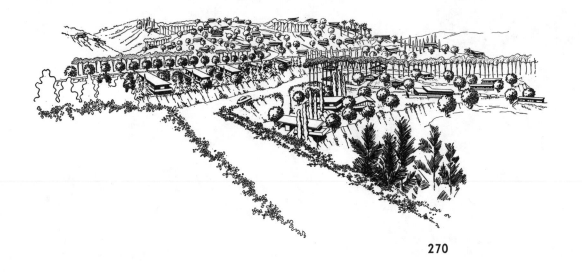

270

Soil Conservation Service

WHAT NEXT

CHAPTER XV

FROM ART TO PLANNING

THE ALLIED ARTS

The existing distinctions between the various fields of planning and design are based largely on the *techniques* with which they work. The expansion in the complication of these techniques since the Industrial Revolution has been one of the wedges tending to force these fields apart from their pre-industrial unity. Architecture, painting, and sculpture were unified activities in Greek, Gothic, Renaissance and Baroque times. In the last two, landscape design, as an architectural extrusion into the landscape, was also integral. Le Corbusier and Frank Lloyd Wright, each in his own way, have projected a reunion of painting, sculpture, and architecture. One purpose of this book is to project an expansion of that union into a landscape that is both architectural and natural.

A simplified theoretical reorganization of the various fields of planning and design concerned with the shaping of our physical environment can be made most rationally in terms of SCALE, or size of the operation, units, or elements, in relation to human size and activity. This is rational because, while some virtuosos can project work at all scales from paintings to cities, sustained practical production for most of us will tend to concentrate within certain broad zones of scale: that of house, school and neighborhood, of the objects and furnishings within them, of the city and region which contains them. To these we must add the direct human scale of such presentations in time and space as drama, dance, music. It is not our intent to prohibit the twentieth century Leonardo from doing everything, but only to suggest a rational structure within which all of us can move and work freely and productively.

The grouping of the design and planning fields in terms of scale will emphasize the areas of agreement, rather than the points of difference, between them. It will emphasize problems rather than techniques, and social usefulness rather than personal expressiveness. Our intent is not further complication or confusion, but rather to simplify and clarify the relations between the many, many fields of art and design which one finds listed in school catalogs and art books. Grouped in terms of the scale of their work, the various fields of conscious creative activity will come together about as follows:

LAND-USE PLANNING—The understanding, control and harmonization of the uses of more than one site, or piece of property in land (real estate), and the working out of the problems produced by the relations between several or many site uses; the rationalization of individualism on the land; subdivision planning, town planning, city planning, regional planning; horizontal scale predominant, control by maps, charts, diagrams, and the law. Today the most practical, the least esthetic, the most politic of the arts; tomorrow the major creative vehicle for the good society.

SPACE ORGANIZATION—The enclosure or definition, partial or complete, for reasons both functional and esthetic, of three-dimensional space within the boundaries of a single site, or piece of land in one ownership. This includes architecture, structural engineering and other less developed kinds of building design; various other kinds of engineering—site, earthwork, bridge, dam, highway, railway, electric, et cetera; landscape architecture and design of all sorts, professional, commercial, and amateur; and various special fields such as recreation planning, the design of mobile space units— autos, airplanes, ships, trains, buses—stage design, interior decorating or design, etc.

TIME-SPACE PRESENTATIONS—All those arts most directly involved with social expression and communication, and popular culture; having a fourth dimension or continuity of production in time, involving the occupancy of space, a direct human scale, and some direct relation between producers and observers: theatre, movies, music, dance, radio, literature, poetry, etc.

OBJECT DESIGN—All the multiform and endlessly varied furnishings, equipment, art objects, and enrichment which go into the enclosed space, indoor or outdoor, once its basic organization is established. This is a broadly inclusive field, and some may bridle at such catholicism. It includes both "fine" and "applied" arts and all degrees of machine and handicraft production: painting, sculpture, the graphic arts, typography, book-binding, furniture design, industrial design and mechanical engineering (equipment and utensils), ceramics, weaving, fashion and costume design, and such garden elements as come under the heading of enrichment: flower borders, rock and driftwood arrangements, ornamental pools, and so on.

It is obvious that, like any rational classification made for working convenience, these are not positive separate entities, flat areas with fixed boundaries, but rather that they represent a continuous space-scale which divides rather naturally into these quadrants in relation to the scale of the human being. These are horizontal divisions which are most closely related to the pattern in which social problems are presented and organized for solution. The problems and the total technical and esthetic organization for their solution are more homogeneous horizontally than vertically. While talented personnel—like the architect who paints, does furniture, buildings, and city planning—may move vertically through these divisions with great freedom and productivity, the changes in scale between levels are greater, more qualitative, and require more conscious adjustment than do the more quantitative horizontal changes in technology.

The one serious vertical split in this fine theoretical structure is that between the approaches to indoor and outdoor space-form and arrangement. The modern sculpture is lost in the period garden or the empty back yard, the modern house sits self-consciously among the same haphazard foundation plants as its dingbat neighbors, and the group of modern buildings floats aimlessly, adrift on a sea of shapeless green. This vertical split is continuous, from object design to land planning; it is the physical expression of the philosophical separation of man and nature. It has been bridged somewhat at the large planning scale by men with a fine sense of site scale, as Corbusier, Wright, and Mendelsohn; and it has been bridged somewhat at the smaller object design scale by a decorative use of natural materials. But these are only straws in the wind. One objective of this book is to lay the groundwork and chart a course for the complete healing of this split, the bridging of the gap which blocks free horizontal movement at every level, and which therefore blocks the most complete solutions.

Perhaps the clearest presentation of these horizontal and vertical relations between the various fields of art and design would be to

232

project a theoretical complete school. Such a school, organized on our basis, would have four primary departments—land-use planning, space organization, time-space presentation, and object design—organized diagrammatically as four wings radiating from a central administrative unit, or perhaps more literally as four floors with a connecting tower. Each of these departments would include, as divisions, all of the various fields closely related to them, as we have described. It should be clear that this would be a most functional structure: all the divisions in each department would be of maximum direct assistance and inspiration to each other in the solution of our main problems, to most of which most of them would prove relevant; nevertheless broad and active vertical liaison between the departments would also be essential to the complete grasp of problem solutions.

The space planner-designer (architect, engineer, landscape architect) is impelled in two directions from his central position in the design field. Whether he is in pursuit of profits, fine plastic esthetics, or social service (or all three) he tends to expand his interests in the direction of city planning of some sort, since it houses his work, and to contract his interests in the direction of object design of some sort, since it completes the interior and is often an essential structural detail of his work.

FROM PLANNING TO DESIGN—The distinction between land-use planning and space organization today is arbitrary, based on the arbitrariness of real estate property lines dividing up the land into parcels whose size and shape have little relation to their use, and function as obstacles to the effective harmonization of the uses of various parcels. Planning today is a kind of diplomacy, concerned with coaxing a minimum co-operative relation out of the anarchy of laissez faire land use; it is restrictive, prohibitive, negative, and advisory, rather than constructive, creative, positive, and mandatory. Actual physical space organization can only occur, as a unified program under one direction, on one piece of real estate. One of the primary struggles of all our efforts at housing development and urban redevelopment has

been to devise techniques for getting the land together in sufficiently large parcels to make possible the benefits of modern planning and mass construction. However, as these units get larger and yet remain small in relation to the size of the community, they tend to become arrogant, intolerant of social co-operation, and to create greater and more discordant splits in the body municipal. Stuyvesant Town in New York, ". . . a vast housing project covering 72 gross acres in some 18 East Side blocks" (Breines in Task), is an excellent example of this arrogant bullying of the community by monopolized high finance.

If we may be allowed the theoretical (if radical) projection of a situation in which the property lines on the land within the area covered by a municipality or other governmental unit were to be eliminated (by thoroughly democratic methods), thus bringing all the physical development of the municipality under the simple direct control of the citizens through their local government, it will be seen that the separation between space organization and land-use planning would immediately become much less arbitrary. Indeed the two would tend to merge, as in the imaginations of so many architects and city planners, as comprehensive three-dimensional space planning projects for town, city and country, up to a point at which the horizontal dimension so far overshadowed the vertical as to render that irrelevant and reduce the project to mapping or charting land use. Thus land-use planning falls between space organization and geography.

FROM ARCHITECTURE TO LANDSCAPE— The inherent tendency of achitecture to expand its concepts beyond the structural shell is expressed simply and directly in the following:

ERNEST J. KUMP

Architecture represents an organic unity of all space in planning considerations. The elements consisting of structurally enclosed, semi-enclosed and open spaces, in reality are parts of a wholeness or total space environment. It is apparent, then, that in this wholeness, the buildings themselves constitute merely particularized spaces in which it is desired to provide controlled environmental conditions, i.e.—visual, climatic, audio, in addition to shelter.

233

However, the expansion is not quite that simple. Architecture can expand rather readily to take in complexes of building and engineering elements of almost any scale up to full communities, because the problems continue to be human, functional, structural. Thinking has to develop quantitatively, but the qualitative terms remain the same. But when it comes to the actual treatment of open ground, the actual form relations in areas between buildings and planted landscape, architecture encounters certain contrasts between itself and landscape design. These are more than the mere technical contrast between structural know-how and planting know-how.

They are contrasts: between design in which specific function is a major determinant of form, and that in which it is minor or negligible in form decisions, therefore in which the free choice of forms and arrangements is minor or major; between design in which the scale comes primarily from a relation between the human form and structural elements, and that in which the scale is a relation between these and that of the site and the surrounding landscape; between design in which there is a fairly consistent relation between horizontal and vertical dimensions, and design in which the former may tremendously exceed the latter; and between design in which all the parts have an actual, physical, supporting connection with each other, and design in which most of the parts have only a visual connection with each other. These are aspects of the contradiction between architecture and landscape design, which can be resolved into a higher art if all aspects receive appropriate consideration. The present theoretical separation between the two, expressed in an actual separation of structure and site, may be considered a kind of demand by history for the resolution of these contradictions.

The primary dichotomy with which we struggled during the nineteenth and the first half of the twentieth centuries was that between architect and engineer (artist:technician). Now that we can see the way to mending that, in principle at least, we find ourselves confronted with another at the more expanded scale of site and region. This is the technical or professional expression of the man:nature dichotomy we have discussed. It may perhaps be phrased thus: architect-engineer:landscape design. This is sometimes the same artist:technician relation, in which the architect-engineer expects of the landscape man merely the technical development of his romantic and/or functional concept of landscape development. At other times this relation is reversed, and the landscape man becomes the artist, the "nature poet" who weaves a network of lyricism, illusion, and natural wonder around the hard, practical fact of the building, "softening its harsh lines," "healing the scarred site," and so on.

Occasionally there is a relation of co-operative teamwork, equal artist-technicians working side by side toward complete solution of all site-development problems, complementing and supplementing each other and maintaining mutual respect for each other's creativity. In all of these relations, however, there is a split; there are two things, not one; there are two different kinds of thinking, both technically and esthetically, going on in the structural and landscape spheres, in spite of the fact that they are united in function by necessity, and in space potentially. We have, at best, house-and-garden; we have no word in our language comparable to the Persian "bagh," house and garden conceived as one inseparable entity, one complete unity of space for living.

We are on the threshold of realizing that our concepts of architecture (including creative engineering) and of landscape design (or landscape architecture) are in reality two halves, or two sides, of a greater art. This is, or will be, an art of site-space organization, of spatial continuity at the truly functional scale of site, neighborhood, and community. It has been historically, and will be again, a creative unity greater than the mere addition of structural design and landscape design, as "bagh" is a concept greater than house-and-garden. In the great formal periods we are able to call this unity of site-space "architecture." The unity of the future, growing out of architecture, engineering, and landscape design as they are practiced today, may well still be called architecture, but it will be greater, richer, and more magnificent than any historical precedent.

It is not our intent to be impractical or utopian; we are not about to ascend into a new ivory tower in which one cannot distinguish indoors from outdoors. We are not projecting a streamlined Suburbia of the twenty-fifth century, in which all climate is synthetic, all production is automatic, and there is only free food, free love, and free space with various combinations of structures and plants just for fun. We are merely saying that architecture and landscape design are both growing in their theoretical and practical concepts, that they are already overlapping each other, and that therefore it may be fruitful to consider what may come of continued growth.

The relations between all these professions must be of teamwork rather than of competition —of real teamwork which allows free movement of individuals between fields, as their talents and understanding direct them. Such freedom and co-operation will, of course, develop only in any quantity where there exists an actual shortage of qualified professionals, a surplus of jobs, over a period of time long enough to dispel the competitive attitudes produced by a shortage of opportunities in the planning and design fields. It is necessary to stress the distinction between competition in quality and quantity of production of ideas and solutions, and competition for livelihood which descends to competition between personalities, contact techniques, and so on. The former is socially productive, the latter socially wasteful because it places competition on a footing of irrelevancy.

The rationalization of professional practice, which is an evident necessity in the nature of the problems of our physical environment, is so closely related to the rationalization of the building industry, a project close to the hearts of architects and housers, as to move hand-in-hand with it. It is the bringing of order and organization into the construction field which is the essential prerequisite to the release of professional energies from the tangle of technology to the full and creative grasp of the problems

and potentialities of the space we live in. When architects and engineers no longer feel it necessary to develop new construction systems for each specific job—because there exists no co-ordinated centralized industrial structure to develop systems big enough and flexible enough to meet all problems—they will be able to concentrate on the job of space planning and design which is their primary social function. The rationalization of building, which will fix the responsibility for technical development where it belongs, on the shoulders of an industrial organization rather than on those of each isolated individual architect, together with the rationalization of the problems of the social environment, which will demand the concentration of professional energies where they are most needed, will promote and make possible that rationalization of our practices and relations which is so badly needed.

FROM SPACE TO OBJECT—Interior design is the bridge between object design and space design. This includes sometimes landscape design, which is interior design out-of-doors when it does its job completely. The link between object designers—including painters and sculptors—and spatial designers is that every painting, every sculpture, every object of any sort has to have a home in space and establish relations between itself and some three-dimensional enclosure. In doing this it participates in the space organization, and changes it qualitatively. That is one of its functions—the refinement of space experience. That function is unavoidable.

There is one way in which the analogy between "interior" design indoors and outdoors— or between structures and trees, communities and landscapes—is incomplete: nature supplies the detail of tree and landscape, we merely arrange and maintain them. But structures and communities have to be consciously detailed down to the last corner and nail, and there is an integral progression from the scale of the parts to the scale of the whole.

The general tendency of all the arts in the twentieth century has been to expand their frontiers, to push toward their maximum scientific potentials in terms of materials, spatial control, and human experience in an abstract sense. Where these frontiers have occurred between the arts, as between architecture and landscape design, the result has been for each to find itself in the other's territory, with mutually beneficial results. Thus sculpture, which since the seventeenth century has only been able to expand by blowing itself up to monumental scale, while remaining an isolated object, can now begin again to think of expanding horizontally to become integrated with its setting, and to produce actual sculptural or plastic effects on that setting. Landscape design, recognizing more and more the plastic or sculptural content of its space organization, can begin to produce refinements in scale and complexity in portions of its work. These refinements, without becoming separated from their context, can at a certain indefinable point, become truly sculptural. In the informal tradition sculpture and a sculptural use of rock and of structural elements were very important in Chinese gardens, and the Japanese garden at its best was a complete sculptural conception: earth forms, rocks, plants, water basins, and the fine formal lanterns were all moulded, grouped, carved, and trained together into fully mature plastic entities. Through all the great formal traditions—the western from Egypt to Baroque France, the Chinese, the Hindu, the Mayan—sculpture and sculptural architectural detail were inextricably integrated in the controlling patterns of architecturally ordered open spaces.

FRANK LLOYD WRIGHT, 1939

Sculptors and painters ask me: 'What place has sculpture and painting in your building?' I reply: 'My buildings are painting and sculpture. But painting and sculpture that is architecture could enter and carry architecture further where I am compelled to leave off for want of more highly specialized technique. . . .' To carry the building higher in its own realm is the rightful place of painting and sculpture wherever they or architecture are rightly concerned.

IMAGINATION TO REALITY—It would be cynical, arrogant, or irresponsible to discuss the allied arts without mentioning the more or less handicraft arts of construction, installation, and maintenance which are essential to the final

236

realization of our fine concepts of space and materials on the ground. The architect and the landscape architect don't "do" the house and the garden; they don't, or at least they seldom, build or plant it with their own hands. They plan it, establish the general concepts, the functional and esthetic relations desired, detail it with varying degrees of completeness on paper, and, often but not always, supervise the production of the final house and/or garden from those drawings. There is many a slip betwixt plan and realization. The final quality of the job is an intimate compound of the skill, competence, and conscience of the construction and installation organization, plus the technical intelligence and creative imagination of the professional planner-designer. Neither can function well without the other.

SITE PLANNING

The bridge from the three formally separated spatial arts which exist, to that expanded concept of site-space form which is implicit in our thinking, is site planning as it is beginning to be understood today. The proof that this is the unifying concept for the spatial arts is the fact that each of the three tends quite automatically to assume that it is the natural one to expand to the control of overall site planning. Each one thinks that its kind of thinking is naturally the kind which should establish the overall concepts of site form and arrangement. The competitive contradictions which ensue when all three arts arrive on the site with this same preconception in mind have in them the germ of a greater art of site-space design in the future.

Site planning has been forced on our attention by expanded problems involving groups of buildings—housing, schools, universities, hospitals, industrial plants—but the bridge from the separate space arts to site-planning exists at smaller scale. Practically all of the problems of general site planning exist in symbolic embryo in the private home-site problem. This home-unit, actually fragmentary, expanded to organic completion, becomes the neighborhood.

The neighborhood is the bridge from site planning as it can be done today to city planning, the great spatial art of the future. Thus site planning becomes the bridge from our system of pigeonholes—the house, the garden, the utilities, the subdivision—to complete environmental concepts.

Site planning should not be thought of as merely placing buildings on the land and connecting them with roads and utilities (architectural), or as merely developing a skeleton of roads and utilities on the land and fitting the buildings to it (engineering). It must be thought of as the organization of the total land area and air space of the site for best use by the people who will occupy it. This means an integrated concept in which buildings, engineering construction, open space and natural materials are planned together at one time by one thoroughly co-ordinated team of technicians, to form a complete, balanced, wholesome and pleasant development or community. If we think of a neighborhood of homes as the ideal site planning concept, its basic skeleton would be composed of public open space or "commons" (rather than streets); its heart the community center: shopping, management, meeting place, recreation rooms, nursery, school, et cetera. Roads or streets for vehicular access might be thought of as a circulatory system which serves this basic skeleton *from outside;* the homes, to continue the simile, as vital nerve centers based on the inner skeleton and served by the heart and circulatory system. To complete the simile, we have an outer skin or greenbelt of planting which protects the neighborhood, insulates it from an unpredictable context, or maintains its integrity in size and area.

Site-planning problems simpler in content—school, hospital, university, public or private multi-family housing—have established the general primary principle, valid both functionally and esthetically: the open space center landscaped for pedestrians only; buildings surrounding it; vehicular circulation and services outside them, even if they take the longer way around. This is the means by which open space becomes a positive element, to be shaped for its own sake by buildings and roads, rather than a negative by-product of architecture and engineering.

Who does the site planning? Everybody—and nobody. It is just beginning to be considered a specific, coherent field of design activity. Hitherto it has been a by-product of the overlapping of town planning, architecture, landscape design, and engineering. There has been no specific training for it, and little specific thought given to it as a complete kind of design problem, and the integrator of all other design problems. For the potential of site planning is not just to fit together all the architectural and engineering objets d'art in a workable fashion, and lubricate them with landscaping to eliminate friction. Its potenial is the potential of any and all art—to put together any series or collection of elements in such a manner that the total will be greater than the mere sum of the parts.

Site planning and space design proceed within a specific social framework of decisions and actions. In every construction or development operation concerned with the human environment these steps are almost invariably followed: first, some sort of program, covering needs and wants, is prepared; second, a site is selected upon which this program is to achieve concrete form; third, the processes of design—putting down on paper the actual form projected for the site development—go on; fourth, construction and installation proceed, controlled more or less by the paper designs; fifth, management, either public or private (a housewife is a manager) takes over and directs the use and maintenance of the project from that time on. Each of these five steps is of nearly equal importance to the final success of the project, and it is a practical impossibility to separate one from another, or to eliminate any one. For instance, if a program is not written at the beginning, the designer has to write it as he proceeds with his work, and if he fails to achieve a clear understanding of the problem, management is very likely to find itself writing the program for the problem which is supposed to have been solved. The first two steps, program and site selection, establish the limits within which the designer must work, and are therefore the primary determinants of the quality of the solution. Programs which are bigger than their sites—as most urban programs —present problems which are insoluble within their own limitations, no matter how ingenious the designer, and point the way toward the kind of collective imagination forecast in Le Corbusier's Ville Radieuse. Sites bigger than their programs involve a conspicuous consumption of land and landscape by the programmers. Programs include not only specific statements of wants and desires, but such things as budgets, general planning standards, building and other ordinances, profit expectations or hopes, and so on. Thus the form and arrangement of most commercial housing (built to sell or rent) is based on standards of profit, rather than standards of planning.

The direction and implications of site planning are toward continuously more complete integration of buildings and grounds, structure and site, indoor and outdoor space. It is within the thinking and the operations of site planning that it becomes possible for us to establish final coherent and unifying relations between plane, plastic, structural, and spatial design. From the potential of site planning as the integrator of the spatial arts, within property line boundaries, emerges the need for one overall design concept: the integrity of the site, or the site-space concept. This is a concept which lays primary emphasis on the complete form given to the total block of three-dimensional air-space bounded by the vertical projection of the property lines, and its visual relationship to the landscape beyond. This concept includes and supersedes, brings to maturity so to speak, the smaller architectural, engineering, and landscape design concepts which tend to accumulate in competitive fashion on most sites. This larger concept of the integrity of the site is important for a number of reasons.

1. It is important technically, because of the overlapping of technical problems on any site, typically the establishment of relations between floor and grade levels, foundations, drainage, surfacing, topsoil, etc. Cost, too, is a technical complication.

2. It is important functionally, because the functional problems likewise overlap. The development of any one site or piece of land is one continuous problem. When we break it into fragments (house, garden) we are apt to leave loose functional ends trailing: how to get in and out, by foot and by car; where do the doors go, what do the windows look at; where DO the clotheslines and garbage cans (the orphans on every job) go. Landscape and structural questions become related most intimately with the introduction of doors and glass in the exterior walls of a building. As we go from the concept of a box with holes punched in the sides to the concept of a building as composed of free and flexible roof, floor, and wall planes, some of the latter glass, the intimacy of this relationship increases. Doors create problems of access and of circulation. Glass in general pushes the problem of controlling privacy and views out beyond the foundation lines of the building. Control of who can look in, and what is seen out through, glass areas becomes a landscape problem although it may, of course, be solved by structural means. Some indication of the failure to plan for such control can be found in the heaviness of the curtaining the residents of multi-family housing units, public or private, find necessary over their windows.

3. It is important esthetically, because the building only exists, visually and spatially, in relation to the site and the surrounding landscape. Conversely, the site only exists, in its visual and spatial relation to people, through the introduction of the building which establishes a permanent relation between people and site. The building and the site are one in fact and in use. The extent to which this unity is strengthened or ignored, expressed or confused, is a function of the design process, and therefore of the designer's pre-conceptions or theories about the relation between building and site.

LE CORBUSIER

"The Exterior is Always An Interior" To sum up, in architectural ensembles, the elements of the site itself come into play by virtue of their cubic volume, their density, and the quality of the material of which

238

they are composed, bringing sensations which are very definite and very varied (wood, marble, a tree, grass, blue horizons, near or distant sea, sky). The elements of the site rise up like walls panoplied in the power of their cubic co-efficient, stratification, material, etc., like the walls of a room. Walls in relation to light, light and shade, sadness, gaiety or serenity, etc. Our compositions must be formed of these elements.

4. Finally, the concept of the integrity of the site is important psycho-biologically, because it gives us a framework of thought, a philosophy of approach, a technique for synthesis of complete cellular units, within which we can more intelligently pursue more complete solutions to the problem of the good environment, the wholesome human habitat. This problem is simply: what do people need in their homes, workspaces and playspaces, in terms of scale, form, color, texture, control or lack of control of climate, degree of refinement of materials, relation to nature, the soil, plants, the sun, the wind, views, solitude and sociability, recreation and relaxation, work and play, objectivity and subjectivity, and so on?

This is not a problem which can be solved by the designer alone, or by the people alone. The designer represents imagination, the people reality, and the contradictions between them have to be resolved by closing the gap. The abstract intellectuality of much modern design, the narrow practicalism of the amateur- or commercial-designed house or garden, both tend toward sterility when separated. There is no abstract man, woman, or child; there are only people, infinitely variable, infinitely analogous, sadly vulnerable to superficial generalization and unrealistic caricaturing both vicious and pollyanna. Behind the problem of integrating structure with site lies the problem of integrating people with site-space. That is the core of our design processes, the reason for our activity, and only complete concepts of habitat or environment can bring all its implications to full fruition.

HOME AND NEIGHBORHOOD—This concept of maximum organization of the total site space will change many approaches to house planning, even the most modern. The house plan will recognize the land and atmosphere around it with more than picture windows, stepping-stone walks, and casual shrubbery. Likewise this site-space concept will provide the key to the remodeling of many millions of existing American homes: homes which, however well built, bathroomed, and kitchened, have more or less completely ignored the potential usefulness of the space between their foundation lines and property lines.

However, neither the apartment, the house, nor the house-and-garden can make up for the unpredictability, the inadequacy, or the chaotic instability of the typical neighborhood, whether old and "just grown," or new and "planned." The city planning profession has worked its way downward to the neighborhood as a minimum planning unit or cell; it is time for the architects and landscape architects to work their way up to the neighborhood as actually the minimum home unit. This fact is indicated in a primitive way by the necessity of planning every house in relation to its neighborhood in economic and social terms, and by those home-buyer's manuals which give checklists for the selection of lots or houses in terms of their proximity to school, shopping, transportation, "nice neighbors," etc. It is further indicated, in reverse, by that excessive concentration, that loving lavish attention to every detail, which is focused by the space-planning professions on the house and/or garden, as a prototype or as an actual specific problem. These fragments make strenuous efforts toward self-sufficiency; they struggle bravely to make up for all the deficiencies of the typical neighborhood; in the hands of skilled designers the home becomes a serene microcosm, a little castle of peace and repose in a restless and unstable world, a completely equipped production plant of household comforts (with the housewife at the controls fourteen hours a day), stocked up, closed in, and ready to survive the collapse of society around it at any time. However, these home units are not complete, self-sufficient, or independent, any more than the individuals or families who live in them. Such illusions tended to vanish during the last depression, and will vanish still more in the future. Even as the house laps over into the lot or garden in functional-esthetic relations, so does this home unit lap over into the neighborhood. The neighborhood is the only unit which makes possible complete thinking about home planning; any planning done for a portion of this unit, as for a house or for a house-and-garden, can only be fragmentary.

ENDS AND MEANS—Surfacing, enclosure, shelter, enrichment—those elements we have outlined as the practical vehicles for the actual development of space organization, are also the vehicles for the continuity from detailed space to site space, at whatever scale. The general problem of site planning as it becomes married to spatial design is the establishment of harmonious and comfortable relations between the individual, the group, the crowd, and the spaces they occupy at every scale from that of the intimate room to that of the biggest wild landscape. Thus surfacing expands from the floors and their coverings within rooms and buildings through the paving and lawns, ground cover and flower beds of refined garden spaces, the greater paved, cultivated or grassed areas of park, playground, and farm, to the grassland, shrubland, and forestland which surface the hills and valleys, plains and mountains of most of the world.

Enclosure expands analogously from the four walls of the closed room, with their doors and windows, through: the freer relations of vertical planes of various heights, materials, and degrees of solidity or transparency under the spreading roof, varying from the widespread one-story building to the multi-story skyscraper; the still freer relations of screens and shrubbery, fences and walls and hedges and tree trunks, in garden and park; the qualitative expansion in scale by which two or more buildings establish enclosure relations between themselves and acquire third dimensions by the force of roof spread, building mass, or structural tension; the still further qualitative expansion by which a building or building complex establishes enclosure relations between itself, as a kind of spatial unit or nucleus, and other elements, man-

made or wild, comparable in scale but somewhat removed in space, which can be seen from it; the humanized landscape scale of considerable areas dominated by planting: grassland, cropland, shrubland, berryland, chaparral, scrubby desert, orchard and windbreak, meadow and savannah, alpine, temperate, and tropical forest; and finally the enclosure scale of the basic land forms—the openness of plain and plateau, the infinitely variable relations of hills and mountains.

Shelter expands in the same way from the ceiling, plain or complex, of the single room, and the interior of car, truck, trailer, or other vehicle, through the hovering roof, at every scale from the little cottage to Willow Run; the expanded structural shelter without sides—covered walk, arbor, pergola, ramada, pavilion, fair building, grandstand, circus tent; the more or less open shelter of trees, scattered or continuous, vertical or horizontal, deciduous or evergreen, meadow, orchard, or forest, from the fifteen-foot spread of the little plum tree to the two-hundred-foot spread of the giant tropical banyan; the greater scale of great works of engineering, bridges, power structures, etc.; and finally (the scale of shelter being more restricted than those of surfacing and enclosure), the shelter illusion of overhanging cliffs and narrow valleys, and the actual solid plastically sheltered space of caves, caverns, and tunnels.

Enrichment expands from the furniture, equipment, utensils, objets d'art, and potted plants of the room and the interior of the building, and the furniture, play equipment, water, rocks, flowers, specimen plants, and sculpture of garden and park; through the people and their clothes, the primary and most important source of enrichment of all space for human living; the treatment, in terms of material selection, color, texture, detailing, and so forth, of the surfacing, enclosure, and shelter elements; all the more or less accidental exedrae and impedimenta of town and city—traffic lights, hydrants, curbs, billboards, neon signs, traffic or other utility structures, vehicles of all sorts; and finally the endless wealth of enriching de-

240

tail in the rural and wild landscape—rocks and water, flowers and specimen plants, animals, birds, the light, moisture, and dust content of the atmosphere.

SCALE—Reciprocal relations in scale between landscape and human development are most important. To sprinkle fine rolling hills with single-family houses of haphazard design, and single-family roads however carefully curved, is to destroy the scale and character of those hills. But if the houses can be in some way grouped, whether in an actual multi-family structure or in some sort of spatial relations, rhythmic or continuous, which tends to fuse them into larger-scale units which have a scale relation to the form of the hills; and furthermore if tree patterns can be developed which have a continuity and a force comparable to those of buildings and hills and which articulate their important parts and elements; then the contradictions between development and site can be resolved, and a result greater in quality than their mere accumulation produced. Nor does this overall pattern have to regiment the individual or subvert democracy, as some may say.

The three-dimensional community unit which is in scale with its landscape context is projected in the works of Corbusier and other architects in Sweden, Brazil and elsewhere. Beyond that the great reclamation projects of the present and the future, in remaking the landscape as a total site for society, will establish entirely new relations between man and nature. Our projected or actual Tennessee Valley, Missouri Valley, Mississippi Valley, Columbia Basin, Colorado Basin, and Central Valley (California) developments; the great All-Russian River control project of the Soviet Union; the Reber earth-fill dams project for San Francisco Bay; the fine work of our Forestry and Soil Conservation services, and the great shelter belt afforestation projected for the Russian steppe in the 15-year agricultural plan of the Soviet Union; all these are milestones on the way to a future humanized, conserved, and stabilized landscape finer in scale and content than we can now visualize.

RELATIONS—In general, the concentration of a truly serious, scientifically esthetic art of site-space planning and design, especially as it expands in scale to sites larger than one acre, will be on RELATIONS rather than patterns or forms. This is a distinction which can be easily confused: it is obvious that relations will always be developed in forms and patterns. But the relations must be primary and controlling; form and pattern must not precede them, ignore them, or supersede them. Nor does concentration on relations imply a diagrammatic simplification; the nature of the relations depends precisely on the precise detailing of the elements which establish them. The primary relation is that between people and the space they occupy, people in numbers, space in cubage with qualitative as well as functional modifications.

In doing this job, site planning works with, resolves, and develops all the other more or less contradictory relations which are embodied or implicit in this occupation of physical space by physical people. The general relation of man to nature receives physical expression in each site-planning project; buildings are related to grounds, and structure to site. Relations between site forms are improved; relations between buildings in the plural, circulation, and open space are developed. Between structural and natural materials and elements, frame structures and plants, masonry and the earth and rock; between program, site, and material resources; between needs and desires embodied in ends, and available means; between the specific social unit and society in general; between site, neighborhood, and community; between specific functions and indeterminate functions; between active and passive, organized and unorganized use of space; between formal as form, and informal as relaxation; between classicism as intellectual order and romanticism as emotional satisfaction; between abstraction as the universal analogy and realism as the content of life; between geometry as simple geometry and biology as complex geometry; between form and content—relations exist which are expressed in complete site planning. All these relations exist already in our environment, but

241

they can certainly be improved. There is no ceiling on the ratio of space to people, or on the rate of improvement of its organization for use; but there must certainly be floors for both. That is where our problems begin.

FROM PLANNING TO ART

CITY PLANNING—In the ladder from site planning through neighborhood, town, city, and regional planning to national planning the city is the central concept, because cities are our major concentrations of population, and our worst physical muddles. City planning is the great creative work of the great future, that magnificent art of the human environment toward which all three space-planning professions gravitate automatically in the course of their work. Today, in America at least, it is a process, frustrating to the participants and mystifying to the observers, of using mammoth conceptions to wrest minute reforms from the city fathers; the real estate heirarchy, the "operative" (speculative) builders, the materials producers, and the mortgage bankers; the FHA which is the official defender of the special interests of these four; and the various owners of utilities, transit and railroad lines, shopping facilities, etc., who constitute that potent pattern of private vested interests which dominates the shaping of our communities. As Fortune said in February 1949: ". . . . For better or worse, a city is the image of its businessmen."

However, we must not forget, in our projection of planning theory, that as of 1940 only 56.5 per cent of the population lived in urban territory (places of 2,500 to 1,000,000 or more population); 43.5 per cent lived in rural territory, and 36.4 per cent in unincorporated territory. The larger cities (five of 1,000,000 or more; nine of 500,000 to 1,000,000; 23 of 250,000 to 500,000; 55 of 100,000 to 250,000) account for our major urban problems and our major urban planning activity; but they still represent only 28.8 per cent of our total population. To assume that conditions get better as places get smaller is a fallacy; some of the

worst slums in the country are rural, and it is the rural population, particularly the children and adolescents, which is most underprivileged in terms of recreational and cultural opportunities. The opportunity to commune with the birds and the bees is not enough, any more than is the opportunity for close communion with the neighbors in congested urban conditions. The antithesis between town and country comes to a head in these social relations; our theory of planning must be derived from, and applicable to, all the range of conditions from extreme urban to extreme rural or primeval. Only the universal analogy of human needs and values will serve to eliminate such antitheses, and equalize the opportunities for personal-social development for all the population.

We need no remote historical research to determine how most of our towns and cities developed the forms they have: they are historically so new that the forces which shaped them are still operating right before our eyes. This is true of practically all our American communities, except the pre-Revolution colonial cores of the older cities of the eastern seaboard. Now, in the middle of the twentieth century, the real estate man and the builder, with the engineering or architectural technicians whom they may hire, are the real primary—because most physically effective—city planners and land planners of America. They write the programs for the development of new land and building, they make the basic decisions as to form and arrangement, they either manage developments after completion or create the climate of concern with values which dictates the attitudes of owner management. The real estate man is the middleman between the land and its potential consumer; the builder is the middleman between that consumer and the development of the land; the banker and the materials men are the middlemen between the consumer and builder and the means to development. The mammoth human erosion, expressed in slum and blight, crime and disease and delinquency; and the piddling conservation measures, housing projects and zoning ordinances and scattered parks, which exist all around us are direct results of processes in which these middlemen have been very active.

REAL ESTATE—Since our land planning, both existent and forthcoming, is dominated by the incentives and the techniques of real estate, a prime qualification for one venturing into the planning field today should be familiarity with the principles of that enterprise. The land, and all the structures on it, are a set of commodities, constantly subject to the activities of the market, either directly if they are rental properties, or indirectly through economic pressures on the owners. Subdivision is a technique for converting the unbreakable continuity of the land into a series of free and flexible pieces of merchandise, subject to all the skill and cleverness of the entrepreneur. The lot, and anything on it, is a commodity, a piece of merchandise; the street provides access to the merchandise; the block is a by-product of the relations between street and lot and a system for grouping the merchandise. That is the principle which is clearly revealed by any objective examination of the typical American community pattern. It is true that this pattern is inhabited by people, by a social pattern which dictates certain minimum standards of space and equipment. But the pattern of subdivision, speculative building, profitable renting makes only the minimum mandatory concessions to these standards. That is the basis for the existence of the gap between the physical reality of our communities, and the theoretical optimums which are projected by all serious planning technicians, from conservative to radical, as desirable standards for a decent and wholesome environment. Land is almost never developed for a specific client who controls its plan to suit his own use-needs; most buildings are developed for general clients, the faceless (and voiceless) public. Hence decisions as to physical plan, form, and arrangement are made by the developers in terms of their own program for lack of anything more specific. Obviously they develop the land and buildings as space for living for people, but thereafter all their decisions as to physical realities are activated by their own approach to development.

If we take for granted a particular pattern covering the layout of streets, public transportation routes, boarding points, and the like, it can be said that rents and market prices obtainable for various tracts of land provide the most serviceable indexes of their relative importance to the community as a whole. Within this sphere, market competition, which tends to force land into the uses from which the greatest returns can be secured, affords the most workable device for deciding the alternative uses to which these land resources may be put. While some qualifications are necessary, such as those arising from a given type of income distribution, it can be said that the use which can pay the most for a given site is the use which will be most advantageous for the community as a whole.

Thus we find our urban environments dominated in their basic planning by (a) the lot, (b) the block, and (c) the street. Inasmuch as lots are grouped into blocks which are defined by streets, the street emerges as the dominant element, the controlling factor, the basic skeleton of our cities, towns, and villages. This is a fact which is obvious to anyone who experiences them. Some may say that the emphasis on street pattern has grown with the automobile. But the gridiron subdivision was here before the auto, and any competent planner can produce plans for communities which will handle any volume of traffic without allowing the streets to dominate the lives of the citizens as ours do. One third of urban land in street use (see Bartholomew) is a sad and irrational waste of badly needed space in our congested communities. It is comparable to the waste in halls and odd corners in old houses or badly planned new ones, and it sets up a comparable problem in municipal housekeeping. Well-planned redevelopment could save at least half of this valuable space by the application of the superblock principle. We must, however, remember that the acreage of asphalt in our communities can be reduced only partially by functional redesign. Much greater reductions will proceed from proper balancing of good automotive and good mass transit facilities. Relation to landscape design is obvious: as asphalt expands, green cover recedes. It is time to reverse this process.

The gridiron is the subdivision of the land on the basis of certain assumptions as to use: "market analysis." However curvilinear, however irregular, however carefully segregated into through streets and quiet residential streets (all of which are definite improvements over the old mechanical rectangular gridiron), however hard to find one's way through, the subdivision of the land into lots, blocks, and the resulting street patterns is still a preconceived gridiron, an oversimplified playing with property-line abstractions. We are so accustomed to this situation as a kind of Act-of-God which controls planning that only occasionally do we realize that perhaps the houses, or other buildings, and the desirable relations between them, should determine the pattern of land-use division. The design process, by which forms of spatial organization are carefully derived from the detailed study of specifically programmed functions, needs and desires, is absent from subdivision, which nevertheless establishes a permanent overall control of all subsequent design processes. Not only that: it establishes an arbitrary framework within which those processes must function, atomizes them into fragments which are only partially functional, and makes it practically impossible to design any physical relationship between the fragments. The subdivision becomes a framework of arbitrary pigeonholes, however varied in size and shape, into which all the potential richness of relations between private and community life must fit. The street, that access corridor across the open faces of the pigeonholes, must carry all the manifold complexity of social relations between the pigeonholes—not only the circulation, which is its function, but the temporary storage of vehicles, social intercourse between the occupants of the pigeonholes, the play of children and adolescents, and so on.

It all adds up to an unnatural separation of planning from design. Planning becomes the generalized solution for the general middle and low standard problems; design remains the specialized solution for the high standard problems. Planning remains areal, two-dimensional,

diagrammatic, and legalistic, no matter how advanced the planner's theoretical grasp of community form and function may be. It starves for lack of continuity into spatial, three-dimensional, specific, and humane design including actual construction. The planner rationalizes his divorce from the design of specific forms and relations by condescending to it as something arty; the designer rationalizes his divorce from planning the continuity between elements by condescending to it as something stuffy; and neither is able to complete his work, or produce whole physical conceptions. You cannot separate planning from design without sterilizing both; you cannot determine realistic land-use in terms of abstract zones and property lines without direct specific reference to architectural, landscape and engineering design; and you cannot realistically determine land-use or physical space-organization without direct reference to specific individuals or organizations who intend themselves to occupy the development.

SOCIETY—The present relation of the private lot to the community is an exact physical expression, a symbol, a diagram, of the social relation between individual and society. The theory of competition places the individual in opposition to society. The world is his apple; it owes him a living; "what's your racket?"; the economic jungle, the happy hunting ground for free enterprise, inhabited by timid consumers who don't understand business. Society remains a no-man's-land from which every individual has the right to extract what he can; a place in which human nature doesn't change, and the race is to the swift, the strong, or the smart (especially if they happen to know the judges). Elaborate planning, both economic and physical, goes on within the limits of each specific productive, distributive, or service enterprise, and sometimes among several as the trend toward monopoly breeds collusive practices. But the planning stops at the limits of the enterprise or group of enterprises, and beyond that tends to become intolerant of other planning. We still think of the world as a jungle into which we venture, boldly or stealthily, to bring home the bacon. Business resists overall controls, overall planning, until the pressure gets too great; then endeavors to force those controls and plans to function to bring order and regularity into its own operations. That has been, and still is, the typical pattern in housing, planning, urban redevelopment, rent control, price control, public recreation, education, health, and so on.

These latter movements, promoted by "public-spirited citizens," reflect an opposing theory of co-operation, termed radical, crackpot, or dreamy by the hard-headed entrepreneur. Yet this is the basic pattern of society. Nothing would be produced or distributed, there would be neither culture nor services without a very considerable pattern of co-operation between all the citizens involved. It is becoming clearer day by day that this theory of competition between individuals for every good thing in life, of society as a kind of raiding preserve for those most enterprising, and of government as merely the police power which prevents those raids from going to extremes, is really an overlay on the basic co-operation of people making and producing a living. Even as this primary human co-operativeness persists in showing through the synthetic mesh of the theory of the combative and acquisitive human animal, so too will the essential patterns of sociability and productivity, of work and play and relaxation, persist in showing through, and eventually overflowing, the mechanical, oversimplified, inflexible gridirons, and the cycle from new slum to old, in which we are mired today. The world does owe me a living, but in return I owe the world my best productive work; or, the world owes me a living for my best productive work. The suspicious, competitive, unfriendly atmospheres of so many neighborhoods; the daily struggle of the auto, jockeying at traffic lights, racing down boulevards, bluffing at intersections, passing on the right, cutting in; the vandalism which so shocks responsible citizens; all of these symptoms of the persistence of a theory or an ideology which sets man against man, and against society, are due to pass on into history. The realities of human decency, sociability, and potential for development will grow

up around them, over them, and swamp them.

To contrast subdivision with planning does not necessarily imply a contradiction between the property line and community relationships. We need not advocate a sudden return to primitive communism, or a sudden advance to utopian communism. The subdivision and zoning of the land is not in itself bad, nor is the lumping together of many parcels into larger units, as projected by urban redevelopment legislation, any guarantee that a better pattern will emerge. The results of such redevelopment may be no better and perhaps much worse in their impact upon the social patterns of our communities. We must understand the relation between *ends* and *means*. It is not a question of *how* the land is divided up, of what *tools* are to be used, but of *who* is to do the dividing and use the tools, and what their objectives are—*what for*. Private property in land existed before the principles of urban real estate, and may well exist after them. The contradiction between social relations and individual land use, which exists in all our communities, is not between subdivision in itself and the community pattern, but rather between subdivision for unreasonable profit, and land-use needs. The admission by all parties concerned, including most members of the banker-builder-realtor trinity, that earlier subdivision and development practices have been unfunctional, unrealistic, or irresponsible, is in itself an admission of this contradiction. The question now has become how much better we are to make these practices. The "community planning" of the operative (speculative) builders and the FHA is supposed to represent the sudden bursting of the Promised Land upon our dazzled eyes. But any objective examination of the plans produced by these operations will indicate what a truly minute step forward they have taken.

PLANNING—But what about professional planning? Surely there is a well-organized and growing body of city planning technicians, commissions, and realistic activity throughout our land? Aren't there even certain universities giving specialized professional curricula in city planning? Surely we are moving from slum clearance and traffic control through master planning to urban redevelopment? Aren't the business community, the Chambers of Commerce, the Real Estate Boards, the Home Builders' Institutes, accepting the idea and the need for planning? Isn't it being presented to the general public through fine exhibits such as the recent one in Philadelphia?

All of this is quite true. There is a great deal of activity about planning problems (which include housing problems) at the citizen level, the professional level, and the official level. Reference to the four national planning organizations, to the great volume of books, pamphlets and periodicals published in the field, to the work being done in schools (whether as separate curricula or as parts of architecture, engineering, or public administration), and to the activities of many competent and active planning commissions at the city and regional level (Chicago, New York, Los Angeles) indicates a great deal of sincere and determined concern with the conditions under which too many of us have to live. Planning, formerly the field toward which all space-planners (architects, engineers, landscape architects) gravitated as their ambitions and their grasp of problems expanded, has become a specialized field offering economic and service opportunities to serious young people willing to train themselves for it.

The trouble is that it is all on paper. "Modern planning" (as distinguished from the old City Beautiful movement which came out of the Chicago Fair of 1893) has been in existence for some thirty years without noticeable effect on the physical form and arrangement of our cities and towns. They are still sprawling at the peripheries and decaying at the centers; they are still full of aggressive slum and blight developments, crime and delinquency, fire and health hazards, traffic congestion and smog, frustrated children and sterilized adults. These conditions have been investigated over and over again; city hall files are loaded with reports and statistics and facts; the technical staffs keep busy merely keeping up with the spread of the elements they are so anxious to correct. Investigation rather than correction seems to be our characteristic.

246

Every mayor or governor who is pressured to correct some outstanding evil within his bailiwick can appoint a commission to investigate and make a full report and recommendations. But nothing; or something too little and too late; or something showy but irrelevant; gets done about it. Our files are full of fine master plans and studies for redevelopment; but the cities still look the same. To be sure there may be a terrific new express highway connecting the suburbs and the downtown business and shopping center; a civic center which is a collection of pretentious and unrelated buildings; a new park here and a lakeshore development there; but, in terms of the scale and the needs of the problem, practically nothing at all. There is too much talk and too little action; land planning or space allocation which does not proceed by direct and regular steps to detailed three-dimensional design and actual construction and installation has little meaning; it dies because it is never born; it never gets out of the planning commission's offices; or if it does it is only a slick and showy exhibit or publication which leaves a comforting feeling of action, a convincing substitute for the real thing, in the minds of the observers. One splendid project after another bursts upon us; we are dazzled, it is jammed down our throats with fanfare and high glee; and on the morning after the city still looks just the same. We must always ask: Does the master plan project the future—or generalize the past? Is its open space permanent—or merely raw land waiting for "higher and better development?" Does it orient toward more wholesome habitats—or more orderly subdivisions?

CIVIC ART—Town, city, and regional planning are arts to the extent that they give actual form to our physical environments, and they are nothing to the extent that they fail to give such form. The theory that the city planner merely establishes a framework for other designers is only a rationalization of the frustration of planning. There is no art in which the general contradiction between imagination and reality, many special contradictions, and hence the potential vitality, are greater or stronger. The resolution of one primary contradiction—that of the isolation of the artist-planner-designer from the needs of the people—is basic to the production of actual live new or renewed cities, because city planning is a social art in the fullest sense of the word. Theories of city planning which are closest to actual practice emphasize reality (real estate practice) and minimize imagination. Let us move from reality toward imagination, as we have begun, and as is the tendency of all frustrated artists.

Civic art is more than the design of streets, intersections, and settings for architectural monuments. It is likewise more than the design of freeways, parkways, civic centers, or parks, although all those are elements in civic art. It is, and must be, the design of complete physical frameworks housing the primary functions of community life: dwelling, work, recreation, and the circulation between them. No lesser unit, such as neighborhood without workspace, can be called more than a fragment of civic art, although perhaps an engrossing problem in site planning and housing design. This makes possible the accurate definition of the civic unit, the community or metropolitan amalgam of communities, in terms of all such triangular relations occurring more often than once a week. Following this, one definition of region might be an area covered by these same primary relations less often: the shifting of seasonal work in industry or agriculture, the itineraries of traveling salesmen or administrators, week-end and vacation travel. The rural community is expanded in space and time, the ultimate in decentralization. It includes homes, farms, schools, plus those nuclear country towns to which the rural population resorts for weekly shopping and entertainment. Thus we have an art expressing organic units of human activity and social pattern, units which are functional and structural and deliberate, rather than sentimental and amoebic and accidental. The biological content of the community is the people and the animals and plants which it houses; no more and no less; that is enough and to spare for the most magnificent organic integrity of form and content that one could desire.

The central problem of urbanism today is the struggle between the forces of concentration and dispersion, the contradiction between centralization and decentralization which must be resolved before we can have healthy communities. The inherent sociable gregariousness of people, their need for social, productive, and cultural intercourse which is still facilitated primarily by direct physical concentration of population (with all due apologies to auto and telephone); and on the other hand their need for fresh air and sunshine and free open space, for direct contact with earth and plants at the scale of natural landscape, for some privacy and occasional solitude by contrast with gregariousness —these are the primary elements of the new urbanism toward which we are groping. One other need we must not forget: the need for familiarity which conveys security, for a bridge between those familiar well-worn forms and patterns of the old home town (however blighted and substandard they may be), and those sparkling patterns for the brave new world, which may look like a village on Mars to the startled average citizen.

FORM—In a most rich and flexible way, then, we must develop the concept of organic cellular municipal structure, insofar as it both reflects, expedites, and directs the social pattern:

The residential neighborhood—a recreational unit in the broadest sense of the word: 500–1500 families, centering around school, shopping, park, and/or other common facilities (not necessarily all the same families for all facilities) at every level of density from Le Corbusier's 1600-person apartment house ("Living Unit of a Proper Size") in Marseilles, to the rural neighborhood of sixty-acre family farms linked up over square miles of landscape by the school bus system.

The community—a more complete relationship between home, workplace, and recreational and cultural facilities, involving one or more neighborhoods, higher education at least through high school, administrative centers, and a pattern of transportation and other services. This too has its specific expression throughout the range of urban, suburban, rural, and primeval conditions. The urban worker who lives in the suburbs (or vice versa) may commute as much as thirty miles each way each day from home to work. The farmer may live in solitude with his family, but his work is just outside the door, and only his children commute to school.

The metropolis—a complex of several or many communities, physically grown together or closely related around common interests and activities. It results in a consequent pyramiding enrichment and complication of shopping, cultural, educational, and recreational facilities for the third of the population who can afford them: a parallel pyramiding of blight, mediocrity, squalor, decay, filth, and depravity for the two-thirds of the population "down under."

The region—a variable relation between one or more metropolitan units, several or many satellite communities, and a rural and/or primeval hinterland whose size and shape are determined by geographic, economic, and social factors which condition its primary orientation toward the metropolitan center or centers. A flexible yet organically realistic concept which seldom establishes exact boundaries, and exists only in embryo and in such emergent forms as the Tennessee Valley Authority and California's Central Valley Project. (See Mumford and Odum.) This concept of a regional pattern of units of varying sizes, developed from a thorough scientific investigation of the relations between land, people, resources, production relations, cultural and recreational patterns, and so on, has a strange and contradictory relation to our established system of county and state governmental units.

The nation—a cumulation of these contradictory political units and physical-economic regions into a total which has a political-social unity and consciousness greater than the sum of these parts, and great enough to overshadow any contradictions between political and physical-economic units. Thus, although North America, composed of Alaska, Canada, and the United States, seems to be a physical and economic unit, and the political boundaries between them are quite relaxed and friendly, we

still speak of America and the United States as synonyms, excluding likewise those Latin Americas south of the border which have their own regional unities. (We even tend to exclude from Americanism those three million or more Mexican-Americans who are symptomatic of the violent overlapping of Anglo and Latin cultures in our southwest in 1846–8.)

FUNCTION—More valuable than the above cellular pattern, in fact superseding and including it because more flexible and realistic, is the CIAM breakdown of urbanism into the functions of Dwelling, Workplaces, Culture of Body and Mind, and Circulation, as presented in the inimitable rhetoric of English translations from Le Corbusier's French, the language of a great intellectual urbanist whose only weakness is a lack of contact with the aspirations and expectations of the actual specific people for whom he plans (witness the villagers' rejection of his elegant skyscraper scheme for the reconstruction of St. Die).

LE CORBUSIER IN UN HEADQUARTERS

These four operations—dwelling, working, the culture of body and mind, circulation—must be performable in their entirety with neither waste nor delay, beneficial alike to the individual and to the collectivity.

Life for most of us breaks down into worktime and recreation-time (re-creation for more and better work, or, work for more and better recreation). Thus recreation includes such functions as eating, sleeping, bathing, and relaxing, in addition to the play and entertainment normally considered recreational. As physical planners we are concerned with places, surroundings, and facilities for work and for recreation. Workplaces are factories and offices, stores and farms; recreation places are parks and movies and community centers and private homes. For the housewife home is both workplace and recreation-place; for children school, as a place for development into good workers (citizens), may be called their workplace. Whether or not the reader agrees that the purpose of life is productive or creative or useful work, honest participation in the indispensable

248

patterns of social cooperation (parasites will say that its purpose is just to LIVE), this analysis of living makes possible the establishment of sound *relationships between* the various elements physical planners deal with: basically between workplaces and recreation places (which are mainly home neighborhoods) and between the public and private portions of the recreation places. The easy or mechanical approach to planning is to concentrate on the connections between these places as they exist (traffic, transit, transportation); while the hard, scientific and humane approach is to concentrate on these primary elements themselves, in terms of quantity and quality, and to endeavor, by improving them internally, and re-organizing their relations to each other, to reduce the problems of connection.

LE CORBUSIER

DWELLING is to live alone, in the real sense, or with the people of one's home, during the twenty-four hour solar day which encompasses human existence and sets the rhythm of man's labor; that short span of time that can be filled with success or bring failure in its course. . . .

The home is the basic social cell containing that inestimable side of life, intimacy, the feeling that one is master, king of one's domain, dependent not on others but on one's self alone or on those whom one has merged into the structure of one's life; wife, children, hearth, both material and spiritual shelter. . . .

Sun, space, greenery—these with stone, brick, steel, and cement are the real elements which go to create man's dwelling.

Sociability will yield its rewards not only for practical ends, but will enrich mind and feeling by communal experience. Men form groups to help each other and to experience gladness.

The intangible and sacred solitude of the home, the pleasures of sociability—such is the binomial problem set for architecture and urbanism. . . .

Dwelling—this is what is known (depending upon the circles you move in) as The American Home, Real Estate Resources, The Housing Problem, The Residential Neighborhood. It is composed of all the places where people live: trailers and tents and shacks, garages and stores and hotel rooms, apartments and flats, rowhouses and duplexes and courts and single-

family houses, housing projects and "garden apartments," slums and blighted neighborhoods and "planned communities." It is composed also of all the variations among those places in size, number of people per room, equipment, age, state of repair, site coverage, amount and kind of open space immediately adjacent, kind, quantity, and quality of community facilities (public or commercial) in the neighborhood, relation to traffic, to occupant income, to landlord demands, and so on. It is the American home to the upper third who can afford some approximation of the standards implied; real estate resources to some 25,000 proprietors and 116,000 agents and brokers in the field (as of 1940); the housing problem to the lower two-thirds who cannot afford "our" standards, and particularly to the lower third who cannot afford even the still-decent hand-me-downs from the upper third, or the new miniature dingbats, in which the middle third is able to live; and the residential neighborhood, in terms of some sort of segregation to the FHA and the banker-builder-real estate trinity, and in terms of organic community integration to the more specific and humane section of the professional planners. Thus in terms of the interests of the democratic majority, the housing problem is the primary concept we must consider today: the American home represents the ideal toward which the American people have been educated to look; the planner's residential neighborhood represents the theoretical concept of the minimum unit for sound home planning or re-planning; and finally, dwelling is real estate resources, including the segregated neighborhood, to those dominant forces which are in general responsible for, and in control of, the situation which exists.

LE CORBUSIER

WORKING is contributing one's living intelligence to others, and thus to one's self. Work may be efficacious or sterile according to whether its program is well or badly drawn up. It can be accomplished in an atmosphere of ease and freedom or on the contrary in one of constraint and discomfort. It can absorb the vital intensity of the worker and strengthen him but it can also overwhelm, exhaust him, ruin his physical

249

and moral health. . . . There is no real happiness if work has not been raised to a level of dignity. . . .

WORKPLACES—The other half of life's habitat for most Americans, the alter ego to their housing problem or dwelling solution or neighborhood relation, is the place where they work, spend their major productive or creative energies and the most active parts of their lives forty hours more or less a week. From the 1940 census reports, the following rough classification of workplaces can be derived:

Total paid labor force	52,020,023
On land or water	13,758,406
In factories or shops	16,680,819
In offices, stores, or equal	15,091,385
In homes or equal	
personal services	4,439,257
housewives (unpaid labor)	26,570,502
In schools—ages 5–20	26,293,224

This somewhat arbitrary reclassification of the census figures breaks the labor force, including housewives but not the school ages, in terms of the nature of the workplace, roughly into fifths: one fifth on the land in agriculture, forestry, fishing, mining, or construction; one fifth in factories or shops; one fifth in offices, stores, or equal; and two fifths in homes or lodgings. That is to say, one fifth in primitive environments or surroundings, one fifth in more or less rough, dirty, mechanized surroundings, and three fifths in more or less clean and refined surroundings. In these various types of surroundings four fifths (including housewives) do manual work which gets their hands dirty, one fifth is the white-collar type which does not get its hands dirty.

LE CORBUSIER

CULTURE OF THE BODY is to care with wisdom for one's bodily frame—the human body, the most perfect machine in the world, the physical prop of our whole existence. The body can thrive or wither, be resplendent or decay in sickness and deformity. . . . CULTURE OF THE MIND is to partake of the works of nature and of the works of men. There is no limit to the knowledge which is ours to grasp, although we need not set ourselves pretentious goals. We must realize that miracles are always possible. Understanding can spring from any soil where seeds have been planted. . . .

250

CULTURE OF BODY AND MIND, a phrase perhaps strange to practical American ears, embodies all those features and facets of public recreation and relaxation, active play and passive contemplation, health care, all the endlessly expanding richness of arts and crafts, museum, theatre and ballet, church and community social life, which have come to be thought of as filling in the gaps in space and time between work and dwelling, or as making up for the deficiencies in opportunity for personal development in either or both. Perhaps we should say more fully still that cultural activities expand the richness of life by another third beyond the satisfactions of good work and rich home life. When either of these becomes mechanical, oppressive, or frustrating, the cultural sphere is called on to restore the balance. But we are learning that this does not work: parks and museums and baseball games cannot compensate for dreary blighted housing, sweatshop factories where the speedup keeps pace with wage raises, or the stale frustration of unemployment. Whether we work in order to recreate or recreate in order to work, most certainly the future richness of an expanding democratic standard of living in all communities must be compounded of an expansion in all spheres of dwelling, work, and group culture. The first two cannot stand still while the last expands beyond them to become the primary reason for living, as some experts seem naïvely to expect.

Basically there are two contradictory trends in recreation programs. One is the creative participation of all those present in the development and continuity of the recreative activity; the other is known as spectatoritis, the segregation of a mass audience from an expert performance. Without calling for the complete elimination of the latter (which would obviously be undesirable), we must stress that the former is the primary democratic pattern, the pattern which is truly recreational for those involved, of all ages from pre-school to senior citizens. Typical of the former are most public park and playground activities, particularly for adolescents and adults. Children's play areas and apparatus tend to become mechanically stereotyped in forms which minimize or eliminate creative participation by the child. Typical of spectator sports are professional and, sadly enough, competitive academic sports. The division is not necessarily between public and commercial: pool and bowling, skating and dancing, even the games and rides of amusement strips at the beach, are participating recreative activities, which should be healthy were it not for the slum and blight atmospheres, and the sharp merchandising elements, which gather around them.

LE CORBUSIER

CIRCULATION is precisely solving the problem of contact, putting into contact without waste motion and wastage of men's lives. Waste takes two forms: absorption of one, two, or three hours each day in transportation by car, train, bus, or subway, wearing down the person and irretrievably losing time in the relentless circuit of the solar day. And, on top of this, the dreadful waste of modern times which strikes so heavily in mechanized societies, above all in the United States of America: Time,—work,—enforced each day and upon each one of us to pay for the fatal error of excessive urban distances. . . .
Man, having succeeded in rationally grouping and locating his establishments, would regain the use of his legs, and by his decisions place urban problems on a new basis. Mechanization liberates. It is used at will. It will cease to be the despot which, often to man's sorrow, places man on wheels.

Traffic and transit and transportation, the flow (or constipation) of motorized vehicles, has been a primary concentration of planners and experts and administrators of all sorts both amateur and professional ever since the funny horseless carriage started suddenly to breed strangely and monstrously variable progeny, like the rabbits in Australia. These problems of circulation, most evident to most people, experienced by all of them in common, most noticeable as an urban characteristic to the visitor from afar, and least controversial as between sections of the people, likewise most concerned with practical mechanics (that great American preoccupation) of all planning problems, have become a common concern, a common annoyance which must be solved, whether or not we think about housing and work and recreation

while doing it. It is not for us to duplicate or repeat the traffic and planning experts, but only to say this: we don't believe you can ever solve these problems without at the same time solving the problems of dwelling and work and culture which are at their ends. Furthermore, if the problems of those three primary functions are solved by comprehensive planning processes which place them in functional and convenient relations to one another, the problems of circulation will be so reduced and simplified as to become a cinch to solve. Further still more, as long as traffic and transportation are played with and tinkered with for their own sakes, on their own terms, or rather on the terms of the uncontrollables at their ends, they will remain insoluble. It will be like trying to control floods without reforestation above and dams below: no one ever caught a snake by holding it in the middle. The whimsies of industry at one end, and of land development at the other, will always be apt to upset any traffic systems, no matter how smoothly streamlined.

URBAN REDEVELOPMENT—During and since the war a new technique has been developed for attacking the physical decadence and obsolescence of urban communities. This is known as urban or community redevelopment. In 1944 Catherine Bauer, that long-time activator in the housing-planning field, said:

In the sacred name of 'master plans,' 'bold reconstruction', 'saving cities', and whatnot, it is proposed to bail out with Federal subsidy the owners of slum and blighted property—not in order to rehouse their present tenants properly, but to stimulate another wave of speculative over-building for the well-to-do and thus, it is naïvely hoped, to turn the tide of decentralization and preserve down-town property values based on high densities and even higher hopes.

The qualitative results of urban redevelopment are wide open and unpredictable. It can produce those brave, magnificent, and humane communities which we idealists project; or it can produce such a pattern of organized economic, social and political segregation, such an exaggeration of the traditional over-building for the upper brackets and miserable congestion for the lower, such a methodical shrinkage of "un-

251

profitable" community facilities (such as schools), such a mechanical acceleration and three-dimensional expansion of the gridiron subdivision of living space, such a sterile leveling out of whatever human richness exists in our urban communities, as we have never seen, but as is demonstrated for us in that prototype for private redevelopment, Stuyvesant Town. The smugness with which this monster has been received by the majority of American space planners and designers is appalling.

POLITICS—If this seems over-gloomy, consider the implications of the accepted sound principles of urban real estate, when teamed up with the public power of eminent domain, the public planning and police power, and the scale of control projected in the legislation. Experience, and a whole generation of muckrakers and debunkers, have proved to us that we cannot rely on the integrity of either private enterprise or elected public officials to produce for us that wholesome new environment for the common man. The results that come out of urban redevelopment will be determined by one simple relation: what interests apply the most pressure in the most effective places at the most appropriate times. That is our traditional pattern by which things get done: it is very simple: the only practical problem involved is just who is to apply the pressures in the interests of sound planning for the people. The basic principle of democracy is not reliance on law, elected officials, or private enterprise; it is reliance on informed and activated public opinion, the needs and desires of the people.

Since few Americans are sufficiently powerful to bring appreciable pressure as individuals, the pressures which determine our social pattern and its physical expression operate through organization. Planners and all those who support the objectives of planning for people must learn the lessons of practical politics in America today, as they are known to every successful business man, trade union leader, or public official. These are the lessons of organization, of education, and of action. Good urban redevelopment will come about through political action; there are no other routes.

252

HENRY R. CHURCHILL

For a master plan to be of influence, it must have a direction and a philosophy—the one implies the other. Most planning commissions are so puzzled about the economics of accomplishment, so confused as to their objectives, and so scared of the real estate interests and the 'practical men,' that they have found no direction, much less evolved a philosophy upon which to rest, for good or ill, the foundation of their planning. They draw back from the attacks they know will be made on any long range ideas, no matter how tentatively presented, they fear the sneers of the men of immediacy. These up-and-doers are in the saddle, they have immediate objectives and need no direction since they are not going anywhere except where they are. . . . Master planning is not for them. The sands of time run out too quickly.

PATERNALISM

BAUER

. . . the crude conflict that has for a generation made schizophrenia the occupational disease of planners on both sides of the Atlantic: the conflict between those who consider the purpose of city planning to be the improvement of the general welfare and amenity, and those who set out to preserve property owners from the degrading and devaluing influence of hoi polloi.

We must beware of the tendency toward intellectual arrogance and paternalism. The planner's function is not to decide—he is not the executive—his function is to advise, to lead, to clarify, to present alternatives and maximum potentialities, to understand, to merge his organized imagination with the disorganized imagination of the people—in a word, to develop the most complete possible approximation of the private designer-client relation with the people who will actually live in the projected development or redevelopment. It is paternalism, plus intellectualism, estheticism, and the rejection of human emotion, which produces the incredible arrogance of designers who think that a world which rejects or refuses to conform to their ideas of form and arrangement must be wrong. This is a sure way to guarantee the death of the best along with the worst of modern design and planning. We cannot put farmers into apartment houses or urbanites out on farms; we cannot decentralize those who like the gregariousness of congestion, or recentralize those who love great open spaces; we cannot put children into elevator apartments or oldsters out on the land, without creating resentment, resistance, and non-cooperation, UNLESS we treat these people as clients, consult with them in a professionally responsible manner, and either sell them our ideas, buy theirs, or both. It is doubtless excellent intellectual exercise for us to struggle with the theoretical resolution of all the contradictions between centralization and decentralization, apartments and houses, pedestrians and autos, housing and industry, zoning, planning, and design, public and private recreation and services, children and adults, economics and sociology, private cars and mass transit, elevators and the good earth, structure and function, mobility and stability, oldsters and youngsters, sociability and solitude, horizontality and verticality, indoors and outdoors, town and country, and so on. But we alone are not going to resolve these in actuality.

The professional designer-planner must be concerned with the people in society as the source of his livelihood; he must also be concerned with them as producing the culture which is the basic foundation and inspirational root-medium for his work. This relation has been very clear in the past: great cultural peaks, as the Greek, the Gothic and the Renaissance, have been the peaks of broad and spreading pyramids, the bulk of whose bases were the folk art and the folk culture of the common people of the times. The high fine art was only the most developed and clarified expression of these broad cultures. All its forms and arrangements were drawn from a popular base, all its plastic enrichment, its carving and decoration and painting and subjective forms had meaning in their time; they were symbolic and emotional forms which were socially expressive to many people.

Today this pyramid has been decapitated. The professional fine artists and designers float on a rich and elegant flying carpet, of authentic period or futuristic design, high above the coarse and vulgar world, fed by a thin pipeline which they studiously avoid noticing or mentioning. The broad base of the pyramid has been steam-rollered, juggernauted, flattened out and smashed down to make foundations and floors for the great mass-production assembly lines of our industrial production system. Popular taste has gone with the wind of commercialism, with the monstrous split between design and production, to be supplanted by the slick and oily sterility of sales management and advertising. The professional artists and designers have no roots, no broad world to function as a source of inspiration, discipline, and experience for expression, only the vacuum of their isolation and the dusty academies which stand between them and the world. It is no wonder that egos expand, that we get inflated personal expressions, the thick richness of Frank Lloyd Wright's structural space-sculpture, the elegant fantasy of Le Corbusier's classicist constructivism.

But the world is still there, the base of the pyramid is still there, the people are still there. They come into the world new and fresh with magnificent potentialities daily, in every generation, ready to be formed by their environment and to participate in forming it. The pyramidal base of integrated culture will come up out of the rich flatness of the American scene like Paracutin out of the meadow—indeed it has already well begun—and the undernourished esthetes on the flying carpet of fine art can slide down their food-line to the rich sustenance of mother earth and common humanity once again. People, the common people, the bulk of the population, are the richest and most interesting things in our world, the basic source of esthetic inspiration, the factor of content which brings any physical environment—from Hooverville to Broadacre City and La Ville Radieuse—to life, gives it its final richness, warmth, vitality, movement, inconsistency, change, and unpredictability, its pulse of life. The people are not going to inhabit our New Towns and Cities in order to give us the pleasure of seeing free human movement in our orderly conceptions; we are building them in order to give the people that good environment which they need, in order to provide society with that good cultural medium, that rich soil and clear quiet air, adequate moisture and fertilization, proper drain-

253

age, maximum growing season, and protection from pests, in which it can foliate most vigorously and luxuriantly and produce its most magnificent cultural flowers and fruits. Just as the horticultural enthusiast plans his garden ever bigger and better because he loves the growth in it, and because he finds it rich and exciting, so must the planner and designer of space for people to live in be primarily concerned and fascinated with the content, the crop. The product of his efforts and his inspiration is not, finally, magnificent space and beautiful enclosure, but the people who expand and grow and develop within it.

BIBLIOGRAPHY

Abercrombie, Patrick.
    GREATER LONDON PLAN 1944. *London: His Majesty's Stationery Office, 1945.*
Adler, Alfred.
    UNDERSTANDING HUMAN NATURE. *New York: Greenberg, 1946.*
Agee, James; and Walker, Evans.
    LET US NOW PRAISE FAMOUS MEN. *Boston: Houghton Mifflin Co., 1941.*
American Geographical Society.
    THE FACE OF THE EARTH AS SEEN FROM THE AIR. *New York: A.G.S., 1922.*
American Institute of Architects.
    ARCHITECTURE—A PROFESSION AND A CAREER. *Washington: A.I.A., 1945.*
    ————— EUROPEAN AND JAPANESE GARDENS. *Philadelphia: Henry T. Coates & Co., 1902.*
American Planning and Civic Association.
    AMERICAN PLANNING AND CIVIC ANNUAL. *Washington: A.P.C.A.*
American Public Health Association, Committee on Hygiene of Housing.
    PLANNING THE NEIGHBORHOOD. *Chicago: Public Administration Service, 1948.*
American Society of Landscape Architects.
    LANDSCAPE ARCHITECTURE (a quarterly magazine). *Boston: A.S.L.A. Publication Board.*
American Society of Planning Officials.
    AMERICAN SOCIETY OF PLANNING OFFICIALS ANNUAL. *Chicago: A.S.P.O.*
Architectural Forum, November, 1948.
    New York: 1948.

Architectural Review, May 1947.
    "Gardens in Brazil." *London: 1947.*
    ————— December 1947. "Gardens in Sweden."
    ————— July 1947. "Gardens in China."
Arquitectura, July 1945.
    Mexico, D.F.: 1945.
Angyal, Andras.
    FOUNDATIONS FOR A SCIENCE OF PERSONALITY. *New York: Commonwealth Fund, 1941.*
Bailey, Liberty H.
    HORTUS. *New York: Macmillan Co., 1941.*
    ————— CYCLOPEDIA OF HORTICULTURE. *New York: Macmillan Co., 1930.*
Bartholomew, H.
    URBAN LAND USES. *Cambridge: Harvard University Press, 1932.*
Bauer, Catherine.
    "Planning Is Politics—but—Are Planners Politicians?" PENCIL POINTS, March 1944.
Behrendt, Walter Curt.
    MODERN BUILDING. *New York: Harcourt Brace & Co., 1937.*
Benedict, Ruth.
    PATTERNS OF CULTURE. *Boston: Houghton Mifflin Co., 1934.*
    ————— RACE, SCIENCE AND POLITICS. *New York: Viking Press, 1943.*
Bernal, J. D.
    THE FREEDOM OF NECESSITY. *London: Routledge and Kegan Paul, 1949.*
Biederman, Charles.
    ART AS THE EVOLUTION OF VISUAL

KNOWLEDGE. *Red Wing, Minnesota: Biederman, 1948.*

Blumenstock and Thornthwaite.
Article in CLIMATE AND MAN (1941 Yearbook of Agriculture). *Washington: U.S. Department of Agriculture, 1941.*

Braun-Blanquet, Dr. J.
PLANT SOCIOLOGY. *New York: McGraw Hill Book Company, 1932.*

Breines, Simon.
"Stuyvesant Town" (Task No. 4) *Task Magazine. New York: 1938.*

Brown, Esther Lucille.
THE PROFESSIONAL ENGINEER. *New York: Russell Sage Foundation, 1936.*

Brunhes, Jean.
HUMAN GEOGRAPHY. *Chicago, New York: Rand McNally, 1920.*

Bureau of Reclamation, U.S. Department of Interior.
RIVER BASIN STUDIES. *Washington: Superintendent of Documents.*

Bureau of Urban Planning (Melville C. Branch, Director).
URBAN PLANNING AND PUBLIC OPINION. *Princeton, N.J.: Princeton University Bureau of Urban Research, 1942.*

Butler, George D. (for National Recreation Association).
RECREATION AREAS. *New York: A. S. Barnes & Co., 1947.*

Byne, Mildred Stapley; and Byne, Arthur.
SPANISH GARDENS AND PATIOS. *Philadelphia: J. B. Lippincott Co., 1924.*

Caudwell, Christopher.
ILLUSION AND REALITY. *New York: International Publishers, 1947.*

Census Bureau, U.S. Department of Commerce (Morris H. Hansen, Statistical Assistant to the Director).
U.S. STATISTICAL ABSTRACT ANNUAL. *Washington: Superintendent of Documents.*

Chambers, Sir William.
A DISSERTATION ON ORIENTAL GARDENING. (*Typed copy in Library of Division of Landscape Design, University of California at Berkeley*). *1772.*

Chamber of Commerce of the United States.
YOUR CITY IS YOUR BUSINESS (A report on Business Men's Conference on Urban Problems). *Washington: Chamber of Commerce of the United States.*

Church, Thomas D.
"Landscape Architecture Series," *House Beautiful, 1948–50.*

Churchill, Henry S.
THE CITY IS THE PEOPLE. *New York: Harcourt Brace, 1945.*

Churchill, Henry S., and Ittleson, Roy.
NEIGHBORHOOD DESIGN AND CONTROL. *New York: National Committee on Housing, Inc., 1944.*

Clelland, T. M. THE MUNSELL COLOR SYSTEM. *Baltimore: Universal Color Standards, 1931.*

Colvin, Brenda.
LAND AND LANDSCAPE. *London: John Murray, 1948.*

Commonwealth Club of California, City Planning Section.
IS THE COMMUNITY REDEVELOPMENT ACT WORKABLE? ADEQUATE? FAIR? *San Francisco: The Commonwealth, 1946.*

COMPTON'S PICTURED ENCYCLOPEDIA. *Chicago: F. E. Compton, 1950.*

Cornell University Faculty.
CONSERVATION IN THE UNITED STATES. *Ithaca, N.Y.: Comstock Publishing Co., 1940.*

Cotton, C. A.
CLIMATIC ACCIDENTS. *Christchurch, N.Z.: Whitcomb & Tombs, 1942.*

——— LANDSCAPE. *New York: Cambridge University Press, 1941.*

——— GEOMORPHOLOGY. *New York: John Wiley & Sons, 1945.*

Creighton, Thomas H.
BUILDING FOR MODERN MAN. *Princeton, N.J.: Princeton University Press, 1949.*

Crisp, Frank.
MEDIEVAL GARDENS. *New York: Brentano's, 1925.*

Croce, Benedetto.
PHILOSOPHY OF THE PRACTICAL. *London: Macmillan Co., 1913.*

Ditchfield, P. H.
PICTURESQUE ENGLISH COTTAGES AND THEIR DOORWAY GARDENS. *Philadelphia, John C. Winston Co., 1905.*

Dunham, Barrows.
MAN AGAINST MYTH. *New York: Little, Brown & Co., 1947.*

Eckbo, Garrett.
Review of books PARK AND RECREATIONAL STRUCTURES. *Magazine of Art,* December 1938. *Architectural Record,* December 1938.

Eckbo, Garrett.
Articles on Landscape Design.
——— *Architectural Forum,* May 1942, February, March 1946.
——— *Arts and Architecture,* October 1945.
——— *Gardens and Gardening* for 1949.
——— *Magazine of Art,* October 1941.
——— *Pencil Points,* September 1937.
——— *Sunset Magazine,* July 1940.

Eckel, Edwin C.
BUILDING STONES AND CLAYS. *New York: John Wiley & Sons, 1912.*

Ecology (Quarterly). Brooklyn Botanic Gardens (through 1948); *Duke University Press (1949–).*

Eliot, C. W.
CHARLES ELIOT, LANDSCAPE ARCHITECT. *Boston and New York: Houghton Mifflin Co., 1903.*

Emerson, Frederick V.
AGRICULTURAL GEOLOGY. *New York: John Wiley & Sons, 1928. London: Chapman & Hall, 1928.*

Emerson, Fred.
BASIC BOTANY. *Philadelphia: Blakiston Co., 1947.*

Faure, Elie.
THE SPIRIT OF THE FORMS. *New York: Garden City Publishing Co., 1937.*

Fenton and Fenton.
THE ROCK BOOK. *Garden City, N.Y.: Doubleday, Doran & Co., 1942.*

Finkelstein, Sidney.
ART AND SOCIETY. *New York: International Publishers, 1947.*
———— JAZZ: A PEOPLE'S MUSIC. *New York: The Citadel Press, 1948.*

Fitch, James Marsten.
AMERICAN BUILDING. *Boston: Houghton Mifflin Co., 1948.*

Fortune Magazine: "Housing." April 1946; January, June, August, September 1947.
———— "The Dynamic Men Of Dallas." February 1949.

French and Eberlein.
THE SMALLER HOUSES AND GARDENS OF VERSAILLES. *New York: Reinhold, 1926.*

Frey, Albert.
IN SEARCH OF LIVING ARCHITECTURE. *New York: Architectural Book Publishing Co., 1939.*

Fromm, Erich.
ESCAPE FROM FREEDOM. *New York: Rinehart & Co., 1941.*
———— MAN FOR HIMSELF. *New York: Rinehart & Co., 1947.*

Gallion, Arthur B.
THE URBAN PATTERN. *New York: D. Van Nostrand, 1949.*

Gallotti, Jean.
MOORISH HOUSES AND GARDENS OF MOROCCO. *New York: William Helburn Inc., 1925.*

Gay and Parker.
MATERIALS AND METHODS OF ARCHITECTURAL CONSTRUCTION. *New York: John Wiley & Sons, 1946.*

Giedion, Siegfried.
SPACE, TIME AND ARCHITECTURE. *Cambridge: Harvard University Press, 1941.*

Goldfinger, Erno.
"The Sensation of Space." *The Architectural Review,* November 1941.

Goodwin, Philip L.
BRAZIL BUILDS. *New York: Museum of Modern Art, 1943.*

Gothein, Marie Louise.
A HISTORY OF GARDEN ART. *New York: E. P. Dutton & Co., 1928.*

Graham, Dorothy.
CHINESE GARDENS. *New York: Dodd, Mead & Co., 1938.*

Graubard, Mark.
MAN THE SLAVE AND MASTER. *New York: Covici-Friede, 1938.*

Gray, George Herbert.
HOUSING AND CITIZENSHIP. *New York: Reinhold, 1946.*

Greenough, Horatio.
FORM AND FUNCTION. *Berkeley and Los Angeles: University of California Press, 1947.*

Grinter, Holmes, Spencer, Oldenburger, Harris, Kloeffler and Faires.
ENGINEERING PREVIEW. *New York: Macmillan Co., 1945.*

Gromort, Georges.
JARDINS D'ESPAGNE. *Paris: A. Vincent, 1926.*

Gropius, Walter.
THE NEW ARCHITECTURE AND THE BAUHAUS. *New York: The Museum of Modern Art, 1936.*

Guptill, Arthur L.
COLOR IN SKETCHING AND RENDERING. *New York: Reinhold, 1945.*

Haffner, Jean-Jacques.
COMPOSITIONS DE JARDINS. *Paris: Vincent, Fréal et Cie, 1931.*

Hamblin, Stephen F.
LISTS OF PLANT TYPES. *Cambridge: Harvard University Press, 1929.*

Hamlin, Talbot.
ARCHITECTURE THROUGH THE AGES. *New York: G. P. Putnam's Sons, 1940.*

Harap, Louis.
SOCIAL ROOTS OF THE ARTS. *New York: International, 1949.*

Harwood, W. S.
LUTHER BURBANK AND NEW CREATIONS IN PLANT LIFE. *New York: Macmillan Co., 1906.*

Haskell, Douglas.
"Beauty for Us." *Architectural Record,* June 1948.

Hegemann, Werner.
CITY PLANNING AND HOUSING. *New York: Architectural Book Publishing Co., 1936.* (3 vol.)

Hilberseimer, L.
THE NEW CITY. *Chicago: Paul Theobald, 1944.*

Hitchcock, Henry-Russell.
IN THE NATURE OF MATERIALS. The Buildings of Frank Lloyd Wright. *New York: Duell, Sloan & Pearce, 1942.*

Hogben, Lancelot.
FROM CAVE PAINTING TO COMIC STRIP. *New York: Chanticleer Press, 1949.*

Hopkins, Andrew Delmar.
BIOCLIMATICS. *Washington: Superintendent of Documents, U.S. Department of Agriculture Miscellaneous Publication No. 280, 1938.*

Howard, Edwin L.
CHINESE GARDEN ARCHITECTURE. *New York: Macmillan Co., 1931.*

Hoyt, R. S.
ORNAMENTAL PLANTS FOR SUBTROPICAL REGIONS. *Los Angeles: Livingston Press, 1938.*

Hubbard and Kimball.
AN INTRODUCTION TO THE STUDY OF LANDSCAPE DESIGN. *New York: Macmillan Co., 1917.*

Huberman, Leo.
MAN'S WORLDLY GOODS. *New York: Harper & Brothers, 1936.*

Hudnut, Joseph.
"Space in the Modern Garden." *Bulletin of the Garden Clubs of America,* May 1940.

Imlay, Catherine.
"Reid Garden: 'Landplanning' Knits House and Site Together." *Sunset Magazine,* May 1946.

Inn, Henry.
CHINESE HOUSES AND GARDENS. *Honolulu: Fong Inn's Ltd., 1940.*

Jackson and Jones.
THE PROFESSION OF ENGINEERING. *New York: John Wiley & Sons, 1929.*

Jellicoe, G. A.
BAROQUE GARDENS OF AUSTRIA. *New York: Charles Scribner's Sons, 1932.*

Jensen, Jens.
SIFTINGS. *Chicago: Ralph Fletcher Seymour, 1939.*

Johnson, Philip C.
MIES VAN DER ROHE. *New York: Museum of Modern Art, 1947.*

Kellog, Charles E.
THE SOILS THAT SUPPORT US. *New York: Macmillan, 1941.*

Kepes, Gyorgy.
LANGUAGE OF VISION. *Chicago: Paul Theobald, 1944.*

Kitao, H.
NEW STYLE IN CHASHITSU (Tea-cult House). *Tokyo: Toko-do Shoten.*

Klingender, Francis D.
ART AND THE INDUSTRIAL REVOLUTION. *London: Noel Carrington, 1950.*

Kryzhanovsky, Ivan.
BIOLOGICAL BASES OF THE EVOLUTION OF MUSIC.

Kuck, Lorraine E.
THE ART OF JAPANESE GARDENS. *New York: John Day.*

——— ONE HUNDRED KYOTO GARDENS. *London: Kegan Paul, Trench, Trubner & Co., 1935.*

Kump, Ernest J.
Guest editorial, *Journal of the American Institute of Architects,* September, 1948.

Lamprecht, Sterling P.
"Man's Place In Nature." *American Scholar,* January 1937.

L'Architecture D'Aujourdhui. "Jardins." April 1937.

Le Corbusier.
THE CITY OF TOMORROW. *London: Architectural Press, 1929.*

——— CONCERNING TOWN PLANNING. *New Haven: Yale University Press, 1948.*

——— NEW WORLD OF SPACE. *New York: Harcourt Brace & Co., 1948.*

——— OEUVRE COMPLETE. *Zurich: Les Editions D'Architecture Erlenbach. 1946.* (4 vol.)

——— TOWARDS A NEW ARCHITECTURE. *New York: Payson & Clarke Ltd., 1927.*

——— U.N. HEADQUARTERS. *New York: Reinhold, 1947.*

Lescaze, William.
ON BEING AN ARCHITECT. *New York: G. P. Putnam's Sons, 1942.*

Lobeck, A. K.
GEOMORPHOLOGY. *New York: McGraw Hill, 1939.*

Lockwood, A. G. B. (compiler and editor).
GARDENS OF COLONY AND STATE. *New York: Charles Scribner's Sons, 1931–1934.* (2 vol.)

Lord, Russell.
TO HOLD THIS SOIL. *Washington: U.S. Superintendent of Documents, Soil Conservation Service, 1938.*

Lunz, L. B.
PARKS OF CULTURE AND RECREATION. *Moscow-Leningrad: Gosstroyizdat, 1934.*

258

Lurçat, André.
TERRASSES ET JARDINS. *Paris: Charles Moreau, 1929.*
MacVeagh, Mrs. Charles.
FOUNTAINS OF PAPAL ROME. *New York: Charles Scribner's Sons, 1915.*
Martin, Nicholson, Gabo.
CIRCLE. *London: Faber & Faber, 1937.*
Marrast, J.
MCMXXV JARDINS. *Paris: Editions D'Art, Charles Moreau, 1926.*
Merrill, George P.
STONES FOR BUILDING AND DECORA-TION. *New York: John Wiley & Sons, 1910.*
Mickey, Karl B.
MAN AND THE SOIL. *Chicago: International Harvester Co., 1945.*
————— HEALTH FROM THE GROUND UP. *Chicago: International Harvester Co., 1946.*
MODERN ART, DOCUMENTS OF. *New York: Wittenborn, Schultz, Inc., 1944.*
Moholy-Nagy, Ladislaus.
THE NEW VISION. *New York: Wittenborn, Schultz, Inc., 1930.*
————— VISION IN MOTION. *Chicago: Paul Theobald, 1947.*
Mumford, Lewis.
THE CULTURE OF CITIES. *New York: Harcourt, Brace & Co., 1938.*
Munro, Thomas.
THE ARTS AND THEIR INTERRELA-TIONS. *New York: Liberal Arts Press, 1949.*
Munsell, A. H.
A COLOR NOTATION. *Baltimore: Munsell Color Co., 1926.*
National Housing Agency, F.P.H.A.
PUBLIC HOUSING DESIGN (A review of experience in low-rent housing). *Washington: U.S. Government Printing Office, 1946.*
National Resources Planning Board.
PLANNING STUDIES. *Washington: U.S. Superintendent of Documents.*
Neumeyer and Neumeyer.
LEISURE AND RECREATION. *New York: A. S. Barnes & Co., 1936.*
Nichols, Rose Standish.
SPANISH AND PORTUGUESE GARDENS. *Boston: Houghton Mifflin Co., 1924.*
Odum, Howard W., and Moore, Harry E.
AMERICAN REGIONALISM. *New York: Henry Holt & Co., 1938.*
Olmsted, Frederick Law Senior.
FORTY YEARS OF LANDSCAPE ARCHI-TECTURE. *New York: G. P. Putnam's Sons, 1928.*
Olmsted, Frederick Law; Coville, Frederick V.; and Kelsey, Harlan P.
STANDARDIZED PLANT NAMES. A catalogue of approved scientific and common names of plants in American commerce. *Salem: American Joint Committee on Horticultural Nomenclature, 1923. New York: A. T. De La Mare Co., 1923.*
O'Neal, Cora M.
GARDENS AND HOMES OF MEXICO. *Dallas: Banks Unshaw & Co., 1945.*
Osborn, Fairfield.
OUR PLUNDERED PLANET. *Boston: Little Brown & Co., 1948.*
Ozenfant, Amedie.
FOUNDATIONS OF MODERN ART. *London: John Rodker, 1931.*
Pack and Gill.
FORESTS OF MANKIND. *New York: Macmillan Co., 1929.*
Parsons, Samuel.
THE ART OF LANDSCAPE ARCHITEC-TURE. *New York: G. P. Putnam's Sons, 1915.*
Peattie, Donald Culross.
FLOWERING EARTH. *New York: G. P. Putnam's Sons, 1939.*
Peets, Elbert.
"The Landscape Priesthood." *American Mercury,* January 1927.
Person, H. S.
LITTLE WATERS. *Washington: U.S. Superintendent of Documents. U.S. Soil Conservation Service. 1936.*
Pevsner, Nikolaus.
PIONEERS OF THE MODERN MOVEMENT. *London: Faber & Faber, 1936.*
Platt, Rutherford.
OUR FLOWERING WORLD. *New York: Dodd, Mead & Co., 1947.*
Pope, Arthur Upham.
"Persian Gardens: Formative Factors in Persian Art" from his INTRODUCTION TO PER-SIAN ART SINCE THE SEVENTH CEN-TURY A.D. *London: P. Davies, 1930.*
Price, Sir Uvedale.
AN ESSAY ON THE PICTURESQUE, AS COMPARED WITH THE SUBLIME AND THE BEAUTIFUL. *London: J. Robson, 1794–98.* (2 vol. Later revisions incorporated in Lauder edition of 1842).
Public Administration Service.
Publications on Planning. *Chicago.*
Ramann, Dr. E.
THE EVOLUTION AND CLASSIFICATION OF SOILS. *Cambridge: W. Heffer & Sons, Ltd., 1928.*
Raunkiaer, C.
LIFE FORMS OF PLANTS. *Oxford: Clarendon Press, 1934.*

Rayner, M. C., and Neilson-Jones, W.
PROBLEMS IN TREE NUTRITION. *London: Faber & Faber.*

Read, Herbert.
ART NOW. *London: Faber & Faber, 1933.*

Repton, Humphrey.
THE ART OF LANDSCAPE GARDENING. *Boston and New York: Houghton, Mifflin Co., 1907.*

Robinson, Florence Bell.
PLANTING DESIGN. *New York: Whittlesey House, 1940.*

Rose, James C.
Articles on Landscape Design. *Pencil Points,* October, November, December 1938; February, April, December 1939.

Rose, James C.; Kiley, Daniel Urban; and Eckbo, Garrett.
Articles on Landscape Design. *Architectural Record,* May, August 1939; February 1940.

Roth, Alfred.
THE NEW ARCHITECTURE. *Zurich: Dr. H. Girsberger, 1940.*

Roux-Spitz, M.
EXPOSITION DES ARTS DÉCORATIFS, PARIS 1925. *Paris: Editions Albert Levy, Batiments et Jardins, 1925.*

Saarinen, Eliel.
THE CITY. *New York: Reinhold, 1943.*

———— THE SEARCH FOR FORM. *New York: Reinhold, 1948.*

Sale, Edith Tunis.
HISTORIC GARDENS OF VIRGINIA. *Richmond: William Byrd Press, James River Garden Club, 1923.*

Salisbury, Rollin D.
PHYSIOGRAPHY. *New York: Henry Holt & Co., 1946.*

Sanders & Rabuck.
NEW CITY PATTERNS. *New York: Reinhold, 1946.*

Sandburg, Carl.
THE PEOPLE, YES. *New York: Harcourt Brace & Co., 1936.*

San Francisco Museum of Art and A.L.A.
LANDSCAPE DESIGN, SAN FRANCISCO REGION. *San Francisco: 1948.*

Sartoris, Alberto.
ENCYCLOPEDIE DE L'ARCHITECTURE NOUVELLE. *Milan: Ulrico Hoepli, 1948.*

———— GLI ELEMENTI. *Milan: Ulrico Hoepli.*

Sauer, Carl Ortwin.
THE MORPHOLOGY OF LANDSCAPE. *University of California Publication in Geography, Vol. II 1919–1929. Berkeley: University of California Press, 1929.*

Schillinger, Joseph.
THE MATHEMATICAL BASIS OF THE ARTS. *New York: The Philosophical Library, 1948.*

Schumann, Charles H.
DESCRIPTIVE GEOMETRY—A TREATISE ON THE GRAPHICS OF SPACE FOR THE SCIENTIFIC PROFESSION. *New York: D. Van Nostrand Co. Inc. 1946.*

Sert, J. L. and C.I.A.M.
CAN OUR CITIES SURVIVE. *Cambridge: Harvard University Press, 1942.*

Sharp, Thomas.
TOWN AND COUNTRYSIDE. *London: Oxford University Press, 1932.*

———— TOWN PLANNING. *New York: Penguin Books, 1940, 1945.*

Shepherd, J. C., and Jellicoe, G. A.
ITALIAN GARDENS OF THE RENAISSANCE. *New York: Charles Scribner's Sons, 1925.*

Shiga, Naoya; and Motoi, Hashimoto, editors.
GARDENS OF JAPAN. *Tokyo: The Zauho Press, 1935.*

Shuler, Ellis W.
ROCKS AND RIVERS. *Lancaster, Pa.: Jacques Cattell Press, 1945.*

Sirén, Osvald
GARDENS OF CHINA. *New York: Ronald Press, 1949.*

Sitte, Camillo.
THE ART OF BUILDING CITIES. *New York: Reinhold, 1945.*

Smith, Janet K.
DESIGN: AN INTRODUCTION. *Chicago-New York: Ziff-Davis Publishing Co., 1946.*

Soil Conservation Service Publications.
Washington: U.S. Superintendent of Documents.

SOILS AND MEN: 1938 Yearbook of Agriculture.

Soltynski, Roman.
GLIMPSES OF POLISH ARCHITECTURE. *London: Maxlove Publishing Co.*

Stegner, Wallace.
ONE NATION. *Boston: Houghton Mifflin Co., 1945.*

Stern, Bernhard J.
THE FAMILY—PAST AND PRESENT. *New York: D. Appleton Century, 1938.*

Stonorov, Oscar; and Kahn, Louis I.
YOU AND YOUR NEIGHBORHOOD. *New York: Revere Copper and Brass Inc., 1944.*

Straus, Nathan.
THE SEVEN MYTHS OF HOUSING. *New York: Alfred A. Knopf, 1945.*

Studio Annual.
GARDENS AND GARDENING. *New York: Studio Publishers Inc.*

Sullivan, Louis.
AUTOBIOGRAPHY OF AN IDEA. *Washington: American Institute of Architects, 1924. New York: Peter Smith, 1949.*
——— KINDERGARTEN CHATS. *New York: Wittenborn, Schultz Inc., 1947.*

Tamura, Tsuyoshi.
ART OF THE LANDSCAPE GARDEN IN JAPAN. *Tokyo: Kokusai Bunka Shinkokai, 1936.*

Task Magazine.
Cambridge, Mass.

Teague, Walter Dorwin.
DESIGN THIS DAY. *New York: Harcourt Brace & Co., 1940, 1949.*

Tubbs, Ralph.
LIVING IN CITIES. *London: Penguin Books, 1942.*

T.V.A.
Publications. *Knoxville, Tenn.*

Tunnard, Christopher.
GARDENS IN THE MODERN LANDSCAPE. *New York: Charles Scribner's Sons, 1948.*

United Auto Workers, C.I.O.
MEMORANDUM ON POST WAR URBAN HOUSING. *Detroit: U.A.W., C.I.O., 1944.*

Van Dersal, William R.
THE AMERICAN LAND. *New York: Oxford University Press, 1943.*

Van Dyke, John C.
NATURE FOR ITS OWN SAKE. *New York: Charles Scribner's Sons, 1921.*

Villiers Stuart, C. M.
GARDENS OF THE GREAT MUGHALS. *London: Adam and Charles Black, 1913.*

von Engeln, D. D.
GEOMORPHOLOGY. *New York: Macmillan Co., 1942.*

von Puckler-Muskau, Prince.
HINTS ON LANDSCAPE GARDENING. *New York: Houghton Mifflin Co., 1917.*

Weaver and Clements.
PLANT ECOLOGY. *New York: McGraw Hill, 1929.*

Weimer, Arthur M.; and Hoyt, Homer.
PRINCIPLES OF URBAN REAL ESTATE. *New York: Ronald Press, 1948.*

Weir, L. H., editor.
PARKS (A manual of municipal and county parks, compiled as a result of a nationwide study of municipal and county parks conducted by the Playground and Recreation Association of America.) *New York: A. S. Barnes & Co., 1928.* (2 vol.)

Weir, Wilbert W.
SOIL SCIENCE. *Chicago-Philadelphia: J. B. Lippincott Co., 1936.*

Welcker, Carola Giedion.
MODERN PLASTIC ART. *Zurich: Girsberger, 1937.*

Whitson & Williams.
LUTHER BURBANK. *New York & London: L. B. Press, 1914.*

Whitney, Milton.
SOIL AND CIVILIZATION. *New York: D. Van Nostrand Co., 1927.*

Whitman, Walt.
LEAVES OF GRASS. *New York: The Modern Library.*

Wight, F. S., in Le Corbusier
NEW WORLD OF SPACE. *New York: Harcourt Brace Co.; Boston, Institute of Contemporary Art, 1948.*

Wilenski, R. H.
THE MEANING OF MODERN SCULPTURE. *New York: Frederick A. Stokes Co., 1935.*

Williams, Clement C.
BUILDING AN ENGINEERING CAREER. *New York: McGraw Hill, 1934.*

Wills, Royal Barry.
THIS BUSINESS OF ARCHITECTURE. *New York: Reinhold, 1941.*

Wright, Frank Lloyd.
ON ARCHITECTURE. (Selected writings edited by Frederick Gutheim.) *New York: Duell, Sloan & Pearce, 1941.*
——— AN AUTOBIOGRAPHY. *New York: Duell, Sloan & Pearce, 1941.*

Wright, Richardson.
THE STORY OF GARDENING. *New York: Garden City Publishing Co., 1938.*

Yale Directive Committee on Regional Planning.
THE CASE FOR REGIONAL PLANNING (with specific reference to New England). *New Haven: Yale University Press, 1947.*

Zucker, Paul.
NEW ARCHITECTURE AND CITY PLANNING. *New York: Philosophical Library, 1944.*

REFERENCES WHICH DO NOT APPEAR
IN THE TEXT

HUMAN NATURE—Adler, Stern
WORLD WE LIVE IN—Amer. Geo. Soc., Census Bur., Ecology, Emerson, Hopkins, Pack, "Soils and Men", Van Dersal, Whitney
ALLIED ARTS—A.I.A., Brown, Grinter, Jackson, Lescaze, Munro, Williams, Wills
HISTORY, PRE-INDUSTRIAL—A.I.A., Arch. Rev., Chambers, Crisp, French & Eberlein,

Gallotti, Gothein, Graham, Gromort, Howard, Jellicoe, Kitao, Lockwood, Nichols, O'Neal, Pope, Price, Sale, Villiers-Stuart

PLANNING—Abercrombie, Amer. Pub. Health Assoc., A.P.C.A., A.S.P.O., Bur. of Urb., Bur. of Rec., C. of C., Comm. Club, Fortune Mag., Gallion, Gray, Hilberseimer, Nat'l Housing, N.R.P.B. Pub. Admin., Sanders, Stonorov, Straus, Task, Tubbs, T.V.A., U.A.W., Yale, Zucker

HISTORY, MODERN—Arch. Rev., Jensen, L. Arch Dauj., Soltynski, Studio Annuals

MODERN ART AND ARCH.—Behrendt, Frey, Goodwin, Gropius, Hitchcock, Martin, John-son, Mod. Art, Ozenfant, Pevsner, Read, Roth, Sullivan, Valentiner, Welcker

COLOR—Munsell

CONSERVATION—Cornell Univ., Lord

MAN AND NATURE—Eckbo-review, Haskell

ROCK—Eckel, Fenton, Merrill

PLANTS—Emerson, Peattie, Rayner, Bailey, Amer. Joint Comm., Robinson

PRACTICE—Imlay

SPACE—Schumann

PARKS & RECREATION—Butler

NINETEENTH AND TWENTIETH CENTU-RIES—Haffner, Lurcat, Marrast, Roux-Spitz, Sartoris, Weir

262